NEW MEDIA AND RELIGIOUS TRANSFORMATIONS IN AFRICA

NEW MEDIA AND RELIGIOUS TRANSFORMATIONS IN AFRICA

Edited by Rosalind I. J. Hackett and Benjamin F. Soares

Foreword by Francis B. Nyamnjoh

Indiana University Press

Bloomington and Indianapolis

This book is a publication of

Indiana University Press
Office of Scholarly Publishing
Herman B Wells Library 350
1320 East 10th Street
Bloomington, Indiana 47405 USA

iupress.indiana.edu

Telephone orders   800–842–6796
Fax orders   812–855–7931

Library of Congress Cataloging-in-Publication Data

New media and religious transformations in Africa / edited by
Rosalind I. J. Hackett and Benjamin F. Soares; foreword by Francis
B. Nyamnjoh.
     pages cm
   Includes bibliographical references and index.
   ISBN 978-0-253-01519-8 (hardcover : alk. paper) —
ISBN 978-0-253-01524-2 (pbk. : alk. paper) —
ISBN 978-0-253-01530-3 (ebook)   1. Mass media in religion—
Africa.   2. Social media—Religious aspects.   3. Social media—
Africa.   4. Africa—Religion—21st century.   I. Hackett, Rosalind I. J.
II. Soares, Benjamin F.
   BL2400.N47 2015
   302.23096—dc23

                                                    2014021491

1 2 3 4 5 20 19 18 17 16 15

Contents

Foreword

Francis B. Nyamnjoh

Pʀɪᴏʀ ᴛᴏ ᴛʜᴇ ᴄᴜʀʀᴇɴᴛ ᴘʀᴏʟɪꜰᴇʀᴀᴛɪᴏɴ of information and communication technologies (ICTs) since the 1990s, "God"[1]—singular, plural, and delegated—was accessible in standardized, routinized, and predictably more conventional ways, with a clear hierarchy of credibility and infallibility. The technologies of communication available at the time were relatively tame and embodied so as to ensure and assure such a system of communication and sense of hierarchy and authority. There was face-to-face transmission of knowledge of "the divine" by and through priests, pastors, imams, and other religious figures from and to members of their congregations, schooled to internalize and reproduce beliefs and practices on and around "salvation" and its possibilities as shaped by virtue and vice. Previously, there was the conventional printed word such as books—the Bible and the Quran, for example; newspapers (popular and religious, tabloid and broadsheet) owned by or sympathetic to churches, mosques, or religious authorities; newsletters, bulletins, tracts, pamphlets, hymnals, and sermons; and music (in audio- and videocassettes). Terrestrial national radio and national television were there to ensure a measure of mass communication beyond the modesty of the loudspeaker. Places and spaces demarcated and delineated as holy and for worship (churches, mosques, shrines, sacred monuments, etc.) were understood to be where one went to pray seriously and where the spirit world, regardless of beliefs about omnipresence, omniscience, and omnipotence, was most likely to be present or accessed, to answer prayers, and to demonstrate power, benevolence, and munificence.

Today, Africa bears witness to individuals, acting alone or as part of religious groups or communities committed to various causes (often without instigation or encouragement from their religious leaders), combing the internet, downloading and sharing (via email, as cell phone text messages, Facebook postings, printouts, faxes, and word of mouth in prayer sessions or in other face-to-face contexts) prayers, inspirational spiritual texts, religious music, ringtones, photos, podcasts, and videos. Away from the church, mosques, or formal prayer grounds, ordinary Christians and Muslims are able to evoke, sense, and access the divine presence on their own terms and without always feeling that they need the "enabling" presence or "blessings" of the hierarchy of the churches, mosques, and temples. Media technologies themselves become intermediaries through which humans can experience "the divine." They have provided for a greater sense of openness and interreligious conviviality as religious contents spread across digital platforms providing opportunities to interact with other religious communities, particularly among youth. Alongside the openness and conviviality is increased animosity across religious differences (which are sometimes blurred with political agendas) that are voiced on digital platforms. They have also allowed for nationals to connect and bond with diasporic communities in the celebration of religious events and in forging ecumenism. It is only by understanding modern media as enablers capable of simultaneously accelerating the pursuit of social transformation and social continuity that one is able to make sense of apparently contradictory and conflicting tendencies in how they are appropriated.

In Africa, perhaps more than anywhere else, the new does not always replace the old. Emphasis tends to be rather on accommodation, conviviality, and composite identities than in zero-sum games in which one person's gain is another person's loss. This is as true of religion as it is of media, where the old and the new not only coexist and are interdependent but are often inextricably entangled. When Africans embrace new religions such as Islam and Christianity (in their various forms) and new media forms, this is to bring the new and the old in conversation in a process of creative domestication and innovation. They may not always succeed in their bid to privilege accommodation and conviviality over conflict and dichotomies, being part of an interconnected world of hierarchical relationships—an often marginalized one at that—in which zero-sum games of power and dominance tend to prevail. Scholars who seek neat dichotomies and binary oppositions will not find it in African life-worlds.[2] This is clear in this volume.

Edited by Rosalind Hackett and Benjamin Soares—leading scholars on the intersection of the anthropology and history of religion in Africa—*New Media and Religious Transformations in Africa* charts a long-overdue multidisciplinary conversation about how to research and debate the changing landscapes of religion and new media in Africa. In view of the interconnections and interdependencies between various and changing media forms and different religious practices, the book highlights the conceptual and methodological terrain related to mediation and its role in understanding histories of religious pluralism in Africa. Hackett and Soares map a conceptual and methodological landscape through which to understand the interconnections and intricacies between varied religious practices and media in African societies. And this is the key contribution: the richness in themes and perspectives together with the range and breadth in religions and their geographies are explored historically and empirically in 15 case studies. The promise to the reader is clearly an intellectual adventure. *New Media and Religious Transformations in Africa* challenges readers to engage in systematic contemplation of religion and the media in Africa, and in turn, what Africans make of the religion and media that target them.

All of the contributors begin the process of providing a critical historical ethnographic overview of African encounters with religions and media technologies, and the mutual shaping between religions and technologies from the fixed telephone to the cell phone, through radio, television, fax, computer, the internet, and social media. African archives—oral and textual, embodied and institutionalized—to contemporary formations, the essays are rich in euphoric associations between media and social transformation. The contributors examine how the euphoria of mediation has been repeatedly tempered, mitigated, or punctured by a more complex and often more nuanced reality. Technological determinism is too stubborn a bedfellow, and we are often too hopeful for mitigated euphoria. Dazzled by its promise, we seldom bring ourselves to question or to put into perspective technology's messianic pretensions.

This book reiterates the need not only for multidisciplinary perspectives but also for a sense of history and the ethnography of everyday relations among different religious actors and between religion and the wider society, as well as the place of technologies of information and communication therein. Researching the social appropriation of communication technologies for religious purposes in Africa provides considerable data to pronounce upon the relevance of technologies to religion. This book provides food for thought on how and the extent to which information and communication technologies can enable various religious practitioners to make choices and decisions about their religious lives.

It is true that all over Africa today, for many an individual and a community, ICTs are mobilizing and democratizing religion in ways unprecedented and unanticipated just over 20 years ago. Prior to the 1990s, when satellite television and the internet were still very much in their infancy and the cell phone a pipe dream, "the divine" was at best a present absence if not an absent presence. The normalized linear hierarchy of the faithful, with major religious figures at the helm, enjoying and managing privileged or monopoly access—both directly and through the departed ancestors—determined and often imposed the structures, strictures, and confines of how "the divine," in its sacredness, could be evoked and concretized for the sinful and the undeserving by the appointed and the anointed. However, just as the media are likely to enhance the mysterious workings of God, so too are they amenable to the devious ways of the Devil.

This appropriation of modern media by individuals, laypersons, and religious activists is as empowering (enabling) as it is threatening (subversive or disabling). Thanks to their creative and innovative appropriation of social media, ordinary Christians and Muslims might be able to lay claim to a closer and more intimate, direct relationship with God. Their actions at the same time may make religious leaders—conventional religious authorities and the hierarchies of credibility and authority they seem to represent—feel increasingly irrelevant and marginal (unless they are able to reinvent themselves, their professions, hierarchies, and authority). The situation is only compounded by the rise and proliferation of new forms of religiosity that are often overtly subversive of established religious traditions, practices, and authorities. It is not beyond contemplation that even God is expected to adapt or perish, as many a gadgeted believer would dearly love an instantly accessible and affordable God, available anytime, anywhere. In communities where ancestral veneration is practiced, burying the dead with cell phones and accessories—or in coffins designed to take the form and shape of cell phones as is done in Ghana—might keep the lines of communication open beyond shrines and sacrificial spots.

It is hardly surprising, therefore, that while ordinary individuals, laypersons, and activists are using ICTs to negotiate and navigate new religious freedoms, the traditional hierarchies of their religions are either joining the bandwagon of innovation and change or exploring how best to harness the new technologies to reinforce their authority and traditions. Although some phenomenally powerful leaders of religious groups continue to claim that they have special access to the divine, others in similar leadership positions are committed to empowering the people they lead as opposed to lording over them. Some among them have joined the ranks of those writing books on how to domesticate ICTs to serve more egalitarian religious ends. Castor Goliama, a Tanzanian priest of the Roman Catholic Church, is one of them. In his book on mobile phones and the church in Africa,[3] Goliama notes that contrary to the past, where the power of presence in simultaneous multiplicities was the prerogative of God alone, the ability of ICTs such as the cell phone to compress time and space means that ordinary Christians can mimic Godlikeness by using these new media to achieve the power of presence in many places simultaneously. While some may perceive this as subversive to divine omnipresence, omniscience, and omnipotence, Goliama invites the church to explore creative and innovative ways of harnessing this potential for ecclesiastical ends. If priests are able to use their capacity for simultaneous presence, they could participate in multiple conversations with people and places separated by distance and time in ways unfathomable over 20 years ago. Thus, just as ICTs can enable Christians, Muslims, and followers of other religions to feel eternally available and reachable by God and messages about God from others, so too are the institutional messengers of the divine—priests, pastors, imams, prophets, and so on—in a position to initiate and sustain conversations between the old and the new, across and within various religious divides. Some studies in this volume suggest such media-facilitated spiritual and interreligious conversations may already be underway.

A cursory look at the fascinating and rapid developments pertaining to the appropriation of different media forms for different religious ends suggests further research themes that, together with those broached in this volume, could lay a firm foundation for the multidisciplinary study of relations between media and religion. It is evident that the accelerated deregulation of the 1990s and early 2000s across Africa has increased media pluralism and provided for significant involvement by religious organizations in the ownership and control of newspapers and radio and television stations, among other media outlets. In some countries, this has led to a proliferation of religious publications, radio stations, and television channels, not to mention virtual/web/internet sites. To what extent such developments have significantly reconfigured the skewed power relations and nonparticipatory "church and state" communication models they have sought to replace or serve as alternatives to is yet to be empirically substantiated. In some countries, opening up the airwaves has led to pluralism in ownership and outlets but not necessarily to diversity in media content. In certain situations, the only functioning television channels in public places such as hotels and bars are religious ones. Many national stations continue to struggle for local content, while others have been more successful in generating local religious programming.

Africans may have new media options to enable presence and participation, but they are not always in a position to influence content or to participate on their own terms. If and when they are able to determine content—such as in popular representations of religion and in the representation of religion in popular locally produced media (e.g., in gospel music or films—such as Nigerian Nollywood and Ghanaian cinema)—one finds portrayal of everyday life in its multiple dimensions and contradictions. Religion remains a popular and contested theme in these popular expressions, as Africans, however religious they may be, are not monolithic in their religious beliefs and practices. They are capable of creatively building their religious worlds around a buffet of values drawn from a range of traditions and practices. Religious conflicts notwithstanding, Africans, like many humans these days, cherish religious conviviality and seek to accommodate a range of worldviews just as they seek to be accommodated by others and their religions. *New Media and Religious Transformations in Africa* raises provocative questions about creative processes at play. It points to the hunger and thirst among Africans to seek to domesticate and democratize modern media forms and religion, as well as to shape the dynamism of change as it relates to Africa, the world, the sacred and the everyday, and both the predictability and the vagaries of the mundane and our place in it.

Notes

1. My reference to God is deliberately ambiguous. Although the nature and character of God for each religion may be particular, I emphasize the shared idea of God and the sense that

all roads lead to the same God, who may be perceived and identified in particular ways from different vantage points.

2. For a critique of such an approach, see M. Mamdani, *Citizen and Subject: Contemporary Africa and the Legacy of Late Colonialism* (London: James Currey, 1996); M. Mamdani, *Good Muslim, Bad Muslim: America, the Cold War, and the Roots of Terror* (Dakar: CODESRIA, 2004).

3. Goliama, C. M., *Where Are You Africa? Church and Society in the Mobile Phone Age* (Bamenda: Langaa, 2010).

Acknowledgments

Most of the chapters in this book are papers that were first presented at an international conference, New Media and Religious Transformations in Africa, in Abuja, Nigeria, in July 2008. The conference was hosted by Centre for the Study of African Culture and Communication (CESACC) in Port Harcourt and received generous funding from the Royal Netherlands Embassy in Abuja and the Afrika-Studiecentrum, Leiden. We thank Robert A. White for introducing us to his former students and colleagues working on religion and media who helped us with the conference. We are particularly grateful to Patrick Alumuku, who ran the local organizing committee for the Abuja conference. Along with his assistant Ema Odu, and a team of affable volunteers and advisors, Patrick managed the local coordination and hosting with aplomb and abundant good cheer. We benefited enormously from the collaboration of our colleague Walter Ihejirika from CESACC. We would like to single out Ambassador Arie van der Wiel, the Dutch ambassador in Abuja at the time, for his support. While preparing the book for publication, we received valuable assistance from Andrea Brigaglia, Kim van Drie, Jayanni Webster, and Erin Wiegand. We thank the contributors for their essays and their patience as we brought the book to publication. Robert Launay was a characteristically insightful and constructive reader of the manuscript, and for this we are most appreciative. Finally, Dee Mortensen has been steadfast in her support for this project from the outset, and we thank her for this. Permission to reprint David Chidester's article from the *Journal of Material Religion* (4(2) (2008): 136–159) was kindly granted by Bloomsbury Publishing Plc. We would like to dedicate this collection to the future generation of scholars of religion and media in Africa.

NEW MEDIA AND RELIGIOUS TRANSFORMATIONS IN AFRICA

Introduction

New Media and Religious Transformations in Africa

Rosalind I. J. Hackett and Benjamin F. Soares

THE MAIN GOAL of this book is to cast a critical look at Africa's rapidly evolving religious media scene. In doing so, we also underscore the importance of studying the media when studying religion in Africa, and vice versa. The case for an interdisciplinary study of religion, media, and culture has been made effectively by a number of scholars over the last two decades.[1] The study of media development in Africa has also become a burgeoning field.[2] However, such studies almost always ignore religion in Africa despite the fact that religious actors have long been in the forefront in taking up new media technologies in Africa.[3] Indeed, as many scholars have convincingly argued, understanding media is vital to understanding religion and the history of Christianity in Africa, not to mention other religions.[4] Brian Larkin recently contended that religious transformations in Africa, particularly in relation to Islam, cannot be analyzed without taking into account the media forms that help to shape religious practice.[5] Yet, most of the existing studies on media in Africa tend to be concerned with questions of democracy and development, and religion has long been treated as marginal to these areas (Hyden, Leslie, and Ogundimu 2002; Nyamnjoh 2005).[6]

Therefore, we provide new and much-needed historical and empirical data about religion and media in Africa. In addition to filling in some of these gaps in knowledge in this burgeoning field, we offer theoretical and methodological reflections on the intersections of religion, media, culture, and politics. Indeed, the rich materials about Africa in this book provide much that is useful for thinking comparatively about media and religion and help us to hone the analysis of their complex mutual imbrications in the world today.

Since the early 1990s, with the end of one-party rule and many authoritarian regimes and subsequent political liberalization in many places in Africa, the media landscape has changed radically.[7] This followed deregulation of the media, which in many places had been subject to strict state control, and the emergence and proliferation of new information and communication technologies (ICTs). The number of newspapers and magazines; radio and television stations, including satellite television; computers; and mobile telephone networks (on mobile telephones, see de Bruijn, Nyamnjoh, and Brinkman 2009) increased rapidly. New opportunities for ownership, production, and participation accompanied this media diversification and the creation of new media worlds (Ginsberg, Abu-Lughod, and Larkin 2002). Religious activists, leaders, and laypersons have appropriated such technologies and new media outlets to strengthen and expand their communities and to gain public recognition for their organizations, activities, and various agendas. In some, more competitive, public spheres, the media have also been used to defame or marginalize and restrict the media access of religious "Others," which has sometimes led to tension, conflict, and even violence. In rarer cases, the media have developed programming to promote inter-religious dialogue and conflict resolution—most famously perhaps in the case of the so-called Imam and the Pastor, a Muslim cleric and a Protestant minister, respectively, from Kaduna in Nigeria, who have worked together to defuse religious tensions and conflict in that country.[8] Not surprisingly, given the context of the current media revolution, the challenges of balancing freedom of expression and freedom of religion and belief in Africa's fast-growing media sector are more apparent than ever (see Hackett 2011).

Any study of the twenty-first-century media scene in Africa must take into account the history of media technologies in Africa and the recent proliferation of new media, which have spread far and wide across the continent (on new media, see Tomaselli 2009). However, Africa is a place where some "old" media, such as print media (see Soares 2007; Zappa, chapter 2 this volume) and radio broadcasting, remain key sites for religious expression (see also Gunner, Ligaga, and Moyo 2011; J. Brennan and Haron, chapters 1 and 4 this volume). The history of such older media forms is important for understanding the expanding range of media that religious actors and communities are employing in a globalizing Africa. Until two decades ago, state broadcasters in most countries in Africa tended to provide rather limited and restricted religious broadcasting, which might feature recordings of Sunday services for Christians and the call to prayer for Muslims and recitation of passages from the Quran (see Adama, chapter 7 this volume). Such religious programming generally increased during Christian and Muslim holidays. Practitioners of so-called African "traditional" religion—"traditionalists"—and other minority religious groups were commonly excluded from these arrangements. Until recently, given the prevalence of modernizing impulses, broadcasting authorities were rather reticent about inviting practitioners of "traditional" religions onto the airwaves. The practitioners themselves were also reluctant to engage with mass media and new media technologies (see Mndende 2009; de Witte, chapter 11 this volume). With media deregulation in many countries, the state no longer necessarily dominates the national or local broadcast or print media scene. Africans now have access to a wider variety of media forms and technologies that range from the small-scale and informal to the large-scale and formal. The broadened range of media forms today include audio- and videocassettes; films; CDs and DVDs; loudspeakers; pamphlets and flyers; posters; banners; billboards; telephony; photography; radio and television, including satellite television; and computer-mediated communication and information—websites, emails, blogs, listservs, discussion boards, SMS (Short Message Service), social media such as Facebook and Twitter, and so forth. Although the difference between "old" and "new" media is anything but straightforward, attempts to limit definitions of "new" media to digital media forms that allow interactivity notwithstanding, the empirical materials from Africa presented in this collection clearly demonstrate how all media forms are at least initially "new." In this way, the newness of a media form depends on context and history rather than on a particular medium and anything inherent in its form. What is striking is how some "old" media forms such as print media or private radio and television broadcasting are relatively new in some contexts in Africa (see Zappa, chapter 2 this volume). At the same time, other media forms such as digital and computer-aided media, which are conventionally considered "new" media, are increasingly important in Africa. Although such media forms are perhaps less developed and less prevalent than elsewhere in the world, there is a real need for further empirical study of such forms and how they intersect with religion.[9]

Given the increased technological capacities for transmission and reception now available on a global scale, and in Africa in particular, media creation, circulation, and consumption are now less confined to local, regional, and national contexts than they were until quite recently. Not so long ago, radio and television broadcasting frequencies were often quite limited, and the relatively weak power of signals was such that targeted audiences tended to be both restricted and limited. The example of radio broadcasting in late colonial Kenya helps to illustrate this (see J. Brennan, chapter 1 this volume). However, there has long been religious broadcasting over shortwave radio available to African audiences, most notably Radio Vatican and Radio ELWA (Eternal Love Winning Africa), the first Christian radio station based in and transmitted from Liberia since 1954, until interruptions in service from the 1990s with the advent of the civil war in that country (Stoneman 2012). But such audiences have always been difficult to quantify. Today, radio and television broadcasts can be streamed via the internet, allowing for the remediation of programming to much wider viewing and listening communities in Africa and in the diaspora. In the space of a couple of decades, the newer-generation evangelical and Pentecostal churches and some Muslim preachers, including some Sufi leaders, in Africa have gone from recording sermons on audiocassette to videocassette to DVD, all of which could be purchased for personal consumption. Now such sermons or public pronouncements are frequently available on websites, especially those of the mega-churches and various charismatic media personalities such as the Mauritanian Muslim scholar Ould Dedew or the Egyptian preacher Amr Khaled, and some churches even offer live streaming of sermons and church services.[10]

Research on Africa's rapidly changing media landscapes is finally recognizing the involvement of religious organizations, whether in terms of acquiring licenses, purchasing airtime, or influencing broadcasting policy.[11] A growing, albeit limited, body of academic research has taken shape over the last decade or so, with a stimulating spectrum of monographs and articles on particular media, religious communities, and countries (see, e.g., Mfumbusa and White 2009; Iherjika 2009). It has mainly been anthropologists and religion and media scholars who have produced this international scholarship, which is frequently based on research in Africa. With a number of notable exceptions (e.g., Launay 1997; Mndende 1999; Haron 2004; Soares 2005; de Witte 2008a; Larkin 2008a; Schulz 2012b; Ibrahim 2013), these works have tended to focus on Christianity (see the references in note 1). The contributors to this volume deepen the study of media among Muslims and help to broaden the perspective by including African "traditional" religion (see Merz and Chidester, chapters 5 and 15 this volume). The book also attempts to bridge the artificial divide between North Africa and sub-Saharan Africa by considering the proliferation of Arab Islamic satellite channels in North Africa, the influence of which extends well beyond North Africa to many places in sub-Saharan Africa where they are often viewed (see Galal, chapter 9 this volume).

Furthermore, our intention is not to limit the discussion to explicitly religious programming, channels, and outlets. Rather, we seek to take a broader perspective that also encompasses the different ways people are engaging with various media forms, particularly in situations of religious diversity (see Eisenlohr 2012). Deregulation and liberalization of the media have also opened up more spaces for creativity for some media consumers, sometimes allowing them to be producers of media, for example, in creating customized CDs and sound files of devotional music for personal listening or sharing. At the same time, we are particularly interested in the ways in which seemingly secular entertainment in the media can be suffused with religious ideas, sounds, and symbols (see, e.g., Pype, chapter 6 this volume). In some cases, such entertainment seems more akin to what we might call devotional entertainment for listeners, spectators, and producers. Some seem to use such media to create personal, customized spaces of devotion and a sense of security and familiarity for themselves and their communities. The use of some new media—such as obviously Christian and Islamic ringtones on mobile phones—unambiguously index the mobile phone's owner's religious affiliation to those within hearing range and might be perceived as a form of proselytization. Such ringtones are equivalent to statements about one's religious proclivities that also might be expressed through dress, adornment, food, and language use in interactive social fields that are frequently fraught with tension and sometimes competition and even outright conflict between different religious communities.

Religious Transformations

In this collection we focus on the diverse religious transformations being generated by the explosion of media technologies—both old and new—across Africa. We highlight a number of the most important of these transformations that have been observable and documented in some of the contributions to this book.

First, in many places we are witnessing changes *of* religion. It is clear that exposure to new religious orientations via media outlets can lead to changes in religious affiliation and processes of conversion and reconversion. This is perhaps most clearly evidenced in the so-called "born-again" phenomenon that is widespread among Christians (Ihejirika 2006) and even among some Muslims, especially youths, as with the Nasr Allah al-Fatih Society of Nigeria (NASFAT), which is a large modern-style Islamic organization that has been compared with Pentecostalism (see Soares 2009).[12] The deregulated media scene in many African countries has helped contribute to the development of a marketplace of religions or religious market. Such a market has more religious options on offer than before, and it is often much more competitive. This is not to say that media have helped reduce religion to the logic of the market. Rather, different media forms have facilitated changes in religious affiliation.

Second, in addition to the change of religion, there has been considerable change *in* religion. Evidence suggests that exposure to new religious orientations via media forms and outlets can influence and result in changes in religious values, behaviors, practices, styles, attitudes, expressive modes, voices, and authority. For example, the Roman Catholic Church in various places in Africa uses mobile phones to promote social justice and interconnectedness (Goliama 2010). The Ghanaian video film industry has contributed significantly to the emergence of a Pentecostally infused—or what Birgit Meyer (2004) terms a "pentecostalite"— public culture. Charles Hirschkind (2006) has shown how cassette sermons in Cairo have served as vehicles of ethical self-improvement and recalibration to the contemporary era. The South African Muslim cleric Ahmed Deedat used Christian styles of communication (pamphlets and electronic media) to strengthen Muslim defenses against Christian evangelism (Larkin 2008b; Sadouni 2011), and NASFAT uses SMS in Nigeria to communicate with its Muslim members about religious comportment and devotional practice (see also Taiwo, chapter 10 this volume).

Third, media frequently create more space for other religious actors and engagement. In some places, modern media technologies provide the capacity for a greater range of religious actors and organizations to be seen and/or heard in the public sphere, potentially supplementing or supplanting prevailing religious voices. Media can facilitate the social and political engagement of certain actors (cf. Schulz 2012a on the controversial "public presence" of female radio preachers in Mali). For example, the Afrikania Mission, a neo-traditional revivalist movement in Ghana, has utilized a range of local and global media to defend the *trokosi* system (the sending of young virgins as objects of sacrifice and atonement to traditional shrines) in Ghana's Volta Region against claims and interventions from mainly Christian human rights organizations that it constitutes a form of female ritual servitude (de Witte 2008a: 311–317; on Afrikania, see also de Witte, chapter 11 this volume).[13] But as scholars of modern public spheres have pointed out (e.g., Warner 2002, Soares 2005; cf. Eickelman and Anderson 2003), the opening up of the public sphere frequently leads to new forms of exclusion, as, for example, in the increased marginalization of African traditional religions in many places in Africa (Mndende 1999; Hackett 2012, 2014).

Fourth, Africa's changing media landscape has facilitated the rise of new religious publics. Indeed, the development of new listening and viewing communities, networks, and online communities has been occasionally sudden and rather dramatic. For example, Dr. Mensa Otabil, the founder of International Central Gospel Church in Ghana, has many followers and new publics that came first through radio and television and then via social media such as Facebook and Twitter, as does Malian Muslim preacher and media star Ousmane Madani Haïdara (on Haïdara, see Soares 2005, Schulz 2012b). Followers of the Mouride Sufi order based in Senegal sometimes watch videos and DVDs of pilgrimages to sacred sites in Senegal together as a means of constructing their religious community in diasporic contexts (Buggenhagen 2010). "Traditional" Yoruba religion has been able to extend its sphere of influence beyond southwestern Nigeria and Benin to practitioners and seekers through various websites and online publications.[14]

Fifth, such new religious publics and various entrepreneurial individuals have helped to create new religious spaces. Media outlets sometimes provide new spaces for religious expression, communication, practice, and encounter that frequently blur the distinctions between public and private, potentially enhancing and/or challenging conventional religious sites, boundaries, organizations, and styles. Birgit Meyer (2008: 87) writes of how "the popular Christian imaginary is affirmed, extended, and actualized in public and private space" through a "forest of [mass-mediated] pictures and sounds" in southern Ghana (see, also, de Witte 2008b). Some vivid examples of this are the multitude of religious posters and signboards, especially in urban locations and even attached to vehicles, for example, in Nigeria (Ukah 2008), and elsewhere.

Sixth, media, and "new" media in digital forms in particular, have been central to some of the new religious debates in Africa. In some cases, media have created greater opportunities for intra-religious debates and public critique of religious "Others"—for example, heated exchanges over the so-called gospel of prosperity associated with the new wave of Pentecostalism and questions of authority and authenticity (see, e.g., Asamoah-Gyadu 2009). The controversial Nigerian TV healer T. B. Joshua, founding pastor of The Synagogue, Church of All Nations (SCOAN), is frequently attacked in the popular print and online media for fraud and so-called occultism. Many of the films generated by Nollywood, Nigeria's successful movie industry, which is one of the largest in the world, demonize traditional religious practices (Krings 2005).

Seventh, media have helped to change the configurations between different religious groups. What might be called mainstream religious groups and those who previously had privileged access to regulated state media outlets have sometimes been overshadowed or eclipsed by newer religious organizations, such as Pentecostals, that have been more adept at (and are usually more economically empowered in) exploiting modern media technologies, as have some modernist and reformist Muslims who have usually taken up the use of media before the other Muslims they have critiqued (Brigaglia 2007; Larkin and Adama, chapters 3 and 7 this volume). Media domination or saturation can also lead to resentment, potentially disrupting interreligious cooperation. Additionally, the granting of licenses and airtime can be instrumental in empowering or disempowering various religious actors and organizations.

Eighth, media have been crucial to changes in state and/or popular recognition of religious groups. Positive or negative media representation can influence state organs and/or popular opinion in according public roles and benefits to different religious groups. Muslims and traditional religious leaders in post-apartheid South Africa have challenged the South African Broadcasting Corporation over programming bias (Hackett 2006; Mndende 2009). New religious movements, such as ECK—the science of sound and light—in Ghana[15] or the Mormons in Uganda[16] can try to counter popular so-called anti-cult fears through informative, internationally linked websites. Increasing numbers of "traditional" healers and diviners in many places in Africa have sought to enhance their credibility through an online presence—for example, in websites and on YouTube and through radio advertising and publicity.[17]

Outline

Part 1 of this book focuses on what is conventionally understood as "old" media. All four chapters examine how African Muslims have engaged with and taken up mass media, particularly print media and radio, in various contexts and the audiences and various publics that have emerged around such media. In his very detailed study of the Voice of Mombasa, James Brennan traces the history of Islamic radio broadcasting in Mombasa in coastal Kenya from the late colonial to the postcolonial period. After Axis powers introduced radio programming dealing with Islamic topics during World War II, Islamic programming became part of pro-colonial British propaganda broadcasting. By the 1950s, the semi-independent radio station in Mombasa created a popular radio format and radio celebrities that appealed to a broad Muslim public. After independence, state broadcasting ostensibly aimed toward nation-building marginalized most Islamic content, and this caused much consternation and resentment among Muslims in coastal Kenya.

In his history and ethnography of the Mali's major Islamic bookshops, Francesco Zappa shows the great importance and influence of Islamic print media in a country where levels of literacy and reading remain very low. He argues that the market for Islamic print media suggests two dual processes. On the one hand, short catechism-like publications provide basic information about Islam and contribute to the standardization of ways of being Muslim and attitudes to religious knowledge. On the other, there is a trend toward increased diversification and pluralism as illustrated in the partisan doctrinal trends of contemporary Islam in Mali as represented in the print media available on the market.

Brian Larkin focuses on Nigeria's foremost Muslim reformist cleric, Sheikh Abubakar Gumi, who was one of the first Muslim clerics in Nigeria to actively embrace mass media. Gumi wrote a newspaper column, made radio broadcasts, and circulated his texts in audio and later video recordings, and inspired a major Islamic reform movement in Nigeria and beyond. Larkin considers "the ways media technologies shape the character and practice of Islamic movements"—for example, in the kind of rational argumentation and discussion in a public sphere that Gumi actively promoted as part of his broader Islamic reformist project. However, he cautions against "being subsumed by the language of rupture" that such reformists—as well as many in media theory and scholars of religion—often espouse. Indeed, as he demonstrates, such stated objectives and teleologies are frequently contradicted in practice.

Muhammed Haron's contribution discusses two Muslim community radio stations in post-apartheid South Africa, one in Cape Town and the other in Johannesburg. As he argues, such community radio stations targeting South Africa's small but diverse Muslim minority spend considerable time promoting what they consider Islamic values and an Islamic lifestyle. If the conservative Muslim theologians associated with one of the stations were resistant to state-sanctioned gender equality mandates requiring women to broadcast on the station and adamant about the incompatibility of Islam and homosexuality, the other station dedicated itself to cultivate religious tolerance and demonstrate respect toward the rights of other communities.

In part 2, the authors examine the appropriations of various "new" media by a range of religious and social communities and the resultant transformations in experience, communality, political engagement, and entertainment. Johannes Merz traces the recent success of locally produced films across West Africa to the cultural resonance of the special visual effects used to communicate the presence of transcendence. He discusses how these films mediate a religious experience to their audiences and act as transcendent mediators between the local or "traditional" and the global or modern. Katrien Pype examines how well Pentecostal Christianity thrives on television. Her particular ethnographic focus is the fictional melodrama in post-Mobutu Kinshasa in the Democratic Republic of Congo. She explores, first, the symbolic structure shared by Pentecostalism and the melodrama, and second, the central role of emotions both in the evangelizing project as well as in Kinshasa's TV fiction.

In his history of Islamic communication and media in Cameroon, Hamadou Adama shows how state-sanctioned "traditional" Muslim religious leaders—so-called *marabouts*—who were taken to be pliable and quiescent had almost exclusive access to state media outlets for Islamic religious programming during the long period of one-party rule. As in Nigeria, it was Muslim reformists who first actively embraced new media technologies. In the era of political liberalization and media liberalization, young media-savvy Muslims in Cameroon have used a popular, didactic Islamic publication, as well as the internet, to disseminate knowledge about being Muslim and modern in ways that contest those who had been close to the one-party state but that are not the mere importation of models of how to be Muslim from the Arab world.

In his contribution, Kwabena Asamoah-Gyadu discusses how Ghanaian Pentecostal churches have appropriated the internet as a major tool of evangelization, translocal and transnational outreach, marketing, and identity formation. He attributes their enthusiastic embrace of this new medium not only to its potential for enhancing the status of Pentecostal leaders and their congregations but also to the strands of dominion and prosperity theology in Pentecostalism. He provides several examples of Pentecostal church founders who claim that God created the internet for the purposes of religious communication or that it can be appropriated and sacralized to such an end.

In his study of Arab satellite television Ehab Galal considers how various privately owned Arab Islamic satellite channels have become new and important players in mediascapes in North Africa but also much farther afield in the Muslim world, where satellite television has become pervasive and influential. Even though these private satellite channels seem to challenge the authority of states and state-controlled secular media outlets, the Islamic satellite channels have often promoted a version of Islam that is apolitical and therefore often palatable and nonthreatening to the authoritarian regimes of North Africa that were replaced since the so-called Arab Spring. After the new Egyptian regime took steps to close down several of the satellite stations with ties to ousted president Morsi and the Muslim Brotherhood, what place the other channels might take in the new political dispensation remains unclear.

The revolutionary impact of mobile telephony in Africa has recently been much noted, and this is no less the case in religious spheres. In his contribution, 'Rotimi Taiwo investigates the profound influence of the mobile phone on religious communication in southwestern Nigeria. In his study of emerging Christian, predominantly Pentecostal, communities of SMS users, he discusses the typical linguistic forms and socio-linguistic functions of religious SMS. He demonstrates the impact of text messaging for proselytization and the fulfillment of social responsibilities.

Part 3 covers arenas of exchange, competition, and conflict in African mediascapes. If the first section, which largely focuses on Islam, and the second, which concentrates on Pentecostalism and reformist Muslims, this final part of the book is more explicitly comparative in approach. It begins with Marleen de Witte's insightful account of the media activities of a neo-traditional religious movement, the Afrikania Mission, in Ghana's Christian-dominated public sphere. Analyzing Afrikania's changing position in and interactions with the public sphere in relation to shifts in Ghana's political, religious, and media landscape, de Witte shows how new constraints and opportunities have compelled Afrikania to adapt its strategies of accessing the media and its styles of representation.

Vicki Brennan explores the dynamic relationships between religious publics in the Nigerian mega-city of Lagos and the tensions that animate these relations from the perspective of genre conventions as an aspect of musical style. Drawing on insights from ethnomusicology and linguistic anthropology about the relationships among genre, intertextuality, and audience, she analyzes how gospel musicians use a diverse array of musical genres that are designed to "grab" certain listeners to circulate their Christian message into Nigeria's urban spaces. In doing so, she elaborates on the implications of the use of musical styles and genres for the kinds of religious audiences and publics produced through the circulation of their music and the impact this circulation has on the nature of religious practice in urban Nigeria. Also writing on Nigeria, but focusing on the practices and policies of the Nigerian Television Authority and the National Broadcasting Commission (NBC) vis-à-vis religious broadcasting in a multireligious society, Asonzeh Ukah considers some of the controversial processes of regulating deregulation. At the center of these controversies is the ban on the broadcast of what the NBC termed, without explanation, "unverified miracles" and its implications for conflict management. While the NBC claimed to be perturbed about entrepreneurial pastors who used the broadcast media to deceive unsuspecting Nigerians, many Pentecostals interpreted this as a strategy to limit their religious freedom.

In his contribution, Samson Bezabeh looks at what he calls the "digital landscapes" in Ethiopia where Muslims and Orthodox Christians have been engaging in increasingly polemical discussions (see also Abbink 2011). He focuses on Dr. Zakir Naik, the Mumbai-based medical doctor cum preacher and founder of the very influential *PeaceTV* broadcast on satellite television, some of whose lectures have been translated into Amharic and circulated on VCD/DVDs in Ethiopia. As Bezabeh notes, the rhetorical and polemical language about Muslims and their plight in Zakir Naik's media productions and their translations are inserted into a setting where tensions might rise as Muslims begin to think they are being marginalized and Orthodox Christians increasingly assert that Ethiopia is a Christian country, despite the presence of a very large Muslim population.

Several of the contributors have shown the longstanding and important influence of media coming from outside Africa on the continent. In contrast, in his contribution, David Chidester (2008) illustrates the transnational media flows emanating from Africa in his case of a Zulu shaman influencing New Age media outside Africa. Chidester treats the reinterpretation of dreams, visions, and extraordinary spiritual experiences by such Zulu neo-shamans as Credo Mutwa in a globalizing South Africa. He shows how they engage the human sensorium and electronic media in three ways: as limit, as potential, and as validation of this new Zulu shamanism. He situates the media-saturated dreamscape, with its abundant and extravagant sensory engagements with extraterrestrials and ancestral spirits, within what he terms "a new energetics of global exchange and global orientation."

In contrast to much of the recent research about media that tends to downplay or even ignore religion, particularly in Africa, the contributors to this book underscore the importance of analyzing the mutual imbrications of media and religion amidst rapid technological and social change on the continent. Not only do these historically and ethnographically rich studies point to new sites of religious learning, participation, expression, and modes of belonging, but they also enrich broader conversations on representation, authentication, commodification, de- and/or re-regulation of media, and censorship, as well as inter- and intra-communal conflict. Moreover, such research on religion and modern media in the African context is especially productive for understanding the local, regional, and global interplay of ideas, discourses, agents, and networks. It also points to the need for additional research in this field given the rapidity of transformations in both media and religion.

Notes

1. See, especially, Hoover and Lundby 1997; de Vries and Weber 2001; Ginsberg et al. 2002; Hoover and Clark 2002; Mitchell and Marriage 2003; Hoover 2006; Meyer and Moors 2006; Morgan 2007; Hirschkind and Larkin 2008; Campbell 2010.

2. See, for example, Bourgault 1995; Fardon and Furniss 1997; Frère 2007; Njogu and Middleton 2009.

3. On the absence of religion in media studies more generally, see Engelke 2010: 377.

4. See, for example, Hackett 1998, 2012; de Witte 2003; Ukah 2003; Meyer 2004; Asamoah-Gyadu 2005; Ihejerika 2006; Marshall 2009: 137–141.

5. Medianthro discussion, December 4, 2012 (email to list).

6. For example, the leading journal in the field, *Journal of African Media Studies*, has devoted little attention to religion. The Pew Forum on Religion and Public Life report (*Tolerance and Tension: Islam and Christianity in Sub-Saharan Africa*) contains a chapter, "Interreligious Harmony and Tensions," that fails to consider how media are often a major factor in shaping negative perceptions of religious "others" and how media can fuel or exacerbate tensions and conflict.

7. On such broader recent changes in Africa, see Otayek and Soares 2007.

8. See, for example, the innovative children's multifaith program shown on SABC in South Africa, "Siyakholwa—We Believe" (Scharnick 2012) and https://www.facebook.com /SiyakholwaWeBelieve. On the Imam and the Pastor, see, for example, https://www.iofc.org /imam-pastor.

9. We are grateful to Robert Launay for encouraging us to clarify these issues. See the special issue of *Culture, Theory and Critique* on "The Newness of New Media" (Gershon and Bell 2013).

10. On Ould Dedew, see Ould Ahmed Salem 2013 and his website, www.dedewnet.com. On Amr Khaled, see Haenni and Holtrop 2002 and his website, www.amrkhaled.net.

11. See, for example, reports by the BBC World Service Trust, *African Media Development Initiative* (2006) and the Panos Institute of West Africa, *Médias et religions en Afrique de l'Ouest* (2009). Compare to the recent Cambridge Arab Media Project (2010) report on religious broadcasting in the Middle East.

12. See, for example, their Facebook page, https://www.facebook.com/pages/Nasfat-Youth -WING-Abuja/165556936800588?sk=info, and related video clips and social media.

13. See, for example, http://www.voanews.com/content/a-13-2006-10-12-voa28/398073 .html.

14. See, for example, Prince (Babalawo) Adigun Olosun's Ibile Faith Online Congregation, http://www.zoominfo.com/p/Adigun-Olosun/1142751525.

15. http://www.eck-ghana.org/.

16. http://allafrica.com/stories/201303060138.html.

17. http://www.traditionalhealer.co.za/ and http://www.newsfromafrica.org/newsfrom africa/articles/art_7486.html.

References

Abbink, Jon. 2011. "Religion in Public Spaces: Emerging Muslim-Christian Polemics in Ethiopia." *African Affairs* 110(439): 253–274.

African Media Development Initiative: Research Summary Report. 2006. London: BBC World Service Trust.

Asamoah-Gyadu, J. Kwabena. 2005. "Reshaping Sub-Saharan African Christianity." *Media Development* 42(2): 17–21.

———. 2009. "Did Jesus Wear Designer Robes?" *Christianity Today*. http://www.christianitytoday.com/globalconversation/november2009/.

Bourgault, Louise M. 1995. *Mass Media in Sub-Saharan Africa*. Bloomington: Indiana University Press.

Brigaglia, Andrea. 2007. "The Radio Kaduna 'tafsir' (1978–1992) and the Construction of Public Images of Muslim Scholars in the Nigerian Media." *Journal for Islamic Studies* 27: 173–210.

Buggenhagen, Beth. 2010. "Islam and the Media of Devotion In and Out of Senegal." *Visual Anthropology Review* 26(2): 81–95.

Cambridge Arab Media Project (CAMP) and the Prince Alwaleed bin Talal Centre of Islamic Studies (CIS). 2010. *Religious Broadcasting in the Middle East. Islamic, Christian and Jewish Channels: Programmes and Discourses*. Cambridge: University of Cambridge.

Campbell, Heidi. 2010. *When Religion Meets New Media: Religion, Media and Culture*. New York: Routledge.

Chidester, David. 2008. "Zulu Dreamscapes: Senses, Media, and Authentication in Contemporary Neo-Shamanism." *Material Religion* 4(2): 136–159.

de Bruijn, Mirjam, Francis Nyamnjoh, and Inge Brinkman, eds. 2009. *Mobile Phones: The New Talking Drums of Everyday Africa*. Bamenda: Langaa RPCIG; Leiden: African Studies Centre.

de Vries, Henk, and Samuel Weber, eds. 2001. *Religion and Media*. Stanford, CA: Stanford University Press.

de Witte, Marleen. 2003. "Televised Charismatic Christianity in Ghana." *Journal of Religion in Africa* 33(2): 171–202.

———. 2008a. "Spirit Media: Charismatics, Traditionalists, and Mediation Practices in Ghana." PhD dissertation, University of Amsterdam.

———. 2008b. "Accra's Sounds and Sacred Spaces." *International Journal of Urban and Regional Research* 32(3): 690–709.

Eickelman, Dale F., and Jon W. Anderson, eds. 2003. *New Media in the Muslim World: The Emerging Public Sphere,* 2nd ed. Bloomington: Indiana University Press.

Eisenlohr, Patrick. 2012. "Media and Religious Diversity." *Annual Review of Anthropology* 41: 37–55.

Engelke, Matthew. 2010. "Religion and the Media Turn: A Review Essay." *American Ethnologist* 37(2): 371–379.

Fardon, Richard, and Graham Furniss, eds. 2000. *African Broadcast Cultures: Radio in Transition*. Oxford: James Currey.

Frère, Marie-Soleil. 2007. *The Media and Conflicts in Central Africa*. Boulder, CO: Lynne Rienner.

Gershon, Ilana, and Joshua A. Bell. 2013. "Introduction: The Newness of New Media." *Culture, Theory and Critique* 54(3): 259–264.

Ginsberg, Faye, Lila Abu-Lughod, and Brian Larkin, eds. 2002. *Media Worlds: Anthropology on New Terrain*. Berkeley: University of California Press.

Goliama, Castor M. 2010. *Where Are You, Africa? Church and Society in the Mobile Phone Age*. Bamenda: Langaa.

Gunner, Liz, Dina Ligaga, and Dumisani Moyo, eds. 2011. *Radio in Africa: Publics, Cultures, Communities*. Johannesburg: Wits University Press.

Hackett, Rosalind I. J. 1998. "Charismatic/Pentecostal Appropriation of Media Technologies in Nigeria and Ghana." *Journal of Religion in Africa* 26(4): 1–19.

——. 2006. "Mediated Religion in South Africa: Balancing Air-time and Rights Claims." In *Media, Religion and the Public Sphere,* edited by Birgit Meyer and Annelies Moors, 166–187. Bloomington: Indiana University Press.

——. 2011. "Regulating Religious Freedom in Africa." *Emory International Law Review* 25: 853–879.

——. 2012. "Devil Bustin' Satellites: How Media Liberalization in Africa Generates Religious Intolerance and Conflict." In *Displacing the State: Religion and Conflict in Neoliberal Africa,* edited by James H. Smith and Rosalind I. J. Hackett, 153–208. South Bend, IN: University of Notre Dame Press.

——. 2014. "Traditional, African, Religious, Freedom?" In *Politics of Religious Freedom,* edited by Winnifred Fallers Sullivan, Elizabeth Shakman Hurd, Saba Mahmood, and Peter Danchin. Chicago: University of Chicago Press.

Haenni, Patrick, and Tjitske Holtrop. 2002. "Mondaines spiritualités: Amr Khâlid, 'shaykh branché' de la jeunesse dorée du Caire." *Politique Africaine* 87: 45–68.

Haron, Muhammed. 2004. "The South African Muslims Making (Air)Waves during the Period of Transformation." In *Religion, Politics, and Identity in a Changing South Africa,* edited by David Chidester, Abdulkader Tayob, and Wolfram Weisse, 125–159. New York: Waxmann.

Hirschkind, Charles. 2006. *The Ethical Soundscape: Cassette Sermons and Islamic Counterpublics.* New York: Columbia University Press.

Hirschkind, Charles, and Brian Larkin. 2008. "Introduction: Media and the Political Forms of Religion." *Social Text* 26(3): 1–9.

Hoover, Stewart M. 2006. *Religion in the Media Age: Religion, Media and Culture.* New York: Routledge.

Hoover, Stewart M., and Lynn Schofield Clark, eds. 2002. *Practicing Religion in the Age of the Media.* New York: Columbia University Press.

Hoover, Stewart M., and Knut Lundby, eds. 1997. *Rethinking Media, Religion, and Culture.* Thousand Oaks, CA: Sage.

Hyden, Goran, Michael Leslie, and Folu F. Ogundimu, eds. 2002. *Media and Democracy in Africa.* New Brunswick, NJ: Transaction.

Ibrahim, Musa. 2013. "Media, Religion and Public Sphere: A Study of Muslim Programmes on Ghanaian Radio and Television Stations." Master's diss., University of Cape Town.

Ihejirika, Walter Chikwendu. 2006. *From Catholicism to Pentecostalism: Role of Nigerian Televangelists in Religious Conversion.* Port Harcourt: University of Port Harcourt Press.

——. 2009. "Research on Media, Religion and Culture in Africa: Current Trends and Debates." *African Communication Research* 2(1): 1–30.

Krings, Matthias. 2005. "Muslim Martyrs and Pagan Vampires: Popular Video Films and the Propagation of Religion in Northern Nigeria." *Postscripts: Journal of Sacred Texts and Contemporary Worlds* 1(2–3): 185–205.

Larkin, Brian. 2008a. *Signal and Noise: Media, Infrastructure, and Urban Culture in Nigeria.* Durham, NC: Duke University Press.

——. 2008b. "Ahmed Deedat and the Form of Islamic Evangelism." *Social Text* 26(3): 101–121.

Launay, Robert. 1997. "Spirit Media: The Electronic Media and Islam among the Dyula of Northern Côte d'Ivoire."*Africa* 67(3): 441–453.

Marshall, Ruth. 2009. *Political Spiritualities: The Pentecostal Revolution in Nigeria.* Chicago: University of Chicago Press.

Médias et religions en Afrique de l'Ouest. 2009. Dakar: L'Institut Panos Afrique de l'Ouest / The Panos Institute of West Africa.

Meyer, Birgit. 2004. "'Praise the Lord': Popular Cinema and Pentecostalite Style in Ghana's New Public Sphere." *American Ethnologist* 31(1): 92–110.

——. 2008. "Powerful Pictures: Popular Christian Aesthetics in Southern Ghana." *Journal of the American Academy of Religion* 76(1): 82–110.

Meyer, Birgit, and Annelies Moors, eds. 2006. *Religion, Media, and the Public Sphere.* Bloomington: Indiana University Press.

Mfumbusa, Bernardin, and Robert A. White, eds. 2009. Special issue, "Media and Religion in Africa," *African Communication Research* 2(1).

Mitchell, Jolyon, and Sophia Marriage, eds. 2003. *Mediating Religion: Conversations in Media, Religion, and Culture.* Edinburgh: T & T Clark.

Mndende, Nokuzola. 1999. "From Racial Oppression to Religious Oppression: African Religion in the New South Africa." In *Religion and Social Transformation in Southern Africa,* edited by Frank Kaufmann and Thomas G. Walsh, 143–155. St. Paul, MN: Paragon House.

——. 2009. *Tears of Distress: Voices of a Denied Spirituality in a Democratic South Africa.* Dutywa, South Africa: Icamagu Institute.

Morgan, David. 2007. *The Lure of Images: A History of Religion and Visual Media in America.* New York: Routledge.

Njogu, Kimani, and John Middleton, eds. 2009. *Media and Identity in Africa.* Edinburgh: Edinburgh University Press.

Nyamnjoh, Francis B. 2005. *Africa's Media: Democracy and the Politics of Belonging.* London: Zed Books.

Otayek, René, and Benjamin F. Soares. 2007. "Introduction." In *Islam and Muslim Politics in Africa,* edited by Benjamin F. Soares and René Otayek, 1–24. New York: Palgrave.

Ould Ahmed Salem, Zekeria. 2013. "Mohammed El Hacen Ould Dedew." Oxford Islamic Studies Online.

Sadouni, Samadia. 2011. *La controverse islamo-chrétienne en Afrique du Sud: Ahmed Deedat et les nouvelles formes de débat.* Aix-en-Provence, France: Presses universitaires de Provence.

Scharnick, Lee-Shae. 2012. "Siyakholwa: A Study in Religion, Education and Media in South Africa." MSocSc. Religious Studies, unpublished thesis, University of Cape Town.

Schulz, Dorothea. 2012a. "Dis/Embodying Authority: Female Radio 'Preachers' and the Ambivalences of Mass-Mediated Speech in Mali. *International Journal of Middle East Studies* 44(1): 23–43.

——. 2012b. *Muslims and New Media in West Africa: Pathways to God.* Bloomington: Indiana University Press.

Soares, Benjamin F. 2005. *Islam and the Prayer Economy: History and Authority in a Malian Town.* Ann Arbor and Edinburgh: University of Michigan Press / University of Edinburgh Press for the International African Institute.

——. 2007. "Saint and Sufi in Contemporary Mali." In *Sufism and the "Modern" in Islam,* edited by Martin van Bruinessen and Julia Howell, 76–91. London: I. B. Tauris.

——. 2009. "An Islamic Social Movement in Contemporary West Africa: NASFAT of Nigeria." In *Movers and Shakers: Social Movements in Africa,* edited by Stephen Ellis and Ineke van Kessel, 178–196. Leiden: Brill.

Stoneman, Timothy. 2012. "Radio Missions: Station ELWA in West Africa." *International Bulletin of Missionary Research,* October 1.

Tomaselli, Keyan G. 2009. "Repositioning African Media Studies." *Journal of African Media Studies* 1(1): 9–21.

Ukah, Asonzeh. 2003. "Advertising God: Nigerian Christian Video-Films and the Power of Consumer Culture." *Journal of Religion in Africa* 33(2): 203–231.

———. 2008. "Seeing Is More than Believing: Posters and Proselytization in Nigeria." In *Proselytization Revisited: Rights Talk, Free Markets and Culture Wars,* edited by Rosalind I. J. Hackett, 167–198. London: Equinox Publishers.

Warner, Michael. 2002. *Publics and Counterpublics.* New York: Zone Books.

PART I

"Old" Media: Print and Radio

1 A History of Sauti ya Mvita (Voice of Mombasa)

Radio, Public Culture, and Islam in Coastal Kenya, 1947–1966

James R. Brennan

S*AUTI YA* M*VITA*, Swahili for "Voice of Mombasa," marks an odd but revealing chapter in the proliferation of radio technologies and religious publics in African history. It was a colonial radio station initially designed to quash local rumor and counter external criticism, but it was also one in which programming was largely produced by local volunteers. During the 1950s, a vibrant radio culture emerged in Mombasa, centered on the idea of a community station that would support and defend "coastal" values by valorizing the local dialect, celebrating Arab and Swahili cultural mores, and entrenching Muslim sensibilities in the station's basic sound and schedule. Sauti ya Mvita was not an Islamic station per se, but rather one purposely designed to meet and reflect the needs of what its programmers imagined to be a coastal Muslim audience situated within a larger sea of non-Muslims. The larger political and cultural significance of the station lay less in its theological content than in its daily format, which sought to amplify what Charles Hirschkind terms the "pious soundscape" (Hirschkind 2006) through sonic rhythms that juxtaposed prayer, recitation, and Muslim debate. At its center in Old Town Mombasa, this pious soundscape today still comprises, according to Andrew Eisenberg's (2009) ethnography, "amplified calls-to-prayer and religious sermons that crackle from loudspeakers mounted on mosques, and recitations and sermons that emanate from radios, boom boxes, and computer speakers in shops and homes" (95). Yet, Sauti ya Mvita also extended beyond the pious to include heavy doses of colonial didacticism, international news, and popular music. Its community monopoly enveloped religious expression and debate within the secular projects of postwar colonial Africa, where a relatively well-funded colonial radio station like Sauti ya Mvita could enlist local developmentalist energies and late imperial loyalties in order to counter international anti-colonial hostilities and the more basic anarchy that characterized shortwave broadcasting. The station's programming independence disappeared in 1959 as it had first appeared in 1947: through arbitrary decisions made in the Kenyan capital of Nairobi. Stripped of its local programming autonomy, Kenya's coastal Muslim listenership responded by demanding more explicitly Islamic programming content from Nairobi programmers during the 1960s and after.

Radio, Propaganda, and Counterpropaganda in Eastern Africa

Local vernacular radio across Africa began as a defensive colonial response to hostile external broadcasting. Anti-British radio broadcasting reached East Africa shortly before the outbreak of the Second World War. The world's shortwave bands were filled with hostile polemics railing against British imperialism, but only a few radio sets in East Africa could receive them, and only a tiny sliver of the population could understand the dominant languages. Colonial officials were most anxious about the potential effects of hostile Arabic-language broadcasts from Italy and Germany. In the early years of the war, large numbers of Arabic speakers in Nairobi and Mombasa would gather around radio sets to listen to Radio Berlin's Yunis al-Bahri preach Holy War against the British Empire.[1] Hyder Kindy, a high-ranking African civil servant in Mombasa, reminisced that neighbors would crowd into his home to hear al-Bahri's broadcasts. "More than 75 percent of the non-European Mombasa population of all religions were pro-German," Kindy (1972) explained, "and were saying quite openly that Britain would be defeated" (116). Little is known about the hostile broadcasts in Swahili emanating daily from Italian-controlled Addis Ababa in 1940–1941 except that they were judged hostile enough in Zanzibar and Tanganyika to seek restrictions on playing enemy broadcasts in public places.[2]

What little British-controlled radio that did exist was poorly positioned to respond to these unprecedented attacks. In 1939, East Africa had only one radio station that the British corporation Cable and Wireless operated in Nairobi on concessionary terms to serve the needs of the region's European and (to a lesser extent) Indian listeners. General policy before the war had been to discourage bringing wireless radio closer to African subjects.[3] The outbreak of war drove Nairobi's information officers to use this station (call-lettered "7LO") to make semi-regular broadcasts in Swahili and other vernacular languages to distribute propaganda about general wartime developments and to counter rumors of imminent Axis power attacks or alleged British defeats.[4] These efforts were joined by BBC's launch of a Swahili shortwave service from London in 1940.

Hostile external broadcasting to East Africa momentarily ceased at war's end—and with it the sense of urgency that had animated wartime colonial broadcasting. Swahili broadcasts from London grew less regular, but the British Broadcasting Corporation (BBC) did exert greater regional influence through its English, Hindustani, and Arabic broadcasts with larger and more regularized programming. What little international competition existed was weak. Global English-language broadcasts from the Soviet bloc went largely ignored. After

1947, Delhi's All India Radio used their English-language broadcast to criticize the British Empire, but in East Africa it was its Hindi, and particularly its Gujarati, programs that had the largest impact, and they were concerned mostly with music and cultural programming. Local radio development was complacent. A BBC engineer's recommendation to form an East African broadcasting scheme was rejected as too centralized and grandiose by territorial governments in 1949; radio would instead develop along separate territorial lines.[5] Radio ranked low in each government's spending priorities, and decision makers attached little urgency to matters of propaganda or counterpropaganda. Radio listening in immediate postwar Mombasa—this chapter's site of study—meant tuning into programming designed elsewhere, from Nairobi, the Armed Forces Broadcasting Station based in Mombasa, or one of the many signals coming from abroad.

Origins and Growth of Sauti ya Mvita, 1947–1959

Like its wartime predecessor, postwar radio programming in colonial East Africa grew largely in response to internal and external political threats. In Mombasa, the key threat was the January 1947 dockworkers' strike, which made the colony's transport nexus grind to a halt. Prevention of future disruptive strikes—sometimes tipped into action, officials felt, by swirling rumors—guided the regional government's new information as well as its labor policy. The new policy's linchpin was to establish a local radio station, which made its first broadcast on November 5, 1947.[6] Controlled by Mombasa's Municipal African Affairs Officer and broadcasting three times a week, the station was established as an arm of Mombasa's information control network, alongside its barazas, propaganda van, Sauti ya Pwani newssheet, and regular consultation with chiefs and presidents of tribal societies.[7] Beginning with public listening points, the government expanded its commitment to make local radio widely available—Coast Province was later allotted 500 "saucepan" radio sets as souvenirs of Queen Elizabeth's coronation, to distribute to African and Arab organizations with the understanding that they would tune into government broadcasts.[8] But other investments were paltry. Mombasa's initial studio and equipment were amateurish, even by prevailing regional standards, and its production methods were crude; "news" was little more than translating *Mombasa Times* items into Swahili. Into this void of production underinvestment stepped Arab volunteers, led by the *liwali* (literally "governor," the leading non-European administrator on the coast, theoretically subject to the Sultan of Zanzibar) of Mombasa, Sheikh al-Amin bin Said. These volunteers filled the thrice-weekly, hour-long Arabic broadcast with Quran readings and talks by imams from all over the Muslim world passing through Mombasa. The Provincial Information Officer in Mombasa freely admitted that the station "caters primarily to Arabs."[9] In 1952, the Mombasa station was renamed Sauti ya Mvita (Voice of Mombasa) by Muhammad Suleiman al-Mazrui, scion of the town's most important political family, who adopted the radio moniker "Abu Suleiman" (Kindy 1972: 164).

Founded to counter internal threats from transport strikes, Sauti ya Mvita blossomed in the mid-1950s with funding designed to defend against external threats from Radio Cairo. Vehemently anti-colonial Arabic broadcasts had entered East Africa from Cairo even before the July 1952 Free Officers coup and had moved the Kenyan government to inaugurate an Arabic broadcast on the Mombasa station.[10] But Cairo became a matter of regional security following the launch of its sharply anti-colonial Swahili-language broadcast, Sauti ya Cairo (Voice of Cairo), in July 1954 (Brennan 2010). Immediately following the launch of Cairo's Swahili program, Mombasa programming was extended first to 8:00 P.M. and then to 9:00 P.M. to "prevent our Swahili listeners tuning immediately to Radio Cairo," as well as to compete against All India Radio's Swahili broadcasts and Radio Moscow's English broadcasts.[11] Arab officials leveraged colonial anxieties to extract greater investments, noting that while Cairo and New Delhi were clearly audible on the northern and southern parts of the coast, Sauti ya Mvita's shortwave transmission was hard to hear at night along the coast, and its medium-wave range barely covered Mombasas Island.[12] The Deputy Governor agreed, adding that "the political importance of better reception of our broadcasts on the coast cannot be put too high."[13] Plans were laid to increase the strength of the broadcasting signal, in what was a thin, oval-shaped transmission pattern to fit the coast, to increase the listenership from 20,000 in Mombasa to some 100,000 along the coast.[14] Anxious officials utilized Sauti ya Mvita's Arabic and Ki-Mvita (Mombasa-dialect Swahili) programs after the Suez Canal hostilities broke out to berate Gamal Abdel Nasser's actions and credibility.[15] Funds soon spilled in from London; just two weeks after the British, French, and Israeli attack on the Sinai and Suez, Sauti ya Mvita was broadcast on a far more powerful shortwave transmitter.[16] The transmitters of Radio Cairo were bombed during the attack; when the signal reappeared a few days later, many Arabs began listening to it again, suggesting that Sauti ya Mvita had not in fact drawn away "any large numbers of listeners" from Cairo.[17]

Unique factors of local programming autonomy and sizeable colonial investment inaugurated a fascinating regional experiment in which consciously "coastal" programming attempted to connect Mombasa with a wider audience to create an international Swahili listening public. Formatting and scheduling were tasked to unite the listeners of the Swahili coast around programs emanating from Mombasa, Zanzibar, and Dar es Salaam. The liwali opposed a plan to shift broadcasting hours to an earlier time because it would conflict with Sauti ya Unguja (Voice of Zanzibar).[18] Programming followed a symbolically Islamic format. Broadcasts would begin with the Sultan of Zanzibar's anthem (the coast formally being under his sovereignty), followed by Quranic recitations. Indeed,

Quran readings would occupy 15 minutes of daily programming, although the station closed each night with the song "God Save the Queen."[19] Some non-Muslim African listeners resented this aspect of Sauti ya Mvita programming and preferred to listen to the implicitly Christian "African" broadcasts from Nairobi.[20] Sauti ya Mvita, which had initiated daily programming in 1954, had moved at last to a professional studio in Treasury Square in 1956, marking its ascent to competitive regional broadcasting.[21]

In interviews, former Sauti ya Mvita employees stressed the wide-ranging editorial freedoms they had enjoyed during the 1950s.[22] The Arab clique that had volunteered early on reaped enormous fruits for their initiative. The dominant personalities were mostly Arab ulama who worked on a volunteer or part-time basis. U. M. M. Bawawzir was the most popular Arabic broadcaster, while Sheikh Muhammad Suleiman Mazrui or "Abu Suleiman" (see above) was both a popular broadcaster as well as a producer on Ki-Mvita broadcasts. The liwali and his officers took close interest in Sauti ya Mvita's programming and staff.[23] European officials, mainly the station manager and the Provincial Information Officer, only oversaw the editing of the daily news. All other programming was left in the hands of local staff, whose loose project was to vindicate Arab culture, help propagate coastal Islam, and assert Mombasa's leading cultural role in the Swahili world. An Arab Broadcasting Committee was established in 1956 to advise on programs in Arabic, which grew into an advisory subcommittee that controlled the station's entire programming.[24] This establishment of formal control occurred just before Sauti ya Mvita began broadcasting from a powerful 5-kW shortwave transmitter, which considerably expanded the station's reach along the Swahili coast.[25]

The station's formal mission was to offer enlightened entertainment appropriate for its target audience. A typical month's programming would include news, music, religious talks, and local public announcements. In February 1956, for example, the 62.5-hour broadcast included talks by Mtoo Ghulum of Tanga, Sheikh Arif Tamir of Syria, Sheikh Mohamed bin Kassim Mazrui, the *kadhi* (judge) of Malindi, and Sheriff Abdulrehman Shatry (on his impression of Mecca and the Middle East); ten Arabic songs from Cairo; and acknowledgment of receipt of 340 letters, 317 of which were from Mombasa.[26] Sheikhs wielding enormous regional authority would also tape sermons for Sauti ya Mvita. Sheikh Abdulla Saleh al-Farsy of Zanzibar, later appointed Chief Kadhi of Zanzibar (1960) and Kenya (1966), recorded eight religious talks during a visit to Mombasa in October/November 1955.[27] By 1955, music had become the station's most popular program in the form of Ahmed Idha's "Mr. Music" on Saturday nights, which relied upon new Arabic records lent to the station for taping by other Sauti ya Mvita Arab volunteers.[28] In 1957, music comprised 44 percent of the Sauti ya Mvita's programming time, followed by 16 percent news and commentary,

15 percent religious programming, 8 percent relay of BBC Arabic, and the remaining 17 percent consisting of various features, plays, quizzes, and BBC rebroadcasts.[29] Popular records were whisked upon arrival at Kilindini Port to Sauti ya Mvita studios for taping.[30] Prohibited from seeking commercial revenues, the station relied heavily on such volunteerism in general. Local bands such as Lulu Orchestra donated their Swahili records for local publicity, while others such as Jowhara Orchestra were paid for in-station performances and recordings, though ever-rising band fees frequently led to the cancellation of such arrangements. Western music also had its proponents, but the station's advisory committee took care that it was not mixed with Arabic music by giving it a separate program.[31] This weekly half-hour slot was far out of proportion to the numerous Western music requests, and by 1959, the matter had become a public controversy.[32] Opponents claimed that Western music featured heavily in other programs such as "Down Your Street" and "Abdullah Presents," thus surpassing its half-hour quota. Strong demand was irrelevant, they argued, because other popular music (e.g., Hindi music) abided by similar restrictions.[33] Most controversial was the playing of rock and roll music. Hundreds of Arabs in Mombasa signed a petition, organized by Faraj Dumila, to ban the practice in early 1959 on the grounds that it spoiled "the thoughts and behaviour of our people and worse still disgrace and bring into disrepute our culture and tradition."[34] Another correspondent countered that he was not disturbed by rock and roll music, and found Kiswahili "Mtungi" and "Mgomba" songs far more immoral.[35]

"African" radio broadcasting in Kenya, meanwhile, was in the hands of the Nairobi-based Information Department under the banner of the African Broadcasting Service, or ABS. Broadcasting not only in Swahili but other vernaculars such as Kikuyu and Jaluo, ABS had a strong following up-country, particularly through its "ABS Club" members scattered throughout Nairobi, Kisumu, Nyeri, and Mombasa.[36] Its main personality was Kipanga Athumani, a young Maasai and former bus driver who came to fame by "ridiculing and guying the Mau Mau and their ceremonies," which allegedly "made more impression on the African mind than all the high-powered government propaganda and rehabilitation schemes put together."[37] ABS's all-European advisory committee aimed to lure away its "African" audience along the coast from the attractions not only of Cairo but also Radio India and Radio Madras. The favored means to do so was to employ modern and traditional musical attractions. "Spanish American music style was more popular than American jazz," the board concluded, and "hillbillies had an appeal for the African," but above all they felt that "attempts should be made to keep alive the interest and pride of the African in his own traditional music."[38] Religious programs on ABS were entirely Christian. The European denominational heads in Nairobi competed for airtime and served on the ABS advisory council; they also provided programming and broadcasting services without charge.[39]

Just as the Nairobi-based ABS worked to standardize Swahili pronunciations, the Mombasa-based Sauti ya Mvita worked to popularize "Ki-Mvita," conventionally understood to be a local dialect of Kiswahili spoken in and around Mombasa. It was, however, much more than this. Ki-Mvita constituted what Birgit Meyer has termed an "aesthetic formation," or the "formative impact of a shared aesthetic through which subjects are shaped by tuning their sense, inducing experiences, molding their bodies, and making sense" (Meyer 2009: 7). In both specific accent and general sensibility, Ki-Mvita pronounced a distinctive Muslim coastal culture asserting itself in relation to the simplified (or "barbarized") Swahili of the largely non-Muslim interior, which raised into relief a pious coastal soundscape. In closing a weekly roundup, Abu Suleiman offered a homily on the paradoxical meaning of "Mvita"; literally the word refers to war (*vita*), but in its properly understood sense for those who had grown up in the "country" (*nti*) of Mombasa, Mvita means to live peacefully.[40] The rapid expansion of Ki-Mvita programming coincided with the station's most influential years. In 1956, Ki-Mvita consisted of 34 percent of programming, compared to Arabic (44 percent) and mostly Swahili "African" programs (22 percent).[41] By 1957, the percentage of Ki-Mvita programming expanded enormously, to 60.5 percent of all programming (vs. 23.5 percent Arabic and 16 percent "Standard Swahili"); by 1958, Ki-Mvita comprised 56 percent of all broadcasting, Arabic 26 percent, and "standard" Swahili 17 percent.[42] This coincided with a massive increase in private radio ownership; radio, along with gramophone, provided "perhaps the most important form of relaxation to the African, and he greatly enjoys listening to the vernacular broadcasts" (Wilson 1958: 414). Listening was increasingly a domestic activity. As early as 1954, the audience turnout at the city's public listening points was in decline.[43] At that time, 53.1 percent of "Arab-Swahili" households in Mombasa had a radio—nearly twice as many as the next-largest "tribe" (Kikuyu/Embu/Meru) in town and three times that of "Coastal" Africans.[44]

Religion and Racial Politics at Sauti ya Mvita, 1956–1963

Sauti ya Mvita's sonic presence had the capacity to sacralize both public and domestic spaces, which sharpened listeners' mental geographies of a Muslim coast standing athwart a vast non-Muslim interior where political power lay. Through its format, Sauti ya Mvita also amplified the particular rhythms of Mombasa's pious soundscape by synchronizing its content around prayer times, Friday sermons, and major festival broadcasts. Sauti ya Mvita developed as a public institution that strengthened identifications with coastal Muslim culture, as well as one in which religious programming carried significant therapeutic value for individual listeners. Yet Sauti ya Mvita was never afforded any nonstate financing, either commercial or communal, but instead was a public service that was infrastructurally produced by late-colonial political structures, upon which local broadcasting volunteers were ultimately dependent.

Among Sauti ya Mvita's program volunteers, Sheikh Muhammad Suleiman Mazrui or "Abu Suleiman" had the most direct influence over popularizing Islamic themes through entertainment programs such as educational plays.[45] Like the Nigerian cleric Sheikh Abubakar Gumi (see chapter 3), Abu Suleiman embraced modern mass media of radio and newsprint to pursue a reformist agenda that was critical toward Christianity as well as Sufism and other "traditional" Islamic practices in which access to knowledge, often thought to be mystical or esoteric, is sharply hierarchical. One of Abu Suleiman's first radio plays, "How the Caliph Omar Embraced Islam," was lavishly praised for its "perfection of ingenious purity and divine truth that atoned for all its shortcomings in the way of drama."[46] Scripts of talks from late 1953 and early 1954 cover such themes as "giving birth to daughters," for which Abu Suleiman dutifully translates and explains a variety of Islamic concepts and practices in Ki-Mvita dialect.[47] The broadcasting project of Abu Suleiman was to carry on the reformist struggles of his paternal uncle, Sheikh al-Amin bin Ali al-Mazrui, a "modern reformer" who challenged the Sharifian elite of Lamu and was arguably the most influential figure among Kenya's ulama in the twentieth century (Pouwels 1981). One of al-Amin's several social issues was to reform coastal marriage practices by purging them of their expensive and "wasteful" excesses. Abu Suleiman similarly protested lavish feasts through humorous radio sketches to show that whatever advantages there may be, "they were heavily outweighed by the disadvantages." Abu Suleiman hosted a live radio debate on the topic in 1954, in which several interlocutors made quick recourse to al-Amin's 1930 writing on the subject in the latter's self-published pamphlet *Sahifa*. For Abu Suleiman and Sauti ya Mvita, this topic was less a matter for genuine debate than an attempt to fulfill al-Amin's intellectual work through a powerful new popular medium.[48] Abu Suleiman further used radio to promote a vigorous conservative defense of the treatment and status of women, speaking at length in support of the veiling of Arab women and demanding that Mombasa treat such women with "chivalry."[49] The "emancipation" of women, he explained in a live radio debate, was destroying coastal culture; citing the West's greater divorce rate [sic] and the religious grounds of purdah, he appealed that "the boot of motherhood . . . should remain indoors."[50] He also declared cinema harmful to female morals, although other debaters changed his mind by stressing the emotional needs that cinema can convey without need for women's mastery of English or Hindi.[51] Pursuing another long-standing campaign of Sheikh al-Amin led to Abu Suleiman's suspension. Sheikh al-Amin had sought to "clear the name" of Arabs in regards to slavery in East Africa, and he took aim at mission schools that hung "gruesome paintings of alleged atrocities perpetrated by the Arabs against the Africans." Abu Suleiman sought to vindicate "the pioneering Arab colonist here, the first ray of light into the Dark Continent" through a series of long arguments. In a voice "shaking with emotion," he concluded that "if history must feature in our politics here, and in our social and cultural discourse, let's hear more of the Arab civiliser and less of the slave-trader."[52] Abu Suleiman's favorable comparisons between Arab and Christian slavery apparently angered Christian listeners; he subsequently withdrew (voluntarily or otherwise) from Sauti ya Mvita for nearly a year, at great protest from hundreds of coastal listeners.[53]

If Abu Suleiman was Sauti ya Mvita's most powerful personality, Maalim Said was its most popular. Maalim Said Ahmed al-Kumri (d. 1980) started at the station in 1952 as a volunteer like everyone else, but as monies flowed in, he eventually became the station's highest-paid broadcaster. Sheikh Ahmad Msallam described Maalim Said as an average student of Sheikh Mohammad Kassim al-Mazrui (see Kresse 2003) before he entered radio. Msallam attributed Said's radio success to his smooth voice rather than his education. Whenever difficult theological questions arose, Maalim Said immediately turned to Sheikh Mohammad Kassim for answers before giving any on the air.[54] But thousands of listeners in Mombasa and elsewhere turned to Maalim Said for his advice on all aspects of Muslim life. He specialized in what Faraj Dumila terms "fantasies," which involved painting enticing pictures of the paradise awaiting his listeners after their life on earth, with rich references to *miraaj,* the Prophet Muhammad's Night Journey, and dispensing advice on the most popular of radio queries: those concerning love. Maalim Said's great popularity—Dumila claimed that he received a thousand letters a month—bred contempt among more intellectual ulama such as Abu Suleiman, but it also guaranteed that Sauti ya Mvita could never dispense with his services.[55] It was his voice, "a beautiful voice, a natural voice,"[56] that secured his fame. In mid-1957, the Provincial Information Officer attempted to reduce the station's payments to religious broadcasters, but the station's advisory committee, led by the liwali of Mombasa, Sheikh al-Amin bin Said el Mandhry, opposed applying this principle to Muslim religious broadcasts. He insisted that it was not possible to compare Muslim and Christian broadcasters' circumstances, since the latter nearly always gave talks for free because they were backed by "highly organised Christian associations and churches." Muslim broadcasters, in contrast, "were very poor men and could not be expected to do this." Maalim Said was eventually paid Shs. 150/- (approximately US$21.00 at the time) per month for his talks—roughly three times the average wage of a Mombasa dockworker at that time.[57] He became the station's one indispensable personality.

Newly amplified in 1957, Sauti ya Mvita gained a much wider reputation across East Africa. One listener in Zanzibar stated that the station's reception was so clear and the programming so good that "he himself and many whom he knows all tune to S.Y.M."[58] As far away as the Hadhramaut in Yemen, Sauti ya Mvita "was being listened to extensively" after 9:00 P.M., when interference on the station's signal subsided.[59] Inevitable comparisons between regional stations bred competition and jealousy. During a visit in 1959, Faraj Dumila, a journalist and broadcaster at Sauti ya Mvita, was deeply impressed with Radio Zanzibar's (Sauti ya Unguja) equipment, staff, and professionalism. He enviously noted that its *shairi* poets were paid Shs. 7/50 (approximately US$1.05) per poem and Holy Quran readers paid Shs. 10/– (approximately US$1.40) per recitation.[60] But Sauti ya Mvita had also launched local artists to wider fame throughout East Africa. Ahmed Nassir Juma Bhallo, Mombasa's finest shairi poet, came to regional prominence through Sauti ya Mvita broadcasts, while in Mombasa the broadcast of his poetry became an integral part of local Ramadan observance.[61]

Colonial radio stations were effective monopolies that wielded power to either include or exclude various "community" programs. Debates over Sauti ya Mvita's format and scheduling increasingly reflected the complex political terrain that characterized the late colonial Kenyan coast. Pressures to address African audiences grew slowly but steadily. The post-Suez infusion of funds raised issues of public investment and programming service among those Africans who lived in Coast Province but did not identify with "Arab-Swahili" cultural institutions. Mijikenda politicians like William Chimwaggah protested that despite the new transmitter, "we find that the major portion of time is given to Arabs at the cost of African programs."[62] During 1957, the population nominally served by Sauti ya Mvita included 21,000 Arabs, 13,000 Swahili, 390,000 Coastal Africans, and some 45,000 "up-country" Africans; yet Ki-Mvita took up 24.5 hours per week, Arabic took up 12.5 hours per week, and "up-country Swahili" took only 7 hours per week.[63] Criticism of the generous time allotted to Arabic language broadcasting grew particularly strong. If Sauti ya Mvita was celebrated as Kenya's first regional broadcasting station, then why, one writer asked, was its program "full of Koran only. . . . We do not enjoy this program, as it also talks about Arab songs which we—Rabai, Giriama, Duruma, and Teita people—do not understand."[64] Africans remained excluded from the Sauti ya Mvita advisory committee, and their official "representative"—a British colonial official— was tasked to oversee the station's "up-country" Swahili programming.[65] Ronald Ngala, Kenya's leading Mijikenda politician, argued in Legislative Council that Sauti ya Mvita would better serve its African audience by providing a Giriama vernacular service.[66] His lobbying efforts led to the establishment of an hour-long "African Programme" in November 1957 and also created a bitter debate about the place of African representation on Sauti ya Mvita's Arab-dominated advisory council.[67] Arabs on the council resisted African appointments, and the Information Department instead formed an "African" advisory council meeting, thus formally separating "African" Swahili programming from Arabic and Ki-Mvita programming within Sauti ya Mvita's structure.[68] The distinction was implicitly religious—Hyder Kindy identifies the former as the "African Christian section."[69] Yet, Sauti ya Mvita's "African" listenership increased steadily over 1958, particularly in Coast Province.[70]

Racial politics and religion proved inseparable elements in defining the station's aesthetic formation. Taveta's District Officer complained that the content of its "African" hour was "so interlaced with Muslim music which does not commend itself to the Africans here. . . . They would like the program to be wholly of African or Western music but not Muslim."[71] Like most colonial radio stations, Sauti ya Mvita steered clear of emerging African party politics, refusing announcement requests from Francis Khamisi's Mombasa African Democratic Union (MADU).[72] Yet, politics were increasingly difficult to avoid. In 1959, the Coast Provincial Commissioner polled officials on the popularity of the hour-long "African Programme" to gauge whether or not to increase "truly coastal or Islamic programmes in Ki-Mvita or Arabic."[73] He suggested that few Africans were listening to Sauti ya Mvita's "African Programme" and preferred ABS from Nairobi and TBC (Tanzania Broadcasting Corporation) from Dar es Salaam because both provided "a continuous programme comprehensible to Africans and of music enjoyed by Africans." Even the station's most popular program, "Listeners' Choice," was dominated by Arabic music, "no doubt at the request of Swahilis, which means that even this hour is not entirely African in content and contains music which is not popular with the African."[74]

A bureaucratic showdown occurred in May 1959, shortly before Sauti ya Mvita was folded into the new Kenya Broadcasting System (KBS) regional network. The Arab-dominated advisory committee recommended, not for the first time, that the "African House" and all other African programming be cut on the grounds that this audience was "catered for perfectly adequately" by African programs from Nairobi. The director of broadcasting in Nairobi, however, vetoed this suggestion and furthermore demanded that the station "take positive steps to avoid giving the impression that the words 'Coast Regional Programme' are synonymous with 'Arabic Regional Programme' or even 'Muslim Regional Programme,' an impression that the membership of the Coast Province Broadcasting Advisory Committee does little to belie."[75] The Provincial Information Officer agreed in principle but warned

> there is no doubt whatever that the Arabs (and ipso facto the Muslims) do and always have looked upon "Sauti Ya Mvita" as their own particular station, and they do unquestionably adopt a strong "parental" attitude toward it. . . . But my own experience here suggests that a Committee of this nature, above all in the light of what may now be regarded as almost an established precedent locally, might not function efficiently if both Arab (Muslim) and African views were

represented simultaneously. . . . [Any "widening" in scope of local broadcasts] will need to be handled carefully.[76]

With little care or tact, the government announced on July 1, 1959, that Sauti ya Mvita no longer existed. The station was subsumed within the KBS and redesignated the Coast Regional Station of the KBS.[77] With the establishment of KBS, both the advisory subcommittee and the Provincial Information Officer lost effective control over the major programming decisions to Nairobi.[78] The creation of KBS finally introduced commercial programming to Kenya (hitherto limited to "spot" advertisements), though this was limited to one hour per day, "in order to assess the effect on African audiences."[79]

The response from loyal Sauti ya Mvita listeners was a revealing befuddlement. Seventy Muslim signatories from the northern towns of Witu and Mkunumbi simply did not know what to make of the absence of "The Week in Mombasa and Its Coast," a weekly review featuring the movements and social events along the coastal strip that had long been a fixture of Sauti ya Mvita programming.[80] They asked it to be returned, for without it they had no way of getting news about their neighbors and family that Abu Suleiman had provided for so long. Updates on the price of rabbits, they bitterly noted, did not help them at all, but knowing who was traveling to Mecca—a regular feature of the weekly social review—did profit them greatly.[81] Most African listeners along the coast continued to prefer Dar es Salaam or Nairobi over the new Coastal KBS service. The aesthetic formation that surrounded Ki-Mvita programming had been stripped of its local institutional backing, seriously disrupting the pious soundscape that had developed over the preceding five years. British programmers in Nairobi attempted to rationalize and streamline national broadcasting, asking, "Is the Ki-Mvita Program on the Coast really necessary?"[82]—to which another official agreed by replying, "The languages we should use at the Coast should be KiUnguja [the Zanzibari dialect, upon which standardized Swahili is based], and this should satisfy everybody."[83] Resentment at this loss of local control became a defining feature of radio listenership along the coast in the decade that followed independence.

Coast Province Radio after *Uhuru* (Independence), 1964–1966

The rise of a nationalized radio monopoly in KBS, quickly renamed the Voice of Kenya (VOK) within the Kenya Broadcasting Corporation, combined with the reduction in plainly "coastal" format and scheduling, sharply raised the stakes for both religious and regional representation. In 1963, the Coast Regional Station was renamed the Mombasa station of the Kenya Broadcasting Corporation "to avoid any possible suggestion that our present Regional Stations will be serving only 'regional' interests."[84] Mijikenda political activists, mostly supporters of the regionalist Kenya African Democratic Union (KADU) party, styled themselves as the genuine citizens (*wananchi halisi*) of the coast and petitioned the new African DC in Mombasa to begin radio announcements in "indigenous languages" such as Kidigo, Kipokomo, Kitaita, and Kigiriama. They argued that Arabic and Ki-Mvita broadcasting should be removed entirely, likening the use of both languages to be as irrelevant to the indigenous inhabitants as Nairobi's Hindi language broadcasts were.[85]

They soon had their way. Both Arabic and Ki-Mvita broadcasts were removed from VOK's Mombasa station in July 1964, not only canceled as programs but effectively broken as aesthetic formations. Mombasa radio was no longer instantly identifiable by its sonorous texture of Islamic acoustics that represented local communitarian ideals of coastal life. Its programming was now thoroughly subsumed within the Kenya national network; "African" sounds quickly grew dominant. Stripped of their Sauti ya Mvita format, coastal listeners shifted their energies to defend and entrench most explicitly Islamic programming. At that year's *maulid* (celebration of the Prophet Muhammad's birth), the Islahil Islamiyyah resolved that the Minister of Broadcasting restore Islamic religious programs "by way of recitals of passages from the Holy Quran followed by translation into Swahili and commentaries by learned theologians in the mornings and evenings as it was before." The body also urged sympathetic consideration "before the feelings of Muslims start to run riot, since already they feel they are being dragged into forcibly listening to Christian prayers only during the opening and closing of the station."[86] The Minister replied that VOK was still broadcasting daily Islamic religious programs with an addition of four half-hour programs per week and asked the community to take up the matter with Maalim Said.[87] Some Ki-Mvita programming was briefly and partially returned, but in March 1965, a ministerial committee directed VOK to replace all foreign music programming in its National (i.e., Swahili) Service with "our local music."[88] Nairobi programmers were instructed to focus on "introducing a large measure of 'Africanness' in all Voice of Kenya programs," particularly by introducing "African" music into the background of English and Hindustani programs.[89] Mombasa radio remained a battlefield for religious representation. The following year, I. M. Mathenge, Coast Provincial Commissioner, relayed complaints he had received "from several people in the Province" that the Mombasa station "is putting far too much emphasis on Muslim religious activities viz. the recital of Holy Koran almost every day," and he suggested that the local Mombasa program replace Quranic recitations with nondenominational religious programs, as well as "religious songs and hymms."[90] The Information Office concurred, wryly observing that there "appears to be some resentment over the fact that all the local items put over this station are Muslim-dominated."[91]

This decision led to the cancellation of Maalim Said's thrice-weekly program "Kipindi cha Dini ya Islam kwa Radio," setting off a firestorm of coastal protest.

Two Muslim MPs, S. M. Balala and Mohamed Jahazi, explained that "Muslims were angered by this arbitrary action" and that they "shall not tolerate such a disgraceful action to be directed against our religion in independent Kenya."[92] They were upset by the action of "certain elements" who, they felt, were trying "gradually to eliminate the influence of Islam in the country."[93] Despite these protests, Mathenge held his ground, describing the changes as "not only beneficial to the public but educative."[94] The Islahil Islamiyya of Mombasa protested directly to the Ministry of Information that cancellation of Maalim Said's program was a particular loss to "women staying indoors."[95] Petitions poured in. Abadalla Said Ahmed and 53 other signatories explained that Said's cancellation had "crippled the hope of many a Muslim of his only source of obtaining Islamic knowledge that he hungrily seeks for after being unfortunate to attend proper Islamic schools." Maalim Said was also the "only widely publicised source of solving some of the most controversial and difficult religious problems encountered by Muslims." The contraction of Quranic recitation from 10 to 15 minutes to only 3 to 5 minutes was deemed insufficient, "as quite often the reader is stopped at the time when it is conveying a very important message."[96] A community club in Siu declared VOK leaders who had removed Maalim Said to be "enemies of Muslims" who were waging a war against Islam (*kupiga vita Uislamu*) and, less bombastically, appealed to the government's sense of equality by arguing that Muslim citizens had rights just like other Kenyan citizens.[97] Rather than continuing to risk a needless religious controversy, the Ministry of Information and Broadcasting reinstated the program to its thrice-weekly schedule but withdrew its payments to keep it in line with other religious broadcasts.[98]

The loss of coastal radio independence was thus seen as tantamount to religious dispossession and described most incendiarily as a "war against Islam" waged from Nairobi. But the centralization of radio broadcasting had come to bother even those otherwise inclined toward an "up-country" aesthetic formation. A group of KANU elders complained that the shift of programming control from Mombasa to Nairobi had left local listeners to seek other countries' broadcastings, including the anti-Kenyan vitriol of Radio Mogadishu.[99] National broadcasting programmers in Kenya had casually marginalized Muslim voices because they could afford to do so. Muslims constituted a little over 10 percent of the nation's population and figured only marginally in the country's complex ethnic political arithmetic. But to the extent that there *was* programming space, it was now reconfigured in explicitly religious terms, rather than in the broad terms of coastal culture. These new terms were accepted, indeed embraced, by disgruntled coastal listeners who now viewed explicitly Islamic programming as the best means to retain what little influence they held within the postcolony.

* * *

People involved directly with Sauti ya Mvita and still resident in Mombasa today insist that the station's control was removed from Mombasa to Nairobi because up-country politicians feared the political power that coastal people might obtain by using radio as an instrument for the realization of their separate cultural values and political institutions.[100] The displacement of Ki-Mvita programming from Mombasa's radio waves was, in this view, a deliberate policy to centralize cultural control in Nairobi by requiring all announcers to adopt the simplified Swahili of the ex-ABS for all Kenyan radio broadcasts.[101] This combined sense of retrospective optimism and contemporary disillusion similarly colors memories of the coastal autonomist *mwambao* movement, which simultaneously unfolded alongside Sauti ya Mvita during the late 1950s and early 1960s in Mombasa and along the Kenya coast. Although mwambao was not explicitly discussed at the time on Mombasa radio because of colonial prohibitions against political party endorsements, its primary aim—to use the legal status of the coast's ten-mile strip as a protectorate of the Sultan of Zanzibar in order to claim political privileges vis-à-vis "up-country" Kenya during decolonization—closely overlaps with the aesthetic goals of Sauti ya Mvita's Ki-Mvita broadcasts (Brennan 2008). To many Mombasan minds, the coast was and remains exceptional and demands recognition as such—"Pwani Si Kenya" ("The Coast Is Not Kenya"), as the slogan of the separatist and currently proscribed Mombasa Republican Council declares. The revival of Ki-Mvita broadcasting in Mombasa since the liberalization of Kenya's media, however, has rendered Sauti ya Mvita's nationalization more of a long and regretted interlude rather than a conclusion. Local hopes are now pinned on the success of the two apparent heirs to Sauti ya Mvita launched in the mid-2000s: Radio Rahma and Radio Salaam. Yet, these new stations operate under audience expectations that took shape during the 1960s, and more recently under the wider liberalization pressures to create successful niche markets, and thus present themselves first as Islamic radio stations rather than simply as stations appropriate for a coastal Muslim community. Radio Rahma's programming is eclectic, including local and foreign sung poetry or *qasida,* Quranic recitation, and English- and Swahili-language sermons from both local and foreign sources. Several older Swahili and Arab men regret that such programming by Radio Rahma and similar stations lacked, as Andrew Eisenberg (2009) discovered, "attention to the sounds of *local Swahili culture*" that had characterized Sauti ya Mvita (182). The disappearance of Sauti ya Mvita was not only nostalgized by elders as "a case study in the rise and fall of a culture," but also represented the physical loss of a vast tape library that was transported to Nairobi following its 1959 "nationalization" within the KBS system, from where invaluable recordings have since dissipated into private collections or were discarded entirely (Eisenberg 2009: 183).

The work of cultural and physical recovery of this sonic legacy remains an important task for those in Mombasa, yet it is also one that can only begin in Nairobi.

Notes

1. Director of Intelligence and Security to Information Officer, May 21, 1941, Kenya National Archives, Nairobi (hereafter KNA) AHC/18/1.
2. Chief Secretary (hereafter CS) Zanzibar to Secretary of Governor's Conference, September 10, 1940, Tanzania National Archives, Dar es Salaam (hereafter TzNA) 27436/f.28; Governor of Tanganyika to Colonial Secretary, October 7, 1940, Colonial Office, UK National Archives, Kew (hereafter CO) 323/1805/1/1.
3. For one summary, see minutes of Hone to DAS, April 5, 1941, TzNA 29541.
4. Memorandum enclosed in Northcote to Cameron, September 28, 1942, CO 875/6/17/83; Baker to CS, October 31, 1939, TzNA 27436/f.8.
5. The scheme was effectively derailed by Tanganyika's new governor, Edward Twining, who championed broadcasting autonomy for each territory. Twining to Creech Jones, October 20, 1949, CO 875/67/6/f.3.
6. *Mombasa Times,* November 5, 1957; Kindy: 163.
7. See 1948 Mombasa District Annual Report (hereafter DAR), KNA DC/MSA/1/5; and Chief Native Commissioner to All PCs, May 23, 1951, KNA CA/16/107/f.1.
8. Provincial Information Officer (hereafter PIO) Coast to DCs Kilifi et al., May 26, 1953, KNA DC/Lamu/2/21/13/f.15.
9. Memorandum of PIO Mombasa, September 4, 1954, KNA CC/23/5/f.116.
10. DC Mombasa to Executive Officer, African Information Services, June 6, 1952, KNA CS/2/8/50.
11. Reiss to Administrative Secretary, Secretariat, July 15, 1954, KNA AHC/10/68/f.174.
12. Minutes of Governor to CS, November 22, 1954, KNA AHC/10/66/f.5; record of Secretariat meeting, December 3, 1954, KNA AHC/10/66/f.15.
13. Deputy Governor to CS, November 25, 1954, KNA AHC/10/66/f.9.
14. PC Coast to Administrative Secretary, Secretariat, March 28, 1955, KNA AHC/10/66/f.29.
15. DO Malindi to DC Kilifi, November 19, 1956, KNA CB/18/27/f.115.
16. PIO Mombasa to all DCs, November 12, 1956, KNA CC/23/5/f.126.
17. Minutes of GWJ, November 16, 1956, KNA AHC/10/66/f.130.
18. PIO Mombasa to DCs Mombasa et al., March 31, 1955, KNA CB/18/27/f.35.
19. Monthly Report, April and May 1956, PIO to Director of Information, June 8, 1956, KNA DC/MSA/2/20/25/f.5.
20. Loyal African Lamu to DC Lamu, June 29, 1953, KNA DC/Lamu/2/21/13/f.27.
21. 1954 Mombasa DAR, KNA DC/MSA/1/5; 1956 Mombasa DAR, KNA DC/MSA/1/5. The studio later moved to Shah Mansion on Digo Road in 1958.
22. Author's interview with Faraj Dumila, Mombasa, July 20, 2006; interview with Abdalla Mbwana, Mombasa, July 20, 2006; interview with Omar Bassadiq, Mombasa, July 21, 2006. See also Kindy: 164. Faraj Dumila worked at Sauti ya Mvita as an occasional news contributor; Abdalla Mbwana primarily as a translator; and Omar Bassadiq as a program assistant.
23. PIO Mombasa to DC Mombasa, January 5, 1955, KNA DC/MSA/2/20/10/f.2.
24. March 1956 Monthly Report, in DC Mombasa to PC Coast, 1956, KNA CA/16/62/f.10; Ag. PC Coast to Asst. CS, July 16, 1957, KNA AHC/10/66/f.169.

25. 1957 Annual Report, PIO Coast to Director of Information, January 14, 1958, KNA DC/MSA/2/20/10/f.4. This was reflected in letters received, which increased from 294 in January 1957 to 1,616 in October 1957.

26. February 1956 Monthly Report, PIO Coast to Director of Information, March 1, 1956, KNA DC/MSA/2/20/25/f.3.

27. October and November 1955 Monthly Reports, PIO Coast to Director of Information, December 3, 1955, KNA DC/MSA/2/20/25/f.1.

28. December 1955 Monthly Report, PIO Coast to Director of Information, January 6, 1956, KNA DC/MSA/2/20/10/f.3.

29. 1957 Annual Report, PIO Coast to Director of Information, January 14, 1958, KNA DC/MSA/2/20/10/f.4.

30. October and November Monthly Reports, PIO Coast to Director of Information, December 3, 1955, KNA DC/MSA/2/20/25/f.1.

31. January 1956 Monthly Report, PIO Coast to Director of Information, February 7, 1956, KNA DC/MSA/2/20/25/f.2; minutes of Coast Broadcasting Advisory Sub-Committee meeting, June 14, 1957, enclosed in Reiss to Asst. CS, July 2, 1957, KNA AHC/30/8/f.3.

32. *Mombasa Times,* March 16, 1959.

33. Letter of Ali Abdallah, *Mombasa Times,* April 9, 1959.

34. "Arabs Want to Stop the Rock on Mombasa Radio," *Mombasa Times,* January 21, 1959.

35. Letter of "Nose Poker," *Mombasa Times,* January 22, 1959.

36. Reiss to Asst. CS, July 2, 1957, KNA AHC/30/8/f.3.

37. *Mombasa Times,* September 4, 1954.

38. Minutes of 7th advisory committee meeting on African Information Services, June 29, 1956, KNA OP/E/1/895/f.27.

39. Minutes of 11th advisory committee meeting on African Information Services, November 30, 1958, KNA OP/E/1/895/f.34.

40. Script entitled "Kitangulizi cha Week Mvita" by Abu Suleiman, January 11, 1954, KNA AHC/18/9. Original reads, "Yote ni kua nti yetu ni MVITA na kwa hivyo ntaeleza kidogo nnini hio MVITA na ndia gani mtu akiwa ataka ishi salama na yapi afanye akiazimia kuwatumikia umma."

41. 1956 Mombasa DAR, KNA DC/MSA/1/5.

42. Annual Report 1957, PIO Coast to Director of Information, January 14, 1958, KNA DC/MSA/2/20/10/f.4; Annual Report 1958, PIO Coast to Director of Information, January 20, 1959, KNA DC/MSA/2/20/10/f.5.

43. Information Services 1954, enclosed in PIO Mombasa to DC Mombasa, January 5, 1955, KNA DC/MSA/2/20/10/f.2.

44. Question and Answers, Mombasa Social Survey, G. M. Wilson, November 7, 1958, KNA DC/MSA/2/1/3/f.12.

45. March 1956 Monthly Report, PIO Coast to Director of Information, April 3, 1956, KNA DC/MSA/2/20/25/f.4.

46. Letter of Subzali Supalo, *Mombasa Times,* June 3, 1952. See also Kindy (1972): 164.

47. These scripts are in KNA AHC/18/9. Abdalla Mbwana said that Abu Suleiman's core work was translating Arabic works into Ki-Mvita for broadcasts. Interview with Abdalla Mbwana, Mombasa, July 20, 2006.

48. *Mombasa Times,* September 22, 1954.

49. *Mombasa Times,* January 27, 1954.

50. *Mombasa Times,* May 19, 1954.

51. *Mombasa Times,* August 25, 1954.

52. *Mombasa Times,* April 20, 1955.

53. *Mombasa Times,* May 4, 1955.

54. Interview: Sheikh Ahmed Msallam, Berlin, May 23, 2007.

55. Interview: Faraj Dumila, Mombasa, July 20, 2006.

56. Interview: Abdalla Mbwana, Mombasa, July 20, 2006.

57. Minutes of Coast Broadcasting Advisory Sub-Committee meeting, June 14, 1957, enclosed in Reiss to Asst. CS, July 2, 1957, KNA AHC/30/8/f.3.

58. April 1957 Monthly Report, PIO Coast to Director of Information, May 4, 1957, KNA DC/MSA/2/20/25/f.13.

59. *Mombasa Times,* July 23, 1959.

60. *Mombasa Times,* August 5, 1959.

61. Interview with Faraj Dumila, Mombasa, July 20, 2006. For Ahmed Nassir's career and work, see Kresse (2007).

62. Letter of William Chimwaggah, *Mombasa Times,* November 27, 1956.

63. Legislative Council Question No. 39, n.d. (ca. late 1957), KNA AHC/10/67.

64. Letter of D. M. Mati, *Mombasa Times,* April 12, 1957.

65. Ag. PC Coast to Asst. CS, July 16, 1957, KNA AHC/10/66/f.169.

66. Eggins to Reiss, June 21, 1957, KNA AHC/10/66/f.164.

67. 1957 Annual Report, PIO Coast to Director of Information, January 14, 1958, KNA DC/MSA/2/20/10/f.4; Evans to Asst. CS, November 2, 1957, KNA AHC/10/67/f.3.

68. Minute of M. N. Evans to Asst. CS, November 7, 1957, KNA AHC/10/67/f.7.

69. Kindy: 165. This section was headquartered with the Information Office staff; its main announcer was Arthur Changawa. Ibid.: 166.

70. This is reflected in the main statistical criteria available at the time, letters to the radio station. See PIO Mombasa to Director of Information, Nairobi, January 20, 1959, KNA DC/MSA/2/20/10/f.5.

71. I. R. Thompson (DO Taveta) to PC Coast, 6 July 1959, KNA DC/Lamu/2/21/13/f.250.

72. January 1959 Monthly Report, PIO to Director of Information, February 18, 1959, KNA DC/MSA/2/20/25/f.35A.

73. Hall to DC's Kilifi et al., June 16, 1959, KNA DC/Lamu/2/21/13/f.240.

74. DO Kaloleni to PC Coast, June 27, 1959, KNA DC/Lamu/2/21/13/f.245.

75. Ag. Director of Broadcasting to Regional Organiser, Kenya Broadcasting Service, Mombasa, May 8, 1959, KNA DC/MSA/2/20/42/f.2A.

76. Watkins-Pitchford to Director of Broadcasting, KBS, May 12, 1959, KNA DC/MSA/2/20/42/f.5.

77. *Mombasa Times,* July 2, 1959.

78. PIO Coast to Information Services, Nairobi, January 15, 1960, KNA DC/MSA/2/20/10/f.6.

79. *Mombasa Times,* July 2, 1959, in KNA DC/MSA/2/20/42/f.13A.

80. Mohamed Abdulla, via DC Lamu to PC Coast, July 23, 1959, KNA DC/Lamu/2/21/13/f.253. Kindy (165) described this 15-minute weekly summary of weddings, deaths, arrivals, departures, and functions as "extremely popular."

81. Witu and Mkunumbi Sauti ya Wilaya ya Pwani's Listeners, Witu (Abderehman Omar and 29 others from Witu; and Mohamed Manazil and 39 others from Mkunumbi) to Broadcasting Officer, Sauti ya Wilaya ya Pwani and Sheikh Mohamed bin Suleiman (Abu Suleiman), Mombasa, July 15, 1959, KNA DC/Lamu/2/21/13/f.252.

82. Minute of Richard Coltart to KBS Director, April 13, 1961, KNA RQ/1/18.

83. Minute of Wink to KBS Director of Planning, May 19, 1961, KNA RQ/1/18.

84. M. S. Said, Station Controller, Mombasa to All Heads of Departments, Mombasa, March 25, 1963, KNA CB/18/29/2/1 /f.37.

85. "Wananchi wa Pwani" (Mohamed Bakari, Salim Nassor, Mohamed Abdalah and Kombo Mzee) to DC Mombasa, March 30, 1963, KNA CB/18/29/f.38.

86. Mbarak Salim Hazir, Ag. President, Islahil Islamiyyah, Mombasa to Minister of Information, August 10, 1964, KNA AHC/18/25/f.3.

87. John Ithau to Mbarak Salim Hariz, August 19, 1964, KNA AHC/18/25/f.4.

88. Koske (VOK Director) to PermSec, Ministry of Information and Broadcasting, March 11, 1965, KNA AHC/18/53/f.59.

89. Gachathi to Director of Broadcasting, March 15, 1966, RQ/1/17.

90. Mathenge (PC Coast) to PIO Mombasa, April 28, 1966, enclosed in Muhanji to Director of Broadcasting, April 29, 1966, KNA AHC/18/53.

91. Muhanji (PIO Coast) to Director of Broadcasting April 29, 1966, KNA AHC/18/53.

92. *East African Standard,* July 6, 1966.

93. *Daily Nation,* July 6, 1966.

94. Muhanji (PIO Coast) to Director VOK, June 6, 1966, KNA AHC/18/53/f.143.

95. Mbarak Hiriz (President, Islahil Islamiyya, Mombasa) to Minister of Information and Broadcasting, June 6, 1966, KNA AHC/18/53/f.143.

96. Abdalla Said Ahmed and 53 other signatories (Mombasa) to Ministry of Information and Broadcasting, June 13, 1966, KNA AHC/18/53/f.147.

97. Raisi, Siu Community Social Club, Mombasa to Ministry of Information and Broadcasting, June 9, 1966, KNA AHC/18/53/f.146.

98. Kikumu (VOK Controller of Programmes) to PIO Coast, July 6, 1966, KNA AHC/18/53/f.153; PIO Coast to Permanent Secretary, Ministry of Information and Broadcasting, July 11, 1966, KNA AHC/18/53/f.156.

99. Baraza la Wazee wa KANU, Mombasa (list of names nearly illegible) to Jomo Kenyatta, September 2, 1966, enclosed in Njiri to DC Mombasa, November 12, 1966, KNA CQ/1/30/f.30.

100. Interview with Faraj Dumila, July 20, 2006; interview with Abdalla Mbwana, July 20, 2006.

101. Interview with Abdalla Mbwana, July 20, 2006.

References

Brennan, James R. 2008. "Lowering the Sultan's Flag: Sovereignty and Decolonization in Coastal Kenya." *Comparative Studies in Society and History* 50: 831–861.

———. 2010. "Radio Cairo and the Decolonization of East Africa, 1953–1964." In *Making a World after Empire: The Bandung Moment and Its Political Afterlives,* edited by Christopher J. Lee, 173–195. Athens: Ohio University Press.

Eisenberg, Andrew. 2009. "The Resonance of Place: Vocalizing Swahili Ethnicity in Mombasa, Kenya." PhD dissertation, Columbia University.

Hirschkind, Charles. 2006. *The Ethical Soundscape: Cassette Sermons and Islamic Counterpublics.* New York: Columbia University Press.

Kindy, Hyder. 1972. *Life and Politics in Mombasa.* Nairobi: East African Publishing House.

Kresse, Kai. 2003. "'Swahili Enlightenment?' East African Reformist Discourse at the Turning Point: The Example of Sheikh Muhammad Kasim Mazrui." *Journal of Religion in Africa* 33: 279–309.

———. 2007. *Philosophising in Mombasa: Knowledge, Islam and Practice on the Swahili Coast.* Edinburgh: Edinburgh University Press.

Meyer, Birgit, ed. 2009. *Aesthetic Formations: Media, Religion, and the Senses*. New York: Palgrave Macmillan.

Pouwels, Randall. 1981. "Sh. al-Amin b. Ali Mazrui and Islamic Modernism in East Africa, 1875–1947." *International Journal of Middle Eastern Studies* 13: 329–345.

Wilson, Gordon. 1958. *Mombasa Social Survey*. Mombasa: Government Printers.

2 Between Standardization and Pluralism

The Islamic Printing Market and Its Social Spaces in Bamako, Mali

Francesco Zappa

Mali's Literacy Environment, "Secular" and "Islamic"

A chapter devoted to the discussion of print in a book about *new* media may sound rather puzzling to some readers, especially if the focus is on printed books and pamphlets rather than newspapers and periodicals. Yet, in many parts of sub-Saharan Africa, especially in the Islamic religious domain, the impact of printed literature is still a relatively recent phenomenon that has not yet completely superseded the role of handwritten manuscripts, although coexisting with the rise in newer media, be they oral, visual, or electronic.

Like most Sahelian countries, Mali is usually portrayed as a predominantly illiterate one, where orality is still the main channel for the articulation and transmission of both "traditional" and modern culture. In sharp contrast to an often idealized precolonial past—evoked through references to the Arabic-manuscripts heritage of Timbuktu—since independence, this country has consistently ranked among the bottom ten for world literacy rates and educational standards, in addition to most other development indexes. In particular, reports by both development agents and academic scholars unfailingly lament a low rate of book reading and selling and, at a deeper level, the lack of a "literate environment," even in the urban setting. According to Dumestre (1997: 34–35), the presence of writing is rather sporadic in the social landscape. Books and newspapers are rare even in literate persons' houses, and even then, they mostly serve as ornaments and displays. Yet fortuitous visits to one of the Islamic bookshops or the more informal bookstalls in the capital city, Bamako, give the impression of a rather flourishing market.

What are we to make of such an apparent contradiction? A partial explanation lies, arguably, in that books in Arabic—and indeed Islam-related books in general—are not considered "books" in the full sense of the term by most of those in charge of commissioning or carrying out inquiries on literacy and reading habits in francophone West Africa; their unexpected presence thus tends to pass unnoticed, and their places of sale, distribution, and consumption are not usually visited by the enquirers nor by their informants.

This omission is part of a more general attitude vis-à-vis Islamic and Arabic education, which, according to Bouwman (2005: 2), "is not even mentioned in some of the literature concerning education in Mali. Foreign researchers and funding partners are often not aware of its significance," in spite of the fact that "some 30 percent of school-going children in Mali are enrolled in modern Arabic education, and another unknown but estimated large proportion receives a traditional Islamic education."

Even scholarly accounts of Mali's socio-linguistic dynamics (e.g., Canut 1996), unless specifically focusing on Islamic issues, hardly mention any role of Arabic, partly due to their tendency to privilege oral over written uses of languages, though more recent assessments tend to redress the balance (e.g., Mbodj-Pouye 2007: 24–42; 2013: 31–40). In terms of historical heritage, especially outside the specific field of Islamic studies, literacy in Arabic in precolonial West Africa is often belittled, following Goody's (1968) influential definition, as "restricted," both in its social basin and in its uses, thus not fully developing its potentialities. And while the very notion of "restricted literacy," with its normative overtones, has been contested since the 1980s by a wave of so-called "new literacy studies," the implications of this theoretical debate have started only very recently to be applied to Arabic literacy in sub-Saharan African contexts.[1] With such a biased attitude toward "traditional" Arabic literacy and Islamic education, most scholars who did not specialize in Islam were all too ready to acknowledge French as the sole written and learned language of colonial and postcolonial Mali (only to be occasionally joined by timid experiments in the local vernaculars) and were ill-prepared to allow for more than a residual role for Arabic in modern education and literacy.

I am not implying here that Islamic publications, in Arabic or otherwise, can rely nowadays on a mass readership, nor that their readership outnumbers that of the remaining, mostly francophone literature circulating in Mali, but only that their impact may be wider and deeper than is usually acknowledged by local and foreign observers. Moreover, the public of this kind of publication, however restricted in number it may be, is not such a close-knit, delimited, and exclusively urban-based group as one might suspect: even though the distribution of Islamic publications outside the main towns is not regularly assured, and bookshops, especially Islamic ones, are rare outside the capital city, a stop at an Islamic bookshop is not so unusual for rural dwellers visiting Bamako or some provincial markets. And if the growing network of madrasas ensures an outlet for publications in Arabic, some readers who are literate in French (or, more recently, even in Bambara) and educated in secular educational institutions have shown, in their turn, an interest in Islamic publications in these languages.

This is probably a good example of how often literacy skills are geared by social actors to serve purposes very far removed from those imagined by the mostly secular-oriented promoters of mass literacy campaigns, who are usually indifferent or suspicious about anything Islamic.

Not surprisingly, in the light of the literacy policies hinted at above, the networks of secular and Islamic bookshops tend to run parallel almost without ever overlapping: Arabic books are completely lacking from the secular network, where it is also very rare to find Islam-related books, except occasional Western-oriented academic works; as for Islamic bookshops, they sell publications in all the main written languages that are read in Mali (Arabic, French, and Bambara), but profane items are virtually confined to a few madrasa textbooks for secular subjects and to sporadic, expensive modern encyclopedic works in Arabic.[2] This sort of mutual compartmentalization also resonates with Soares's (2006: 79–82) vivid description of the social landscape of downtown Bamako as one character-ized by "jarring juxtapositions" of icons of Islam, so-called African "traditional religions," and secular culture, rather than by a shared, consistent repertoire of common references.[3] And yet (former) students of madrasas and secular franco-phone schools are not such discrete groups; rather, they are often found inside the same household, since parents not infrequently diversify their educational choices for their children by dividing them among the different kinds of schools available (including the option of not enrolling them at any) so that the family as a whole can benefit from each experience thanks to the skills and career chances it provides.[4] Moreover, the Malian educational landscape is presently charac-terized by what Tamari (2002: 104) defines as a "relatively free flow of students between state [secular], modernizing, and traditional Islamic schools," which fosters a mixture of educational experiences, skills, and influences in the very same individuals. It is perhaps exactly this paradoxical alternation of mixing and compartmentalization among different languages, models of knowledge, forma-tive tracks, and printed items available that must be kept in mind when exploring the Islamic printing and media market in Bamako. In other words, if pluralism, as shall be seen, may be identified as a salient feature of the inner dynamics of Islamic bookshops, it also characterizes, with all its contradictions, the wider social landscape in which they are placed.

Bamako's Islamic bookshops can be looked at both as physical places that embody the thriving market of Islamic printing and as spaces of social interaction among booksellers, writers, customers, and society at large. The following sec-tions examine some of the printed commodities that are displayed and sold there, which include some Islamic oral media items. Then issues of standardization of religiosity and attitudes toward religious knowledge on the one hand and doctrinal and linguistic pluralism on the other are discussed, with an eye on the local and global processes in which such trends engage.[5]

Islamic Bookshops as a Social Space: The Ongoïba Example

At the time of my fieldwork, all of Bamako's Islamic bookshops were situated in an overcrowded downtown area, within a range of a few hundred meters. The oldest and largest one was the Librairie islamique El-Hadj Isa Ongoïba, which was established in 1952. In size and book supply, it was certainly not inferior to the city's main "secular" bookshops, which, in their turn, were not huge either. It had started as a simple *tabali* ("stall" in Bambara) on the same spot where the two-story building in which the bookshop resides. The building is strategically located at the beginning of the arterial road serving the eastern half of the city, opposite a bustling minibus station and a recent monument to the Palestinian martyrs, halfway between the old colonial city center, the Bagadadji market, and some densely populated neighborhoods.

Its owner and founder, the octogenarian el-Hadj Isa Ongoïba, born to a family originating from the ostensibly "pagan" Dogon region of Mali (colonial Soudan Français at the time), settled down in Bamako after traveling through several Sahelian countries for educational and working purposes, as well as on his way to Mecca, which he reached by crossing the Sahara on foot like the pilgrims of old. After several humble jobs, including a water hawker, he started selling Islamic books in the last decade of the colonial era in a climate marked by heated clashes between "traditionalist" and "reformist" Muslims in the city. Since that time, his activity developed into a full-blown bookshop, steadily increasing its supply and customer base. By the time of my fieldwork, his three sons had taken over the business, but he still spent most of his time at the bookshop, sitting in a corner aloof from the counter and revered by the numerous visitors. In spite of the enviable success of his enterprise, which a regular visitor quantified in an income of around 1 million CFA francs (approximately €1,500) a day,[6] none of his sons worked in the bookstore full time, since all of them had other jobs, ranging from a small stationery shop to a construction firm. His many married daughters, who were scattered among Mali, Burkina Faso, Sudan, Saudi Arabia, Italy, and elsewhere, ensured the family—and probably the bookshop—a sort of private transnational network.[7]

While all his family members proudly professed their espousal of Wahhabi doctrinal trends, they also exhibited a concern for pluralism and emphatically underscored, at least in my presence, their lack of militancy for an "Islamic state."[8] In informal conversations, they often compared the sincerity of the growing religious commitment of many Malian Muslims to what they described as the rather hypocritical observance of the Saudis, arguing that democracy and freedom of expression are more effective than government-enforced orthodoxy in shaping pious Muslim citizens. The same preference for persuasion over coercion was extended to the private sphere—for instance, in discussions about appropriate female behavior according to Islamic standards. Such a pluralistic leaning was mirrored in the bookshop's patrons, as well as in the collection of publications available: the general ambience was predominantly Wahhabi-oriented, but all trends were represented, with no special tensions.

The patrons of this oft-crowded bookshop were actually very diverse not only as to doctrinal leanings but also in geographical, social, and educational background; age; attire; and even gender, although men were the overwhelming majority. While most customers were passersby who just stopped in for the time needed for their shopping, a significant number of them were regular visitors who enjoyed staying longer and engaging in conversations with the booksellers and other customers. Among the latter were locally renowned religious intellectuals and Malian authors of some of the publications for sale who sometimes also used the bookshop as a sort of publisher, or as a place to meet individual readers who occasionally asked them for explanations on ambiguous points in their writings. In the mostly cordial conversations taking place in this lively setting, the kind of peremptory mutual excommunications between followers of opposing doctrinal trends (especially between "Sufis" and "Wahhabis") that are so common in some of the publications sold in the bookshop and in other forms of public discourse often took on a more inoffensive tone of jesting and ritualized insult that was reminiscent of modalities of verbal exchange typical of locally pervasive forms of joking relationships (*senenkunya* in Bambara).[9]

While this climate might well be understood as part of a larger trend toward a lightening up of sectarian tensions between Muslims of different allegiances, the very existence of contending doctrinal trends may still be perceived as rather disorienting by some ordinary Muslims, as illustrated by the paradoxical case of a regular visitor of the bookshop who, as a friend to one of the booksellers, would spend a very long time in the store, while proudly maintaining that he had never read any of the publications for sale there. He explained to me with some humor that his friend had repeatedly offered him books as gifts, but he consistently refused, because—he said—"if I start reading books about Islam, I will have to decide whether to become a Wahhabi, a Tijani, or whatever; I prefer to remain a normal Muslim who prays every day rather than getting perplexed about what to choose." While this attitude may be viewed as an example of the increasing appeal of what Soares (2005: 224), after Eickelman, defines as "a generic Islam of assumed universals," it is also marked by a disengagement that contrasts sharply with the religious commitment of other Islamic experiences, similarly lacking doctrinal specificity, that are increasingly successful in present-day Mali, like the *Ançar Dine* movement, led by the popular media preacher Chérif Ousmane Madani Haïdara (Schulz 2003: 156–160; 2006: 216).[10]

Inside the Market of Religious Knowledge: The Book and the Books

For those who, unlike this rather extravagant visitor, were there precisely to buy books and other printed items, the choice was by no means limited. Not surprisingly, the Quran was available in great supply, mainly but not exclusively in the standard Saudi-authorized edition, as well as in French versions, invariably by Muslim translators. Occasional lithographed reproductions of handwritten copies of the whole Holy Book or, more frequently, of a singular portion (*juz'* or *hizb*) in booklet format were also for sale as sort of luxury editions; such versions conform to locally established, time-honored calligraphic styles and to Warsh's version (*riwāya*) of Nāfiʿs reading variant (*qirāʾa*), which predominated throughout West Africa up to recent times, until the diffusion of printed copies from the Middle East popularized Hafs version of ʿĀsim's reading variant. Next to French translations, though usually in a different section, since the 1990s the first printed samples of Bambara translations of portions of the Quran have become available thanks to the work of al-Hajj Modibo Diarra, the most prolific of the very few authors of Islamic publications in Bambara. At the time of my fieldwork, only the last juz' (corresponding to one-thirtieth of the whole Quran) had come out, together with a couple of short anthologies of scattered verses and suras; however, during a later visit in early 2010, I found that in the intervening time, the latter half of the Book had been fully published in two installments.

The main classical collections of *hadiths* were also widely available in spite of their huge size and considerable cost. And the choice was not confined to the two most authoritative ones—the *Sahīhs* of al-Bukhārī and Muslim—or to the *Muwatta'* of Mālik, the founder of the school of Islamic law that predominated unchallenged in Mali until only recently. The availability of ponderous works in several volumes, sometimes occupying an entire shelf, was not limited to these collections of hadiths and commentaries to them; it extended to a remarkably wide array of medieval encyclopedic works, including treatises of Quranic exegesis (*tafsir*), Muslim jurisprudence (*fiqh*), theology (*tawhīd*), Arabic lexicography, and linguistics (traditionally conceived as an essential tool for all Islamic religious sciences). Moreover, in the shelves holding classical medieval works, authors like al-Suyūtī (died 1505), who were central to the understanding of classical Islam that was widespread among West African Sufis and traditionally trained scholars, were not less represented than, say, Ibn Taymiyya (died 1328), from whose teachings most present-day reformist trends claim intellectual descent. One could even find, for instance, the tafsir of Fakhr al-Dīn al-Rāzī, (died 1209), which, due to its predominantly philosophical orientation, its comparatively free resort to personal opinion (*ra'y*), and its very complexity, is less and less fashionable in the curriculum of exegetical studies in contemporary West Africa as elsewhere in the Muslim world (Brigaglia 2005: 379). Less surprisingly, the bookshop contained all the main classical works that are part of the standard curriculum of advanced traditional Islamic studies. Among these, the *Risāla* of al-Qayrawānī (died 996), which is considered the handbook of Maliki law *par excellence* throughout West Africa, is also available in French; in 2000, it was translated into Bambara, thus becoming the most voluminous Islamic book (and maybe the most voluminous book *tout court*) ever published in that language. A few one-volume works of Sufi devotion and hagiography, well rooted in the local tradition since precolonial times, were also available in lithographed reproductions: these included *Dalā'il al-khayrāt,* a famous collection of prayers for the Prophet Muhammad by the Moroccan Sufi Muhammad al-Jazūlī (died 1465), and *Jawāhir al-maʿānī,* the authorized biography of Ahmad al-Tijānī (died 1815), which was compiled by his disciple ʿAlī Harāzim b. Barrāda and on the margins of which is printed the famous *Kitāb al-Rimāh* written by the nineteenth-century West African jihadist leader al-Hajj ʿUmar Tall.

As noted above, the classics of Arabic nonreligious literature were almost totally absent, except for a few works that are part of the standard curriculum of traditional education in Mali, such as the *Maqāmāt* of al-Harīrī (died 1122), a collection of picaresque tales that are often used as references for Arabic rhetoric and lexicography due to their highly sophisticated literary elaboration.[11] I witnessed an Algerian customer ask in vain for an Arabic copy of *One Thousand and One Nights,* and I could not find any works of contemporary Arabic fiction. This resonates with Bouwman's (2005: 127–128) remark that although the spread of modernizing Arabic education in Mali has led many Malians to consider Arabic as a "secular," ordinary language of everyday life, Arabic is still learned almost exclusively for its role as the language of Islam, without any special interest in Arab culture broadly conceived. In fact, the only Arabic modern "secular" books available in this bookshop were madrasa textbooks for secular subjects.

Religious books from contemporary authors ranged, doctrinally speaking, from the writings of the Grand Mufti of Saudi Arabia, ʿAbd al-ʿAzīz bin Bāz (1910?–1999), whose stance as an uncompromising guardian of the monarchy's official Wahhabi doctrine and whose role in Wahhabi global *daʿwa* are well known, to the works of Cheikh Ahmadou Tall (1943–), a Senegalese descendant of al-Hajj ʿUmar Tall, who published a series of books in French illustrating Islamic "secrets"—namely, the "magical" uses of special petitionary prayers (*duʿāʾ*), Quranic verses, and "names of God." As the last example shows, while translations into French were more numerous for contemporary books than for classical ones, some of the contemporary religious literature available was composed directly in French, and the proportion of French-language publications was even higher among booklets.[12]

Nuggets of Islamic Knowledge: Booklets and Tracts

Indeed, booklets and tracts occupied the lion's share of the local Islamic printing market and enjoyed higher visibility than any other item in the bookshop. According to Soares (2005: 231), "Since the 1980s, the range of subjects [they] cover has broadened considerably." Because ordinary Muslims (or even, in a few cases, candidates to conversion) are their main target, including those with no formal Islamic educational background and only a basic command of written Arabic, French, or Bambara, it is no surprise that many of them deal with the rudiments of Islamic doctrine and uncontroversial rules for proper worship and ritual purity. Topics of basic religious instruction in these publications can be broadly divided into the following categories:

- Worship and ritual practices (*'ibādāt*).
- Moral edification, legal issues of practical import and proper conduct (*adab*) in daily life.
- Basic tenets of doctrine (tawhīd) and rudiments of sacred history.
- General catechisms.

The first category consists essentially of booklets or pamphlets illustrating the "five pillars of Islam," followed by others detailing wedding and funeral rituals. Most of the booklets that focus on only one "pillar" deal with ritual daily prayer (*salāt*), including norms of ritual purity. This emphasis on the observance of worship duties is consonant with a more general trend toward the adoption of standardized ritual practices by all Muslims alike, which has been in progress since the colonial era (Soares 2003: 207–213; 2005: 66–68); however, it might also be ascribed to an influence of the Wahhabis' reassertion of the crucial role of ritual prayer, as opposed to the litanies of the Sufi orders, for the sake of salvation. While some of these booklets have a very simple and systematic layout, others reproduce or translate more difficult medieval legal compendiums that are part of the traditional Malian curriculum, like the *Mukhtasar fi'l-'ibādāt* by the Algerian scholar al-Akhdarī (died 1576).

The second category includes small anthologies of short, edifying hadiths, with a very didactic explanation of the meaning and practical implication of every single hadith. Some booklets center on more specific domains of daily life and quite often on gender-specific prescriptions. Among publications focusing on legal issues, the most popular topic is probably marriage. Such a concern for proper everyday behavior, alongside ritual observance, as a prerequisite for the attainment of both individual salvation and the common good is part of a widespread sense of individual moral accountability characterizing Islamic religiosity in present-day Mali and further contributing to its standardization (Schulz 2003: 157; 2006: 212–216). In addition, the reassertion of the centrality of the Prophet's

Sunna as a behavioral model may also be considered, at least in part, as an outcome of Wahhabi influence.

Booklets from the third category include short tracts glossing the Muslim profession of faith (*shahāda*) and biographies of the Prophet Muhammad, other prophets mentioned in the Quran, and prominent Muslims from the idealized first generations. In these biographies, one can hardly find traces of the legendary material filling up classical Islamic narrative genres like *qisas al-anbiyā'* (prophets' stories), which in their turn are echoed in many West African oral, non-scholarly literary texts (Zappa 2009b). Moreover, the prophets are not so much proposed here as objects of devotion, as in the locally rooted Sufi tradition, but rather as models of piety and individual conduct to be imitated, in line with more severe understandings of Islam.

Finally, general catechisms tend to mix elements from all the aforementioned categories, usually adding a few shorter suras and Quranic verses of common use.

Booklets from all these categories were available in all of the three languages of Islamic printing that are read in Mali (Arabic, French, and Bambara). In a few cases, the very same text was available in only two or in all three languages, usually in separate editions. In most other cases, the French or Bambara version was presented alongside the Arabic original in the same edition. However, not all booklets in French or Bambara were translated from Arabic, some being relatively original compositions. More interestingly, many French and Bambara booklets dealing with prayers or reproducing excerpts from the Quran or the Sunna include, after (or even in place of) the relevant Arabic texts, a rough phonetic transcription in Roman script adapted to the phonology of the main language in which the booklet is written, usually followed by a translation into that same language. If the aim of this mixing process is to ensure a correct pronunciation of such liturgical texts (especially of the ones that have to be uttered in the ritual daily prayers) by Muslims illiterate in Arabic, together with an understanding of their meaning, it also contributes to undermining the notion of a quintessential link among the Arabic language, the Arabic alphabet, and the Quran.

While most of these very basic, popularizing booklets may seem to be dealing mainly with uncontroversial subjects (at least from a Muslim point of view), some elements of their content lay themselves open to disagreement, as is the case with certain slight differences in the performance of the ritual daily prayers that have developed into veritable hallmarks of belonging to contending Muslim factions in Mali since the mid-twentieth century. Thus, the amount of factionalism of a given publication can be effectively measured by the way it tackles such sensitive issues. To continue with the example of ritual prayer, while some booklets vehemently underscore that a given posture (either crossed arms or hanging arms during the phases that must be performed in standing position, Arabic *qiyām*) is the only acceptable one, others content themselves with prescribing that same posture with no further comment, and still others avoid specifying altogether.[13] Since, as observed by Soares (2005: 187), the symbolic import of this matter has lessened over time, publications of the second and third kinds have increasingly outnumbered those of the first one. On other sensitive issues, however, like belief in intercession, visits to the Prophet's tomb or to the saints' tombs, notions of sanctity, and so forth, a tendentious presentation of partisan views as if they were shared by the consensus of the whole Muslim community is sometimes more clearly detectable. Indeed, many of the Wahhabi-oriented pamphlets are in the disguise of "neutral" catechisms.

Still other booklets exhibited a more avowedly militant orientation. Some of these, though, centered around topics that allowed a cutting across doctrinal differences among contending Muslim groups, since their main target of polemics are secularist ideas or non-Muslim religious groups. One such topic is female excision, which has recently come at the forefront of national debate (Soares 2006: 89), as reflected also by the high visibility of publications dealing with this issue inside Islamic bookshops. All these publications invariably aim at countering, with an uncompromising tone, campaigns for eradicating excision led by international and local women's rights activists, which are perceived as a threat to the integrity of the local Muslim community.

Another genre that is cultivated, in rather lengthy and detailed tracts, by authors of disparate doctrinal allegiances is anti-Christian doctrinal polemic. This inspired, for instance, at least two booklets in French written by the influential Sufi reformer Saada Oumar Touré,[14] one in French written by the Sufi-oriented young writer Aboubacar Ballo, and two in Bambara written by the Wahhabi-minded al-Hajj Modibo Diarra. This preference for languages other than Arabic in dealing with this subject, even by an author like Touré, who composed most of his writings in Arabic and gave a decisive contribution to the revival of Arabic education, is very telling. In my view, while the influence of anti-Christian motives permeating the global da'wa movements is undeniable, these tracts are arising primarily as a local response to the initiatives of Christian missionaries, both Catholics and Protestants, who for the past century have been particularly active in promoting religious instruction through literacy and publications in both French and the local vernaculars. Indeed, it is no accident that the only author extensively published in Bambara is from a province, Bélédougou, where Christian missionary presence is much stronger than in most other regions of Mali. One of his anti-Christian pamphlets is framed as a point-by-point response to a Catholic publication in Bambara and is also one of the first booklets he has published. Even one of Touré's booklets starts with a reference to a Bambara catechism dating from 1947. This is somewhat striking in that, though writing several decades later, the author prefers to quote some strongly anti-Islamic statements from such an old publication, rather than consider the changes that have occurred in attitudes toward Islam that the Catholic Church has adopted since the Second Vatican Council and, in particular, the many initiatives for the promotion of interreligious dialogue carried out by Catholic missionaries in Mali. Be this as it may, the amount of publications devoted to Christianity is significant considering that Christians make up less than 2 percent of Mali's total population.

Another category of booklets gave voice to partisan doctrinal trends of contemporary Islam in Mali. Wahhabis were not the only ones to resort to such popularizing publications; Sufi authors from different Sufi orders also contributed to them to a large extent.

Brief Wahhabi publications included short theological compendia and polemical pamphlets; their authorships range from Muhammad b. 'Abd al-Wahhāb himself (died 1792) to less well-known (mostly foreign) contemporary scholars, while their language coverage extends from Arabic to French and Bambara. Some of them were published and distributed for free by Islamic NGOs based in the Gulf States or in Saudi Arabia as part of da'wa campaigns.

As for Sufi publications, they usually did not engage in doctrinal polemics, even though occasional apologetic motives crept into some of their booklets. While most of these texts centered on illustrating the basic litanies of a given order, some also added general considerations of the merits of Sufi devotion in general or of the founder of the relevant Sufi order. A case apart were booklets in French by the highly mediatized, young, "rasta-looking" Malian saint Cheick Soufi Bilal, which, as observed by Soares (2007: 85), propose "a veritable *bricolage* of ideas and techniques from different Sufi orders, especially from the Qādiriyya and the Tijāniyya," while being "very much focused on [the author] as an individual religious figure whose claims to superior, secret, esoteric knowledge are proclaimed."

Since many of the Sufi booklets are in French, the texts of the litanies are often written in the same style as ordinary daily prayer in the more generic booklets mentioned above: the Arabic text is followed by a Romanized transcription and a French translation.[15] Such a popularizing treatment is all the more puzzling for these esoteric liturgical texts that, according to the doctrines and praxis of the Sufi orders, are to be transmitted personally in an initiatic way, in the context of an intimate relationship between master and disciple.

Analogous considerations apply to more doctrinally ambiguous publications concerning names of God and invocations (*dhikr*), which receive the same rationalizing treatment. Their doctrinal ambiguity lies in that they present themselves as utterly nonsectarian, since the formulas they propose are drawn, for the most part, from the Quran and the Sunna, rather than from the repertoire of Sufi orders or other esoteric circles. Furthermore, while these booklets suggest that the recitation of such formulas has practical, beneficial effects in worldly life that the reader is encouraged to pursue, they still present themselves as manuals of devotion. The ritual practices accompanying the recitation of every such formula and the specific purpose it serves, which are usually detailed under its heading, are often supported by the example of the Prophet himself, or, at any rate, do not depart from the practices followed and authorized even by uncompromising religious reformers like Ibn Taymiyya and his faithful disciple Ibn Qayyim al-Jawziyya, the spiritual ancestors of present-day Wahhabis.[16] One of these publications, which is featured among the best sellers in Malian Islamic bookshops, goes so far as to explicitly warn against the use of amulets made up with Quranic verses, and, in an introduction to the ninety-nine "names of God," emphatically rejects the idea that His one hundredth and "most exalted" name is a secret revealed to only a few saintly individuals, who, thanks to this knowledge, claim to be able to penetrate the occult and accomplish wondrous things.[17] Such a straightforward attack undermines one of the pillars of Sufi doctrine, since every Sufi order claims to be the holder of the "most exalted" name of God. Thus, with all these caveats, these outwardly esoteric publications appeal to a broad public, including mistrustful Wahhabi-minded readers who must be reassured about the lawfulness of what is proposed.

Still other booklets, however, dealt more explicitly with "esoteric sciences," and sometimes even with the word "magic" (or its Arabic equivalent *sihr*) appearing in the title. The few such publications for sale at Ongoïba bookshop were not openly displayed, but the booksellers, although showing their embarrassment and disapproval, were quite willing to sell them. However, since those available at Ongoïba were not numerous, the following discussion is based mainly on "esoteric" publications found in other Islamic bookshops in Bamako. Unlike the latter category of publications we just examined, their contents are not usually organized according to a listing of prayers and formulas but rather under more outspoken headings pointing to different practical purposes, each followed by the relevant recipes. When the recitation or manipulation of Quranic verses and petitionary prayers is involved, sometimes these are also transcribed in Romanized script and translated into French, according to the same procedure at work in other publications, thus further erasing the aura of mystery surrounding the sacred word.

While the morality of some of the objectives proposed in these booklets is potentially ambiguous, I could not find any publications dealing with matters of so-called "black magic" or recommending ritual practices deemed illicit by shari'a standards (like writing or invoking names of devils, or mixing the writing of the Quran with ritually impure materials) in any of Bamako's bookshops. This was somewhat surprising, since this branch of magic has been extensively cultivated in some treatises of Muslim (including West African) authorship (Hamès 1998) and is still widely present in the everyday lives of Malian Muslims

(Dumestre 2007).[18] Some booklets even contain occasional warnings to use these recipes for licit purposes according to shari'a standards. One astonishing case is a booklet in Arabic titled *The Exemplary Way to Counter Magicians and Sorcerers*, written by a Malian madrasa teacher, with the stated goal of fighting "pagan" magic and sorcery by perfectly licit means. The booklet is full of references to a seemingly very institutionalized "Ibn Taymiyya center for traditional medicine," founded and run by the author in Bamako. This is no doubt a very astute naming strategy that allows him to appeal simultaneously on the one hand to the secularist rhetoric of self-development attained through the rediscovery of the "traditional" "folk" heritage and on the other hand to a legitimizing Islamic discourse, invoking conformity to the teachings of Ibn Taymiyya to escape criticism from the Wahhabi side.

Variations on a Theme: Exploring Other Islamic Bookshops

To complete our virtual tour of Bamako's Islamic bookshops at the time of my fieldwork, the second biggest one was, beyond any doubt, the Librairie el-Hadj Bakary Sow, which was situated just behind the Great Mosque and close to an Islamic radio station, about 200 meters away from Ongoïba. Though more recent, it was almost as crowded as the latter. Its patrons were also rather varied, as were the books for sale; however, although my direct experience with this bookshop as a place of social interaction was admittedly much more restricted than with Ongoïba, I saw a more severe ambience and a more outspoken Wahhabi orientation. Most publications for sale were almost the same as those in Ongoïba,[19] but their comparative visibility was slightly different. For instance, among the collections of hadith, the most visible was Muhammad Nasiruddin al-Albanī (1914–1999), an influential Salafi scholar whose rigidly selective criteria in assessing the authenticity of the hadiths aroused a lot of controversy for his censoring attitude toward much of what the classical scholarly tradition had widely accepted. This bookshop also sold nonprinted (and nonverbal) "religious commodities," although in a much less varied array than the ones described by Starrett (1995) as filling the markets in Cairo. The most widespread were men's and women's clothing, mostly imported from Southeast Asia, of the kind worn, at least in Mali, almost exclusively by those identified as Wahhabis.

A few meters away, in an overcrowded avenue with plenty of shops, one could feel a different atmosphere in a smaller bookshop called Miftāh al-Islām (the key of Islam) and also known by the name of its owner, Mouminou Wattara. This welcoming man from Sikasso (in southern Mali), who was not literate in Arabic, had studied in a French-language school and did not conceal his Sufi likings, even though he was not formally affiliated to any Sufi order. His bookshop, established in 1990, displayed a more limited but still remarkably varied choice of publications. Booklets here tended to outnumber bigger books, publications on Sufism took pride of place, and booklets on magic were much more numerous and visible than elsewhere.

The whole area between the Great Mosque and the market was punctuated by small Islamic bookshops and bookstalls that mainly sold booklets, copies of the Quran, and other basic Islamic publications. Some smaller bookstalls even mixed Islamic printed commodities with other, non-Islamic items, like school manuals and other secular publications.

The only Islamic publications that were exclusively sold outside the network of Islamic bookshops were those written in Malinké in the N'ko alphabet, which, probably due to the rather sectarian character of the N'ko movement, were almost exclusively available in bookshops specialized in N'ko publications of all subjects.[20]

Audiotape Islamic commodities were also more commonly found outside the network of Islamic bookshops, usually at small shops or stalls specializing in the selling of audiotapes of any kind, from African pop music to oral performances by local bards (*griots*).[21] Among such Islamic oral items, the most popular were undoubtedly sermons by local preachers, usually delivered in Bambara, while lectures in French by francophone, sometimes European or Europe-based Muslim, intellectuals appealed to a more elitist audience.[22] However, in Islamic bookshops these items were less regularly distributed than audiocassettes reproducing sessions of Quranic exegesis (*tafsir*) in Bambara, which is probably considered a more scholarly genre.[23] Some of these audiorecorded tafsirs extended through several dozen cassettes, embracing the whole Quran. Their authorship was at least as doctrinally diverse as that of the Islamic publications examined so far, including even a member of the tiny Shi'ite community of Mali, which owed its very recent existence to the proselytizing activities of the Iranian cultural center.

When I was doing fieldwork (albeit with a different focus) in early 2010, I noticed that this media sector of Islamic religious commodities, by now extending also to CDs and DVDs, had considerably expanded over the preceding several years, so much so that it would indeed deserve a separate study.

Mass Literature and Reconfigurations of Islamic Knowledge: Standardization or Pluralism?

Assessing the impact of this unprecedented supply of affordable and easily readable publications on locally rooted attitudes toward (and representations of) Islamic religious knowledge is a rather delicate task that requires some comparative considerations. Anthropologists and historians discussing the rise of printing in disparate parts of the Muslim oecumene and in different periods of contemporary history—from early-nineteenth-century India (e.g., Robinson 1993) to twentieth-century Middle East (e.g., Eickelman 1992) or present-day sub-Saharan

Africa (e.g., Loimeier 2005)—all agree that the impact of this new technology on religious knowledge, coupled with the progressive spread of mass education and the adoption of Western-style methods of teaching (Brenner 2001), tends to lead to an erosion of the authority of the established scholarly élites, who are increasingly marginalized and bypassed in their role as intermediaries between scriptural texts and their socially accepted interpretations.

In many cases, one further outcome of these processes seems to be a standardization of religiosity, entailing the adoption of more literalist, rigid, and impersonal understandings of religious doctrines, as well as a pressure toward a more uniform practice of Islam (Starrett 1996; Soares 2005). Nevertheless, some observers also highlight a hardening of sectarianism, provoked by a "fragmentation of religious authority" (Loimeier 2005: 413) and leading to an irreconcilable opposition of contending doctrinal trends that are increasingly objectified as mutually exclusive, self-contained systems. While these two trends may appear to contradict each other, they can actually coexist in the same context, since they are sometimes pinpointed by the very same scholar. Indeed, it is precisely the act of presenting one's systematized reading of Islam as anti-sectarian that is conducive to excluding the possibility of any alternative reading.[24] This competition among equally standardized doctrinal trends for attracting the largest possible following is further stirred by processes of transformation of the public arena of debate into a market of ideas and by the parallel transformation of access to religious knowledge into a market of religious printed and media items. Thus, while the success of new religious texts (both written or oral) ultimately depends on a given author's ability to persuade his or her public by clear, simple, and compelling arguments, it also relies on a sense of individual moral accountability that is increasingly cultivated by social actors who feel compelled to choose one of the available ready-made religious identities as a model of behavior to be staged in public (Schulz 2003).

The question remains whether these kinds of sectarian confrontations among competing religious views might or not be ultimately conducive to some kind of pluralism. According to Eickelman and Anderson (1997: 61), "Participation in a plural, multivocal world is not the same as acknowledging or even embracing it." However, the social context of Malian Islamic bookstores shows, in my view, a deeper acceptance of the coexistence of different Islamic identities, coupled with an effort to reach a consensus on some sort of common denominator. It is also true that—as observed by Soares (2005: 247; 1999)—this consensus tends, in its turn, to exclude from the public sphere certain categories of social actors whose practices were more tolerated, or even valued, in the recent past.

From our exploration of the contents and outlook of the publications available in Bamako's Islamic bookshops, we can gain a more specific insight into issues of religious pluralism, sectarianism, standardization of religiosity, and attitudes toward Islamic knowledge. I think the main, somewhat contradictory trends that emerge can be conveniently outlined as follows:

> The promotion of a "generic Islam" through a series of catechism-like publications of basic religious instruction that, in spite of their stress on seemingly uncontroversial issues, show a certain influence of Wahhabi ideas. All the more so that, by presenting Islam as a fixed, simple set of rituals, beliefs, and rules to be understood and consciously adopted by every responsible individual believer, these booklets do not leave much room for imagining the acquisition of further religious knowledge as a progressive unveiling of a multilayered truth, to be achieved within the tracks of the established scholarly hierarchy.

There is also a tendency to avoid or downplay issues of disagreement that can be detected in some of the more partisan publications. To recall some examples:

- Some publications by Wahhabi-oriented authors reduce to a minimum the space they devote to blaming ritual practices that Muslims of different orientations follow. Sometimes they are even silent on this subject. An increasing number of Wahhabi authors also translate or quote from books that are well rooted in the curriculum of local traditional education, including works of Maliki *fiqh*, though in principle they disavow the established schools of law and claim a right to autonomous interpretation of legal sources. At most, these authors content themselves with indicating some singular points of disagreement by way of glosses.[25]
- Most Sufi publications, in their turn, also avoid engaging in doctrinal polemics with their opponents.
- Some publications on *dhikr* and "names of God" refrain from hinting at the more esoteric and even "magical" practices associated with these formulas, or even explicitly condemn them.
- Some authors of publications explicitly dealing with the esoteric sciences strive to appear in line with "orthodox" standards, even by invoking the authority of Ibn Taymiyya.

In spite of all this evidence of a more consensual attitude, many publications show that competition among contending doctrinal trends is still strong. This competition is articulated through different options of consumption in a liberalized market of religious knowledge, thus establishing a close link between reading choices and doctrinal leanings. In this arena of debate, the influence of Wahhabi ideas and attitudes seems to put Sufis and experts of esoteric sciences on the defensive.[26] Defensive strategies, as they emerge from their publications, include the following:

- Self-censoring some of their perceived "excesses," thus conceding to some of the arguments of their opponents.
- Accepting the catechism-like booklet format as a necessary tool for avoiding being marginalized by rival propaganda.
- Resorting to a depersonalized transmission of "esoteric knowledge" through easily available booklets, which involves an indiscriminate "publication of secrets."[27]
- Marginalizing the importance of Sufi affiliations through a repersonalization of mystical charisma in highly mass-mediated saintly figures (e.g., Cheick Soufi Bilal).

Such a "publication of secrets" is, however, highly selective and only limited to the less hidden part of "esoteric" knowledge, which is usually transmitted during the first stages of Sufi initiation.[28] This partial revelation serves an advertising purpose.[29] Revealing a part of secret knowledge is not a renunciation of the "esoteric episteme" (Brenner 2001) but is rather a price to pay for reasserting it.

For the moment, Wahhabi trends are far from hegemonic in Mali, and although the basic instruction of ordinary Malian Muslims increasingly tends to conform to standardized explanations of a "generic Islam" of the kind one can find in catechism-like booklets, there is still a widespread sense that, at higher levels, knowledge functions in a much different way. Thus, even in the representations of knowledge shared by most of those with only basic religious instruction, the notion of "secret" still seems to play quite an important role.

A Babel of Languages: Secularizing and Diversifying the Articulation of Islamic Knowledge

As we have seen, Islamic publications available in the Malian market are also varied as far as the languages of writing are concerned. This linguistic diversification is, of course, part of a strategy for targeting different publics, thus widening the social basin of Islamic written knowledge. If publications in French appeal to a predominantly urban readership educated in modern secular schools, the emergent Islamic literature in Bambara is consumed mainly by rural readers, who are also the main target for whom it has been conceived.

As a consequence of this shuffle of languages and contents, Arabic is no longer the only written language of Islamic knowledge, and its status as a sacred tongue almost consubstantial with divine revelation, which had already been weakened, rather paradoxically, by its very use as a language of instruction and everyday communication in the madrasas,[30] is further relativized by the concomitant use of other languages as convenient tools for transmitting Islamic knowledge through writing. Resort to Romanized transcriptions of Arabic religious formulas further contributes to this process of the secularization of Arabic, since, according to a long-standing intellectual tradition that is still well rooted in West African traditional education and social practice, the very letters of the Arabic alphabet are credited to be imbued with the sacred power of the divine word.[31]

French, in its turn, ceases to be perceived solely as a colonial legacy of the postcolonial state, conveying a stubbornly secular culture, and is invested with a new status as an "Islamic language."[32] The Malian francophone readership, while more restricted than that of other former French colonies—such as Senegal or Côte d'Ivoire, where French is more widely practiced—is still larger than the social basin of those educated in Arabic and, moreover, has traditionally been less exposed to Islamic messages breaking the hegemony of secularist discourses.

Finally, the access of Bambara to the status of an Islamic language suitable for the written transmission of Islamic knowledge is an even more revolutionary event, since literacy in this language has been promoted, with a limited success, only for a few decades and for rather restricted uses, strictly defined by the policies of "functional literacy" dictated by UNESCO and governmental agencies like Compagnie Malienne pour le Développement des Textiles. For this and other reasons, although its role as a vehicular language for oral communication is rapidly gaining ground throughout the country at all levels of society, its written uses are usually confined to a growing, but still small, portion of an almost exclusively rural population that is often not educated in either French or in Arabic; urban dwellers are very seldom literate in Bambara and tend to dismiss its potentialities as a written language.[33] Thus, while the use of Bambara, together with the other Malian vernaculars, as a language of oral explanation of Arabic texts (including the Quran) is well rooted in the traditional Islamic educational system,[34] Islamic booklets (and, more recently, even a few books) in Bambara have been published only since the mid-1980s, and almost all are by one author, al-Hajj Modibo Diarra (1957–), a rural-based scholar targeting an essentially rural readership.[35] A substantial portion of this readership has never been exposed to any written form of transmission of Islamic knowledge, except sometimes elementary Quranic school. Thus, while audiotaped sermons in Bambara have undoubtedly a more widespread (and perhaps deeper) impact on this population, written publications in the local vernacular are likely to introduce among them new sensibilities toward written and scholarly religious knowledge.

If one keeps in mind the elevated status of literacy in Islamic religious imagination, all these changes are likely to have far-reaching consequences. For instance, the changing religious status of Arabic and other languages is also paralleled by a symmetric process of secularization of Islamic religious knowledge, as well as of the book as the physical object embodying it. This process, triggered by the secularization of Arabic through the rationalizing pedagogy of the madrasa and the diffusion of printed religious books, is accelerated by their translation (or even composition) in French, still perceived as a foreign and prestigious language, albeit associated with secular culture, and is further achieved by their translation or composition in Bambara, the language of everyday communication. Some influential social actors seem ready to draw the full consequences, as in the case of the popular preacher Chérif Ousmane Madani Haïdara, who advocated for adopting Bambara as a language of Islamic liturgy.[36] It is, however, unlikely that such an abrupt departure from established tradition might soon gain widespread acceptance. After all, Islamic publications in French and Bambara still allow for an important place for Arabic, especially when dealing with matters of liturgy and devotion. Different languages tend to coexist within the same texts, playing complementary roles in a way that is reminiscent of the oral uses of the local vernaculars in traditional Islamic education.

The access of new languages to Islamic written uses seems to open up new spaces for different doctrinal trends and understandings of Islamic knowledge to coexist and interact in an ever-widening, increasingly pluralistic public sphere of Islamic discourse. Moreover, the literacy practices of the recipients and consumers of this new literature show a tendency to appropriate and mix disparate (and seemingly irreconcilable) modalities of transmission of Islamic knowledge, also blurring the divide between competing representations of and approaches to that very knowledge. This may well be seen, for instance, in some of the personal notebooks of Bambara farmers from rural southern Mali analyzed by Mbodj-Pouye (2007: 564–571, 577–581; 2013: 223–224, 236–238). In these notebooks, written by villagers with basic but often varied educational backgrounds, excerpts copied from Wahhabi-oriented catechisms in Bambara are written side by side with Tijani litanies in Romanized Arabic, and, to give another example, the numerological value of the Arabic letters composing some names of God accompanies their transcription in Roman characters. The creativity of social actors thus seems to resist any attempt at standardization, showing a remarkable ability to reelaborate different influences in often unpredictable ways.

Acknowledgments

Most of the fieldwork for this chapter was carried out between 2000 and 2001 and in 2005. My last visit to Bamako for a different project was between November 2009 and February 2010. The paper was completed in July 2011—thus before the political and military crises in Mali that began in early 2012. I have been unable to determine the effects of such events on the topic of this research. An earlier version of this chapter was presented at the workshop "Texts, Words, and Images:

New Media and Islam in Africa" that was organized by the Institute for the Study of Islamic Thought in Africa (ISITA) at Northwestern University on October 22 and 23, 2007. I am grateful to all participants to that workshop for their insightful comments. I am also indebted to Islamic booksellers and their constituencies in Bamako, as well as to al-Hajj Modibo Diarra, for their welcoming and helpful attitudes. Fieldwork carried out in 2005 was funded by a grant from Institut Français de Recherche en Afrique (IFRA), based in Ibadan (Nigeria), in the context of the second phase of the research program "Transnational Networks and New Religious Actors in West Africa."

Notes

1. For a general review of new literacy studies by one of their main promoters, see Street (2003); for a discussion of Arabic literacy in Mali in light of this theoretical perspective, see Mbodj-Pouye (2007: 38–42).

2. To these may be added Arabic grammar books, dictionaries, and Arabic-language textbooks, though Arabic language and linguistics, being studied as a tool for understanding the Quran and the relevant Islamic texts, are not conceived of as entirely secular subjects, even by those educated in modernizing madrasas.

3. Eickelman and Anderson (1997: 54) notice a similar separation between secular and Islamic bookshops in Bangladesh, though competing for the same audiences.

4. See Brenner 2001: 238 and Bouwman 2005: 128–129, 156–157.

5. The information presented here is based on fieldwork as part of a project on Islamic publications in Bambara. On the one hand, such a focus may account for the incomplete listing of the bookshops' full collections of printed items, as well as for the lack of quantitative data on the volume of sales and the profitability of the Islamic bookshop as a commercial enterprise. On the other hand, it may also explain, at least in part, the proportional space devoted, even in this chapter, to publications in Bambara and to language issues in general.

6. Their figures, which were not confirmed by the booksellers, are probably exaggerated; however, the volume of sales, about which I do not have reliable data, must be considerable in light of the average attendance I witnessed.

7. During a visit to the bookshop in February 2010, I was saddened by the news of El-Hadj Isa's recent passing. The bookshop, run by his sons, was still thriving, however, and had even opened a rather well-stocked media section.

8. Indeed, like most of those who, in Mali as elsewhere, are called Wahhabis, they tend to reject this label, claiming for themselves the more "universal" name of "Sunnis." However, although the construction of Wahhabi identity as a colonial term of discourse charged with disparaging overtones has been rightly highlighted by Brenner (1993), who argues that this label was and still is applied rather indiscriminately to a variety of Islamic reformists, I find it even more misleading to follow uncritically their self-definition as "Sunnis," which would entail an implicit denial of this attribute to other Malian Muslims, almost all of whom claim a Sunni identity. Indeed, the latter term has an almost performative, legitimizing function in local debates about proper religiosity.

9. For a similar parallel, see Kaba 2000: 203.

10. For similar examples of what I would call "disengaged" practicing Malian Muslims, see Soares 2005: 242–243.

11. On the importance of the Maqāmāt in the curriculum of Malian advanced traditional education (*majlis*), see Tamari 2002 and, more thoroughly, Tamari 2005.

12. The popularity of books by this author, repeatedly reprinted by Senegalese and Lebanese publishers, has also been observed by Soares 2003: 116–117 and 2005: 231.

13. On this sadl/qabd issue in Mali, see Kaba 1974: 23–24.

14. On Saada Oumar Touré as an anti-Christian polemist, see Brenner 1997: 483–485.

15. Since the only prolific author of Islamic publications in Bambara has Wahhabi leanings, no Sufi publications had been issued in Bambara at the time of my fieldwork.

16. On Ibn Taymiyya and Ibn Qayyim as endorsing practices like *ruqya* (incantations), partaking in what he defines "le Coran utile," see Hamès 1997: 139–143.

17. On this booklet, see also Soares 2005: 242. Other booklets of the same kind contain similar warnings.

18. Some examples are "for every need of possession, domination, and control of a thing, a being, or a situation"; "to hedge against any enemy (skipping a control, etc.)"; and "to deliver a prisoner." Other booklets concentrate mainly on conjuring tricks, not always involving specifically Islamic references.

19. Notable exceptions are books published by a particular bookshop, which has the sole right to sell them. Most of the Islamic publications in Bambara are published and distributed in this way.

20. On Islamic publications in the N'ko alphabet, see Amselle 2001 and Oyler 1995.

21. Part of the repertoire of these bards consists, in its turn, of stories of local "marabouts" (see Zappa 2009b).

22. On audiotape sermons in Mali, see Schulz 2003 and 2006, and Soares 2005: 233–235, 252–254.

23. On the diffusion of Islamic exegesis in Bambara through radio broadcasting and audiotapes, see Tamari 1996: 49.

24. An influential starting point for this trend was probably Eickelman (1992).

25. The Wahhabi-oriented writer Modibo Diarra, who translated in Bambara Maliki classics like the *Risāla* of al-Qayrawani together with tracts by Muhammad Ibn 'Abd al-Wahhab, is a case in point.

26. See also Soares 2005: 206–209.

27. On the notion of the "publication of secrets" as a salient feature of contemporary Sufism, see Ernst 2009.

28. See also Soares 2005: 248.

29. Sufi popularizing literature revealing "secrets" is, in turn, part of a wider array of media commodities mobilized to enhance the reputation of individual saints: see Soares 2004a: 84.

30. See Brenner 1991: 23 and Loimeier 2005: 409.

31. See Mommersteeg 1991.

32. On the notion of Islamic languages, see Bausani 1981.

33. See, for instance, Dumestre 1994 and Canut 1996.

34. See Tamari 1996, 2002, 2005.

35. I have dealt elsewhere with this author at some length (see Zappa 2004: 39–86 and 2009a). While Soares (2005: 277) maintains that "a very limited number of pamphlets dealing with Islam are available in Bambara," by the time of my fieldwork, they already outnumbered 80 titles, which is not negligible for the standards of Malian publishing.

36. See Soares 2004b: 219 and 2005: 234.

References

Amselle, J. L. 2001. *Branchements: anthropologie de l'universalité des cultures.* Paris: Flammarion.
Bausani, A. 1981. "Le lingue islamiche: interazioni e acculturazioni." In *Il mondo islamico tra interazione e acculturazione,* edited by A. Bausani and B. Scarcia Amoretti, 3–19. Rome: Istituto di Studi Islamici.
Bouwman, D. 2005. "Throwing Stones at the Moon: The Role of Arabic in Contemporary Mali." PhD dissertation, Research School CNWS, Universiteit Leiden.
Brenner, L. 1991. *Controlling Knowledge: Religion, Power, and Schooling in a West African Muslim Society.* Bloomington: Indiana University Press.
———. 1993. "Constructing Muslim Identities in Mali." In *Muslim Identity and Social Change in Sub-Saharan Africa,* edited by L. Brenner, 59–78. London: Hurst.
———. 1997. "Becoming Muslim in Soudan Français." In *Le temps des marabouts: Itinéraires et stratégies islamiques en Afrique Occidentale Française, v. 1880–1960,* edited by D. Robinson and J.-L. Triaud, 467–492. Paris: Karthala.
———. 2001. *Controlling Knowledge: Religion, Power and Schooling in a West African Muslim Society.* Bloomington: Indiana University Press.
Brigaglia, A. 2005. "Testo, tradizione e onflitto esegetico. Gli 'ulamā' contemporanei e gli sviluppi dell'esegesi coranica nella società nord-nigeriana (Kano e Kaduna, 1960–2002)." PhD thesis, Università degli Studi di Napoli "L'Orientale."
Canut, C. 1996. *Dynamiques linguistiques au Mali.* Paris: CIRELFA—Agence de la Francophonie.
Dumestre, G. 1994. "Introduction: la dynamique des langues au Mali: le trinôme langues régionales—Bambara—Français." In *Stratégies communicatives au Mali: langues régionales, bambara, français,* edited by G. Dumestre, 3–11. Paris: Agence de Coopération Culturelle et Technique (ACTT).
———. 1997. "De l'école au Mali." *Nordic Journal of African Studies* 6(2): 31–55.
———. 2007. *Maléfices et manigances: chroniques maliennes.* Paris: Karthala.
Eickelman, D. F. 1992. "Mass Higher Education and the Religious Imagination in Contemporary Arab Societies." *American Ethnologist* 19(4): 643–655.
Eickelman, D. F., and J. W. Anderson. 1997. "Print, Islam, and the Prospects for Civic Pluralism: New Religious Writings and Their Audiences." *Journal of Islamic Studies* 8(1): 1997: 43–62.
Ernst, C. 2009. "Sufism, Islam, and Globalization in the Contemporary World: Methodological Reflections on a Changing Field of Study." In Memoriam: The 4th Victor Danner Memorial Lecture. Bloomington, IN: Department of Near Eastern Languages and Cultures. http://www.unc.edu/~cernst/pdf/danner.pdf.
Goody, J. 1968. "Restricted Literacy in Northern Ghana." In *Literacy in Traditional Societies,* edited by J. Goody, 198–264. Cambridge: Cambridge University Press.
Hamès, C. 1997. "Le Coran talismanique: de l'Arabie des origines à l'Afrique Occidentale contemporaine: délimitation et inventaire des textes et des procédés linguistiques utilisés." In *Religion et pratiques de puissance,* edited by A. de Surgy, 129–160. Paris: L'Harmattan.
———. 1998. "Magie, morale et religion dans les pratiques talismaniques d'Afrique Occidentale." *Religiologiques* 18: 99–112.
Kaba, L. 1974. *The Wahhabiyya: Islamic Reform and Politics in French West Africa.* Evanston, IL: Northwestern University Press.
———. 2000. "Islam in West Africa: Radicalism and the New Ethic of Disagreement." In *The History of Islam in Africa,* edited by N. Levtzion and R. L. Pouwels, 189–208. Athens: Ohio University Press.

Loimeier, R. 2005. "Translating the Qu'rān in Sub-Saharan Africa: Dynamics and Disputes." *Journal of Religion in Africa* 35(4): 403–423.

Mbodj-Pouye, A. 2007. "Des cahiers au village. Socialisations à l'écrit et pratiques d'écriture dans la région cotonnière du sud du Mali." PhD thesis, Université Lumière, Lyon.

———. 2013. *Le fil de l'écrit. Une anthropologie de l'alphabétisation au Mali,* Lyon: ENS Éditions.

Mommersteeg, G. 1991. "L'éducation coranique au Mali: le pouvoir des mots sacrés." In *L'enseignement islamique au Mali,* edited by L. Brenner and B. Sanankoua, 45–61. Bamako: Éditions Jamana.

Oyler, D. W. 1995. "For 'All Those Who Say N'ko': N'ko Literacy and Mande Cultural Nationalism in the Republic of Guinea." PhD thesis, University of Florida.

Robinson, F. 1993. "Technology and Religious Change: Islam and the Impact of Print." *Modern Asian Studies* 27(1): 229–251, special issue: *How Social, Political and Cultural Information Is Collected, Defined, Used and Analysed.*

Schulz, D. E. 2003. "'Charisma and Brotherhood' Revisited: Mass-Mediated Forms of Spirituality in Urban Mali." *Journal of Religion in Africa* 33(2): 146–171.

———. 2006. "Promises of (Im)mediate Salvation: Islam, Broadcast Media, and the Remaking of Religious Experience in Mali." *American Ethnologist* 33(2): 210–229.

Soares, B. F. 1999. "Muslim Proselytization as Purification: Religious Pluralism and Conflict in Contemporary Mali." In *Proselytization and Communal Self-Determination in Africa,* edited by A. A. An-Na'im, 228–245. Maryknoll, NY: Orbis Books.

———. 2003. "A Warning about Imminent Calamity in Colonial French West Africa: The Chain Letter as Historical Source." *Sudanic Africa* 14: 103–116.

———. 2004a. "Muslim Saints in the Age of Neoliberalism." In *Producing African Futures: Ritual and Reproduction in a Neoliberal Age,* edited by B. Weiss, 79–105. Leiden: Brill.

———. 2004b. "Islam and Public Piety in Mali." In *Public Islam and the Common Good,* edited by A. Salvatore and D. F. Eickelman, 205–226. Leiden: Brill.

———. 2005. *Islam and the Prayer Economy: History and Authority in a Malian Town.* Edinburgh: Edinburgh University Press.

———. 2006. "Islam in Mali in the Neoliberal Era." *African Affairs* 105(418): 77–95.

———. 2007. "Saint and Sufi in Contemporary Mali." In *Sufism and the Modern in Islam,* edited by M. van Bruinessen and J. D. Howell, 76–91. London: I. B. Tauris.

Starrett, G. 1995. "The Political Economy of Religious Commodities in Cairo." *American Anthropologist* 97(1): 51–68.

———. 1996. "The Margins of Print: Children's Religious Literature in Egypt." *Journal of the Royal Anthropological Institute* 2(1): 117–139.

Street, B. 2003. "What's 'New' in New Literacy Studies? Critical Approaches to Literacy in Theory and Practice." *Current Issues in Comparative Education* 5(2): 77–91.

Tamari, T. 1996. "L'exégèse coranique (*tafsīr*) en milieu mandingue: Rapport préliminaire sur une recherche en cours." *Islam et Sociétés au Sud du Sahara* 10: 45–79.

———. 2002. "Islamic Higher Education in West Africa: Some Examples from Mali." In *Yearbook of the Sociology of Islam,* edited by H. Buchholt and G. Stauth; vol. 4, *Islam in Africa,* edited by T. Bierschenk and G. Stauth, 91–128. Münster: Lit Verlag.

———. 2005. "La prose littéraire arabe en traduction bambara: une *maqāma* d'al-Harīrī." In *Paroles nomades: Écrits d'ethnolinguistique africaine en hommage à Christiane Seydou,* edited by U. Baumgardt and J. Derive, 431–463. Paris: Karthala.

Zappa, F. 2004. *L'islamizzazione della lingua bambara in Mali. Tra pubblicistica scritta e letteratura orale.* Supplement n° 2 to *Rivista degli Studi Orientali* 77. Pisa: Istituti Editoriali e Poligrafici Internazionali.

———. 2009a. "Écrire l'Islam en bambara: lieux, réseaux et enjeux de l'entreprise d'al-Hājj Modibo Diarra." *Archives de sciences sociales des religions* 147: 167–186, special issue: *Traduire l'intraduisible.*

———. 2009b. "Popularizing Islamic Knowledge through Oral Epic: A Malian Bard in a Media Age." *Die Welt des Islams* 49(3–4): 367–397, special issue: *Islam in Contemporary West Africa: Literature, Orality and Law.*

3 Binary Islam

Media and Religious Movements in Nigeria

Brian Larkin

THE NIGERIAN REFORMIST CLERIC Sheikh Abubakar Gumi was famous for wearing white, simple robes. This simplicity was a means of displaying a certain egalitarianism. It was, implicitly, a critique of Sufi hierarchy and of royal author- ity by rejecting the elaborate gowns associated with those elites and a staging of that rejection through daily dress. As he described it, "I learned to appreciate simple and functional clothes as against conspicuous and expensive ones. . . . I have always strived to wear clothes that . . . would never discourage a prospective student from approaching me because he is scared by their flamboyance" (Gumi and Tsiga 1992: 68). Gumi famously refused to allow followers to bow or prostrate themselves, a common practice of respect in Nigeria and one especially associ- ated with royal and religious elites.[1] He was known to his followers as *mallam,* a term that means "teacher" but can refer to any adult male and stands in distinc- tion from the more rarified *sheikh,* a status Gumi clearly occupied. But perhaps the most vivid example of this egalitarianism lay in the way Gumi addressed his followers and allowed them to address him. As one said to me, "Anyone, anyone could ask mallam a question. Even a child, so long as they based their question on the Quran and hadiths." Here the follower is emphasizing Gumi's assertion that the right to take part in religious debate comes from individual learning rather than ascribed status and so is available to anyone ("even a child"). In my experience it was rare to speak to a follower of Gumi who did not refer to this openness and Gumi's welcoming of questions and debate. The scholar Ousmane Kane, himself a grandson of a major Sufi sheikh and well versed in the socia- bility of Sufi orders, demonstrates this in his account of meeting Gumi for an interview: "I was quite struck by his egalitarian tendencies. In his living room all the visitors were sitting in armchairs, including young people and people from apparently modest origin. Everybody shook hands with him as a way of greeting. It would never occur to any member of a Sufi order to shake hands with a Sufi *shaykh* or to sit in an armchair in the same room as a *shaykh*" (Kane 2003: 138).

What is going on in these public displays of egalitarianism? Gumi is marry- ing an egalitarian tradition within Islam to the norms of what we often term the "secular public sphere." Gumi (1972; Gumi and Tsiga 1992) attacked the claims of Sufi clerics to have esoteric knowledge that passed down from sheikh to disciple and was unavailable to ordinary Muslims. This claim is, he argued "by far the greatest point of contention" between Sufis and their reformist opponents (Gumi and Tsiga 1992: 142). Knowledge, Gumi asserted, is open. Muhammad bestowed it on all Muslims in the form of the Quran and the hadith, and each Muslim has access to it on the same basis. Gumi sought to actualize this transparency through the use of modern media techniques. He was one of the first clerics to broadcast over the radio and one of the first to write regularly for a newspaper. He translated the Quran and hadiths into Hausa so ordinary Muslims could gain access to them, and he was the first to record these texts and his own writings on audio- and videocassettes so even illiterate Muslims could gain access to religious knowledge. This use of media presumes a world organized by rationality, where individual learning is theoretically available to all in a society made up of equivalent, interchangeable individuals and not divided by inherited rank. There is an affinity here with Habermas's conception of the public sphere where "the authority of status is reduced to the authority of debating skill" (Habermas 1994: 36–37) and where reason emerges from the "public clash of arguments" (Habermas 1994: 97). Gumi's use of media takes their dispersive qualities and ties them to a particular epistemology and theology of religious practice. By downplaying hierarchy, Gumi, it seems to suggest, is an ordinary Muslim, and ordinary Muslims, by corollary, can ascend to the position he occupies. To wear white, then, is to publicly assert this egalitarianism and to split Gumi and his followers from others who wear luxurious gowns and invest in the modes of hierarchy they connote. It is a public performance of equivalence. To encourage questions, "even from a child" is not just to qualitatively increase the exchange of communication; it also congeals a series of claims about knowledge, hierarchy, and individual agency. It metareflexively dramatizes those claims and effects a split between what Gumi would claim to be more modern and less modern forms of Islam.

Gumi embodies the divide between what is often termed "traditional" and "reformist" Islam and partakes in a logic of rupture that is common in analyses of religious movements in Africa. Birgit Meyer (1998), writing about the rise of Pentecostalism, summarized this as "making a complete break with the past," a phrase that has been picked up and amplified in a series of studies since (Robbins 2004; Larkin and Meyer 2006; Keane 2007; Marshall 2009; Piot 2010). Meyer takes the phrase from Pentecostals themselves, particularly their recognition that people are held in the grip of the past and so cannot achieve individual and social mobility without overtly rejecting past practices. As Ruth Marshall (2009) has elaborated, this break is part of the political techniques of religious revival through which congregants are enjoined to work upon their selves to achieve liberation and fulfillment. Charles Piot (2010) has recently taken the concept beyond religion, arguing that the demonization of past practices characterizes the work of NGOs and development workers who identify cultural practices as retardants to development. By doing this, Piot argues, pastors and NGO workers alike have come to take on the power and authority of the state. Making a break with the past becomes a dominant act whereby the relation between citizen and sovereign is "recalibrated."

While the emphasis on rupture has particular relevance in the contemporary era, it draws upon a long tradition of analyzing religious movements in terms of binary distinctions.[2] One problem with this scholarship is that it takes what is often a tactic of religious movement building—seeking to reify the labile nature of opponents into fixed categories that can then be attacked—as an analytic description of the movements themselves. Focusing on binary oppositions frames those movements as cohesive, bounded, and mutually separable, homogenizing what are internally diverse movements and rendering them static. The language of rupture also serves to order religious movements along a historical and moral scale, where one movement comes to represent a backward past and another a modernizing future.[3] As one can imagine, it is usually the newer movements that are most invested in fixing this temporality by stigmatizing their opponents as backward and themselves as modern. Much of the way the study of religion in Africa has been organized has been through such binary logics: "animist" movements are opposed to mission Christianity; traditional (often Sufi) Muslim practice to Salafi reformers; mainline Christian churches to the born-again movement; Islam to Christianity; and, finally, religion to secularism. While the particular content changes, the structural ordering does not.

The concept of making a complete break is clearly part of the dynamic of religious movements but one that scholars have taken too literally. It is a strategy asserted by adherents in order to homogenize and objectify others eliding the many entanglements that tie seemingly opposed movements together. Scholars need to interrogate claims to difference, to see them as forms of objectification that are part of that political contest and not simply descriptions of the state of things.[4]

Binary Islam

The tendency toward binarism is particularly marked in Islamic studies, which has long been oriented around the tension between what John Bowen (1993: 7) refers to as locally oriented "traditionalists" versus nationally and transnationally directed "modernists." This division takes various names: between calligraphic and print Islam (Messick 1993); traditionalists and modernists (Bowen 1993; Umar 2001); esoteric and modernist epistemes (Brenner 2001); Sufis and anti-Sufis (Brenner 1993); or African Islam versus Islam in Africa (Westerlund and Rosander 1997). Yet all share an understanding of a split between two mutually opposed states, and the scholarly effort then goes into identifying the key features that typify and distinguish one state from another.

While these divisions are complexly configured—incorporating theological beliefs, cultural practices, and modes of institutional organization—one of the most constitutive aspects of this divide is the process of knowledge transmission. This places media technologies at the center of analysis as processes of storage, transmission, and retrieval that are core to the operation of media and of religious movements. Brinkley Messick (1993), for instance, in his study of Islam in Yemen, describes a transition from a "calligraphic" world of audition and person-to-person transmission of knowledge to a world dominated by print, modern schooling, and the state. In the traditional mosque circles he observes, pupils sit at the feet of their teacher, addressing him as "our master," displaying the norms of hierarchy, humility, and obedience that were as much a part of learning as the content of the text. The master literally embodied the text and its commentaries, having been taught it himself in a chain of transmission that tracks back to the earliest writers. As Louis Brenner (2001) noted, this form of knowledge transmission is "initiatic" in that it stresses that "Islamic knowledge can be legitimately acquired only through personal transmission" (2001:7). Messick argues that the final aim was to promote "*adab,* a complex of valued intellectual dispositions and appropriate behaviors" (1993: 77) so that learning was not just about assimilating information but about the cultivation of modes of deportment.

In contrast to this world of reed pens, recitation, and memorization, in Western-style Islamic schools, students are instructed by professors according to a set syllabus that, in principle, could be taught by a changing array of personnel. This reorients the educational encounter away from initiatic connection to a particular person and toward printed texts. Authoritative knowledge is reconceived to refer to the content contained in the text rather than deriving from the process of transmission whereby one scholar taught it to another. In this way, religion comes to be conceived of as a system, one among others, rather than as a total way of life (Eickelman 1992). What Messick refers to as a system of circulation based on "closed genealogical networks" gives way with print to one based on "open networks of commercial exchange" (1993: 118). As Dale Eickelman puts it, "With the spread of mass higher education in the Muslim world, access to the Quran as well as to other books and the ways of knowing inculcated by them has shifted in form. Religious authority in earlier generations derived from the mastery of authoritative texts studied under recognized scholars. Mass education fosters a direct, albeit selective access to the printed word and a break with earlier traditions of authority" (1992: 646). Bowen argues that books came to embody "the idea of a supralocal authority" (1993: 29) and thus were central to the reorientation away from local religious practices and an increased receptivity to currents of reform taking place elsewhere in the Muslim world. The shift from memorization, calligraphy, and reed pens to the standardizing technology of print is constitutive of the rupture that scholars see separating traditional from modernist Islam.

In this narrative, print is associated with the forms of rationality, individual interpretation, and transparency associated with modernity and counterposed to the oral, charismatic backwater of Islam's evolutionary past. Michael Warner (1990) argues that the West treasures few myths like the belief that print brings about democratization by fragmenting established forms of power. The locus classicus of this idea is the Protestant use of print to contest Catholic priestly hegemony, but the fantasy that new means of communication allow individuals to think for themselves and contest established hierarchies accompanies each media revolution from electronic media to contemporary digital technologies.[5]

The central tension of this chapter involves taking seriously the ways media technologies shape the character and practice of Islamic movements, while not being subsumed by the language of rupture this promotes. There is an elective affinity here between media theory that has been organized around a sequence of ruptures (the movement from orality to literacy, print, electronic, and digital media, etc.) and theories of religion that have analyzed the emergence of new religious movements in binary terms. The idea of "making a complete break with the past" or identifying a cleavage between a Sufi order and a Salafi reform movement may seem to have more to do with the complex of theology, politics, and religious practice, but because those movements organize that split around medial practices of storing and transmitting knowledge, they are then deeply affected by the normative concepts embedded in technology: that each technological revolution is part of a teleological movement toward progress.

Religious movements are heteroglossic assemblages rather than homogenous blocs contained in self-enclosed silos, mutually opposed to each other. They are dynamic, continually responsive to other movements, and quick to incorporate elements from other movements that are useful to their own. In Nigeria, Salafi movements have borrowed organizational forms from Pentecostal Christianity as well as from mainline missions and secular modernity.[6] Similarly, Sufi movements were never quite the backward, personalist, anti-cosmopolitan traditionalists their opponents claimed. Indeed, many of the innovations we now associate with Salafi reformers and that those reformers claim for themselves had their origins in Sufi renewal movements.[7] All religious movements are internally competitive, containing several lineages of thought, some of which might incline in a more modernist, rationalist direction, and others in a more esoteric one. This does not mean we cannot draw out over all distinctions, but we must recognize the internal diversity and not let the self-narrative of difference overwhelm our understanding of the way these orders overlap and borrow from one another. The rise of Gumi offers insight into this process.

Education and the Modern Nigerian

The literature on Abubakar Gumi and Izala, the movement he inspired, is now considerable,[8] and I will only briefly touch on his biography here. On leaving school, Gumi's skill in Arabic won him a series of government positions as Pilgrim's Officer to Saudi Arabia, then teacher, then judge, ascending to the position of Grand Khadi of northern Nigeria—the seniormost post in Islamic law. As Grand Khadi, he was based in Kaduna, the political center of the Northern Region, and became informal religious advisor to Ahmadu Bello, the Sardauna of Sokoto, leader of the Northern Region at independence. This placed him at the epicenter of the new political class at its moment of coming to power. Gumi also acted as the Sardauna's translator and guide to the Gulf States at the time when those states, and Saudi Arabia in particular, sought to exert greater influence in world Muslim affairs by funding Islamic renewal. To that end the Saudis founded the World Muslim League in the 1960s, and Bello was selected as its vice president, with Gumi as his key advisor. This position gave Bello and Gumi access to important religious and financial networks that could aid their political and religious programs, and in Nigeria it helped associate Gumi with the forms of Islamic renewal associated with the Arab world. After the Sardauna's death, Gumi began to explicitly lay out his theology of Islamic reform by attacking Sufi orders—first, from the pulpit of his mosque in Kaduna and then in newspapers, books, and, perhaps most famously, through the radio. His success there, discussed below, was recognized as so important that leaders of competing Sufi orders (and of competing lineages within each order), who historically had often been bitter opponents, came together to select a preacher, Dahiru Bauchi, to go on the radio to oppose Gumi. In 1979 two followers of Gumi, Sheikh Sanusi Gumbi in Kaduna and Sheikh Ismaila Idris in Jos, formed *Izala*[9]—the mass movement that took Gumi as its inspiration. My interest is not in Gumi's overall theology or in the sociology of Gumi and Izala, but in analyzing how they used modern media as part of their broader reformist theology.

In his autobiography, Abubakar Gumi explains the traditional religious milieu that he grew up in as the son of a mallam in Gumi in Sokoto state. The book opens with a description of an *ilm* (higher studies) school that was run by his father. He describes how students and the teacher did not face each other sitting on chairs but were arranged in a circle, with his father sitting cross-legged in the center "surrounded on either side by his senior students." Some of the students were young, "while others were almost as old as he was." Gumi goes into detail about the deportment required of such an encounter. "The students did not sit with their legs crossed, like the teacher. Instead they sat on their sides most with their feet arranged expertly behind, partly covered with their flowing gowns. Their posture was formal, . . . their eyes gently focused on their own texts" (1992: 1).

The opening of the book depicts a classic scene associated with traditional Islamic education.[10] Pupils sit at the feet of their teacher. The careful placement of feet is a mark of respect, displaying the deference necessary for learning to take place. The ilm school Gumi's father ran was the opposite of a modern school: it "did not have a syllabus or set books," Gumi tells us; students would "travel long distances to study under an acknowledged expert"; "there was no definite time for enrolling into the school or organized classes"; and each lesson had students of mixed ages and abilities (1992: 8). This is the epitome of local, person-to-person transmission, rooted in a specific place. Gumi begins his autobiography this way to structure the pilgrim's progress of his life journey away from this tradition and toward modern education and modern Islam. It is allegorical in that Gumi's trajectory stands for the broader direction of Islamic reform, his experience that of Muslims more generally. And it also repeats the evolutionary logic of media theories of rupture that require as their ground a primitiveness from which subsequent media revolutions can be measured. To understand the distinction of literacy from orality or print from literacy, one needs as a structuring absence a point of origin—usually an "animist," oral society—from which all subsequent media revolutions take their measure. Gumi's father's school stands as that originary moment for the purpose of his life story—the mode of education, media, and cultural norms that together comprise traditional Islam. That Gumi opens his book with this originary moment is significant because it reveals how much he sees revolutions in education and media as central to his life and thought. Gumi dwells on the details of time, organization, (lack of) syllabi, modes of sitting and looking, and the cultural techniques that accompany media forms and the epistemologies they encode, and he orders them along a historical teleology.[11]

The young Abubakar Gumi experienced exactly this split when he left his hometown to attend a series of Western schools designed by the British to cultivate a new modernizing Northern elite—what came to be called the *yan boko* (see below). His father's students tried to prevent this because the school "represented not just education but a different way of life" (Gumi and Tsiga 1992: 14), but Gumi himself thrived at Western-style schools. He attended a series of them, finally moving on to the School of Arabic Studies (SAS, formerly Kano Law School), the first institution in Nigeria to teach Islamic studies using Western pedagogy. Gumi is explicit about the influence of this on his life and on the superiority of this style of schooling from traditional Islamic education. "The Law school (SAS) had an intellectual tradition which made it unique among all the schools that I attended. Very often, we were encouraged to assert our own independence and initiative rather than blind obedience to the views of our teachers. We challenged them frequently if we felt their understanding was faulty" (Gumi and Tsiga 1992: 33). Gumi's implicit comparison is with the norms of obedience and rote learning that marked traditional Islamic pedagogy. "I did not welcome studying with the leading scholars around, because I had now become used to an approach quite different from theirs. Most of my teachers had studied in both the European and traditional Islamic schools, and that made them quite different. They read and interpreted books with regard to their overall meaning, and always listened to my own understanding which sometimes contradicted theirs. At times they would even welcome the chance for me to disagree with them, so that we would compare opinions and together seek out the best" (Gumi and Tsiga 1992: 64).

Gumi puts forward a classic account of the Habermasian public sphere, where status is subject to the scrutiny of intelligence and learning. The ability to question is key to this. He echoes Eickelman's argument that the rise of mass education and literacy alters the "style and content of authoritative religious discourse" by shifting the site of meaning away from ritual contexts and locating it, instead, in the study of texts (Gumi and Tsiga 1992: 648). "Local mallams," as traditional Muslim clerics are sometimes derisively called, could not operate in this world. "As I saw it," Gumi argued, "the city scholars had a less flexible background. They would not be too likely to tolerate this sort of exchange" (Gumi and Tsiga 1992: 648). Gumi is staging openness as constitutive of the break separating his reformism from traditional Islamic practice. Shifts in education are part of a broader transformation of self in which individual agency is manifest in the ability to question inherited practices, to subject them to scrutiny by referring them back to Quranic source material. "Questioning" is not just a means to clarify information but is something to be publicly performed as the visible display of a deeper epistemology. In summing up his time as SAS, Gumi concludes, "The whole experience left a deep impression on my mind, and today there is nothing I love better than to be challenged about my views" (Gumi and Tsiga 1992: 33). It is why even a child could challenge him.

In his study of Christian conversion in Ambon in Indonesia, Webb Keane (2007) argues that the rupture between "traditional" and "modern" religious practices, such as that which marks Gumi's reformism, draws upon a long history of liberalism. In Indonesia, Christian missionaries typified "animist" marapu followers as prisoners of their culture, unthinkingly replicating a traditional way of life and thus abdicating the individual agency proper to modern subjects. To be modern, Keane argues, is to make agentive decisions about the world and to be able to subject hierarchy and fixed rituals to questioning. There are clear echoes here with Gumi's critique that Sufism cultivated blind obedience, unthinking loyalty to a sheikh believed to possess *baraka* (magical charisma), *fayda* (an overflowing of spiritual energy), and *batin* (secret knowledge about the hidden sides of everyday life). Against this Gumi championed classic liberal ideas of transparency and the free flow of information. "The Prophet did not conceal anything in his lifetime," Gumi (1972: 22) wrote. Claims to secret knowledge are thus "void and false; the whole of them are the work of impostors [*sic*] in Islam" (1972: 45).

In his major written critique, *Al-Aqidah Al-Sahihah Bi Muwafaqah Al-Sharia* (*The Right Belief Is Based on the Sharia*, 1972), Gumi argues that the Quran is an open, transparent text and that Muhammad is the seal of all prophets—the last person to receive revelations from God—and, as a messenger, he made public all knowledge he possessed: "Allah says in the Quran, 'He knows the unseen and makes His secrets known to none except a Messenger whom He chooses'" (Q72: 26–28) (1972: 49), and thus "anyone who thinks that the Prophet concealed any- thing during his lifetime which those after him reported is in disbelief" (1972: 23).

In this polemic one sees the link between Gumi's theology and his implicit media theory. Media, in their broadcast, centripetal nature, have an elective affinity with reform Islam in aiding the dispersal of religious knowledge and promoting the ethical responsibility of Muslims to attend to that message. To not do this is to be in thrall to blind obedience. "There is no mysticism in Islam," Gumi argued. "Everything has been laid out, and the individual Muslim never stands in need of anyone else's intercession between him and God" (Gumi and Tsiga 1992: 135). Knowledge lies on the surface. It is transparent and available to all. Nowhere was this more clear than in the 1960s and 1970s, when Gumi first began to use the radio to broadcast his *tafsir* (Quranic exegesis), the single most important event in transforming what was a limited, elite group of reformers into a broad mass movement.

Radio

Gumi's initial foray into radio came at a time when he forcefully began to articu- late the ideological basis of his reform in a variety of different media—newspaper articles, books, audiocassettes, and later videocassettes—as part of the broader aim of extending religious knowledge to more people. Radio Kaduna was and is the largest radio station in West Africa and is for northern Nigerians a major institution organized according to public-service norms: the presentation to an anonymous public; the inclusion of different points of view in a pluralistic soci- ety; and the establishment of a clear, transparent presentation of information. Jonathan Sterne (2003), in his history of sound technologies, refers to this as "rea- soned listening," a practice that developed over the nineteenth century whereby listening was articulated to ideas of science, reason, and rationality. Radio broad- casts are not simply the dissemination of sound but involve practices saturated with their own epistemologies. Reasoned listening prioritizes the adjudication of meaning, and attention to the message over the ritual function of listening as a mode of worship. Gumi was not the first Muslim preacher on the radio in Nige- ria, but he was the first to fully use its possibilities.

To understand this, one must recognize how the emergence of radio was an indissoluble part of the rise of a new power bloc in Nigerian society: the *yan boko*. Located in the political center of Kaduna, these were the emerging elites whose wealth and authority were rooted in the modern sectors of society, rather than the old trading and religious networks. *Boko*[12] (sing. *dan boko*) literally refers to Hausa written in roman script and came to take on the general meaning of the Western-educated elite whose power derived from control of politics, the civil service, and the military. They represented a new type of Muslim subject and were greeted initially with tremendous suspicion and resentment. Ibrahim Tahir (1975), a Cambridge-educated Hausa scholar, argued that as late as the 1970s, *boko* was a term of abuse—he translates it as connoting something "false and unreal"—and *ŷan boko* were seen as "faked people."[13] Auwalu Anwar (1989) writes that traditional ulama derided their Western-educated colleagues as *mallamin gwamnati* ("government mallams") or *mallamin zamani* ("modern mallams"), and Tahir says he himself was dismissed as a *dan takarda*, a "paper person,"[14] and accused of being *zindiq*: someone who is vaguely Muslim but who has abandoned Islam's core beliefs. In turn, in a classic dynamic of nationalism, *ŷan boko* often regarded traditional elites with contempt, seeing them as backward and provincial and themselves as a modernizing vanguard, educated, and cosmopolitan. (Yakubu 1996). Given the intensity of this divide, one can see why Gumi cut such a distinctive figure for his supporters, acting as a figurehead for this newly emerging elite. Gumi offered powerful support for the ideas they were taught in the new colonial schools and the professions they laid out for themselves, and he could repudiate religious attacks by aligning this colonially educated class with Islamic reform movements from the Middle East. It had the practical consequences that the majority of professionals in institutions such as the radio station—the technicians and administrators, presenters and engineers—were strong Gumi supporters. These professionals could recognize themselves in Gumi, and he, in return, saw that elite as his natural power base.[15]

Both Gumi's supporters and his opponents realized it was Gumi's connections with the new political class—a class that he became a de facto religious leader for—that facilitated his appearance in the media. Sheikh Sanusi Gumbi, one of Gumi's most famous disciples, made this point strongly: "Malam [Gumi] knew about tradition, he knew about modern education" and was "part of government. Those ulama working in their houses,[16] they don't know government. . . . That is the difference between him [Gumi] and those people."[17] Dahiru Bauchi, the preacher selected by Sufi orders to oppose Gumi, also argued that Gumi's position in government and his connections with radio professionals was decisive.[18] The professionals working at Radio Kaduna, by contrast, argued that the choice of Gumi was neither religious nor political but purely technical.[19] Unlike nearly all other major clerics, Gumi's position in government meant that he was based in Kaduna, the colonially built city where the station was located, far from traditional Islamic religious centers. He was fluent in Hausa and Arabic and spoke English, meaning he could move in between the different worlds of

Islamic clerics and colonial and postcolonial bureaucrats with facility. His style of explication was clear, aimed at ordinary Muslims, which fit well with the needs of a radio medium. According to Aminu Ahmed, who worked at Radio Kaduna at the time, the choice of Gumi was "neither an act of omission or commission." Gumi was "available, disposed, and keen."

In 1967 Gumi was asked to allow the tafsir he conducted at the Sultan Bello mosque every Ramadan to be recorded and broadcast over the radio. Until mid-century, the ability to give tafsir, the exegesis of the Quran, was passed down in families and usually conducted in the houses of wealthy elites. It was tightly restricted and ritualistic in character (Brigaglia 2009). Broadcasting tafsir over the radio transformed the audience and social function of tafsir and opened it up to a mass audience that nearly all accounts of Gumi see as decisive in his transformation into a mass leader.

From the beginning, Gumi cultivated a style of tafsir that was readily comprehensible to ordinary Muslims. Nearly all the radio professionals active in Radio Kaduna whom I spoke with at that time commented on the difficulty of following the tafsir of more traditional mallams (many of them naming the learned and highly popular head of the Qādiriyya order, Sheikh Nasiru Kabara, as exemplary of this tradition). Brenner and Last refer to this language as *malamanci* or "the vocabulary, grammar, and spelling common to mallams (scholars) when being at their most scholarly" (1985: 443). As Aminu Ahmed argued, Kabara "speaks only to a selected audience who have a very deep knowledge. He is too philosophical, too deep for the ordinary person. His interpretation is more difficult than the original texts itself. He is a mallam's mallam."[20] Gumi, by contrast, was "down to earth and simplistic," which worked for his program of extending religious knowledge, but also fit the needs of a public broadcast radio medium. One official from CTV Kano flatly referred to Kabara's tafsir as "incomprehensible" and complained about Sufi malams who assumed listeners had "read as much or knew as much as" they did.[21] Even Dahiru Bauchi, chosen to go on the radio as a counterweight to Gumi, still presented difficulties because of the "depth of his learning." For these media professionals there was a clear distinction between the style of tafsir given by Gumi and those of Sufi sheikhs, and they saw the latter as using tafsir as an opportunity to demonstrate erudition before an audience and place less weight on whether the audience could understand and internalize the overall message.

Even though Gumi's radio broadcasts were recordings of tafsir that he had long been giving from the Sultan Bello mosque in Kaduna, Gumi recognized that the act of remediating them on the radio effected a transformation from a person-to-person interaction to addressing an anonymous public. "When I addressed only my immediate audience in the mosque, I could say my understanding freely without fear. The people would sit right in front of me, and any one of them who wanted further explanation could ask me. . . . Once my readings were being broadcast to the entire region, however, I lost this privilege. My audience were now no longer in my reach. Indeed, I might never meet more than a few of them in my life" (Gumi and Tsiga 1992: 132). This address to an open, anonymous public rather than an enclosed, knowledgeable community is the hallmark of the public sphere where a public, as Michael Warner (2002) has argued, is figured as a relation among strangers. It is a mode of address that presumes the existence of competing messages, differing forms of argument from which the listener selects that he or she sees as best, and one engineered into the institutional culture of public broadcast services.

Tension between Gumi and his Sufi opponents broke out into physical conflict in the 1970s, and Gumi himself was worried about threats on his life (Gumi and Tsiga 1992; Umar 1993). Initially, the choice of Gumi to give tafsir was uncontroversial because radio belonged to a Christian world of technology and science seemingly far removed from the esoteric practices of Sufis. But his enormous success and the perceived vitriol of his supporters led the Tijāniyya and Qādiriyya, historically fierce enemies, to unite in an effort to drive out Gumi from the radio station and from mainstream Hausa Islamic organizations. Dahiru Modibbo, head of Radio Kaduna at the time, refused.[22] He responded by arguing that the choice of Gumi was practically, not religiously, motivated (few traditional ulama lived in Kaduna where the radio studios were located) and assuaged Sufi clerics by acknowledging that "as a public institution we do recognize the need to ensure that people of all shades of religious, political, and other persuasions" are represented. The situation was finally resolved when representatives of the Sufi orders selected the Tijani cleric, Dahiru Bauchi, to broadcast alternately with Gumi during Ramadan. This resolution was achieved by appealing to classic public sphere norms. Years later, the fit between Gumi's reformism and the needs of a public-service medium was made palpable to me in interviews with media professionals that demonstrated their strong identification with Gumi. "What Gumi was saying wasn't controversial," one said. "It was just the truth." Another stated, "He [Gumi] had no point of view. What you must understand is that all he did was read the Quran and interpret it. He gave no opinions."[23] Yet another referred scathingly to pressure by politicians to give the Sufi orders the "semblance of equal time," which he clearly saw as undue pressure. He continued, "I believe his interpretations of Islamic jurisprudence" are completely innocent and harmless "except for those who want to take offence." All of these were people working in Radio Kaduna at the height of the controversy over tafsir, and they echo the general sensibility of the time. Modibbo appeared to recognize this bias in his instructions to staff. "Members of staff involved must *never, ever* attempt to judge the correctness or otherwise of the interpretations; whatever personal religious convictions may be, we must avoid taking sides on doctrinal issues" (italics in original).[24] "Should we fail to handle this explosive situation," he concluded, "it is all too likely [we will have to] stop the tafsir broadcasts altogether."

After the rise of Gumi, radio broadcasting went from being an irrelevant part of securing religious authority to a bitterly contested one. Gumi himself was well aware of the central place of Radio Kaduna in his rise to prominence. In his autobiography he remarked how one friend confided in him: "You know . . . the last six years during which your readings were broadcast over the air have been far more effective [in spreading your message] than all the years in which you previously spent preaching" (Gumi and Tsiga 1992:149). For the clerics involved, broadcasting tafsir on the media was perceived largely as a means of extending religion—of reaching new audiences unable to attend the mosque. But when tafsir is framed within the space of a public-service broadcast, alternating with the tafsir of another mallam, this introduces a radical change in religious practice. Religion is presented as a series of options the believer chooses between, and the believer is figured as an independent agent who draws on his individual reason to make his choice. This is a far cry from the Sufi maxim that the follower is like a "corpse at the hand of the one who washes him" in that the disciple owes total fealty and submission to his sheikh, a form of relationship that cannot be sustained under the relativist norms of the public sphere. As Sanusi Gumbi put it, once Dahiru Bauchi was on the radio giving his tafsir, now "the people [could] listen to understand [and] choose." If the Sufi orders are correct, then "Dahiru Bauchi will represent their ideas. If Izala are true, then Abubakar Gumi will represent their ideas," almost perfectly expressing the relativist logic of the public sphere.

Porous Distinctions

In both his autobiography and his public life, Gumi emphasized the rupture between his reformism and Sufi orders and made the public staging of rationality a key symbolic marker of that divide. Rationality was, for him, a set of pragmatic forms that bled into all sorts of practices—wearing white, simple clothes; discouraging followers from removing their shoes and bowing; encouraging questions from supporters—that embodied the idea of rationality in a myriad of ways. What Gumi is encouraging, according to this narrative, is the use of independent, agentive reason—reason that can be mobilized because of the spread of religious knowledge and reason that, by inference, is absent from Sufi forms of knowledge transmission. My point is not just that this divide rests upon a medial base—the division between an oral world of rote memorization and calligraphy versus the rational world of print and electronic media—but that religious movements themselves vivify these medial bases as a means of advancing the logic of rupture. When Izala followers deride traditionalist opponents as *mallamin zaure,* for instance, referring to the room at the front of the house (zaure) where ilm lessons are held, they are metareflexively pointing to the means of knowledge transmission as that which defines Sufi orders. Similarly, when traditionalists critiqued modernizing clerics as *yan boko* (or as *dan takarda*), they are highlighting media (paper, Western script) as the symbolic heart of the rupture between the two. It is what separates one group from another. But when these movements do this, they ignore the countervailing practices that undermine the sharpness of this divide and that unite both groups in common sets of practices.

One can see this by returning to Gumi's use of tafsir. His broadcasts fit into the development of "reasoned listening" (Sterne 2003), the inculcation of practices of reason, interpretation, and rationality addressed to a broad public. Yet, in a series of studies, Andrea Brigaglia (2007; 2009) draws on the practice of tafsir to provide an argument that fundamentally counters this point of view. Brigaglia argues Gumi's tafsir operated on an emotive rather than a rationalist basis. Gumi used sarcastic asides and humor to deride Sufi sheikhs and excite his audience. Even when he was pressured not to inflame sectarian tensions, followers used questions and interjections from the audience to trick him into making "explicit (and explosive) pronouncements" about Sufi orders (Brigaglia 2007: 193), contributing to the overall "emotional tension" of the event. When, in his autobiography, Gumi stressed that he was helped in his radio broadcasts "by the interruptions that I frequently received from audiences in the mosque," he was evoking the lineage of thought that allies questioning to rationality and the application of individual reason. But there is a gap between the ideology laying behind Gumi's tafsir and the effect of it that addressed more passionate emotions. Brigaglia concludes that though the question-and-answer session was "intended, amongst other things, to promote a 'rationalized' religious mode, it functioned essentially as a strongly emotional performance" (Brigaglia 2007: 193). It deploys the form of rational debate but enacts a very different pedagogical effect.

One of the basic problems with accepting at face value the argument about rupture is that many of the features typically associated with reform Islam—egalitarianism, breaking the monopoly of religious elites, mass participation, promotion of education and renewal—first appeared in modern Nigeria through the internal dynamism of Sufi movements themselves rather than from their reform opponents, notwithstanding arguments to the contrary that dominate Islamic studies. Emerging work on Sufism has begun to radically question the tendency to homogenize Sufi movements and to take claims of rupture and difference leveled by opponents at face value.[25] Muhammad Sani Umar (2001) has argued that the modernist structure of Izala—holding regular elections, the use of written constitution, the creation of national and local branches—has been used to define it as a modern civic institution in opposition to the personalist hierarchy of Sufi orders. However, the very same features were developed by the

Sufi organization Fityanul-Islam long before Izala ever existed. The first Islamic movements to organize religious participation on a mass basis occurred in the 1950s with the emergence of new Sufi leaders such as the Tijani Ibrahim Niasse and the Qadiri Nasir Kabara (Paden 1973), who turned Sufi rituals into public events, spectacles that drew in a wide audience; sponsored new Islamic schools; and promoted teaching Arabic. Ousmane Kane (2003) argues that the central reforms that constitute the modernism of Izala—egalitarianism, mass mobilization, innovation of modern educational reform, intensified connection to the broader Muslim world, and the use of modern media to media to extend religious knowledge—have their origins here, and the tendency to treat reformers like Gumi as exceptional are misguided. Indeed, Andrea Brigaglia (2009) argues that Niasse's followers, not Gumi's, were the first to innovate public tafsir by using loudspeakers to address a public beyond the mosque. In the 1930s, Brigaglia notes, there were only 3 or 4 places in Kano city where public tafsir was given, but by the 1960s, when Niasse's influence in Nigeria was reaching its apex, it grew to over 50—an expansion attributable to the Niassian Tijani network's sustained effort to broaden religious participation. "The change from sitting on a goat skin to a small podium," Brigaglia concludes, "and the introduction of a loudspeaker . . . concretely marked the transformation of tafsir in Kano from a discipline of indoor learning to a public expression of scholarly talents" (Brigaglia 2009: 361). This took tafsir away from its elite audience and made it "a popular thing and object of discussion in the city" (2009: 362).

Sufism, and indeed all religious movements, is more usefully thought of as a heterogeneous assemblage rather than a fixed, unitary, theologically homogenous entity. Particular orders are internally diverse. They contain elements that certainly fit on the "traditional" side of the divisions we have laid out above, but there are also many other aspects that fit equally well with the modernizing influences that Gumi and Izala supporters would like to claim for themselves. They are often internally contested with countervailing tendencies pushing in differing directions, some mallams emphasizing more charismatic, magical abilities, while others in the same order eschewing them. The language of rupture fails to capture this internal complexity partly because by basing the division between religious movements on medial bases, scholars of religion partake in the logic of rupture that has dominated media theory. In the case of reform movements such as Izala, it also fails to capture the public staging of rationality as a set of pragmatic forms relatively detachable from their content. Scholars often accept this staging at face value, attributing a purified sense of reformism, easily opposed to traditional Islam, without questioning the truth of that opposition. The result is that the bright line that distinguishes one side from the other—one side insisting that they have made a "complete break from the past"—is much muddier.

Acknowledgments

Research for this paper was funded by the Wenner-Gren Foundation for Anthropological Research and the Pioneer Project in Mass Media and the Imagination of Communities, University of Amsterdam. I thank Benjamin Soares and Rosalind Hackett for thoughtful and informed comments on the draft. I also thank Abdullahi Maradun of Arewa House Centre for Historical Documentation for help with interviews.

Notes

1. Bowing, saluting, averting one's eyes when speaking with social superiors, and crouching as one speaks to them are common practices by which social juniors indicate the status of seniors. In these ways children salute parents, wives their husbands, students their teachers, and so on, in what is seen as a common mark of respect and manners.

2. The most extensive analysis of this process is the literature on the "animist" encounter with Christian missionization. See, for instance, Beidelman 1982; Sanneh 1989; Comaroff and Comaroff 1991; 1997; Meyer 1999; Peel 2003.

3. Benjamin Soares argues that the Salafi critique of Sufi movements produces a new teleology. Where modernization theory presumed secularism would replace religion, now the presumption is that "all Muslim societies will necessarily undergo similar processes of Islamization" (2005: 4–5).

4. Ruth Marshall, in her analysis of the politics of the Nigerian born-again movement, has a subtle appreciation of how the self-conscious critique of local cultural and religious practices by born-again adherents is part of a political project of subjectivation, the condition for producing a new political subject. But this is combined with an overdetermined adherence to the concept of "making a complete break with the past." For her, any attempt to deny the depth of that rupture is to assert a "culturalist" emphasis on continuity that denies the political nature of the break. I do not see why this has to be so. While I accept a great deal of her analysis of how subjectivation operates, I see the constant iteration of rupture as a form of objectification made by one set of actors against others, one that overcodes the many entanglements that movements share. To interrogate these entanglements is not to deny politics; it is to examine how the political project of Pentecostalism operates.

5. For a restatement of these arguments in the context of contemporary Islam, see Eickelman and Anderson 1999.

6. In Nigeria the adoption of mission techniques of outreach by the pan-Muslim organization Jamaat Nasrul Islam (JNI), the use of public preaching by Izala that was organizationally modeled on born-again revival techniques (Umar 1993), and the adoption of Christian mission techniques by Islamic da'wa (renewal) movements such as the preacher Ahmed Deedat (Larkin 2008) are all evidence of this borrowing. See Larkin and Meyer (2006) for a discussion. For another striking example of Muslim adoption of Pentecostal techniques in the aim of being "more modern," see Soares's (2009) analysis of the Yoruba Islamic movement NAFSAT.

7. This is especially the case with the Tijāniyya lineage associated with Ibrahim Niasse from Senegal. See Paden 1973; Kane 2003; Wright 2010; Seesemann 2011.

8. See Loimeier 1997; Umar 1988, 1993; Kane 2003.

9. Jamaatu Izalat al-Bida wa Iqamat al-Sunna or the Society for the Removal of Innovation and for the Sunna.

10. See Eickelman 1985; Bowen 1993; Messick 1993; Brenner 2001; Ware 2004.

11. It should be noted that while Gumi does emphasize the traditional nature of this lesson, he is at pains to describe his father as a modernist *avant la lettre*. He notes his father's openness, his welcoming of questions, and his distinction from other mallams at the time.

12. *Boko* refers to Hausa written in roman script. Before British colonialism, Hausa was written in Ajami or Arabic script. Brenner and Last (1985) argue that the introduction of *boko* by the British gave it a governmental and bureaucratic cast in which norms of rationality and modern education are dominant. Ajami, by contrast, came to take on a solely religious register.

13. "The general view of the Western-educated person is that he is devoid of any sense of propriety, is ignorant of religion, is immoral and is destructive of the social order" (Tahir 1975: 32), someone to be contrasted "with true scholars, the ulama" (1975: 37).

14. This is a reference to the medium of education. Paper is contrasted with the wooden allo boards used in traditional Quranic schools.

15. In his autobiography, Gumi says the beginning of his turn to public avocation of reform was when he started preaching from the Bello mosque in an elite area of Kaduna where senior civil servants lived. "I was happy with the mosque, especially because it enabled me to talk directly to those in authority. My aim was to catch the top, as it were, as the first step toward checking the general ills in society. It has always been my conviction that the best way to effect change in any society is to educate those who have power" (1992: 130). There is an irony in that Izala, the group Gumi became associated with, also became known as a genuinely popular movement as many poor Nigerians reacted positively to Gumi's critique of royal authority. But his aim, initially, was to work from the top down.

16. This is a dismissive reference to traditional ilm classes that often take place in the houses of clerics. See Gumi's description of his father's lesson circle above.

17. Interview: Sheikh Sanusi Gumbi, Kaduna, Nigeria, on May 18, 1995, and June 7, 1995.

18. Interview: Sheikh Dahiru Bauchi, Kaduna, Nigeria, on May 14, 1995.

19. Interviews: Halilu Getso, director of Radio Kaduna, on April 24, 1995; Usman Shettima on April 24, 1995; and Ibrahim Baki on April 26, 1995—all in Kaduna, Nigeria. Aminu Ahmed, director of Kano State Ministry of Information, on May 27, 1995, and July 3, 1995; Aminu Isa, head of Programs, City Television Kano, on May 20, 1995; Hassan Suleiman, Kano State Ministry of Information, on July 2, 1995—all in Kano, Nigeria.

20. Interview: Aminu Ahmed, Kano State Minister of Culture, July 1995, in Kano, Nigeria.

21. Interview: Aminu Isa on May 27, 1995, in Kano, Nigeria.

22. Federal Radio Corporation of Nigeria (FRCN) File D60/Islamic Religious Affairs. Letter to the Leaders of the Tijāniyya and Qādiriyya from Dahiru Modibbo, August 14, 1977.

23. Interview: Ibrahim Baki, Radio Kaduna, on April 24, 1995, in Kaduna, Nigeria.

24. FRCN/D60/Islamic Religious Affairs. Memo from managing director to head of Programs, August 11, 1978.

25. Umar 2001; Soares 2005; Brigaglia 2007, 2009; Wright 2010; Seesemann 2011.

References

Anwar, A. 1989. "The Struggle for Influence and Identity: The Ulama in Kano, 1937–1987." PhD dissertation, University of Maiduguri.

Beidelman, T. O. 1982. *Colonial Evangelism: A Socio-Historical Study of an East African Mission at the Grassroots.* Bloomington: Indiana University Press.

Bowen, J. R. 1993. *Muslims through Discourse: Religion and Ritual in Gayo Society.* Princeton, NJ: Princeton University Press.

Brenner, L., ed. 1993. *Muslim Identity and Social Change in Sub-Saharan Africa.* Bloomington: Indiana University Press.

———. 2001. *Controlling Knowledge: Religion, Power and Schooling in a West African Muslim Society.* Bloomington: Indiana University Press.

Brenner, L., and M. Last. 1985. "The Role of Language in West African Islam." *Africa* 55(4): 432–446.

Brigaglia, A. 2007. "The Radio Kaduna Tafsir (1978–1992) and the Construction of Muslim Scholars in the Nigerian Media." *Journal for Islamic Studies* 27: 173–210.

———. 2009. "Learning, Gnosis and Exegesis: Public Tafsir and Sufi Revival in the City of Kano (Northern Nigeria) 1950–1970." *Die Welt des Islams* 49: 334–366.

Comaroff, J., and J. L. Comaroff. 1991. *Of Revelation and Revolution,* vol. 1: *Christianity, Colonialism and Culture.* Chicago: University of Chicago Press.

———. 1997. *Of Revelation and Revolution,* vol. 2: *The Dialectics of Modernity on a South African Frontier.* Chicago: University of Chicago Press.

Eickelman, D. 1985. *Knowledge and Power in Morocco: The Education of a Twentieth-Century Notable.* Princeton, NJ: Princeton University Press.

———. 1992. "Mass Higher Education and the Religious Imagination in Contemporary Arab Societies." *American Ethnologist* 19(4): 643–655.

Eickelman, D., and J. Anderson, eds. 1999. *New Media in the Muslim World: The Emerging Public Sphere.* Bloomington: Indiana University Press.

Gumi, Sheikh A. M. 1972. *Al-Aqidah Al-Sahihah Bi Muwafaqah Al-Sharia.* Kaduna: Ibrahim Dasuki Foundation.

Gumi, Sheikh A. M., and I. A. Tsiga. 1992. *Where I Stand.* Ibadan: Spectrum Books.

Habermas, J. 1994 [1962]. *The Structural Transformation of the Public Sphere: An Inquiry into a Category of Bourgeois Society.* Cambridge, MA: MIT Press.

Kane, O. 2003. *Muslim Modernity in Postcolonial Nigeria: A Study of the Society for the Removal of Innovation and Reinstatement of Tradition.* Leiden: Brill.

Keane, W. 2007. *Christian Moderns: Freedom and Fetish in the Mission Encounter.* Berkeley: University of California Press.

Larkin, B. 2008. "Ahmed Deedat and the Form of Islamic Evangelism." *Social Text* 26(3): 101–121.

Larkin, B., and B. Meyer. 2006. "Pentecostalism, Islam and Culture. New Religious Movements in West Africa." In *Themes in West African History,* edited by E. Akyeampong. Oxford: James Currey.

Loimeier, R. 1997. *Islamic Reform and Political Change in Northern Nigeria.* Evanston, IL: Northwestern University Press.

Marshall, R. 2009. *Political Spiritualities. The Pentecostal Revolution in Nigeria.* Chicago: University of Chicago Press.

Messick, B. 1993. *The Calligraphic State. Textual Domination and History in a Muslim Society.* Berkeley: University of California Press.

Meyer, B. 1998. "'Make a Complete Break with the Past': Memory and Postcolonial Modernity in Ghanaian Discourse." *Journal of Religion in Africa* 28(3): 316–349.

———. 1999. *Translating the Devil: Religion and Modernity among the Ewe in Ghana.* Edinburgh: IAI Press.

Paden, J. N. 1973. *Religion and Political Culture in Nigeria.* Berkeley: University of California Press.

Peel, J. D. Y. 2003. *Religious Encounters and the Making of the Yoruba.* Bloomington: Indiana University Press.

Piot, C. 2010. *Nostalgia for the Future: West Africa after the Cold War.* Chicago: University of Chicago Press.

Robbins, J. 2004. *Becoming Sinners: Christianity and Moral Torment in a Papua New Guinea Society.* Berkeley: University of California Press.

Sanneh, L. 1989. *Translating the Message: The Missionary Impact on Culture.* Maryknoll, NY: Orbis Books.

Seesemann, R. 2011. *The Divine Flood. Ibrahim Niasse and the Roots of a Twentieth Century Islamic Revival.* New York: Oxford University Press.

Soares, B. F. 2005. *Islam and the Prayer Economy. History and Authority in a Malian Town.* Ann Arbor: University of Michigan Press.

———. 2009. "An Islamic Social Movement in Contemporary West Africa: NASFAT of Nigeria." In *Movers and Shakers: Social Movements in Africa,* edited by S. D. K. Ellis and W. M. J. van Kessel, 178–196. Leiden: Brill.

Sterne, J. 2003. *The Audible Past: Cultural Origins of Sound Reproduction.* Durham, NC: Duke University Press.

Tahir, I. 1975. "Scholars, Saints, Sufis and Capitalists in Kano 1904–1974: The Pattern of Bourgeois Revolution in an Islamic Society." PhD dissertation, Cambridge University.

Umar, M. S. 1988. "Sufism and Anti-Sufism in Nigeria." MA thesis. Bayero University Kano.

———. 1993. "Changing Islamic Identity in Nigeria from the 1960s to the 1980s: From Sufism to Anti-Sufism." In *Muslim Identity and Social Change in Sub-Saharan Africa,* edited by L. Brenner. Bloomington: Indiana University Press.

———. 2001. "Education and Islamic Trends in Northern Nigeria: 1970s–1990s." *Africa Today* (48)2: 127–150.

Ware, R. T. 2004. "Knowledge, Faith, and Power: A History of Qur'anic Schooling in 20th Century Senegal." PhD dissertation, University of Pennsylvania.

Warner, M. 1990. *Letters of the Republic: Publication and the Public Sphere in Eighteenth Century America.* Cambridge, MA: Harvard University Press.

———. 2002. *Publics and Counter-publics.* New York: Zone Books.

Westerlund, D., and E. Rosander, eds. 1997. *African Islam and Islam in Africa. Encounters between Sufis and Islamists.* London: Hurst.

Wright, Z. 2010. "Embodied Knowledge in West African Islam: Continuity and Change in the Gnostic Islam of Sheikhs Ibrahim Niasse." PhD dissertation, Northwestern University.

Yakubu, A. M. 1996. *An Aristocracy in Political Crisis. The End of Indirect Rule and the Emergence of Party Politics in the Emirates of Northern Nigeria.* Aldershot, UK: Avebury Press.

4 Muslim Community Radio Stations

Constructing and Shaping Identities in a Democratic South Africa

Muhammed Haron

SOUTH AFRICA'S MEDIA LANDSCAPE radically changed even before South Africa's apartheid government was replaced by a government of national unity in May 1994. The foundations for the changes witnessed in the media sector from that period onward were laid during the phases of negotiations that took place after the De Klerk regime had released Mandela and lifted the ban on the anti-apartheid liberation movements. Although those were trying times, they were also exciting times as non-governmental organizations (NGOs) such as the Campaign for an Open Media began to work proactively toward "freeing the airwaves," something that many of the oppressed communities had yearned for since the mid-1980s (Minnie 2000: 174–175).

One of the many factors that contributed toward the change in attitude during post-1994 South Africa is the role played by religious media—more specifically, the Muslim media since 1994. Muslim radio stations in particular have had substantial input in terms of the ways Muslims perceive themselves in a secular, democratic environment. This chapter focuses on two stations that, I argue, have made significant contributions to both reinforcing and deepening the identity of Muslims in South Africa. The Muslim media, I contend, have helped listeners to deal with the variety of challenges they face in a predominantly non-Muslim environment.

The purpose of this chapter is to (re)visit two of the seven stations that have been established since 1994 (cf. Haron 2002: 121–132). First, it offers a general overview of the Voice of the Cape and Radio Islam. Second, it discusses how these two stations (and their websites) have managed to open up debates and offer reasonable responses to certain themes that were not questioned or discussed openly in the past. Third, the chapter examines ways in which both stations have constructed and shaped the religious identities of their respective constituencies.

South Africa's Muslims reinvented themselves during the post-apartheid period by downplaying, to some degree, their ethnic identity. In their quest

for social integration, they vied for the establishment of community radio stations because they realized the radio's potential to help construct their broader
national and religious identities (see Fardon and Furniss 2000; Dagron 2001).
Community radio played a critical role in democratizing the voices of the South
African people (see Bosch 2006), a people who formed part of a multilingual,
multiracial, multiethnic, and multireligious society. South Africa's post-1994
government supported the establishment of community media through the creation of institutions such as the Independent Broadcasting Authority (IBA) and
the Independent Communications Authority of South Africa (ICASA). This provided myriad opportunities for religio-ethnic communities not only to empower
themselves but also to maintain and celebrate their distinct identities through the
use of communal media. They could do so without undermining or destroying
the overarching nationalist project. Identity is not a fixed or unchanging vari-
able but one that is tentative and contestable and, in fact, always under construction. South Africa's overarching national identity has been dynamic and one that
is tied to subgroup identities (for example, religious communities) that act as
important pillars in the nation-building process (see Chipkin 2007). Like other
religious communities, Muslims took advantage of South Africa's Bill of Rights
as enshrined in the Constitution (South Africa 1996) that grants them the right,
among others, to enjoy the "freedom of [religious] association" and benefit from
the "freedom of the airwaves."

Muslim Radio Stations: Agents of Socio-Religious Change

As soon as the IBA in its 1997 *Position Paper on Four-Year Licenses for Community Sound Broadcasting Services* (see Teer-Tomaselli 2001: 234–235) opened
the opportunity for groups to apply for licenses, eight different Muslim representatives in four of South Africa's main cities submitted applications. Each of
these potential applicants saw itself as an agent of socio-religious change when
it presented its reasons for wanting to set up a radio station. In Johannesburg
the successful stations were The Voice, Radio Islam, and Channel Islam International, and in the Cape they were Radio 786 and Voice of the Cape. The focus of
this chapter is on Radio Islam and Voice of the Cape, stations that belong to two
divergent (theological and jurisprudential) Muslim groups. Radio Islam was
established by the major theologically conservative organization in Gauteng—
namely, Jamiat ul-Ulama of Gauteng (JUG, established in 1923)—and Voice of
the Cape was set up by a more liberal theological organization—namely, the
Muslim Judicial Council (MJC, established in 1945), along with other Western
Cape–based Muslim organizations.

The intention of this chapter is to demonstrate the differences and the com-
monalities that exist between the two and the extent to which they have reinforced

and deepened their respective Muslim identities amidst a socio-politically trans-formed South African society. The formation of these Muslim stations has tangi-bly contributed toward a fairly secure Muslim identity in a post-apartheid period because of their right "to enjoy their culture, practice their religion, and use their language; and to form, join, and maintain cultural, religious, and linguistic as-sociations and other organs of civil society" (South Africa 1996). Throughout the post-apartheid era, both JUG and MJC have been proactive in encouraging mem-bers of their constituencies to vote and participate in civil society activities, and they have effectively done so by using the radio stations that they had set up.

Voice of the Cape: "My Radio Station, Your Radio Station, Our Radio Station"

The Muslim Broadcasting Corporation succeeded during the early part of 1995 in securing a temporary license and in trading as the Voice of the Cape (hereafter VOC). When it was launched during the (fasting) month of Ramadan in 1995, it reached a sizeable number of greater Cape Town's community. Since then, the VOC progressed at a steady pace, and after years of campaigns and requests to ICASA, it was awarded a four-year license in June 2002. This has been a positive outcome for the station, which has had a diverse audience and a listenership that has steadily grown over the years. As a result, it competes favorably with its sis-ter community radio stations such as Bush Radio (www.bushradio.co.za) in the Western Cape, as well as with those located in other provinces (cf. Haron 2002; Bosch 2006, 2010). The VOC's mandate was twofold: to inform and educate the Cape Muslim community about Islam, with an inherent focus on religious teach-ings, and to report in its programming on matters of cultural, political, social, and economic significance.

Since its inception, the VOC has produced a variety of programs, and through a process of trial and error it has been able to improve its program menu over the years. On an annual basis during the months of February and March, the VOC reviews its programs and makes the necessary adjustments; these are usually based on responses from listeners. With the help of AMPS, the radio management team is able to evaluate and reassess the importance and relevance of particular programs. According to Munadia Karaan (2003), one of the promi-nent senior female staff at the VOC, the rationale behind bringing about program changes was "to strengthen our infrastructure and create an engine room of core, well-trained staff which would have a positive impact on our programming." Like all other community radio stations, the VOC was able to present a variety of popular and not-so-popular programs; the station covers the sports, cookery, children's corner, religious lecture, and live phone-in programs. The programs that have attracted a strong listenership since their inception are *Q & A, Say It*

Like It Is, Youth Line, and *Open Line @ 9.* The last is a "talk show" program hosted by Karaan that usually attracts a wide audience because of her animated interaction with guests and listeners on a variety of topics and themes.

Hume (2003: 241) describes "talk show culture" as a "TV or radio program which features a host, sometimes with studio guests, incorporating questions or comments from the audience," and Hendy (2000: 206) mentions Diane Rehm (1993: 64), who confidently argues that talk show listeners are usually individually empowered. Rehm said the following:

> Talk radio is . . . a provocative and even dangerous medium, capable of representing an extreme form of democracy that gives voice and weight to every idea without stifling or censoring. In offering a forum for ideas and the exchange of viewpoints, talk radio contributes to a growing understanding of the complex issues confronting society.

Indeed, while community radio station "talk shows" presented by hosts such as Karaan might not be as provocative as their counterparts on commercial talk radio stations, such as Radio 702, they succeeded in engaging their listeners to give comments and pose critical questions regarding the issues under discussion. On November 1, 2007, for example, Karaan had a panel of three individuals representing different Muslim media to debate ICASA's decision regarding Radio 702's "hate speech." The discussions and phone-ins were informative and lively, mainly owing to the way Karaan handled the debate. The following year, on November 8, 2008, she hosted a program that concentrated on "dying Cape cultural practices," with the objective of making a documentary. Elderly individuals who had specialized in some of these skills, such as masonry handwork, cabinet making, and *taraza* (the laying of floor tiles), eagerly called in to affirm, on the one hand, that these have almost disappeared and, on the other, the need for creating workshops where these skills can be taught to anyone interested in becoming familiar with them. What Karaan managed to do was to revisit aspects that formed part of the Cape Muslims' cultural identity and one that needed urgent attention. These types of talk shows undoubtedly provided callers with "an accessible and non-threatening alternative to interpersonal communication" (see Armstrong and Rubin 1989: 89). In fact, even though sections of the Muslim community were familiar with state and commercial "talk show" programs, the VOC and its sister community stations have helped to make a qualitative difference in this regard, because their target communities have been empowered and given the opportunity to participate and share their own opinions on issues, which they were unable to do previously.

Although the Q & A program does not fall within the ambit of "talk radio" as understood by the aforementioned scholars, it sparked some interesting debates in the community, particularly in reaction to the types of answers given to some of the questions posed. Since the Q & A program draws a fairly vast listenership on Channel Islam International (CII)—the satellite Muslim radio station that broadcasts from Johannesburg—the VOC realized the program's intrinsic value. The VOC recognized that it would not only help to increase its audience but that it would also educate its Western Cape listeners about theological and jurisprudential issues that underpin their Muslim identity. By late 2006, after an agreement was reached between the VOC and CII, the VOC began to air the popular weekly Q & A program. The program, which is anchored by one of the VOC's presenters (Muhammad Zain), welcomes a range of religious questions that are posed to Mufti Abdul-Kader Hoosein, a former lecturer at the KwaZulu-Natal-based Darul-Ulum Newcastle (a theological seminary) and someone who has a "license" to issue a *fatwa* (a legal opinion); he has been CII's head of religious affairs for a number of years. The questions include theological issues, such as whether a woman may travel abroad without her legal guardian, and more intricate legal matters pertaining to death, divorce, and the dissolution of inheritance.

During the month of fasting in 2005, the mufti had a frank debate on CII with Moegsien Hendricks, representative of The Inner Circle (http://theinner circle.org.za), a South African gay and lesbian Muslim organization. After the debate had ended, the subsequent phone-in discussion showed that homosexuality remained a highly sensitive topic linked to how Muslims viewed their religious identity in a secular state. The debate, which was later also discussed on the VOC, concretely proved that the Muslim radio stations were prepared to open up discussions that were publicly considered taboo and that they were willing to interrogate marginal Muslim identities in a reasonably informative way. This debate effectively forced the Muslim community to deal with those groups that see themselves as "proudly South African Muslims" but that have been (theologically) marginalized by their fellow Muslims because of their sexual orientation. Even though the debate has since died down, it has remained an issue of discussion at informal and formal Muslim events such as family weddings and annual general meetings (AGMs) of organizations.

From the aforementioned and other phone-in programs, it is evident that the audience or listeners—as active radio consumers and perhaps as co-producers (Hendy 2000: 140)—play a vital role in the issues that are debated. They have the ability to influence the discussions either way, and this inevitably affects the way the anchorperson or presenter is able to manage the flow of the debate. This critical role of the audience/listeners in terms of the program's content and outcomes was duly acknowledged by VOC's management staff. This usually happens online and on air at the beginning of each year when they review and plan their program schedule. Consequently, the VOC has been mindful of its performance and presentation, with the intention of retaining loyal listeners and increasing its audience. For example, a perusal of the SAARF listenership survey between April and August 2004 shows that the VOC outstripped its sister stations such as Bush Radio, which has been the focus of a number of significant studies (cf. Dagron 2001; Bosch 2006); the latter station, according to SAARF reports, was able to attract only a 3.1 percent listenership as compared to the VOC's 4.9 percent.

These figures illustrate three significant developments. One is that the VOC's management team has become acutely aware of the role that listeners play and the opinions that they express via phone-ins and other surveys regarding its programs. The second is that the VOC has realized that as a community station it competes with commercial/state stations as well as with other community stations to attract its Cape listeners. And the third is that since it considers itself as a bona fide Muslim station, it has to accommodate topical matters that affect and interest the South African Muslim community in particular and the South African society in general. On this point, the VOC is conscious of the fact that its audience also includes a fair number of non-Muslim listeners who regularly tune into its current affairs programs such as *Drive Time;* these individuals listen to these particular programs because they offer alternative views on social and political matters. Since this is the case, the management therefore also tries to cater to this audience in its programming.

A SAARF survey, which regrettably does not give a breakdown of whether the listeners are Muslim or non-Muslim, recorded an increase in listenership for the station between 2006 and 2007; this increase may be attributed to the fact that the VOC obtained more FM frequencies from ICASA during this period and that it began to audiostream. From that period onward, it opened up the station to a wider set of audiences who were unable to access the terrestrial station. Via audiostreaming, the VOC was able to reach "Cape Muslims" who emigrated "home" on a regular basis; they tuned in from countries such as Australia, Canada, and the United Kingdom. For these far-flung communities, the VOC introduced a special program titled "To Hear a Touch of Home"; this program broadcasts twice a month on every alternate Sundays. It targeted the diaspora "Cape Muslims," with the intention of transnationally reinforcing (and perhaps strengthening) their religious and national identity. And it also inadvertently seems to reinforce the ethnic identity of those who still wish to hold onto their ethnicity.

According to the online VOC news (October 13, 2007), a record number of 11,696 online listeners from abroad tuned in from the beginning of September/ Ramadan, and this figure increased to 17,511 by mid-October. These online listeners tuned in from 44 countries around the world, with the United States, the United Kingdom, Australia, Canada, and New Zealand being the top five. The comparative online survey further showed that 43.4 percent of the audiostreamed onliners tuned into specific programs; when compared to the 2006 figure, this percentage was up by 0.3 percent. It should be noted that Ramadan, which is the sacred month of fasting for Muslims, usually affects the way Muslims conduct themselves, and they tune in to listen to, among other things, the recitation of the Quran, the discussions that focus on the month's sacredness, and religious programs reminding them of how they should act and behave throughout that month. For many expatriates, audiostreaming and remaining in contact with the VOC provided a critical lifeline that assists them in reinforcing their identity as Muslim men and women in predominantly (foreign) non-Muslim environments where Islam and Muslims have generally been viewed negatively rather than positively.

To conclude, the VOC website in general and the audiostreaming in particular have made a major difference to the VOC's profile over the past few years. The website, which is updated on a daily basis, has attracted both young and old. While the chat room has turned into an exciting, interactive site for the young, the news service has proved quite valuable for the other age categories. This implies that the VOC has succeeded in serving the religio-cultural needs of South Africa's "Cape Muslims" and assisted in enhancing their religious identity through the diverse radio programs and information that it disseminates on its website. It may safely be argued that the VOC's image has been boosted because of its revamped radio programs and its well-managed, regularly updated website. The same may be said for the Johannesburg-based Radio Islam, to which I now turn.

Radio Islam: "Your Learning Station"

Radio Islam (www.radioislam.org.za), while already registered as a section 21 company by November 1993, was a latecomer into the broadcasting arena. The station's management was granted a license in 1997, even though it had been ready to start broadcasting in 1995. Its first signal broadcast was on April 10, 1997, from Lenasia, a predominantly Indian area in the southern part of Johannesburg (see Murkens 2009). The station carved out its own unique identity in that it was managed by South African theologians—namely, the Jamiat ul-Ulama of Gauteng (JUG)—who were mainly Indian Muslims who strictly adhere to the Hanafi School of Islamic jurisprudence. As a consequence of their restricted interpretation and application of the Islamic primary sources, the Quran and Prophet Muhammad's Sunna, they espoused a conservative Muslim model for identity as opposed to the more liberal one advocated by the VOC toward sensitive and debatable issues such as women's rights, dress codes, and music.

The station used the aforementioned primary sources with the aim of promoting Islam's "pure" message and disseminating Islamic values. And, according to the station's manager, it undertook the ambitious task of dispelling "misconceptions relating to Islam and Muslims in South Africa and abroad" (see Radio

Islam). It is indeed ironic that although the station wished to dispel myths and misconceptions about Islam, it disseminated its own set of misconceived ideas and practices. For example, the presenters would harp on what the length of a person's beard should be when the person leads the *salāt* (ritual daily prayer). When their views and interpretations regarding these types of issues are compared to the understanding of the Cape Muslims, it will be quite obvious that the latter group—who hail from a different jurisprudential and theological school— do not identify with their method of interpreting jurisprudential and theological matters. In addition to the aims mentioned, the management also expressed the view online that the station had become "a beacon of guidance and an invitation to the world" through broadcasting high-quality infotainment that has, in its opinion, "become a bridge across the community divide" (Radio Islam). Critically minded Muslims have challenged the station's management with regard to what it means by such infotainment, since it has adopted specific policies toward the playing of "religious music" that it considers unacceptable according to its understanding of the primary Islamic texts (see Baig 2008). The management interestingly—and quite belatedly—also adopted a policy that squarely opposes any form of discrimination based on gender, race, political persuasion, class, religion, belief, language, and disability. This policy differs from its initial position of not giving women any space on the airwaves due to some of its trustees' ultra-conservative views on the status of women in the public sphere.

However, the station has progressed over the years in terms of the policies that it was forced to revise, the training of individuals that it conducted in the various sectors of radio journalism, and the infotainment programs that it offered. It committed itself as a station to a set of policies that seriously takes into account the concerns and needs of *Batho Pele* (*People First*) (Radio Islam). Whether this has been achieved is hard to tell, since it has not been conducting regular surveys—in the way the VOC does—to gauge the listeners' views. It has, however, occasionally been in contact with its devoted listeners, with whom it discusses these issues at the theological body's AGM. It also communicates through a consultative process via the "Your Feedback" file that appears in the main menu on the station's website; the station management stresses that if it knows what its audience/customers consider important, then it should be in a position to set service standards that are achievable and, of course, realistic.

Radio Islam identified the following objectives on its website: promoting Islam to all via the airwaves; striving to be an authentic Islamic voice; working toward the upliftment of humankind; and providing alternative news and current events programs. The listed programs demonstrate that the station has been able to fulfill the objective of promoting Islam; in fact, one non-Muslim, Kweletsi Maphopha, wrote in the "Your Feedback" file that he was "an ardent listener of Radio Islam (though . . . not a Muslim) and was at first surprised by values and morals of the Islam(ic) religion . . . as compared to the reality . . . people have about Islam" (May 22, 2006). Comments such as these stand the station in good stead because they reflect the Islamic values and identity, which it has been mediating, have been successfully conveyed. This response is bound to enhance the station's profile and support base, which will provide it with the necessary rationale to maintain its status within the community radio station fraternity into the foreseeable future as a competitive and relevant station.

Fortunately for Radio Islam, its frequency has been accessible to the communities that it has targeted, and the audience profile has changed only slightly since the programs have become available via audiostreaming, accompanied by a revamped website. South African expatriates who have accessed the website have been audiostreaming from as far as the United States and Canada, and some of them have made very favorable comments about the station's programs (see Sibar Mohammad's comments in the "Your Feedback" file on September 8, 2007). Yusuf Haffejee, who comes from South Africa and is probably teaching in Saudi Arabia, stated in the "Your Feedback" file that he "had the good opportunity to listen to Radio Islam . . . over the internet. It's wonderful . . . to be able to feel as part of the global *Ummah*" (May 22, 2006). It is exactly this idea that the management had hoped to achieve—that is, being a station that connects with the global Muslim community and reinforces that global Muslim identity.

Another listener, Hajira Nosarka, declared in the "Your Feedback" file, "I am origanally [sic] from SA [and] moved to Canada a few years ago. Insha Allah [God willing] I pray that Radio Islam always broadcast[s] interesting programs so that everyone throughout that is listening can benefit in some way. Shukran [Thanks]" (May 22, 2006). Although this woman did not pinpoint which programs she found informative, her words demonstrate that the station has been able to constitute a focus for Muslims abroad. The quotations from two local listeners are also quite insightful: Farouk Valiallah from Azaadville commended the radio for being "very educative, and very professional," and Fatima Mangel from Lenasia informed the management that "I am glued to Radio Islam. As a lady I have learnt so much about Islam." Unfortunately, there was no indication from any of these listeners as to which programs they considered educational and which contributed more information about Islam than they had already possessed. These ideas were, however, solicited and gathered soon after Radio Islam carried out an important community-needs assessment survey and an overdue listeners' survey prior to handing in its application for a four-year license. According to Romy Murkens (2009: 86), one survey was about need, demand, and support from the community and surrounding mosques, and the other was a second listeners' survey to gauge the community's ideas regarding its programs; both surveys formed part of Radio Islam's annual general meeting's 2007 "composite report" (see *Radio Islam AGM Report*, August 26, 2007).

Radio Islam, like other community radio stations such as the VOC, did not have the necessary expertise when it started out and as a consequence had to train individuals in the different sectors of radio broadcasting (Murkens 2009). However, some of its extremely conservative executive members declared from the very outset that although they were open to individuals being trained for various posts, they were not prepared to accept women. This very problematic and sensitive issue, one that dented the image of Radio Islam, has been discussed and referred to by media studies specialists such as Romy Murkens (2009) and Tanja Bosch (2010).

Members of the station's management board were also members of JUG, a body, as already mentioned, generally associated with a conservative and an ultra-orthodox Muslim position—a position and an interpretation that have been inextricably mixed and fused with South Asian culture. Their ultra-conservative understanding of the primary Islamic sources led them to advocate the view that the place of the woman is not in the public sphere but in the private sector (that is, the home). They thus effectively conveyed a skewed and questionable understanding of women in Islam. In fact, they controversially and incorrectly deduced that a woman's private parts also include her voice! Since they regarded themselves as the spokespersons for and gatekeepers of Islam and Muslims (in South Africa), the impression they created was that all Muslims hold similar viewpoints; this was, of course, far from the truth. When the management's stand was publicized in mosques and on the air, there was a resounding backlash from various Muslim (and non-Muslim) sectors. A small organization known as Youth for Islam, Enlightenment, Leadership and Development took up the case and pointed out that the station violated some of the IBA laws (see IBA *Position Paper on Four-Year Licenses for Community Sound Broadcasting Services* 1997). The management was forced to change its stance; it eventually relented and complied with the IBA decision (see Wessels 1998; Haron 2002).

The outcome of this important episode in the early life of Radio Islam obliged the management to make some substantial changes and amendments to its structures and programs and to include more women as presenters and board members. These changes naturally impacted upon the program content, and the station has since been broadcasting programs that focus on women's affairs (see Murkens 2009: 78–81). In fact, it is ironic to note that as a result of the station's "Women of Wonder" promotion, it was publicly recognized at the first MTN Radio Awards on May 14, 2010. That aside, a few typical examples give an insight into the issues covered: at 8:40 A.M., there is a 10-minute program that offers "Guidelines for Muslim Women," followed by a 15-minute program at 8:50 that reflects on the role of the Sahaabiyat (the Prophet's female companions). At 11:30, there is a 15-minute program titled *An-Nisa* (*Women [Issues]*). Even though these are fairly short programs, it is a clear indication that the station had to reposition and adapt to the current circumstances and show its willingness to empower women.

The question of whether the station succeeded in adopting a less conservative stance toward women remains. One specific issue that was raised in Europe toward the end of 2009 was that of the banning by the French government of the veil that many Arab (and South Asian) Muslim females donned publicly. The government unexpectedly received full support from Shaykh Muhammad Tantawi, who was the Egyptian Grand Shaykh of Al-Azhar University at the time (2010). In response to the French ban, Radio Islam decided to air a series of lectures by prominent JUG theologians Maulana Ravat and Maulana Suleiman. Their presentations were aired during November and December of 2009, respectively. In addition, the station also invited Mufti Siraj Desai, an ultra-conservative theologian who hails from Port Elizabeth. Apart from being a leading member of the Eastern Cape Muslim theological body, the Majlus ul-Ulama of PE, this theologian is also closely associated with the highly controversial paper *The Majlis* (www.themajlis.net), which condemned Muslim radio stations as instruments of the Devil (cf. Haron 2003). Each of these theologians explained what was meant by the donning of the hijab (i.e., the outer covering) of the Muslim female. As far as I know, the station did not ask any of the available female theologians to address the subject. Nonetheless, what is important to bear in mind is that these (male) theologians defended their interpretation and understanding of the issue of women's dress code, and Mufti Desai in particular condemned Shaykh Tantawi's compromised position on the *niqab* (veil) issue. These responses clearly indicate that the station's position remained firmly conservative, and it is doubtful that the station will shift from this position in the near future. It is clear that the interaction between the audience and the station helped to change the management's attitude toward the question of gender and thus shaped it to become more accommodating.

It may be argued that the overhaul of programs that took place over the years and formed part of the empowerment and transformation processes would not have been possible if IBA/ICASA had not intervened. These new developments may also be attributed to the acquisition of new, young presenters who joined the station in different capacities over the years. For example, Ismail Variawa, the station's program manager, demonstrated his willingness to accommodate changes such as producing a refurbished user-friendly and informative website and issuing a free newsletter to its subscribers. The website and online newsletter are additional instruments that have helped to provide the station with an attractive "religious" look and identity. Both the website and the newsletter have complemented the station's broadcasts in more ways than one, and listeners have shown their appreciation via their recorded comments on the website.

The station broadcasts on MW and not on FM like a number of other radio stations, such as the defunct The Voice. Despite the disadvantage of broadcasting to the people in the greater Johannesburg area from its MW frequency, it has been able to attract a large listenership. SAARF's RAMS survey indicates that Radio Islam has about 43,000 listeners, but its management seems to doubt the statistics and estimates that it has a listenership base in excess of 100,000. It should be borne in mind that Radio Islam has to compete with CII, the satellite Muslim radio station located in the same area, as well as with other Muslim stations such as the VOC, which is available via audiostreaming.

The available SAARF data reflect that Radio Islam performed badly compared to other radio stations in the Gauteng region for the period from July 2006 to June 2007. The decline in listenership may be attributed to competition from the aforementioned Muslim radio stations—terrestrial and satellite—both inside and outside the region. In the absence of hard evidence and radio surveys, it may be speculated that with the presence of audiostreaming as another means of accessing the stations, some listeners shifted their loyalties to other stations that mediate more ear-catching religious programs; one is therefore not taken off guard to hear during informal conversations at public gatherings that listeners who were once avid Radio Islam listeners had switched to the Cape Town–based Muslim stations, where they found more exciting programs.

What is also telling about the statistics is that the shift from one Muslim station to another indicates that listeners seem to be comfortable with a more open approach to the understanding and application of Islam. In other words, the conservative Muslim identity displayed by Radio Islam as compared to the more liberal Muslim identity reflected by the VOC appears to have caused listeners to migrate to Muslim stations as and when they became aware of the programs offered and presented by sister stations through audiostreaming; the sister station provided them with an opportunity to listen to, for example, VOC's *Happy Homes* which offers an interesting insight into how Islam has been understood and interpreted from a different (theological) perspective. All of this implies that theological identity within the South African house of Islam has been fluid because of the images that conservatism and orthodoxy reflect in the global arena. The ideas of Zegeye and Harris (2003) that allude to the unstable nature of identity connect well with the theological identity shifts noticed among South Africa's Muslims; in other words, even though Muslims stress the notion of a global *umma,* they cannot overlook the fact that there are tendencies within the house of Islam that pull Muslims in different directions, depending on how the dominant theological groups present their positions in the public arena and how their Muslim media mediate information about those competing tendencies. In the case of South Africa, both stations have continued to show that while they feel extremely comfortable with their national identity and being Muslims in South Africa, they cannot deny the fact that internal and external socio-political, as well as theological, developments have influenced their attitudes and outlooks during the past few years.

* * *

Throughout South Africa's post-apartheid era, the commercial and community radio stations have contributed toward and shaped South Africans' national identity. This ongoing nation-building process has been far from easy to manage, since South Africans have had to adjust to democratic conditions demanding that they shed the racist attitudes they have been accustomed to for many decades. Like everyone else, the Muslim community has been affected by the former apartheid system and is still wrestling to get rid of what remnants are left. The Muslim radio stations have, to a certain degree, assisted in overcoming these legacies by remolding and reshaping the identities of the Muslim communities that they target and serve amidst the formation of the emergent, more inclusive national identity.

In the post-apartheid era, these radio stations have had to accommodate social developments that were stimulated by the democratic system that was put in place and that impinged upon the religious values they expressed. Among the issues that the stations have had to contend with is the provision of equitable and adequate space for marginal voices. This implied that as representatives of the Muslim minority, the stations' management teams had to permit the airing of voices that were generally considered insignificant in traditional Muslim societies. When the question of the empowerment of women was broached, none of the stations could afford to ignore or overlook it because it formed part and parcel of the IBA conditions and agreements for issuing a license. Although this was a nonissue for the VOC's management team, it was a problematic matter for Radio Islam's conservative management team; it was, however, a matter that the latter team could not wish away and had to resolve quickly. The positive outcome enhanced the status of the Gauteng-based Muslim women by granting them opportunities in a variety of sectors that were usually considered off-limits by Islam's gatekeepers—namely, the orthodox Muslim theologians.

And when the debate on homosexuality was placed on the stations' busy agenda, the management teams could not skirt around it, since it had been and remained a topical matter that also affected other religious communities. Providentially, the stations' management teams, which cultivated a culture of theological dialogue as they gained more experience and exposure in the media industry, entertained the idea and permitted the issue to be aired and debated. Even though the debate, as expected, did not sway Muslim listeners to embrace homosexuality, as was noted during the phone-in session that took place soon after the interview, it provided them the opportunity to deal with the matter publicly and sensibly without getting too emotionally embroiled in the affair. The debate also gave those who openly proclaimed themselves as homosexual Muslims the opportunity to find theological answers to their religio-sexual identity challenges in the public arena.

Finally, the stations, which form an integral part of South Africa's democratic culture, provided and continue to afford important platforms via which South African Islam and Muslim identity is debated and discussed; they are forums where these issues are also exposed to a large listening audience, something that was only marginally possible before the formation of these community radio stations. As a consequence of their establishment, the stations have been able not only to reinforce the religious identities of their target audience (that is, the Muslims) but also to share basic Islamic principles and values that constitute a Muslim's identity with non-Muslim listeners who have been interested in knowing what causes Muslims to express themselves passionately in this highly secularized, postmodern world. In conclusion, it may be argued that as a result of the predominantly liberal and tolerant South African environment, the various Muslim groups managed to openly and, to a large extent, respectfully differ from one another and reflect a fairly effervescent and vibrant Muslim identity.

References

Armstrong, C. B., and A. M. Rubin. 1989. "Talk Radio as Interpersonal Communication." *Journal of Communication* 39(2): 84–94.

Baig, Khalid. 2008. *Slippery Stone: An Inquiry into Islam's Stance on Music.* Garden Grove, CA: Open Mind Press.

Bosch, Tanja. 2006. "Radio as an Instrument of Protest: The History of Bush Radio." *Journal of Radio Studies* 13(2): 249–265.

———. 2010. "Community Radio in South Africa 15 Years after Democracy." In *The Citizen in Communication: Re-visiting Traditional, New and Community Practices in South Africa,* edited by N. Hyde-Clarke, 139–154. Cape Town: Juta Academic.

Bush Radio. www.bushradio.co.za.

Chipkin, Ivor. 2007. *Do South Africans Exist? Nationalism, Democracy and the Identity of "the People."* Johannesburg: University of Witwatersrand Press.

Dagron, Alfonso Gumucio. 2001. *Making Waves: Stories of Participatory Communication for Social Change.* New York: Rockefeller Foundation.

Fardon, Richard, and Graham Furniss, eds. 2000. *African Broadcast Cultures: Radio in Transition.* Cape Town: David Philip.

IBA. 1997. *Position Paper on Four-Year Licenses for Community Sound Broadcasting Services.* Pretoria: Department of Communications.

Haron, Muhammed. 2002. "South African Muslims Making (Air) Waves during the Period of Transformation." *Journal for the Study of Religion* 15(2): 111–144.

———. 2003. "Maulana Desai and His Majlis: An Ultra-Conservative Voice in the Eastern Cape Wilderness." *Annual Review of Islam in South Africa* 6: 55–59.

Hendy, David. 2000. *Radio in the Global Age.* Cambridge: Polity Press.

Hume, Ellen. 2003. "Talk Show Culture." In *Encyclopedia of International Media and Communication,* edited by Donald H. Johnston. New York: Academic Press.

Karaan, Munadia. 2003. "Islamic Identity as Perceived by Community Media: A Study of the *Voice of the Cape.*" *Annual Research of Islam in South Africa* 6: 16–19.

Minnie, Jeanette. 2000. "The Growth of Independent Broadcasting in South Africa: Lessons from Africa." In *African Broadcast Cultures: Radio in Transition,* edited by Richard Fardon and Graham Furniss, 174–179. Cape Town: David Philip.

Murkens, Romie. 2009. "The 'Special Interest' and 'Geographic' Models of Community Radio: A Study of the Effectiveness of the Two Models in Meeting the Needs of the Community." Unpublished MA thesis, University of Witwatersrand.

Radio Islam. 2007. *Radio Islam AGM Report.* Lenasia, South Africa: JUG. August 26.

Radio Islam International. www.radioislam.org.za.

Rehm, Diane. 1993. "Talking over America's Backyard Fence." *Media Studies Journal* 7(3): 63–69.

Teer-Tomaselli, Ruth. 2001. "Who Is 'Community' in Community Radio: A Case Study of Community Radio Stations in Durban, Kwazulu Natal." In *Media, Democracy and Renewal in Southern Africa,* edited by S. Keith Tomaselli and Dunn Hopeton, 231–254. Colorado Springs: International Academic Publishers.

The Constitution of the Republic of South Africa. 1996.

The Inner Circle. www.innercircle.org.za.

The Majlis (Voices of Islam). www.themajlis.net.

Voice of the Cape. www.vocfm.co.za.

Wessels, Jakkie. 1998. "Community Participation in Community Broadcasting." *Codicillis* 39(1): 29–35.

Zegeye, Abebe, and Richard Harris. 2003. "Introduction." In *Media, Identity and the Public Sphere in Post-Apartheid South Africa,* edited by Abebe Zegeye and Richard Harris. Leiden: Brill.

PART II

NEW MEDIA AND MEDIA WORLDS

5 Mediating Transcendence

Popular Film, Visuality, and Religious Experience in West Africa

Johannes Merz

WEST AFRICAN POPULAR VIDEO FILMS are often set in a Christian (Pentecostal or charismatic), distinctly modern and urban environment in which the Devil and other powers of darkness and their human agents fight against Christians and God, with the good side winning in the end. A key trademark of such films is their visualization of magic and the revelation of occult powers (Meyer 2003a: 209–210, 2004, 2005b; Ukah 2003). The film industry based in southern Nigeria that produces this "new cultural art form" (Ukadike 2000) is now referred to as "Nollywood" (Barrot 2008; Haynes 2010). Its products are "becoming the most dynamic media form in African history" (Larkin 2008: 174), and they continue to enjoy a growing success, with 1,711 films—the most ever—produced in 2007 for Nigeria alone (Barrot 2008: 32). Ghana and, more recently, the Republic of Benin are also part of this phenomenon.

Factors that contributed to the unprecedented success of the West African film industry include advances in video technology and its increased accessibility, as well as deregulation of the media sector in many countries (e.g., Meyer 2003a). In this chapter I argue that there are also important cultural reasons for the video films' success that are rooted in African culture and experience. A good understanding of the local and traditional aspects of African culture, especially in terms of visuality, entertainment, and religious experience, permits a deeper understanding of the nature of the medium of film, how it functions in African societies, and how it works as a slow but steady catalyst of religious transformation, even in more remote and rural parts of the continent.

I approach the subject from the perspective of contemporary anthropology, which includes my own experience and work among the Bebelibe, who live in a rural area of the northwest of the Republic of Benin.[1] Using the existing literature on popular film in Ghana (Meyer 2003a, 2003b, 2004, 2005a, 2005b, 2006) and Nigeria (e.g., Haynes 2000, 2010; Ukah 2003, 2005; Barrot 2008; Larkin 2008), I attempt to draw some generalizations by interpretively linking the situation of the Bebelibe with the wider West African context. My aim is to show what I consider general trends by relating film to Christianity and traditional religion. In doing so, I consciously accept the risk of omitting details and of not representing all segments of West African society.

I trace different aspects of popular African film back to beliefs, practices, and other traits of African culture and religion that predate the introduction of the new medium to the continent. Traditional rituals not only contain aspects of performance and entertainment but also have a strong transcendental perspective and a religious function. Ritual practices and activities usually have visual characteristics that I think are founded in the presence of an important visuality that touches on many parts of life, including learning processes of rituals, and religion in a wider sense. Today, many of these characteristics of visual and religious culture are mediated and extended through film into modern urban, and often Christian, life. Film, as a mediator between the local and the global (Ukah 2005), has a broad and complex function within society. Following scholars such as Lyden (2003) and Marsh (2004), I examine film from the perspective of functional religion by considering film watching as a religious activity and experience. The narratives of film both mirror society and shape it. In the West African context, film watching itself can be seen as a functional substitute for traditional religion. Popular films depict different aspects and ideas of traditional culture and beliefs—often diabolized from a Pentecostal-Charismatic perspective—by offering an entertainment ritual that takes the place of traditional rituals. Popular films, I argue, mediate a transcendent experience to their audiences.

Film, Religion, and Entertainment

Religion has always played a more or less important role as a subject depicted in film. The medium can use special effects and montage tricks to portray religious and transcendent themes. In the West, Jesus films were among the first commercially produced films, and they continue to be made today (Walsh 2003). Likewise, the first Indian film producer, Dhundiraj Govind Phalke, was inspired to make films depicting Hindu mythology after having watched an American Jesus film in Mumbai during Christmas 1910 (Bakker 2007: 44). Religion has continued to feature in Indian films in the form of filmed mythology (Gillespie 1995: 361) and more generally, even in recent times, by the characteristic song-and-dance sequences that can be considered a direct development of Hindi mythology (Wenner 2002).

Religion in popular West African films cannot be linked directly to dramatized mythology, religion, or ritual, as is the case in India and the West. In spite of this, I see a clear connection between the medium of film and African traditional religions more in terms of a functional mode rather than a representational one: film and religion share aspects of performance, both in a theatrical and an entertainment sense. This is undoubtedly facilitated by the fact that, unlike in Europe (cf. Marsh 2004: 19–20), the boundaries between entertainment and religion, whether traditional or Christian, have remained blurred in Africa and elsewhere (Gillespie 1995: 358 and 363; Collins 2004; Meyer 2006).

Traditional religion often plays a major part in popular West African films, even when it has been affected by Christians imagining it in its diabolized form (see Meyer 2005a, 2005b). In contemporary African society at large, witchcraft beliefs, rituals, sacrifices, and possession ceremonies also remain part of everyday life and can hardly be ignored. Anthropologists have described and analyzed the complexity of African religions in different ways. One of them is to see an element of acting and theatrical performance in traditional rituals, whether they are diabolized or not. Stoller (1995), for example, takes this as a starting point by using a theatrical explanation as the basis for his analysis of the social memory embodied in *Hauka* spirit possession in Niger. Apart from the Hauka, the performative aspect of traditional religion is evident in masqueraded dances, such as those performed by the Yoruba *Egúngún* cult. Besides providing entertainment, the dancers of Egúngún—who are believed to embody the spirits they represent— offer a religious ritual that acts as a mediator between the ancestors and the living (Finnegan 1970: 509–516; Stoller 1995: 86; Lyden 2003: 54 and 79). More generally, the similarities that theater, ritual, and media share, which includes both work and play and different levels of participation (Goody 1997: 99–152), have been described with the term *performance* (e.g., Hughes-Freeland 1998).

A strong performative element in the above sense is also present in rituals and ceremonies performed by the Bebelibe. Among the most important ones are the two main types of initiation rites and the burial and funeral ceremonies. The first kind of initiation, *Tikonte*,[2] is performed yearly for both boys and girls by the Bebelibe and their northwestern neighbors (Huber 1979; Kreamer 1995), while the second, more complex, type—the *Difone* cycle of initiations which lasts four years—is mainly celebrated by the eastern and southern clans of the Bebelibe and their neighbors, the Betammaribe (Sewane 2002). The Difone cycle includes the different initiations called Difone and *Ditentide* for boys and *Dikuntide* for girls. While Difone is considered a secretive and severe initiation, all the other rites (Ditentide, Dikuntide, and Tikonte) remain popular due to their public displays of colorful paraphernalia, music, and dance. Ditentide, Dikuntide, and Tikonte all end with important public celebrations, where the novices are almost playfully dressed in colorful (usually red and white) garments that include cowry shells, beads, hats, towels, sunglasses, and other paraphernalia specific to each initiation. The novices are required to perform the dances they have learned during the initiation to the specific rhythm of drums that are sometimes accompanied by the songs of the relevant initiation rite. The purpose of all these public events is to demonstrate and celebrate the successful completion of the specific initiation.

The initiation usually includes physical and spiritual tests and the revelation of secret information, often of a religious nature (Huber 1979; Sewane 2002).

Among the Bebelibe, burial and funeral rites for adults are even more important than the initiation rites. While the burial rites need to be performed within a day of someone's death out of necessity, funeral rites last three to four days and are organized at least a year later, usually toward the end of the dry season. Their main purpose is the transition of the deceased person to ancestorhood.

Both burial and funeral rites are complex and elaborate, and they can be considered a collection of different rites (cf. Sewane 2003). Often, for example, the specific initiation rites that the deceased person participated in are repeated during both burial and funeral rites through their rhythms, dances, and sometimes songs. These are performed at different times during the three or four days of a funeral. Several genres of songs and dances that celebrate the life of the deceased, or simply entertain, equally have their place. An important part of the funeral involves offering large quantities of pork and millet beer to the paternal, and more importantly the maternal, family of the deceased as well as to guests. The burial itself ends with the body, or these days the coffin containing the body, being placed in the grave, but the funeral culminates in the placing of a large pierced clay pot on the grave.

Traditional rituals, whether initiation, burial, or funeral, usually draw an audience that follows all the proceedings. Ritual, with its element of performance, serves as an important and popular means of entertainment in traditional village settings. Among the Bebelibe most ceremonies and rites, especially funeral rites, remain very popular and well attended, and an informal market for the purpose of amusement and socialization develops at the site of the event.

With the arrival of Christianity (introduced by Western missionaries), this element of traditional entertainment has usually been suppressed, together with traditional religion and its representations, without offering a real alternative (Goody 1997: 42–65; Meyer 1998; Collins 2004). Practicing Bebelibe Christians, an estimated 10 percent of the population, are discouraged from undergoing initiation rites, and many do not even attend the public parts of these ceremonies anymore. Equally, they are advised to follow burial procedures as outlined by their respective denomination, which are much less exuberant, have little religious significance in the traditional sense, and are not usually followed by a funeral.

While this religious entertainment as part of a traditional ritual is, of course, best experienced by actively participating in the ritual itself, it can now be watched as represented and acted in a film. It has become commonplace for people to video both Christian and traditional ceremonies (see, e.g., Gore 1998), and rituals are also frequently featured in popular films. The Beninese film *Yatin: Lieu de souffrance* (2002) by Stedafilm International, for example, opens with a vodu ceremony as celebrated in southern Benin that would not normally be attended by Christians. *Yatin* was written, directed, and produced by Christine Madeleine Botokou and follows the example and conventions of Nollywood films. Botokou spent many years in Nigeria, where she was involved in the production of popular video films. In 1998 she returned to Benin to start her own interdenominational drama and film ministry (Mayrargue 2005: 248–250). Another Beninese film that is popular among the Bebelibe is the commercially produced *Le berger* (2004) by Akoyane Films. *Yatin* and *Le berger* both present city-based pastors as the heroes fighting against witchcraft (*Yatin*) or Mammy Wata spirits (*Le berger*) that are prevalent in rural and seemingly backward villages. After a period of suffering, the pastors claim complete victory, which results in the deliverance and conversion of the afflicted victims.

Local markets in the Cobly area host video clubs and offer a variety of films on DVD from Benin and its neighboring countries, as well as from Asia and the West. Since Cobly, the main town of the Bebelibe, started to receive electricity during the evening hours in early 2005, many people have bought television sets and video-CD or DVD players, sometimes despite severe economic difficulties. This kind of equipment is mainly owned by Christians from different denominations who also constitute the economic force in the town and need to be counted among the wealthier segment of the population. Compared to the more traditional Bebelibe, they do not have the sometimes huge ritual expenses to host a funeral or have their children initiated, even though many Christians financially support their respective church.

The appeal of popular video films is that they have the ability to reveal, contain, control, and re-imagine traditional rituals, together with other representations of evil, and thus render them safe for consumption and entertainment, especially for Christians (cf. Meyer 2005a). In this way the performative and entertainment aspects of traditional rituals can remain part of modern and Christian life, while at the same time they can be rejected as being something from the Devil and the past (Meyer 1998). Through the portrayal of ritual, film mediates transcendence at least to those viewers who have the necessary cultural background or knowledge to exegete the pictures as having a transcendental aspect, which is usually encoded in the proceedings of ritual itself. Film thus mediates ritual to its audiences in such a way that film watching as a group activity can be considered to have become a ritual in itself (see Lyden 2003; Walsh 2003: 11).

While traditional ritual and film can be understood in terms of performance, they are also characterized by a shared importance of visuality. It is therefore important to examine the question of visuality in African culture, as well as in film, and how visuality finds its expression in the specific cinematography of the West African film industry.

Visuality in Tradition and Film

In anthropology and related disciplines, African societies have usually been described as being "oral" due to their often extensive corpuses of orally transmitted literature (see, e.g., Finnegan 1970). Visual culture is often considered as playing a less important role in traditional African cultures as anthropologists have observed a lack of pictures, paintings, and other concrete visual representations of people and objects (e.g., Goody 1997: 3). Among the Bebelibe, for example, the only concrete visual representation I have become aware of in their tradition are small statues sometimes found in the houses of diviners that represent the *siyawesi,* spirits that are believed to mediate between God and the diviner as an essential part of the divination process (Huber 1973: 386–387).

In spite of the supposed lack of concrete visual representations, I consider Bebelibe culture to be strongly visual as well as oral. The visual culture of the Bebelibe touches on many areas, including art, symbolism, ritual, and religion. For the purposes of this chapter, I give only a few examples that directly relate to religious beliefs and practices.[3]

Ancestors (*uhido,* pl. *behidibe*), guardian spirits (*ditenwende,* pl. *atenwiene*), and other spiritual agents all have their visual representations in the form of different mounds of clay or stacks of rocks (cf. Goody 1997: 51–74). Sometimes their construction and maintenance require prescribed rituals through the sacrifice of sorghum beer and different kinds of animals. After each sacrifice, traces of blood, feathers, pieces of animal skin, and the skulls are left on or near the altar, and the person for whom the sacrifice has been performed wears a bracelet on the wrist or below the knee made of feathers or a piece of fur of the animal sacrificed (Huber 1973). They all visually indicate to the wider community what has been happening.

The divination process prescribes exactly what is needed for any kind of necessary sacrifice or the construction of an altar, down to the pattern and color of the animal in question. Divination is to a large extent a visual process, as the movements of the divination rod and the patterns formed by the thrown cowry shells determine the answers to problems and questions posed (Huber 1973: 388–392; Blier 1991). This process needs to be known not only by the diviner but also by each head of a compound, who seeks advice on behalf of those for whom he is responsible.

The Bebelibe also know many different kinds of medicines (*uyanku,* pl. *iyanki*). Their main purpose is to ward off evil and guarantee protection. Sometimes the visual representation of a medicine shows its direct function. For one type, arrows are attached to the pot that holds the medicine. The installation is placed in front of a compound. Its purpose is to ward off witches (*uhua,* pl. *behope*) by threatening to shoot them should they approach the house. The arrows act as a visual symbol of the spiritual protection that this medicine is believed to offer. The same principle can also be observed at neo-traditional anti-witchcraft shrines of *Tigare* and *Nkunde,* which are both found among the Bebelibe (Merz 1998: 25–37). The shrines offer their divinities physical spears that they can use when hunting witches at night. At an urban Tigare shrine, I came across two wooden models of airplanes that, according to a priest, his divinity used to hunt modern witches. Some witches, it is believed, rely on technology, such as airplanes, which renders their evil activities even more vicious and dangerous (cf. Geschiere 1997: 2–3).

These few examples clearly show that the Bebelibe have a strong visual aspect in their religion and culture. Having said this, I see their kind of visuality as having a different focus to the one found in Western societies, which has specialized in concrete and realistic visual representations, such as those found in paintings, photos, and, above all, film. Among the Bebelibe, altars generally have a more abstract, functional, and symbolic visual display that does not directly portray the entity it represents. The divination process is even more abstract in that their visual symbols represent only meaning. Most aspects of visuality are concerned with perceiving objects, actions, and patterns that communicate a specific meaning and that are not always easily identified by outsiders as part of the Bebelibe's visual culture. The focus of the Bebelibe's visuality is thus more symbolic—or, as I prefer to call it, interpretive—than representational.

Lakoff and Johnson observe that most metaphors used in English to express knowledge are based on visual perception (knowing is seeing). They conclude that "we get most of our knowledge through vision" (1999: 238). This observation also seems to apply to languages and cultures beyond the Indo-European ones. The link between "seeing" and "knowing" is present among the Bebelibe and encoded in their language Mbelime. The verb *ya* not only covers the semantic areas of "to see, to perceive," but also "to understand," similar to the English verb "to see" and one of their proverbs states, *A fe nonfe yaa ne tu nne di toode kesime* (The eye that sees is better than the ear that hears).

A strong link between knowing and seeing has also been confirmed by Sewane (2002, 2003) for the Betammaribe, the Bebelibe's closest neighbors. She was often challenged for asking difficult questions when she could simply observe what was happening. Seeing, many Betammaribe claimed, should be sufficient for her to understand what she wanted to know.

Sewane (2003) concluded that "seeing" is the way for the Betammaribe themselves to learn about ceremonies. Rituals, like film, follow a basic narrative structure that is reaffirmed, and sometimes reauthorized, every time the ritual is performed. For the Bebelibe, I have observed that the ritual performance is prescribed and supervised by old men who are recognized as authorities and who are present for the ritual. Often, it is younger men who actually perform a ritual, such as the burial of a body or the sacrifice of a chicken. The older men will make it known if they do not agree with the way things are done. Sometimes opinions differ among several old men, which gives rise to debates that, if possible, are resolved by consensus and in turn reauthorize the current way of performing a specific ritual. Each performance of a ritual provides a learning experience for younger men who observe the proceedings and who in the future will become the authoritative voices in prescribing ritual themselves.

Learning by observation and imitation as it has been described for the Betammaribe (Blier 1991: 78; Sewane 2002, 2003), and as I observed for the Bebelibe, can also be referred to as "visual learning." This approach to learning is not commonly found in Western-style education, but it is widespread in societies that have been labeled "traditional" or "oral" (see, e.g., Harris 1984). Observing a ritual and watching a film have evident similarities, since the same strategy of visual learning can be applied. This is why Harris (1984: 83) considers films to be potentially useful in instructing people who are accustomed to learning visually by observation and imitation. Like a ritual that can be observed over and over, a film can be watched many times.

Visual learning and the specifics of the interpretive nature of African visuality play an important role in how African audiences watch films and how African filmmakers make films. The latter are ultimately determinative for the emerging cinematographic conventions of West African popular video film, giving them an art form that is unique and different from other centers of world cinema, such as Hollywood or India.

At the heart of popular West African cinematography stands the picture. Ogundele (2000: 127) sees a major shift from the importance of the voice in Yoruba traveling theater to the image of Yoruba video films. For Ghana, Meyer (2005a: 278–279) confirms that audiences emphasize the visual aspects of film over its sound and language. According to her, the historical reason for this visual emphasis goes back to colonial times when copies of celluloid films were often so bad that the sound was impossible to hear. When Indian films became popular in Ghana, they were usually enjoyed in the original languages without subtitles, as is still the case in northern Nigeria (Larkin 1997: 412). The sound quality of West African popular video films, particularly the ones made in Ghana, is usually so poor that it is difficult to understand the dialogue (cf. Haynes 2000: 2; Meyer 2005a: 278–279).

Filmmakers of popular videos thus focus their creative efforts on the composition of the picture and, more specifically, what it communicates. With the interpretive visuality of their target audiences, they do not need to deliver a thoroughly aesthetic or meticulously realistic picture, as is usually expected by Western audiences. African audiences rather stress visual patterns and symbols that transmit the intended meaning of the filmmaker.

The best example of this can be seen in the special effects often used in popular video films to visualize the supernatural (cf. Meyer 2005b: 176). In the early days of popular film—namely, during the early 1990s—special effects were, from today's perspective, rather crude. Sometimes they merely consisted of people vanishing or simple arrows or spheres moving across the screen to show the flow of supernatural power. Usually, special effects are also accompanied by sound effects. Contemporary special effects have become technically more sophisticated as the home-computer technology used by filmmakers continues to improve. The Beninese *Yatin: Lieu de souffrance* (2002), for example, uses animated white or bluish lines that are reminiscent of electric sparks and lightning to represent the flow of supernatural powers. Stills of people are moved into or out of the picture to show supernatural displacement, or a (physical) snake is metamorphosed into a (spiritual) person.

While such effects have improved considerably since the early days, they are still barely acceptable to Western audiences, as they appear too obvious or not realistic enough. To the target audiences of such films, on the other hand, they symbolize a sufficient and acceptable visual representation of the presence and relevance of the supernatural in everyday life and allow for a correct interpretation of the meaning intended by the filmmaker (Meyer 2005b). Like the medicines described above for the Bebelibe, special effects act as a representation and reminder of the presence of the supernatural by providing a visual reference. The composition of a picture with its special effects allows the medium to represent life with its constant transcendent presence. Through its cinematography, popular film directly mediates transcendence to its intended audiences the same way traditional religion uses its different visual symbols of altars, rituals, and other processes (cf. Gillespie 1995: 364 and 377–378).

The interpretive visuality of African societies is the place where film and religion converge. This visuality sets film apart from other media, and it provides film with its uniquely persuasive and enchanting power. This brings us back to the nature of film itself and the way it is watched and consumed. Films are primarily made to entertain, but due to their transcendent nature, they provide their audiences with religious experience.

Film Watching as a Religious Experience

Recent studies of film in the West have underlined its link with religion and its religious function (Marsh 2004: 34). Accordingly, film watching can be seen as functioning as an alternative to religion, providing, in a limited way, an experience of spirituality and even worship (e.g., Deacy 2000; Moore 2000; Lyden 2003; Marsh 2004).

The affinity of film watching with religious or spiritual experience can be explained by cognitive science. Accordingly, Lakoff and Johnson (1999: 565) understand a major part of what is commonly called spiritual experience in terms of imaginative empathic projection. This is the cognitive faculty that lets us feel empathy with another person by projecting her imaginative experience to ourselves, thereby enabling us to imagine what it is like to be her and to imitate her. This faculty also comes to bear in watching films. A successful film asks its audience to identify with at least one of the characters portrayed and to project oneself empathically into his situation so his experience can be felt by the audience. In this way, film watching in the West has become "one of the contemporary channels which supplies narratives for people to 'live within'" (Marsh 2004: 11; see also Moore 2000: 11; Meyer 2004: 105).

While in the past Christianity provided a meta-narrative for Western societies that included morals, ethics, and values, it is now films that offer a myriad of different narratives that contribute to society's standards and ideals.

Film can be seen as a dialectical mirror of culture. It reflects how culture really is, while at the same time it shows how it should be according to current cultural ideas and ideals (Lyden 2003). In this way, film picks up on trends in society and then processes and popularizes them to the extent that it influences the way we perceive reality (cf. Appadurai 1996; Deacy 2000). In West Africa, popular video films with a Pentecostal-Charismatic nature are often accepted as accurate documentations and revelations of the spiritual realm (Meyer 2005a: 286–287, 2005b, 2006: 304). The reason for this seems to lie in the comparison that African audiences make between films and "dreams" or "visions." These are the only traditional concepts that are linked to the idea of moving images that come to persons from outside their normal consciousness. Like film, they follow a basic narrative structure. It is not surprising, then, that the Bebelibe usually associate films directly with dreams. They suggest that what they experience both in dreams and in films is comparable. Both can be interrupted: dreams by waking up and films by meddling with the equipment. Many also say that, having watched a film, they experience its pictures in their dreams. On the other hand, the Bebelibe also recognize that there are differences between films and dreams. While dreams are something personal that only the individual experiences, watching films is usually public (cf. Lyden 2003: 51–52).[4]

"Dreams" and "visions" are both accepted as important in a realistic way and as having an immediate influence on everyday life, and thus a direct relevance. Along with trance and possession, they are both seen as means to access the unseen or spiritual realm.[5] While dreams are something that everybody experiences at night, visions are generally believed to be more powerful and are not restricted to sleep. Only some claim to possess the gift of vision, having acquired it either at birth or during initiation. By dreaming or by having a "second pair of eyes" (cf. Blier 1991: 76), people can "see" what is happening in the spiritual realm. Those who possess the gift of vision can then use their special knowledge in normal life for their own benefit or the benefit of their community. Some may use their gift to become active players in the spiritual realm where they can have a direct influence by deciding the life or death of other people, often without even being aware of it. The gift of vision is usually associated with seers, diviners, healers, prophets, and witches.

In contemporary Africa, "seeing" beyond the visible remains popular also among Christians, and some people actively seek to gain the faculty by whatever means necessary (see, e.g., Meyer 2006: 301–302; Merz 2008). Meyer (2003b) reports that many Ghanaian Pentecostal pastors claim to possess the gift of vision, which they use for their sermons and in delivering people from demons and other powers of darkness. Likewise, many Ghanaian video filmmakers claim they have first "seen" their films in dreams before they actually produced them. Such films usually have a Pentecostal-Charismatic theme depicting aspects of the spiritual realm that are normally believed only to be "seen" in visions. By declaring themselves visionary in this way, they claim the authority to make films that appear realistic and true to their audiences, to the point that they are accepted as documentations of the spiritual realm (cf. Meyer 2005b: 166; Ukah 2005: 311).

While the faculty of vision a person has is usually attributed to some kind of mystical force or power, in the cinema it is technology represented by cameras, projectors, or consumer electronics that causes film to appear on screen. Technical commodities, such as television sets and other equipment needed to consume film, are often perceived as being enchanted or having magical connotations (e.g., Lyons and Lyons 1987: 131–132; Hackett 1998: 267; Marshall-Fratani 2001: 93). The technology underlying film takes the place of mystical power and gets identified with it as the means by which vision is mediated through film. In a wider sense, then, film technology is understood as modern magic, which is acceptable for Christians. Hence, "films are able to mimetically reproduce vision itself" (Meyer 2004: 101), and spectators can share in this public vision of "techno-religious realism" (Meyer 2005b) that depicts and reveals the spiritual realm by becoming passive visionaries themselves. Audiences can thus experience film as a collective dream or vision in both a realistic and enchanted way by morally engaging in it and actively interacting with what they regard as a representation of reality (Meyer 2003b: 26, 2004: 104, 2005b, 2006: 303; Ukah 2003: 225).

Popular video films keep their audiences aware of the imminence and transcendence of the spiritual realm and of potential dangers and problems caused by it. Through films people can learn how demonic forces operate and how to counteract them. Each film offers a solution to the specific problems it portrays that is often grounded in Christianity (Meyer 2006: 304). Popular video films are used like visions to confirm beliefs about the unseen world and to gain a better understanding of what is happening there. This insight can then be applied to everyday life. For example, through the Beninese film *Yatin: Lieu de souffrance* (2002), which shows witches attacking their victims from behind, Bebelibe spectators are reminded that they should keep an eye on what is happening behind them in real life. More generally, McCall has observed for Nigeria that popular films in Igbo have become an important source for cultural exegesis and that we "cannot underestimate the degree to which these videos have become a part of popular life" (2002: 92).

Film is a powerful medium because it stimulates our senses both by imitating experiences of the real and by mimicking the way our memory works. We easily remember certain films or parts of them. They can penetrate our memories and haunt us in our dreams. Film happens to us; it can be experienced and understood intuitively without investing any significant processing effort. Film thus delivers a message of pre-processed and intentional images that are supported by language and sounds, straight to our memory. As with any other experience, film can directly imprint itself on our memory and thus shape it, as well as the way we think and how we imagine and perceive reality. Both in Africa and the West, then, films mediate transcendence through their visuality and allow for a religious and distinctly modern experience by dialectically interacting with wider society and thus influencing people's lives and their perceptions of reality (Appadurai 1996; Marshall-Fratani 2001; Lyden 2003; Ukah 2003: 225, 2005; Meyer 2004, 2005b).

Film has become an integral part of modern, and often Christian, life in West Africa, and it has been thoroughly appropriated to the local context (Hackett 1998; Ukadike 2000; Larkin 2008). This is most vividly shown in the still-growing importance of the West African popular film industry. While the recent liberalization of the media market in many countries of West Africa and the advance in digital video technology certainly acted as a major catalyst for the growing industry, I see the real reason for the unprecedented success of popular West African video films in African culture and traditions that are represented and expressed in different ways in film itself. As I have argued, African societies are not less visually oriented than other societies, even though it needs to be recognized that the way visuality is experienced differs among different cultures. African visuality, with its interpretive character, is currently being developed by West African filmmakers and cinematographers. It is being made more concrete, explicit, and representational, while still maintaining its originality and uniqueness as typically expressed in contemporary popular video films with their computer-generated special effects.

Interpretive visuality as found in African cultures has so far largely escaped Western-dominated approaches to culture, and especially film, because it is less representational and does not offer a ready and concrete object of study as, for example, oral literature does. Popular video films have often been criticized and downplayed for their technical simplicity and for content that can appear melodramatic and vulgar and has been accused of portraying "outdated superstitions" (Meyer 2004: 98). Intellectuals especially can sometimes feel uneasy about these films because they do not seem to be compatible with rational modernity, and they are different from the more established celluloid filmmaking that closely follows Western models of film (McCall 2002).

With their growing popularity and importance across West Africa and beyond (Barrot 2008), however, popular video films can no longer be overlooked or downplayed. It needs to be recognized that popular films have gained in importance, that they are developing their own art form and cinematography, and that they are not a cancerous derivative of modernity. On the contrary, I consider them as an extension of tradition into modernity through the continuation of traditional religion and interpretive visuality.

Popular video films are transforming the ever-changing cultural and religious landscape of West Africa, while they continue themselves to develop as part of an enchanted and modern universe. The transcendent character of film links the medium intricately to magic and religion, and its consumption can become an act of religious experience itself. Interest in the spiritual realm, which is an integral part of African cultures and traditions, remains important as part of modern Africa and hardly fades with conversion to Christianity. Conversion in contemporary Africa usually means a transformation of the perception of the world that results in a morally dualized cosmology. In accepting the Christian God, people "make a complete break with the past" (Meyer 1998) by opposing and diabolizing witchcraft, the divinities, and other spirits of traditional religion and, in a wider sense, local village life. Traditional religion is not suppressed but continues to exist within African Christian worldviews under the Devil's authority (see also Marshall-Fratani 2001; Merz 2008: 207–209). Christian life, on the other hand, is often associated with success, wealth, and, above all, modern urban life that is characterized by Western ideals.

The ideals of the successful modern Christian life, together with the machinations of the Devil, are represented in popular video films, thereby glamorizing them (Meyer 2004: 102). By relying on technology, the explicitly modern medium of film becomes itself an integral part of African Christianity, mainly in its Pentecostal and charismatic expressions, and in a wider sense of the urban public square, as Meyer (2006) has shown for Ghana. Ukah concludes for Nigeria that "the medium of video has become one of the preferred channels for the communication of religious truth, hope, ideas, and propaganda" (2003: 226). With this development, popular video films have probably become the most important cultural expression of the religious and spiritual experience of Africans who are inclined toward Pentecostal or charismatic Christianity.

Film helps to maintain an integrated worldview where modernity, Christianity, and traditional religion all have their distinct but nonetheless tightly linked spheres. Film as an exemplary expression of modernity acts as a mediator between the local or traditional and the global or modern (Ukah 2005). In the urban home the television set has taken the functional place of the ancestor or family shrine as a material and visual mediator of transcendence that facilitates the accessibility to the spiritual realm through dream and vision (cf. Lyons and Lyons 1987: 131–132; Gillespie 1995: 362; Marshall-Fratani 2001: 93). In front of the television set, people watch rituals of traditional and modern nature and interact with dreams and visions of the spiritual realm that popular video films supply. By doing so they engage in the entertainment ritual of film watching that functionally replaces traditional rituals of the village and keeps them theatrically alive and remembered in a modern, urban, and often distinctly Christian setting that itself is projected in film as an idealized and dramatized dream. In this way popular video films closely follow different aspects and functions of traditional religion and thereby ensure the continuity of religious experience between the older traditional religion and the newer modern Christianity.

Notes

1. The Bebelibe consist of an estimated 58,000 people, who speak a language they call Mbelime. Both the ethnic group and the language have also been referred to as Niendé or Nyende (Huber 1973; 1979). Between 1995 and 1997, I spent seven months among the Bebelibe doing anthropological research (Merz 1998). In 2002 I moved to their area as part of my work with SIL Togo-Benin, continuing my research on a part-time basis to the present day.

2. For typographical reasons, I use a simplified form of the standard orthography for words in Mbelime, the language of the Bebelibe.

3. Blier (1987) gives a wealth of examples of the importance of visuality among the Betammaribe, both of architectural features and culture more generally, which she interprets through different and multiple metaphors that do not always seem to be based on local realities. Her controversial approach (Sewane 2002: 183n1) reduces the value of her work for this chapter to a mere general affirmation of my premise of the importance of visuality in African culture.

4. This analogy between films and dreams has also been explored and discussed by Western film theorists using psychoanalytic approaches (Lyden 2003: 50–52).

5. In this chapter I treat dreams and visions in a generalized and linked way, knowing that there are differences in their conception and use in West Africa. While I found dreams to be the favored comparison for films among the Bebelibe, where visions play a less important role than dreams, it is likely that in other parts of Africa (such as in Ghana, see below) visions offer a better analogy for film. Although it is theoretically possible to compare films also with trance and possession, I have not found any indication in anthropological literature that this is happening. For the Bebelibe, both trance and possession are only marginal phenomena and usually linked with ceremonies that have come from outside the area, such as the ones celebrated at shrines of Tigare or Nkunde (Merz 1998: 25–37).

References

Appadurai, A. 1996. *Modernity at Large: Cultural Dimensions of Globalization.* Minneapolis: University of Minnesota Press.
Bakker, F. L. 2007. "Shanti Sandesham, a New Jesus Film Produced in India: Indian Christology in Pictures." *Exchange* 36(1): 41–64.
Barrot, P., ed. 2008. *Nollywood: The Video Phenomenon in Nigeria.* Oxford: James Currey.
Blier, S. P. 1987. *The Anatomy of Architecture: Ontology and Metaphor in Batammaliba Architectural Expression.* Chicago: University of Chicago Press.
———. 1991. "Diviners as Alienists and Annunciators among the Batammaliba of Togo." In *African Divination Systems: Ways of Knowing,* edited by P. M. Peek, 73–90. Bloomington: Indiana University Press.
Collins, J. 2004. "Ghanaian Christianity and Popular Entertainment." *History in Africa* 31: 407–423.
Deacy, C. R. 2000. "Redemption and Film: Cinema as a Contemporary Site of Religious Activity." *Media Development* 47(1): 50–54.
Finnegan, R. 1970. *Oral Literature in Africa.* Oxford: Clarendon.
Geschiere, P. 1997. *The Modernity of Witchcraft: Politics and the Occult in Postcolonial Africa.* Charlottesville: University Press of Virginia.
Gillespie, M. 1995. "Sacred Serials, Devotional Viewing, and Domestic Worship: A Case-Study in the Interpretation of Two TV Versions of *The Mahabharata* in a Hindu Family in West London." In *To Be Continued . . .: Soap Operas Around the World,* edited by R. C. Allen, 354–380. London: Routledge.
Goody, J. 1997. *Representations and Contradictions: Ambivalence Towards Images, Theatre, Fiction, Relics and Sexuality.* Oxford: Blackwell.
Gore, C. 1998. "Ritual, Performance and Media in Urban Contemporary Shrine Configurations in Benin City, Nigeria." In *Ritual, Performance, Media,* edited by F. Hughes-Freeland, 66–84. London: Routledge.
Hackett, R. I. J. 1998. "Charismatic/Pentecostal Appropriation of Media Technologies in Nigeria and Ghana." *Journal of Religion in Africa* 28(3): 258–277.
Harris, S. 1984. *Culture and Learning: Tradition and Education in North-east Arnhem Land.* Canberra: Australian Institute of Aboriginal Studies.
Haynes, J., ed. 2000. *Nigerian Video Films.* Athens: Ohio University Press.
———. 2010. "A Literature Review: Nigerian and Ghanaian videos." *Journal of African Cultural Studies* 22(1): 105–120.
Huber, H. 1973. "L'existence humaine en face du monde sacré: rites domestiques chez les Nyende du Dahomey." *Anthropos* 68: 377–441.
———. 1979. *Tod und Auferstehung: Organisation, rituelle Symbolik und Lehrprogramm einer westafrikanischen Initiationsfeier.* Freiburg: Universitätsverlag Freiburg Schweiz.
Hughes-Freeland, F. 1998. "Introduction." In *Ritual, Performance, Media,* edited by F. Hughes-Freeland, 1–28. London: Routledge.
Kreamer, C. M. 1995. "Transformation and Power in Moba (Northern Togo) Initiation Rites." *Africa* 65(1): 58–78.
Lakoff, G., and M. Johnson. 1999. *Philosophy in the Flesh: The Embodied Mind and its Challenge to Western Thought.* New York: Basic Books.
Larkin, B. 1997. "Indian Films and Nigerian Lovers: Media and the Creation of Parallel Modernities." *Africa* 67(3): 406–440.

———. 2008. *Signal and Noise: Media, Infrastructure, and Urban Culture in Nigeria.* Durham, NC: Duke University Press.

Lyden, J. C. 2003. *Film as Religion: Myths, Morals, Rituals.* New York: New York University Press.

Lyons, A. P., and H. D. Lyons. 1987. "Magical Medicine on Television: Benin City, Nigeria." *Journal of Ritual Studies* 1(2): 103–136.

Marsh, C. 2004. *Cinema and Sentiment: Film's Challenge to Theology.* Milton Keynes, UK: Paternoster Press.

Marshall-Fratani, R. 2001. "Mediating the Global and Local in Nigerian Pentecostalism." In *Between Babel and Pentecost: Transnational Pentecostalism in Africa and Latin America,* edited by A. Corten and R. Marshall-Fratani, 80–105. London: Hurst.

Mayrargue, C. 2005. "Dynamiques transnationales et mobilisations pentecôtistes dans l'espace public béninois." In *Entreprises religieuses transnationales en Afrique de l'Ouest,* edited by L. Fourchard, A. Mary, and R. Otayek, 243–265. Paris: Karthala; Ibadan: IFRA.

McCall, J. C. 2002. "Madness, Money, and Movies: Watching a Nigerian Popular Video with the Guidance of a Native Doctor." *Africa Today* 49(3): 79–94.

Merz, J. 1998. "I Seek Life: Witchcraft Beliefs and Moral Dualism in the Northern Atakora of Benin." MA thesis, Leiden University.

———. 2008. "'I Am a Witch in the Holy Spirit': Rupture and Continuity of Witchcraft Beliefs in African Christianity." *Missiology* 36(2): 201–218.

Meyer, B. 1998. "'Make a Complete Break with the Past': Memory and Post-Colonial Modernity in Ghanaian Pentecostalist Discourse." *Journal of Religion in Africa* 28(3): 316–349.

———. 2003a. "Ghanaian Popular Cinema and the Magic in and of Film." In *Magic and Modernity: Interfaces of Revelation and Concealment,* edited by B. Meyer and P. Pels, 200–222. Stanford, CA: Stanford University Press.

———. 2003b. "Visions of Blood, Sex and Money: Fantasy Spaces in Popular Ghanaian Cinema." *Visual Anthropology* 16(1): 15–41.

———. 2004. "'Praise the Lord'": Popular Cinema and Pentecostalite Style in Ghana's New Public Sphere." *American Ethnologist* 31(1): 92–110.

———. 2005a. "Mediating Tradition: Pentecostal Pastors, African Priests, and Chiefs in Ghanaian Popular Films." In *Christianity and Social Change in Africa. Essays in Honor of J.D.Y. Peel,* edited by T. Falola, 275–306. Durham, NC: Carolina Academic Press.

———. 2005b. "Religious Remediations: Pentecostal Views in Ghanaian Video-Movies." *Postscripts* 1(2–3): 155–181.

———. 2006. "Impossible Representations: Pentecostalism, Vision, and Video Technology in Ghana." In *Religion, Media, and the Public Sphere,* edited by B. Meyer and A. Moors, 290–312. Bloomington: Indiana University Press.

Moore, R. O. 2000. *Savage Theory: Cinema as Modern Magic.* Durham, NC: Duke University Press.

Ogundele, W. 2000. "From Folk Opera to Soap Opera: Improvisations and Transformations in Yoruba Popular Theater." In *Nigerian Video Films,* edited by J. Haynes, 89–130. Athens: Ohio University Press.

Sewane, D. 2002. *La nuit des grands morts: L'initiée et l'épouse chez les Tamberma du Togo.* Paris: Economica.

———. 2003. *Le souffle du mort: Les Batãmmariba (Togo, Bénin).* Paris: Plon.

Stoller, P. 1995. *Embodying Colonial Memories: Spirit Possession, Power, and the Hauka in West Africa.* New York: Routledge.

Ukadike, N. F. 2000. "Images of the 'Real' Thing: African Video-Films and the Emergence of a New Cultural Art." *Social Identities* 6(3): 243–261.

Ukah, A. 2003. "Advertising God: Nigerian Christian Video-Films and the Power of Consumer Culture." *Journal of Religion in Africa* 33(2): 203–231.

———. 2005. "The Local and the Global in the Media and Material Culture of Nigerian Pentecostalism." In *Entreprises religieuses transnationales en Afrique de l'Ouest,* edited by L. Fourchard, A. Mary, and R. Otayek, 285–313. Paris: Karthala; Ibadan: IFRA.

Walsh, R. 2003. *Reading the Gospels in the Dark: Portrayals of Jesus in Film.* Harrisburg, PA: Trinity Press International.

Wenner, D. 2002. "Popular Cinema in India." In *Bollywood: The Indian Cinema and Switzerland, English Version,* edited by A. Schneider, 7–10. Zurich: Museum für Gestaltung.

6 The Heart of Man

Pentecostal Emotive Style in and beyond Kinshasa's Media World

Katrien Pype

In their introduction to their groundbreaking book on the intertwinement of religion and new information technologies, Hent de Vries and Samuel Weber (2001) point out that public spheres in many contemporary societies have been invaded by religion. In this colonization of the public, religious authorities and proselytizers use the new information technologies like the internet, print media, radio, and television. The authors argue that "the [electronic mass] medium is not secondary; nor is the religious mere epiphenomenon" (19), hypothesizing "an intrinsic and structural relationship between the new media and the renewed manifestation of religion" (10).

Of the diverse religions on offer on the African continent, Pentecostal movements are the most significant media players (Hackett 1998; Meyer 2004a). Observing the increasing participation of these Pentecostal[1] churches in African media worlds, we are faced with the question of how this type of Christianity thrives so well on television. In this chapter, of which the ethnographic context is post-Mobutu Kinshasa in the Democratic Republic of Congo (formerly Zaire) or DRC, I will analyze how Pentecostalism connects with one TV genre: the fictional melodrama. I first focus on the symbolic structure shared by Pentecostalism and the melodrama and then on the role of emotions both in the evangelizing project as well as in Kinshasa's TV fiction.

The Heart of Man (*Le coeur de l'homme*) is the title of one of Kinshasa's longest-running television serials, produced by the drama group headed by Muyombe Gauche. This theater company is not known for its explicit evangelizing TV serials (Pype 2009c), though most of its serials also comply with a general Christian key scenario that glorifies the power of the pastor; locates evil within households; and thrives upon visualizations of the occult (especially through special effects). In 2003 and 2004, Kinois (inhabitants of Kinshasa) spectators could follow more than 30 episodes about how John, a young man born and raised in the province of the Lower-Congo, arrives in Kinshasa in search of Kindingu, a girl from his village. It was John's deceased father's wish that he marry one of the daughters of a woman named Afia, and Kindingu is one of them. The serial touches on themes like the selection of marriage partners, jealousy concerning others' luck in finding wealthy husbands, and the use of witchcraft to break up existing alliances. The serial's title is also a reference to a very popular proverb in Kinshasa: *One can never know what goes on in the heart of another person (toyebi motema na bato te)*. The proverb is commonly used as a warning or a reminder about the disconnect between one's image, public presentation, and words on the one hand and one's feelings, desires, and actions on the other hand. In Muyombe Gauche's serial, it is shown how jealousy incites Mimi (Afia's sister) and her daughter Kati, who wants to marry John, to use witchcraft and "traditional" healers to inflict harm on their opponents, Souza and Kindingu, Afia's two daughters. The occult actions are performed in secret, often during the night. Nobody can imagine that the two city women, whose lifestyle emanates class, prestige, and ease, could be jealous of Kindingu, their classificatory daughter and sister. The serial ends when, as a result of the occult law that states that prayer sends curses and witchcraft back to its sender, Mimi becomes blind. In order to heal, Mimi visits a pastor, who urges her to confess how she envied Kindingu's future with John and how these feelings pushed her to enter in exchanges with bad spirits. After Mimi has asked for forgiveness, demons are chased out of her body, and John and Kindingu get married. The serial thus shows an association between jealousy and evil spirits, and it portrays confession and remorse as powerful tools to purify the evildoer and to bring harmony back within the family. In this chapter, I focus on the rendition of emotions, so crucial in *The Heart of Man,* and in all other Kinois TV fiction produced since the turn of the millennium.

My decision to examine the representation and meaning of affects and feelings[2] in evangelizing teleserials and in the overall Pentecostal context derives from the central place emotions attain in the mass-mediated melodramas as well as in Pentecostal instructive religious genres like sermons and predications. Pentecostal gatherings are very much characterized by highly emotional events triggered through dance, songs, and trance. One explanation for the importance of the emotional events in these church movements derives from the emphasis Pentecostals put on the experience of the religious. Karla O. Poewe argues that "the Pentecostal fashions his [*sic*] God directly from his feelings" (1994: 192). Furthermore, evangelization is a total project, in the sense that not only are theological notions transmitted to the (converted) audiences, but emotional states and experiences likewise receive considerable attention in religious instructions. It could well be argued that the focus on personal experiences has more sweeping effects than text-centered biblical teaching. This chapter is part of a larger project on the role of TV fiction in the production of the Pentecostal-Charismatic lifeworld in Kinshasa. In Pype (2012: 130–167), I explore the Pentecostal media pedagogics concerning the reception of music video clips, American wrestling

shows, Hollywood and Nollywood films, and locally produced TV serials. Pentecostal Christians attribute meaning to media products concerning the emotions that the spectator experiences when contemplating the footage. This haptic
visuality—that is, the engagement with the bodily ways of watching television—
explains why, according to many Kinois, Pentecostals, and non-Pentecostals,
spectators suddenly can become bewitched or be healed when watching a television program. Feeling calm, excited, or afraid when watching television is, according to the Pentecostals, a sign of how to locate the fundamental meaning of
a media text within the spiritual warfare between the Holy Spirit and the Devil
that is the pillar of Pentecostal beliefs (Pype 2012: 155).

It is striking that when scrutinizing the body of academic literature that has
emerged in the wake of the popularity of Pentecostal Christianity in sub-Saharan
Africa (Gifford 1998; Corten and Marshall-Fratani 2001; Meyer 2004b), the ways
in which religion structures and expresses emotions are often ignored.[3] Notable
exceptions are the works of Thomas Csordas (1994) and Karla Poewe (1994), who
approached the role of emotions in religious experiences and in healing. My
main focus, however, is on the representation of feelings and affects in proselytizing moments. The key question is "How are emotions and bodily sensations
described and interpreted by Kinshasa's evangelizing Pentecostals?"

This chapter connects in the first instance with thriving research on the
public role of Pentecostalism in Africa (Meyer 2004b). As Birgit Meyer convincingly argues, Pentecostalism blurs the boundaries between religion and entertainment, through which a new representational economy has come into being.
Pentecostalism's capacity to absorb and recast popular culture, its skillful use
of visual technology, its narrative in which God is opposed to the Devil, and its
focus on modern life are what Meyer identifies as the key elements of a "pentecostalite style" (2004b: 101). Meyer's use of "style" combines media aesthetics, mode
of thinking, and individual behavior, and thus captures both the relevance of
Pentecostalism in public debates and the Protestant emphasis on the individual.
My ethnography of the individual and personal feelings and emotions in Pentecostal spheres, mass-mediated or not, adds to this analysis of Pentecostal public
discourses about the private and the personal. It thus contributes to the analysis
of the significance of Pentecostal Christianity in public spheres and more private
lifeworlds.

My theoretical focus is in particular influenced by recent theories on the
social construction of emotions. William M. Reddy (1997), a social historian, criticized the writings of feminist-inspired ethnographers such as Lila Abu-Lughod
(1986), Catherine Lutz (1988), and Benedicte Grima (1992). In response to Grima's
statement "Emotion is culture," Reddy disapproves of feminist critiques of essen-
tialism and also of research inspired by Michel Foucault's discourse theories and
Pierre Bourdieu's concept of practice. In his view, "for these ethnographers, there

is no limit to the extent to which personal feelings are socially, locally, culturally constructed" (1997: 329). While Reddy obviously values the premise that interpretations of feelings are culture-dependent, he directs the attention to the way feelings are organized and orchestrated and calls on us to point out the political and social changes that underpin diachronic (dis-)continuities in the attribution of meaning to affect and feeling (1997: 330).

We can question whether such a historical perspective really abandons the constructionist approach. In my view, Reddy's historical interest can be easily wedded to the viewpoint of feminist researchers (Rosaldo 1982; Lutz 1986; Scheper-Hughes and Lock 1987) who assume that human emotion and feeling are never free of cultural shaping and cultural meaning (Scheper-Hughes and Lock 1987: 28). Abu-Lughod, for example, mentions in several of her studies the social and political forces that construct "culture" and thus also forge the apt emotional style and registers of sentiment at play in a given society. Furthermore, not all constructionists claim that without culture people would not know how to feel. Whereas bodily sensations like anger, love, disappointment, and so on are probably universal, the values ascribed to them and the particular social meanings they carry are, as most (feminist) constructionists underscore, inherently intertwined with the major social and political vectors at work in a society and the kinds of "culture" produced therein.

Reddy's major contribution to the study of emotions lies especially in his call for a coherent, politically meaningful historical ethnography of emotions. He invites researchers to scrutinize the political and historical dimensions of emotional regimes, the biographies of emotional styles, and the dynamics in a society's emotional registers.

I should stress that, while a wide variety of emotive styles prevails in post-Mobutu Kinshasa, this chapter is limited to the meanings attributed to affects and feelings within a Pentecostal context. The emotional regime as spread by Pentecostal churches is part of the larger distinct cultural style of these churches that competes with the images of apt personality, feelings, and body language as expressed in, among others, rumba music, school institutions, and, significantly, other Christian tendencies such as Roman Catholic and Kimbanguist Christianity.

Combining semiotics and an analysis of power structures, I reveal some of the strategies in the propagation of Pentecostal Christianity. In particular, I examine the linguistic and visual (re-)presentation of emotional behavior both in sermons and in evangelizing television serials (*maboke, théâtre populaire,* or *télédramatiques*). In line with Meyer (2004), I argue that mass-mediated melodramas occupy a central role in the spread of Pentecostal principles in post-Mobutu Kinshasa. At the same time, I focus on the continuities and ruptures between the Pentecostal emotive style and more locally rooted matrices of public and private self-presentation. In this way I contribute to a better understanding of Pentecostalism in urban Africa. My emphasis on religious media aesthetics also offers a new entry into the study of the intertwinement of media and religion more generally (cf. de Vries and Weber 2001; Meyer and Moors 2006).

The first part of the chapter sketches the emergence of charismatic Christianity in Kinshasa's media world and depicts the transformations of local television drama. In the second part, I examine the fictive representation of emotions as expressions of Pentecostal beliefs. The data for this research were gathered during extensive fieldwork with one of Kinshasa's most popular evangelizing drama groups, Cinarc (Pype 2012). This theater company originated in 1998 after a dream the troupe's leader experienced in which the Christian God asked him to work for Him. Three years later, Cinarc produced its first teleserial and since then has been a fixture in Kinshasa's media world. The drama group consists of about 30 actors, yet the number is not fixed, since old actors leave and new actors arrive. Membership in the group requires first and foremost baptism according to Pentecostal principles. If a novice has not yet been baptized, then several members of the drama group provide spiritual instruction. It is only after baptism that the novice can start the artistic formation and appear in the teleserials.

Cinarc's telenarratives are broadcast on channels that are privately owned by journalists and politicians. In 2005, two Cinarc actors received an award for best female actor as *kizengi* ("fool," a stock character in Kinshasa's serials). The winners of these honors were selected by Kinshasa's dramatic artists working for television. In 2006 and 2007, this group also received the annual "Child of the Country" Award (Mwana Mboka[4] Trophy) for best television theater company. This prize was awarded by audience vote through text messages and emails. These prizes indicate that the group is a significant player in Kinshasa's media world.

For 17 months, I interviewed the actors and participated in their rehearsals and filming.[5] Much time was also spent in the religious gatherings organized by the Church of the Holy Mountain (Eglise de Montagne Sainte), the Pentecostal church to which the drama group was affiliated during most of the fieldwork. Just like all of Kinshasa's television acting groups, Cinarc is firmly embedded in a church, and actors are expected to attend sermons and special prayer events. Furthermore, the drama group also organizes its own weekly prayer sessions, to which fans are invited. Most of Kinshasa's drama groups are counseled by several spiritual advisors, who are all mentioned in the episodes' acknowledgments. Their names are listed after "Jésus de Nazareth" and are complemented by the name and address of the church to which the troupe is affiliated and the name and phone numbers of the leaders of the troupe and the church.

Media and Religion

A census taken in 2005 found that the platform of Congolese charismatic churches (called Eglises de Réveil du Congo—ERC) had 12,000 member churches in Kinshasa.[6] Though one might question the accuracy of this number,[7] the tremendous dominance of this type of church in Kinshasa is a fact. Everywhere one sees walls of compounds with names of small revival churches, advertisements of their weekly programs, and huge billboards announcing upcoming religious gatherings. You can hear people praying when you walk down the small streets of the townships, and if you switch on the TV or tune into a radio channel, you will find sermons, Christian songs, confessions and discussions of spiritual matters, and programs about the social and political roles of Jesus Christ.

As elsewhere in sub-Saharan Africa (cf. Launay 1997; Hackett 1994, 1998; de Witte 2003; Meyer 2004b), audiovisual media are important means for Kinshasa's charismatic leaders to attract followers and to spread their messages. It could even be argued that broadcasts have contributed significantly to the increasing popularity of these types of churches.

Although Pentecostalism is said to have entered Kinshasa in 1967, it is only since the early 1990s that this type of Christianity has found firm ground.[8] The church leaders benefited from a change in Congo's media politics that occurred at that moment. During Mobutu's regime, the president only allowed two television channels, which were used as his own propaganda tool. When his power eroded, Mobutu's controlling grip over local mass media weakened, too. Around the 1990s, he allowed two private channels to broadcast in Kinshasa. Six years later, a law of freedom of the press (1996) opened up the space of the audiovisual media in radical ways. This political decision explains the incredible increase in indigenous Congolese media in recent years.[9] Alternative patterns of patronage and investment in the media space became possible, and setting up a television station became much easier.[10] Wealthy families, politicians, and Christian leaders all created their own TV and radio stations.

Kinshasa's TV stations in the post-Mobutu period can be categorized as "national" (owned by the government) and "private" channels. The latter group makes up the majority of Kinshasa's media world. A further classification of the "private" stations is possible on the grounds of the goals of the channel owners: some are owned by political leaders, who use the media as a tool for propaganda. Several channels have a commercial profile, while others are explicitly linked to a prophet or a church group for whom the medium is an excellent instrument to dialogue with their religious communities and to attract new members. The confessional channels continue to grow because many leaders of the Pentecostal-Charismatic churches attempt to create their own television station, where they can send out taped images of their religious activities. Nowadays, the Kimbanguist Church owns two TV stations, while the Protestant Church and the Roman Catholic Church each broadcast on one television channel. By contrast, ten television channels were in the hands of charismatic leaders.

Apart from shows on Congolese music and their stars, local television serials and shows with guests from these programs are very popular (Pype 2009b). All local television channels have several theater companies working for them. Each of these drama groups produces one episode each week of a serial. Independent of the profile of the channel on which the serials are broadcast (national, commercial, or confessional), all of the serials are framed within a Pentecostal ideology. Some theater companies have an explicit evangelizing profile, like the Cinarc troupe with which I worked, and The Evangelists (on RAGATV), The Trumpet (Tropicana TV), and The Levites.[11] The other drama groups, the so-called secular drama groups (*troupes ya mokili,* "troupes of the world"), also display a trend toward Christianization.

The Melodramatic Mode

The proliferation of Pentecostal churches in the city during the 1990s changed the design of the locally produced teleserials drastically. Before the early 1990s, local televised drama supported Mobutu's nationalist politics, but today, Kinshasa's television serials are inscribed in an apocalyptic experience of the postcolonial reality, as some of the titles suggest: the group Pléiade des Stars produced *Le quartier maudit (The Cursed Neighborhood), Le tombeau ouvert (The Open Tomb), Le cartel de l'obscurité (The Alliance of Darkness),* and *Kinshasa ou sodomie 18 (Kinshasa or Sodom(y) 18).* Groupe Simba produced *Tout se paie ici en bas (Retribution Here and Now),* and Afrik'art produced *La séringue magique (The Magic Needle).* Completely in line with the teachings in churches and broadcasts on radio and television, Kinois are reminded that the Devil is always around and that the social, economic, and political crises are signs of the end of the world. As a result, the morality represented in the TV serials became more and more a religious matter than a result of social movements. And invisible forces were increasingly present on the screen. The Salongo serials—produced on Mobutu's channels—already used special effects to visualize witchcraft, but since the second half of the 1990s, this has become part and parcel of almost every serial (Pype 2006, 2009a, 2012).[12]

Since most of Kinshasa's television dramas follow the same plotlines and display the same fictional characters, I am inclined to group them under one generic rubric: *the Pentecostal melodrama.* I agree with Karin Barber (1987, 1997), who states that the field of cultural creativity on the African continent is difficult to categorize. All of Kinshasa's theater companies producing serials respond (some more than others) to an ideal type of "good serial." They all use the same stock figures, the same plot, and, most importantly, the same closure that spreads a Christian message (Pype 2010). Therefore, the serials produced after the turn of the millennium can best be called "Christian serials." I prefer to define them as "Pentecostal melodramas," for the Pentecostal-Charismatic influence and the symbolical structure of the melodrama are significant.[13]

The concept of the "melodrama" has been elaborated by Peter Brooks, who studied novels and theater plays written by European male and female writers in the nineteenth century.[14] "Melodrama" is, however, not confined to literature or drama; the concept refers to a particular imagination that is translated in narratives. Melodrama, then, is a symbolic structure (cf. Abu-Lughod 2002: 116) that can be manifested in numerous generic formations, like on theater podia, on television screens, in books, at oral counting events, and so on. Characteristics of this symbolic structure are, first, that a story is told over several short episodes (Abu-Lughod 2002). Second, the narrative shows a Manichean universe where good and evil are in a constant battle. This combat often takes place in the invisible realms of reality. Third, the main characters in this fight are not mythic creatures or the heroes of folkloric epic tales but common citizens who have many similarities to the intended audience. Fourth, there is a strong moral justice underlying the plot and the closure of the story. The end of the narrative is therefore always the most important event in the whole script, since it accentuates the ideology. Last, emotions are important both in the story and in the reception of the serials.

As Brooks notes, the melodramatic imagination relates to specific historical contexts, "where the traditional imperatives of truth and ethics have been violently thrown into question" (1976: 15). This is exactly the case in post-Mobutu Kinshasa, where a political, social, and economic crisis is understood as a sign of the Apocalypse, which is prepared in the occult realms of reality (De Boeck 2005). The political impasse, social conflicts within the private circle, illness, and poverty are explained as the outcomes of occult dealings, in particular with witches and demons. Such is the main narrative professed by the Pentecostal churches, which is easily translated into the symbolic structure of the melodrama (cf. Meyer 2004b). The main characteristic of the apocalyptic worldview is a thorough polarization between good and evil and a belief that the demonic evil is the outcome of the Devil's reign. In Pentecostal discourse, the good-bad opposition is played out by Christians and their adversaries, human accomplices of the Devil. The following excerpt from Brooks's (1976) book shows how close Brooks's definition is to the apocalyptic experience:

> We find there an intense emotional and ethical drama based on the man-ichaeistic struggle of good and evil, a world where what one lives for and by is seen in terms of, and as determined by, the most fundamental psychic

relations and cosmic ethical forces. The polarization of good and evil works toward revealing their presence and operation as real forces in the world. Their conflict suggests the need to recognize and confront evil, to combat and expel it, to purge the social order. Man is seen to be, and must recognize himself to be, playing on a theater that is the point of juncture, and of clash, of imperatives beyond himself that are non-mediated and irreducible. This is what is most real in the universe. The spectacular enactments of melodrama seek constantly to express these forces and imperatives, to bring them to striking revelation, to impose their evidence. (12–13)

According to Brooks, the representation of a clash between the Good and the Bad stems from a desire to understand the Real, which itself is hidden and masked. He condenses "the main *raison d'être* of the melodramatic mode as to localize and to articulate the moral occult" (1976: 5).

In line with the teachings in Kinshasa's charismatic churches, the Pentecostal melodramas point out that the occult is nested in the urban interpersonal sphere. Matrimonial conflicts, adultery, the search for a good spouse, rivalry between church members or even between Christian leaders, loss of a job, and unruly offspring are some of the main themes of the TV serials that reflect the hardship of social and economic survival in an urban African precarious society. The fictional characters of Kinshasa's teleserials are rooted in this urban universe: teenagers; Christian pastors; relatives who arrive from the village; colleagues at work; fellow members of the Christian congregation; and diviners, magicians, and "traditional" healers all dwell in these fictional worlds (Pype 2010). Yet, as the unfolding plots uncover, the "real" identities of these fictional characters stem from their connections with the divine or the demonic.

Wicked Emotions

A crucial feature of the melodrama is its emphasis on emotions.[15] I illustrate this point with some scenes from one evangelizing TV drama, the serial *The Maquis Boys and Girls*,[16] though all of Kinshasa's teleserials contain similar scenes and convey the same message. This telenarrative depicts the whereabouts of pupils who have withdrawn to prepare for the state exam. As a "real Christian" girl, the serial's heroine, Charlainne, does not feel at ease in the secluded girls' group that seems to be dominated by "pagans." She prefers to devote herself to study and attempts to keep a peaceful atmosphere within the group. This is, however, rather difficult, since jealousy between two other girls, who have a lesbian relationship, often leads to heated discussions and sometimes even physical assaults. Another girl is envied by some of the other girls, who suspect her of having a sexual relationship with their teacher. Each time these quarrels and fights break out, Charlainne interferes and reminds the girls that their behavior is not "Christian." The message is that Christians do not fight, neither verbally nor physically. She warns the girls that these fights could invite the Devil to settle within the girls' group. Furthermore, if the girls wish to succeed in their final examination, they should focus on Jesus. On all these occasions, Charlainne displays the ideal Christian attitude: she prays, reads the Bible, and instructs other girls on Christian values. When she visits her poor mother, however, Charlainne expresses fear and anxiety. She says to her mother that the school inspector has asked each pupil to pay him $100. Those who pay will be given passing grades. Her mother tells her that the tuition fee was already beyond their means and that she will not ask others for money that will contribute to corruption. "Christians do not corrupt," she states. Charlainne fears she will not obtain her diploma. In true *deus ex machina* form, Pastor Chapy calls on the despairing Charlainne and brings her relief. He reminds her of Psalm 25:3[17] by way of encouraging her to keep the faith and recalls that when he was a pupil, God had somehow made it possible for him to pass the final exam without having to pay a bribe. He also urges her to stop crying, stating that "Christians do not cry." If she read the Bible again, she would receive solace and know that God will help her.

Such an emphasis on the emotional life of fictional characters is often accompanied by an explicit interpretation of the value of certain emotions, in particular anxiety (*bobangi*), jealousy (*nzuwa*), hatred (*likundu*), and anger (*nkanda*). The audience is taught an apocalyptic understanding of "good" and "bad" feelings. In this respect, Christian leaders and artists give meaning to feelings and the social outcome of emotions.

Jealousy in particular is represented in the Pentecostal melodramas as "un-Christian." Envy among multiple wives, within the extended family, between friends, in the neighborhood, or within the church community is the dominant emotion underlying the serials' plots.[18] During the weeks in which the serial *The Moziki Women* was broadcast, on the streets, in stores, in church, and on television, the actresses would hear people shouting the following phrase, which was often mentioned in the fictional narrative: "Women of the Moziki group, [is there] jealousy? No jealousy!" ("*Bamaman Moziki, nzuwa? Nzuwa nde te!*"). The serial speaks about a group of women participating in an urban women's association (*moziki*) and offers a Christian reading of these women's groups. Within the fictional world conjured up by the serial, the shouts remind the women members that they should not be jealous of their colleagues' jewelry, perfume, or clothes. In sum, one should not envy what others have. In the story, however, these women do become jealous. This emotion pushes some moziki women to engage in adulterous relationships with men who can provide them with more luxurious items than their husbands can. One of these women has an affair with the husband of a co-moziki woman. Where joy and ambience governed the initial moziki meetings, envy and anger alter the convivial atmosphere and lead to quarrels and fights. In the end, one woman poisons her rival, and one of the adulterous men kills two women and his rival before committing suicide. Death is shown as the most dramatic, but also the most natural, outcome of jealousy.

Christians and their leaders explain why jealousy has demonic origins in the following way: As an angel of light, the Devil was once very close to God but then wanted to become almighty just like God. His jealousy created the occult world, and jealousy continues to sow evil and wickedness. Jealousy should be suppressed, because it leads to anger (*nkanda*) and hatred (*likunya*),[19] which in turn produce violence (*mbeba*). All these emotions are perceived as demonic agencies and are called "the spirit of jealousy" (*molimo ya zuwa*), "the spirit of anger" (*molimo ya nkanda*), and the "spirit of hatred" (*molimo ya likunya*).

In one scene from the serial *The Open Tomb*, Makubakuba and Kuaku are fighting. Kuaku, Theresia's husband, has just arrived in Kinshasa and is looking for his children. At home in Mbuji-Mayi, he had learned that his wife was living with another man in Kinshasa. Kuaku locates his wife and tries to bring his children back home. The spectators see how Kuaku physically forces his sisters-in-law to tell him where his spouse is: he shouts, beats his children with his cane, and even threatens to put a curse on those who will not assist him. Alarmed by the row, Makubakuba arrives on the scene of the struggle and, recognizing his rival, begins to fight with him as well. The scene shows two older men fighting each other at length.

One of the Cinarc actresses commented on the dramatic behavior of these men:

> Here in Kinshasa, we do not give much social value to people who fight. Fighting is not good. One should control oneself and keep peace within. But people with *mubulu* (chaos) do just the reverse. In fact, both men here act in this way because Theresia has bewitched them. If they were not bewitched, they would not be fighting like this.

This explanation of the two fighting men (Kuaku and Makubakuba in *The Open Tomb*) as "bewitched" invites us to understand the correlation between emotions and witchcraft. The heart (*motema*), the location of the soul, plays an important part in this. It is said that good and evil reside within the heart. The essence of man's morality can be manifested through looks and physical signs. If someone hurts others, is selfish, or posits himself outside of social life and believes himself to be above the social order, it is said that person "has a bad heart" (*aza na motema mabe*). Someone "has a good heart" (*aza na motema malamu*) if she displays appropriate social behavior. The following overview of character idioms displays the central notion of the heart (*motema*) when referring to emotions:

Motema mabe: "a bad heart," bad character, jealous
Motema mokuse: "a short heart," without patience
Motema makasi: "a hard heart," audacious; heartless

Motema likolo: "a high heart," worrisome, anxious
Motema mwindo: "a black heart," depressed
Motema motau: weak character
Motema ndoki: "the heart of a witch," a vengeful person
Motema molai: "a long heart," patient
Motema mpiko: "a persevering heart," courageous and perseverant
Na mitema mibale: "having two hearts," hypocritical
Motema: character and conscience
Kokata motema: "to cut the heart," to die
Kolongola motema: "to remove from the heart," to forget
Kokitisa motema: "to let the heart go down," to calm oneself
Kotuna motema: "asking one's heart," to examine one's conscience
Kokanga motema: "closing the heart," to contain one's emotions

Morality and emotion are interrelated and reflect a condition of the heart. Jealousy stems from "a bad heart," while a witch has "*motema [ya] ndoki*," "the heart of a witch." The interpretations given to emotions and affects are inspired by the writings of Paul to the Galatians in the Bible.

The explanations are not only articulated through religious instruction in the church context, but they are also transmitted by other modern educational institutions. The scheme presented below was copied from a notebook of a young girl who attended a Catholic school in Kinshasa. The notebook dealt with "personal hygiene" and recorded instructions on brushing teeth, combating bacteria, the need to drink boiled water, and so on. The girl had copied this scheme from the blackboard, where the teacher had drawn two grids. The left part sets out the Christian emotions and states, while counterparts on the right side identify negative feelings and actions.

A Christian knows	*A Christian should conquer*
Love (*bolingo*)	Hatred (*motema likundu, likundu:* pancreas)
Joy (*esengo*)	Sadness (*mawa*)
Peace (*kimia*)	Conflict, struggle (*bitumba*)
Patience (*motema monene, motema mulai motema pio*)	Being quick-tempered (*motema moto moto*, a "hot" heart)
Goodness (*bolamu*)	Badness (*motema mabe*)
Benevolence (*kolimbisa*, to forgive)	Anger (*nkanda*)
Faithfulness (*elaka*, "promise")	Unfaithfulness (*kobuka elaka*)
Concord (*boboto*)	Sternness (*motema makasi*, a "hard" heart)

Yet, in Pentecostal discourse, negative emotions are personified in evil spirits, disturb social harmony or *kimia*, and thus constitute the antisocial person. This notion of the spiritual interference in the experience of emotions is not a "new" interpretation but relates to beliefs with a longer history in the area. As René Devisch notes for the baYaka, sudden amorality is seen as the effect of sorcery or possession by a malicious spirit (1993, 141). This perception can probably be generalized for most ethnic groups in the Democratic Republic of Congo. In the Christianized urban setting of Kinshasa, however, this outlook is perpetuated, although in a modified form, along apocalyptic lines: asocial and immoral behavior stems from demonic witchcraft, which "turns the heart black" (*eyinda motema*). It is argued that only the Holy Spirit can chase away the impure spirits that caused the heart to become black. In the instant one comes to know Jesus Christ, the heart is changed (*azolongola motema mabe*, he chases a bad heart). As such, it is explained that an evil person does not necessarily remain so.

Self-Containment

Kinshasa's Christians state that emotions like anger, jealousy, and hatred are in fact very human sensations, inherent in the "earthly" experience. A Christian is expected to transcend the terrestrial and try to connect with the divine. Only a person whose body is regularly inhabited by the Holy Spirit has enough energy to fight against these bad influences. Yet, Christians themselves regularly succumb and need to be "cured," meaning delivered, from these possessions. The spiritual leaders warn believers to allow the Holy Spirit to "keep the door closed" so that the evil spirits cannot enter.

"When you walk with God, you know to control your body," it is argued. Mastery over one's emotions is thus also part of a particular bodily discipline. This quality of self-control is often translated as *maîtrise de soi*. It is assumed that a child of God always preserves an attitude of calmness within herself (*abatela kimia na ye*). *Kimia* signifies peace, calmness, balance, harmony, silence, and serenity, all states implying that self-control concerns bodily behavior, emotions, and thoughts. The Lingala term *komikitisa*, which can be translated as "humiliating oneself, calming oneself, bringing oneself down," is also frequently used when explaining how to preserve this calmness. These meanings denote that certain personal states of mind, emotions, and feelings should be overcome by minimizing or even suppressing them. Another verb more exclusively employed to denote the emotional side of this self-mastery is, for example, *kokanga motema*. This literally means "to lock the heart," and it could best be translated as "to bear, to endure." It is an exhortation "not to react but to keep everything inside." *Komidiscipliner* is another example. This verb is a Lingala pidgin expression based on the French word for "discipline," and it relates this ideal of self-control to modern practices of constituting the subject. This neologism reminds us of Foucault's (1975) discussion of the construction of the subject through disciplining means controlled by the state. The concept "*komidiscipliner*" might stem from the historical project of constructing "colonial subjects," which points out, from a different perspective, that the "Christian subject" is a modern notion.

It is furthermore said that a "real Christian" "knows" (*koyeba*) and shows the following feelings: fear of God (*bobangi ya Nzambe*), remorse (*bomimi*), tranquility (*kimia*), and humility (*bokonde*) before God. These affective dispositions encourage proper moral conduct. The use of "know," as in "a Christian knows humility," implies that emotional states are considered to be the outcome of a particular consciousness (*mayele*) or spiritual knowledge (*bwanya*); these faculties are also located in the heart. Cinarc's pastor once described this quality in the course of an Easter sermon (2005): "What is spiritual wisdom? If you are in front of someone who exaggerates his feelings, stop talking. At that moment you should say: 'You will have no power over me. God above me is watching me.'" One reason to maintain a calm attitude, he explained, is that one might, in a state of emotional distraction, do things that one will not be able to remember later on. Moreover, in the mastery of his emotions, a man shows himself to be strong. "Those who are calm are very strong people. They know how to endure." It is assumed that a Christian possesses a faculty that inspires and aids him to maintain an internal balance through his spiritual affiliation with the Holy Spirit. This stability is necessary to refrain from yelling, reacting to provocation, or slapping someone. In difficult moments, a Christian should maintain a soft voice and ask his opponent for an explanation of his aggressive behavior. In this respect, it is important to draw attention to the concept of "strong men" (*moto makasi*). To repeat the pastor's words: "Those who are calm are very strong people." The notion of "strong men" translates a culturally defined idea of masculinity (Pype 2007). Pentecostal leaders claim to embody the concept of "strong men" and link it to a new behavioral pattern. Instead of adhering to older notions of "strong men," as embodied by today's young wrestlers and sportsmen, these new Christian leaders emphasize that those who fight and conquer earthly desires and feelings are the genuine "strong men." To that extent, the pastor is depicted in the serials as the person who can control himself best.

The Christian management of emotions also influences the discourse of dramatic artists embodying so-called un-Christian emotions (cf. Pype 2009b). The Cinarc actress Mamy Moke, who plays Charlainne, became more and more specialized in weeping. She usually played the role of the victim of evildoers and thus gained much sympathy from audiences. The actress often argued that nobody could express sadness and sorrow better than she did, and she was very proud of this ability. Mamy Moke received the award for best actress in two consecutive years. In her opinion, she deserves this prize, because "no one can cry like she can." Encouraged by the public recognition, the actress forced the troupe's leader to film more close-ups of a crying and despairing Charlainne.[20]

Mamy Moke's explanation of how she acquired this skill reveals much about the Christians' management of emotions. In recent years, this young actress has lost her four older sisters—due to witchcraft, it was said. Her paternal uncle in the village confessed to sorcery practices. Mamy Moke told me that her father's brother (living in a village in Bandundu province) was jealous of his brother's beautiful daughters and had threatened to kill all of them. This was how she explained the deaths of her elder sisters in their early thirties. As the only remaining daughter, Mamy Moke was afraid that her turn would soon come. Consequently, she said, she cried a lot. Things changed for her when she received Jesus. As soon as she really began to pray, her depression and despair disappeared, and she stopped crying. Mamy Moke tried to convince me that as a "real" Christian, she only cries when performing a role because, with her faith and the comfort that Jesus has given her, she has "no reason to cry anymore."

When speaking about her weeping alter ego, however, Mamy Moke emphasized that her characters only cried insofar as they had lost faith in God. She pointed to the evolution of Charlainne's character over several episodes of the *Mayimona* serial that was running at the time of our conversation. In this serial, Charlainne, a married woman, is suddenly confronted with the situation of another of her husband's wives in her house. She cannot accept this state of affairs and seeks the advice of the godparents of her Christian marriage. Despite their consoling words and their admonition to keep praying, Charlainne loses faith in God. Her tears are signs that she is spiritually weakened. The narrative closes with Charlainne's death.

The representation of the emotional subject in the Pentecostal melodrama is thus ambiguous. On the one hand, characters with a vivid and, at times, turbulent inner life are given lengthy and heart-wrenching scenes, like that of a weeping Charlainne. On the other hand, Pentecostal melodramas subscribe to the ideology of the revival churches and teach that a Christian should control his or her emotions.

Kinshasa's Christian leaders, however, do not stand alone in their discouragement of any direct expression of sentiments and emotions in everyday social life. The meanings and values ascribed to emotions and feelings within the Pentecostal ideology perpetuate more local social matrices that also load bodily experiences with significance. The translation given by a Lingala-French dictionary for "emotion" (*mayanga*) emphasizes the disturbing work of emotionalism: *Mayanga:* 1. Trouble, emotion, 2. troubled, moved, "the fact of turning the head" (*tourner la tête*) (Kawata 2003: 151, author's translation). Multiple references to the ideal of self-containment can also be found in ethnographies on ethnic groups in DR Congo and beyond (Harris 1978; Devisch 1990: 129; Riesman 1992; Bekaert 2000: 254–257; De Boeck 2004: 195). In the indigenous approach to social functionality, emotional management characterizes social relationships, conformity to social norms, and social sensitivity (Devisch 1990: 116). Apt emotional management also demarcates "adults" from "non-adults." For Kinshasa's Christians, this balancing of social order remains one of the main aspects of sociability, but new social boundaries are also erected through the control of emotions. What is new in the post-Mobutu urban context, however, is that the importance of this cultural ideal is now explained through a religious lens and with regard to the Pentecostal ideal of the Christian subject. Whereas "adult people" (read: men) distinguish themselves from others by containing their emotions, this bodily discipline has received a religious sense nowadays. The act of self-containment draws a line between Christians and nonbelievers. As the foregoing scenes in the melodramas exemplify, lack of self-control is now presented as a characteristic attributed by Christians to "pagans." Disciplining the emotions constitutes the difference between the two categories and asserts the superiority of "real Christians" over their Others.

Despite these Christian resignifications of emotions and emotionalism, it is nevertheless important to point out that in general, self-control remains in the first instance a feature of masculinity. And this also influences the social evaluation of the actors. Bienvenu, also a Cinarc actor, spoke about the remarks made by his neighbors when he was playing a character (in the serial *The Open Tomb*) that cried a lot because his girlfriend had abandoned him. Playing a crying man transgresses the cultural code prescribing that a man does not weep. The day after the broadcast, the actor's neighbors reprimanded him: "A crying man! You should know better." As the actor stated, the displays of grief and despair were necessitated by the experiences of his fictional alter ego. His neighbor's remarks, however, related not only to the breakdown of the cultural code within the fictional world but also to his own masculinity. They expected not only that the actor would know that such behavior did not suit his fictional character but also that he himself should live up to social expectations even within the context of play. He subsequently stated that, in order not to do his social reputation more harm in the future, he did not want any sequences with lengthy emotional displays.

Here is a significant gendered difference with regard to how people behave toward actors. While Mamy Moke was encouraged by her fans to keep faith in God, Bienvenu was criticized for not meeting up to the standard of masculinity. This means that for most Kinois, emotionalism remains in the first instance a non-masculine behavior. Only when women cry, Christianity is offered as a means to overcome the sadness.

Taking the different registers at play in the propagation of the self-contained person, we can argue that Pentecostal discourse is a kind of palimpsest that adds Christian layers onto local beliefs. The complex emotional style and the registers of sentiments promoted in Kinshasa's teleserials offer a politically meaningful understanding of the management of emotions in post-Mobutu Kinshasa. The

Pentecostal meanings that are assigned to affects build upon local spiritual and social significations that were ascribed to certain persons, actions, feelings, and behaviors.

Religious Scripts of Emotional Behavior

In this chapter, I analyzed the discourse about emotions since it occupies an important place in Pentecostal gatherings and in Kinshasa's Christian popular culture. To conclude, I would like to relate this Pentecostal discourse on emotions to the symbolic structure of melodrama. "Revealing the most real in the universe" and "purging society" are significant terms Brooks uses in describing the key goals of the melodrama. His description highlights the fundamental aspects that the melodrama shares with Pentecostal-Charismatic Christianity. Consider, for example, Pentecostals' most frequently performed rituals: deliverances, sermons, and testimonies of former witches. All of these aim at localizing evil within society (people/places) and expelling it. It comes as no surprise, then, that, according to Brooks (1976: 17), the melodrama resembles a ritual insofar as it deals with experiences of pain and suffering and with expelling their evil causes. Brooks even remarks that melodrama offers a substitute for the rite of sacrifice, "an urging toward combat in life, an active, lucid confrontation of evil" (1976: 206).

Significant for the analysis of Pentecostalism and media is that TV melodramas are important mediators of these new forms of subjective, emotional regimes. Via fictive representations, Kinshasa's TV spectators are instructed about apt and inapt feelings and emotional behavior. Apart from the significance of the melodramatic symbolic structure, visual broadcasting and viewing experiences are important as well. The TV serials not only illustrate particular emotions and render them meaningful, but they also enable the spectator to identify with the fictive characters and their experiences. Viewing audiences become familiar with Christian emotive styles. Fictive subjects thus enable the construction of Christian selves in Kinshasa's living rooms.

Acknowledgments

Field research in Kinshasa was made possible thanks to a position as research and teaching assistant at the Institute for Anthropological Research in Africa (University of Leuven). Many of Kinshasa's drama groups have welcomed me and included me in their artistic and religious work. I greatly appreciate the support offered by the Cinarc group and by Ecurie Maloba and Théâtre Canacu. I feel very much indebted to the church communities of Église de la Montaigne Sainte and Foi-en-Action, who offered me ample opportunities to participate in

Pentecostal gatherings and to gain an insight into their beliefs. Finally, I wish to thank Filip De Boeck and Rosalind I. J. Hackett, who read and commented on a draft of this chapter.

Notes

1. By "Pentecostal," I mean churches inspired by the Pentecostal movement without actually being inserted in the Protestant Pentecostal Church. The churches I am discussing here are part of the so-called third wave of the Pentecostal-Charismatic Christian world, in which pastors start their own churches after having received individual calls from God rather than having followed a theological training within the Protestant Church. In my use of religious appellations I try to follow as closely as possible the vocabulary of my informants. I am aware of the general use in religious studies of the term "Neo-Pentecostalism" to indicate more recent forms of Pentecostalism that originated in the United States during the 1960s (Hollenweger 1972). Other terms I use in this chapter are *Pentecostal-Charismatic churches, revival churches,* and *charismatic churches.*

2. I use "affects" to mean emotional states and "feelings" to mean physical sensations.

3. The social and symbolic values of emotions are not only absent in Pentecostal studies but in the research on African religions in general (cf. Van Beek and Blakely 1994: 13).

4. Lingala is Kinshasa's lingua franca and is thus also the main language in which Kinshasa's telenarratives are set.

5. Fieldwork was spread over four periods: February–March 2003, October 2003–March 2004, November 2004–April 2005, and April–July 2006.

6. Personal communication with Bishop Kankienza, leader of the ERC platform and General Sony Kafuta (leader of the ERC's council of wise men).

7. Alexis Matangila gives a more modest impression of the quantity of revival churches in Kinshasa. He has counted over 3,000 revival churches in Kinshasa, of which only 391 were officially member of the ERC platform (2006: 78).

8. Pentecostalism is said to have taken hold in Kinshasa in 1967, when Jacques Juron, a French pastor, began to organize healing sessions and performed miracles on Pont Kasa-Vubu.

9. Kinshasa's local media world is a highly dynamic terrain. New local and international channels are added regularly, and the government's strong control over the media often suspends or withdraws licenses of channel owners. At the start of my fieldwork (February 2003), the city's population could watch 25 television channels, of which 22 were urban-local. These numbers had increased to 48 and 43 ten years later (July 2013). These data are significant in comparison to the total amount of television channels in Congo. Researchers for the Parisian Panos Institute counted 52 television channels in 2004 on the national territory.

The scope of Kinshasa's postcolonial televised public sphere is local-urban, since most channels can only be received within the city itself. Some of the television stations are also captured in Brazzaville, the capital of the neighboring Republic of Congo. Since October 2005, two TV channels, RTNC and RTG@, are being received through satellite abroad.

10. Today, it only requires US$25,000 and permission from the authorities to create a private television channel in Kinshasa.

11. I translated the French names of these drama groups: *Les Evangélistes, La Trompette,* and *Les Lévites.*

12. Nigerian video films also contributed to this transformation of Kinshasa's teleserials. This issue cannot be addressed here. See Pype (2013) for an analysis of the appropriation of Nigerian films in Kinshasa's media world.

13. The categorization of the serials under the genre of "Pentecostal melodrama" is my own. I am aware of the potential power issue inherent in the designation of a genre, but the use of the label of "melodrama," a concept from literary theory, enables me to convey the character of the post-Mobutu serials and does not imply a preference for certain teleserials or drama groups over others.

14. As a genre in West European literature (novels and theater), Brooks locates its roots around the French Revolution, with the advent of the "post-sacred era." The hidden forces the melodrama reveals are for authors such as Balzac and James located within a psychic interior.

15. Lutz (1988: 3–13) rightly observed that emotion is a master Western cultural category that can misguide the researcher and that a Western cultural schema, with its assignment of particular values to certain emotions, might influence data collection and analysis. The emotions discussed here are those that receive much attention in the serials and the moments of instruction among Pentecostal-Charismatic Christians.

16. The serial was produced by the drama group Cinarc between July and September 2004 and immediately aired on one of the city's private TV stations (RTG@).

17. Psalm 25:3—"No one whose hope is in you will ever be put to shame, but they will be put to shame who are treacherous without excuse."

18. Although the telenarratives also offer a gendered vision of jealousy, here I want to focus on the Christian interpretations of this emotion.

19. Evans-Pritchard, when working among the Azande, described the same three emotions (jealousy, anger, and hatred) as vicious feelings that set witchcraft in motion. According to his informants, these feelings activate the witchcraft substance that can be present in one's body. Evans-Pritchard noted that "a man may not be aware that he possesses this substance, which is the power of witchcraft. Even if he has this power it will remain 'cool' inside of him, unless he entertains vicious feelings against a fellow. But if he hates another, feels anger against him, or is envious of him, grudging his good fortune and resenting his success, the witchcraft becomes 'hot'" (in Gluckman 1972: 8). According to Evans-Pritchard, self-control or self-containment was very important for social management of the person in that the exhibition of these vicious feelings could influence the oracles that determined the causes of occult origins of witchcraft or sorcery.

20. This kind of individualization of the serials' characters is still rare because most of the character types remain allegorical and rather one-dimensional.

References

Abu-Lughod, L. 1986. *Veiled Sentiments: Honor and Poetry in a Bedouin Society.* Berkeley: University of California Press.

Abu-Lughod, L. 2002. "Egyptian Melodrama—Technology of the Modern Subject?" In *Media Worlds. Anthropology on New Terrain*, edited by F. Ginsburg, L. Abu-Lughod, and B. Larkin, 115–133. Berkeley: University of California Press.

Barber, K. 1987. "Popular Arts in Africa." *African Studies Review* 30(3): 1–78.

———. 1997. "Views from the Field: Introduction." In *Readings in African Popular Culture*, edited by K. Barber, 1–10. Bloomington and Oxford: Indiana University Press and James Currey.

Bekaert, S. 2000. *System and Repertoire in Sakata Medicine: Democratic Republic of Congo.* Uppsala Studies in Cultural Anthropology 31.Uppsala: Acta Universitatis Upsaliensis.

Brooks, P. 1976. *The Melodramatic Imagination.* New Haven, CT: Yale University Press.

Corten, A., and R. Marshall-Fratani, eds. 2001. *Between Babel and Pentecost. Transnational Pentecostalism in Africa and Latin-America.* Bloomington: Indiana University Press.

Csordas, T. 1994. *The Sacred Self: A Cultural Phenomenology of Charismatic Healing.* Berkeley: University of California Press.

De Boeck, F. 2004. *Kinshasa: Tales of the Invisible City.* Ghent: Ludion.

———. 2005. "The Apocalyptic Interlude: Revealing Death in Kinshasa." *African Studies Review* 48(2): 11–32.

Devisch, R. 1990. "The Human Body as a Vehicle for Emotions among the Yaka of Zaire." In *Personhood and Agency. The Experience of Self and Other in African Cultures,* edited by M. Jackson and I. Karp, 115–133. Stockholm: Almqvist and Wiksell.

———. 1993. *Weaving the Threads of Life: The Khita Gyn-Eco-Logical Healing Cult among the Yaka.* Chicago: University of Chicago Press.

de Vries, H., and S. Weber, eds. 2001. *Religion and Media.* Stanford, CA: Stanford University Press.

de Witte, M. 2003. "Altar Media's Living Word: Televised Christianity in Ghana." *Journal of Religion in Africa* 33(2): 172–202.

Foucault, M. 1975. *Surveiller et punir: naissance de la prison.* Paris: Gallimard.

Gifford, P. 1998. *African Christianity: Its Public Role.* Bloomington: Indiana University Press.

Gledhill, C. 1987. *Home Is Where the Heart Is: Studies in Melodrama and the Woman's Film.* London: British Film Institute.

Gluckman, M., ed. 1972. *The Allocation of Responsibility.* Manchester: Manchester University Press.

Grima, B. 1992. *The Performance of Emotion among Paxtun Women.* Austin: University of Texas Press.

Hackett, R. I. J. 1994. "African Art and Religion: Some Observations and Reflections." *Journal of Religion in Africa* 24(4): 294–308.

———. 1998. "Charismatic/Pentecostal Appropriation of Media Technologies in Nigeria and Ghana." *Journal of Religion in Africa* 28(3): 1–19.

Harris, G. G. 1978. *Casting Out Anger: Religion among the Taita of Kenya.* Cambridge: Cambridge University Press.

Hollenweger, W. J. 1972. *The Pentecostals.* London: SCM.

Kawata, A. T. 2003. *Bago: Dictionnaire Lingala/Falanse Français/Lingala.* Paris: Éditions le laboratoire de langues congolaises.

Launay, R. 1997. "Spirit Media: The Electronic Media and Islam among the Dyula of Northern Côte d'Ivoire." *Africa* 67(3): 441–452.

Lutz, C. A. 1988. *Unnatural Emotion: Everyday Sentiments on a Micronesian Atoll and Their Challenge to Western Theory.* Chicago: University of Chicago Press.

Matangila, A. 2006. "Pour une analyse du discours des Eglises de réveil à Kinshasa: méthode et contexte." *Civilisations* 54(1–2): 77–84.

Meyer, B. 1999. *Translating the Devil: Religion and Modernity among the Ewe in Ghana.* Edinburgh: Edinburgh University Press.

———. 2004a. "Christianity in Africa: From African Independent to Pentecostal-Charismatic Churches." *Annual Review of Anthropology* 33: 447–474.

———. 2004b. "'Praise the Lord': Popular Cinema and Pentecostalite Style in Ghana's New Public Sphere." *American Ethnologist* 31(1): 92–110.

Meyer, B., and A. Moors, eds. 2006. *Religion, Media and the Public Sphere.* Bloomington: Indiana University Press.

Poewe, K. O., ed. 1994. *Charismatic Christianity as a Global Culture.* Columbia: University of South Carolina Press.

Pype, K. 2006. "From Working Citizen to Praying Christian. Or, Converted Visual Politics in Postcolonial Kinshasa." *A Prior Magazine,* December: 88–96.

———. 2007. "Fighting Boys, Strong Men and Gorillas: Notes on the Imagination of Masculinities in Kinshasa." *Africa* 77(2): 250–271.

———. 2009a. "Historical Routes towards Religious Television Fiction in Post-Mobutu Kinshasa." *Studies in World Christianity* 15(2): 131–148.

———. 2009b. "Media Celebrity, Charisma and Morality in Post-Mobutu Kinshasa. *Journal of Southern African Studies* 35(3): 341–355.

———. 2009c. "'We Need to Open Up the Country': Development and the Christian Key Scenario in the Social Space of Kinshasa's Teleserials." *Journal of African Media Studies* 1(1): 101–116.

———. 2010. "Of Fools and False Pastors. Tricksters in Kinshasa's TV Fiction." *Visual Anthropology* 23(2): 115–135.

———. 2012. *The Making of the Pentecostal Melodrama: Religion, Media and Gender in Kinshasa.* New York: Berghahn Books.

———. 2013. "Religion, Migration and Media Aesthetics. Notes on the Circulation and Reception of Nigerian Films in Kinshasa." In *Global Nollywood: Transnational Dimensions of an African Video Film Industry,* edited by M. Krings and O. Okome, 199–222. Bloomington: Indiana University Press.

Reddy, W. M. 1997. "Against Constructionism: The Historical Ethnography of Emotions." *Current Anthropology* 38(3): 327–351.

Riesman, P. 1992. *First Find Your Child a Good Mother: The Construction of Self in Two African Communities.* New Brunswick, NJ: Rutgers University Press.

Rosaldo, R. 1982. *Knowledge and Passion: Ilongot Notions of Self and Social Life.* Cambridge: Cambridge University Press.

Scheper-Hughes, N., and M. Lock. 1987. "The Mindful Body: A Prolegomenon to Future Work in Medical Anthropology." *Medical Anthropology Quarterly* 1(1), 6–41.

van Beek, W. E. A., and T. D. Blakely. 1994. "Introduction." In *Religion in Africa,* edited by T. D. Blakely, W. E. A. van Beek, and D. L. Thomson, 1–20. London: James Currey and Heinemann.

Vasudevan, R., ed. 2000. "Shifting Codes, Dissolving Identities: The Hindi Social Film of the 1950s as Popular Culture." In *Making Meaning in Indian Cinema,* edited by R. Vasudevan, 99–121. New Delhi: OUP.

7 Islamic Communication and Mass Media in Cameroon

Hamadou Adama

THE NEED TO COMMUNICATE is not only a prerequisite for political parties, established institutions, and ambitious individuals in all fields, but it is also a vital tool for religious leaders and structurally organized networks. Shortly after Cameroon gained independence in 1960, Islamic communication was institutionalized by the newly created state and made operational through the state-controlled radio medium before private associations, activists, and vocal religious leaders took over and, progressively, managed to come up with alternative solutions.

Either way, the focus was geared toward looking for ways and means to reach a much wider audience, including prospective converts to Islam. Whether in national media—Cameroon Radio Television (CRTV)—or in private newspapers, Muslim clerics who were not media professionals were visibly aware of the influence of the media; they devoted themselves to making messages about Islam available through media and experimented with various different alternatives. They took advantage of the international political climate, also known as the "winds of change," in the early 1990s; organized themselves according to the new media regulatory landscape; and conveniently articulated Islamic communication discourse in the public sphere. Nevertheless, the content of the so-called Islamic message was willfully and increasingly controversial on social and political issues. As I will show, religion and media in Cameroon have been very closely connected.

This chapter reviews some of the strategies and itineraries members of the Muslim intellectual elite used to articulate Islamic discourse and interpret the corpus of religious texts in the public arena in a constantly changing social environment. The passage from private to secular, from individual to community through (mass-)mediated processes has been punctuated with sporadic tensions, occasional dialogue, negotiation, and influence. From the early 1960s to the present, the relationships with the state, as well with other Muslim countries and transnational or/and private networks, such as the Saudi-funded World Association of Muslim Youth (WAMY) and the Cameroon Muslim Student Union

(CAMSU), have influenced and framed Islamic discourses on the media land-scape in Cameroon.

This chapter also examines the intellectual background of some prominent individuals dedicated to the reformulation of Islamic communication and to the reinterpretation of the Quran in a new hermeneutics to be aired, broadcast, or printed. From that standpoint, the relations between new religious media and emergent translocal, diverse, and cosmopolitan Muslim communities is taken into consideration, as well as the ongoing dialogue of these within popular culture.

First and foremost, we need to distinguish two important political periods whose separation point is in the early 1990s. The socio-political context of the first period is characterized by the implementation of a one-party political system, and the context of the second period is clearly demarcated by the experience of multiparty politics and an opening up to electoral competition, both constitutive factors that directly influence the mass media.

Monolithism and Its Impact on the Media (1960–1990)

With the accession of Cameroon to international sovereignty in 1960, politics became oriented toward the construction of a new country, emancipated from the inherited colonial state that was then ravaged by guerrilla warfare and insurgency with numerous rebellions waged against colonial rule. This considerably impeded the preservation of national integrity and the subsequent construction of national unity. These goals were upheld by President Ahmadou Ahidjo (1958–1982) to support his idea of nation-building.

Shortly thereafter, Ahidjo proclaimed independence in 1960 and reunification of the former French Cameroon with the British Cameroon to become the Federal Republic of Cameroon. In 1961, he installed an authoritarian centralized regime and split the country into seven administrative provinces, each ruled by an appointed governor. To strengthen state authority, he set up a monitoring security service, which did not hesitate to crack down on all forms of contestation and even resorted to physical elimination of "rebels," or those qualified as such according to the consecrated administrative terminology, for the sake of peace.

Another established characteristic of the authoritarian regime of Ahmadou Ahidjo was the desire to fully control the mass media in order to render it unable to openly criticize the regime, even constructively. The radio broadcasting house, which had become operational a few years before independence, had time to install itself and to become an indispensable tool for political propaganda. It obviously constituted the controversial center of interests as well, the sovereign tool per se through which government activities were made known to the people. From a range of power of less than 5 kilowatts in 1960, the three radio broadcasting stations set up in the major cities of Yaoundé, Douala, and Garoua were rapidly equipped and upgraded by the early 1970s to 30 kilowatts so as to meet the increasing communication needs of the postcolonial political authorities (Tremblay 1974). Administrative decrees and bylaws alongside local government decisions read over the radio at peak listening hours, during midday and evening news programs. Agricultural extension programs aimed at rural populations as well as plays to entertain audiences were also aired over medium-wave broadcast on national public radio to reach the widest number of listeners possible and to effectively achieve the aims of the regime.

By and large, it is within the framework of this classical triple mission of communication—namely, to inform, educate, and entertain—that religious communication, specifically the Islamic media, also fit. It is around these assigned missions that the roles and objectives of media were discussed, debated, and framed during that period of political monolithism. The main observation one can make here is that the religious media emerged in the public sphere during this period and gained popularity as a socio-political reality with complex and expanding influence.

In the mid-1960s, the influence of modern media technologies rapidly increased, and such media reached a large number of Cameroonians, particularly those living in urban areas. This new communication reality engendered a new environment that was deemed both threatening and rewarding. The state authorities and the Muslim intellectual elite were separately looking for ways and means of adopting and adapting radio to take advantage of its inherent qualities and merits. From this perspective, the level of literacy acquired by acting partners was erected as the barometer and the decisive argument in the competition to transform or to surrender to the power of the new media technology. The issue was to leave nothing to chance in order to rapidly learn and domesticate the new regulations and techniques brought about by the so-called "spirit media" (Launay 1997).

For many Muslims, the radio became an indispensable tool per se for the propagation and large-scale broadcasting of Islamic discourse. Therefore, having this medium as an ally was absolutely required to break down existing frontiers—whether along the lines of politics or gender—among Muslims. But even before thinking of how to make judicious use of this new medium that the political authority consents, at times, to accord Muslims some airtime on, one should perhaps question the level of preparedness of the potential users. In other words, were Muslims properly prepared to make good use of the radio within the legal framework implemented by the state? One cannot so hastily come up with a tangible answer to this question without taking a global look at the literacy rate of Cameroonians shortly after 1960.

A rapid glance at the official statistics reveals that the literacy rate in Cameroon during this phase of the one-party political system was considerably higher in the southern Christian-dominated regions (65 percent) than in the northern administrative constituencies (20 percent), molded, in part, by its Islamic culture and history.[1] It is important to underscore that we are dealing here with the literacy rate in the official languages in the case of Cameroon. Before the advent and the installation of the first European colonizers, many Muslims in northern Cameroon could read and write in Arabic. Some of those educated in Arabic are proficient in the use of Arabic: they are known as *moodibbo* (plural: *moodibbe,* literally scholars) in the areas under the influence of the Fulani. Throughout the northern regions formerly ruled by Muslim clerics, Islamic education was operational and effective after the jihad launched; it was coordinated in the early nineteenth century by Modibbo Adama, emir of Yola and one of Shehu Usman dan Fodio of Sokoto's flag bearers (Njeuma 1978). When the Europeans came in and violently imposed a new order after having seized their lands, Muslims almost unanimously rejected Western education, translating thereby their refusal of the imported system and expressing through action their passive resistance to the colonizers. During colonial rule, it was usually only children from the lower social classes who were effectively enrolled in Western schools, which most Muslims shunned and denigrated. It took a number of decades for Muslims to realize their mistake in avoiding Western education. To this day, non-Muslims represent a higher percentage of schoolchildren in Western schools than Muslims in the three northern regions of Cameroon (Far North, North, and Adamawa).

After colonization and the installation of the new political order inherited from the former colonial powers (Germany, Britain, and France) and inspired by secular government in the French tradition, communication over the radio, despite the severe control exerted by the independent State of Cameroon, had to be produced in the official languages of English and French—a situation that obviously did not favor the spread of Islam and Muslim scholars, who had greater proficiency in Arabic than the official languages.

Be that as it may, some educated, talented, and highly competent individual Muslims and self-made religious entrepreneurs managed to make their way. But the question as to whether the microphone would effectively be accessible to this category of "uncontrollable" Muslims who were always feared by the secular state was crucial. Herein lies the tension that has long crisscrossed the Cameroonian Muslim community. Those Muslims with advanced training in Arabic and Islamic studies who upheld a distantiated approach vis-à-vis the state and local clerics were disadvantaged when it came to communicating in the official languages, since most of them, if not all, received higher education from universities in the Middle East. Even those Muslim intellectual elites who were educated and trained in Western higher institutions of learning, the so-called "Europhone" (Kane 2003) scholars and defenders of state authority, had serious difficulties translating the corpus of religious texts into appropriate terms and meanings in the official languages.

This linguistic gap, or rather "colonial gap," between two potentially conflicting positions also hid a profound misunderstanding that was subtly exploited by state authorities over time and in different places. The political authority—for this was an open secret—had always displayed its preference for the traditional Muslim religious leaders, or *marabouts* in the French colonial lexicon, deemed conservatives, more malleable, and respectful by tradition of the established political authority, while the Arabic-speaking scholars trained outside Cameroon, sometimes hastily portrayed as "fundamentalists" or "Wahhabis," were more prone—at least according to popular opinion—to opposition and resistance. Consequently, it was therefore the marabouts who were actually endorsed and selected to pronounce Islamic religious discourse on the state radio. Due to their educational deficiencies in European languages, the messages to be aired could only be in poor French or approximate English or, alternatively, in one of the national languages.

In any case, such Islamic communication was not only difficult to understand by the majority of Muslim listeners, it was also usually a sermon that made no attempt to explain the textual meaning and facilitate its understanding. The audience was therefore often served a rather monotonous sermon with a pedantic vocabulary mostly borrowed from Arabic, if not culled from the lexicon of a past age. In both cases, the language employed was hardly understandable to most listeners. The passage from the mosque—where this kind of sermon is usually made by marabouts, frequently criticized for illiteracy in the Arabic language—to the radio station did not motivate marabouts to adapt methodological or pedagogical approaches for the new medium. This attitude could be understood to some extent and be interpreted as if the mosque and the broadcasting radio house were similar, while in reality the two forums are radically and intrinsically different in nature and scope. If in the mosque, the imam addresses Muslims who come to worship God in a sacred and physically demarcated space, the radio broadcasting house—certainly a privileged place of communication as well—is open to the outside world and its diverse, cosmopolitan, and multi-confessional audiences. Similarly, while the mosque is a closed environment, which does not give room for open debates, the radio is, fundamentally, a forum of dialogue and exchange of ideas, lively debate, and, occasionally, of contradiction, contestation, and dispute. Neither the religious authorities nor the political powers could tolerate such an allegedly deviant and alienating attitude on the radio. Given their shared preoccupations, the state and the marabout had to reach a realistic compromise of mutual interest meant to judiciously use the radio and avoid any friction.

By and large, Islamic communication through the state-controlled media during this period of the one-party system consisted of a monologue that was concerned with taking up airtime without really inciting the interest of the Muslim listener. It made use of an information apparatus heavily controlled by the state without realizing perhaps that religion too had, in itself, become an instrument of state propaganda deliberately diverted with the intention of establishing the loyalty of a religious community. At best, the state encouraged freedom of worship, which in most cases was expected to promote moral values, law and order, respect for the established political authorities, and unchallenged recognition of political supremacy over religious legitimacy. In this sense, the state's intended objectives toward Islam were to render it impermeable to new and imported religious ideologies, suspected—rightly or wrongly—of potentially carrying with them an innovative and heterodox order. It was also to meet up with a hidden agenda that could be dissimulated under ostentatious religious practices and forms that President Ahidjo decided to institutionalize, in 1963, with the creation of the Islamic Cultural Association of Cameroon, widely known by its French acronym ACIC.[2] He conferred upon it the duty of Islamic education and training as well as political supervision of the Muslim community (Adama 1999). Positions of power within this Muslim associational structure were reserved for individuals of the inner circle of the ruling political regime. The ACIC top-ranking staff was composed of civil servants, Arabic-speaking scholars, and active members of the ruling party.

Consequently, and perhaps without even realizing what was happening, the ACIC rapidly became a token organization, an artificial partner whose very existence was solely legitimized by its own trusteeship. It continued, though, to demonize some Sufi orders, such as the Tijāniyya and the Qādiriyya, and organize public discussions on hot Islamic issues such as the relationship of the latter with the state; gender; youth pregnancy; and marriage crisis without gaining large and tangible support from the Muslim community as a whole. The lack of popularity of its leaders among the Muslim masses, manipulation of the lunar calendar, misuse of government subsidies for educational programs, and maintenance of places of worship are only some illustrative cases of the failure to live up to expectations that led to the discrediting and demise of the ACIC.

In short, the inability of the marabouts—due to their poor educational levels in the official languages—to make optimal use of the radio, coupled with pressure from political authorities that was constantly brought to bear on those who conceived Islamic programs, generated little esteem for Islamic discourse over the radio. Increasingly, the audience became indifferent to and distanced itself from Islamic programs over the radio.

Such a situation only seemed to encourage the search for alternatives, and this is indeed what happened. That period also coincided with the production and mad rush for audiocassettes and videotapes by charismatic vocal preachers, with South African preacher Ahmet Deedat's *Crucifixion or Cruci-fiction?* and Cameroonian Modibbo Abdoulaye's *yiite djahannamaye* (Gehenna's fire) among the bestsellers. In both cases, there was a clear search for convincing arguments, controversy, and lively debates, all constituting ingredients that were constantly and regularly censored in the state-controlled radio. In a social context largely influenced and impacted by the religious affiliation of the ruling regime, such arguments were valuable, for they could be employed to defend the weakening position of the religious clerics. Private radio stations expressing the diversity of the Muslim community's views did not exist, nor did alternative forms of Islamic communication such as plays, sketches, or print media. Not a single informal Islamic communication medium was recorded during the first 20 years after independence (excluding audiocassettes and videotapes, illegally imported from neighboring Nigeria).

Thus, failing to inform, educate, and entertain, Islamic communication over the radio reproduced a conservative kind of discourse that was largely devoid of interest and appeal. Islamic print media were nonexistent, and state television was still in its debut, with its coverage limited to the capital city, Yaoundé. After the 1990s, a completely new media landscape emerged in the Cameroonian public domain. The transition was, however, gradual, although at certain points the populace resorted to street demonstrations and violence before claims for civil liberties, freedom of expression, and association were given recognition.

To summarize this first period of the one-party political system, we need to notice that by the end of the 1980s, the state had succeeded in transforming the marabouts by confining them to a defensive role, ostensibly "protecting" them from such "harmful" influences as Islamic syncretism and "Wahhabis." In reality, the state exploited the vacuum created by the lack of administrative structures and organization within the Muslim community and the competition between self-proclaimed religious leaders to implement its policies and reinforce its centrality in the public sphere. Logically, the state ended up subordinating the "happy few" who had embarked on defending the ruling regime, and, in exchange, they were granted certain privileges and perks.

In that respect, the media played an active role in transforming such religious leaders, not only by marginalizing them and anaesthetizing their discourse, but leaders' interactions with the radio also obliged them to rally behind the ruling regime and effectively become civil servant religious leaders. Indeed, the sociopolitical context in which the state strategy was geared toward eliminating any potentially competitive actors in civil society was effective. Paradoxically, the hidden agenda intending to discredit potentially uncompromising religious leaders by exposing them to the media was beneficial to the newly returned scholars educated and trained in Middle Eastern universities and higher institutions of learning.

New Environment, Actors, and Communication Strategies

Directly or indirectly, the geopolitical reconfiguration of the world after the collapse of the Berlin Wall and the end of the apartheid regime in South Africa influenced the political system in many African countries hitherto ruled by self-proclaimed "Founding Fathers" through highly centralized one-party systems. Cameroon is one such country that has been politically and socially influenced by the subsequent "new world order." On the streets, in structurally organized civil society associations, and even at the national assembly and within the ruling party, students, political leaders, and members of parliament across the country were demonstrating, expressing openly their desire for political liberalization; free, fair, and transparent elections; competition; freedom of speech; and the implementation of a democratic process.

For a number of reasons, the 1990s represent an important turning point in the contemporary history of Cameroon. These years also marked a transitional period in the evolution of the country toward democracy. As early as 1990, unprecedented popular pressure compelled the political authorities to open up politics to competition. A series of bills, laws, and regulations bearing on the fundamental rights of individuals were voted and promulgated with immediate effect. This newly created socio-political environment stimulated the setting up of opposition political parties, many of which emerged from community or religious associations with a press organ established for the promotion of its interests.

Civil society became much more diverse. The religious options on offer were both diversified and democratized. Numerous religious organizations emerged. In some urban locales such as Douala, Yaoundé, Maroua, and Garoua, many of the established religious organizations staged preaching sessions in stadiums, marketplaces, and theaters with relative success.

Traditional forms of communication now had to be adjusted and adapted to the new environment and sharing of power. With this emerging new context, young and educated returnees and updated media technology could only imply alternative ways of communicating. Whether the advent of the new information and communication technologies (ICTs) will revolutionize the relationship between religion and society as a whole is foreseeable when their potentially transformational nature is taken into account. But how deep, far, and fast ICTs will transform the religious corpus, leaders, and organizations is much less predictable given the speed of creativity in that domain.

Over the state radio, the transformation process has occurred gradually. Islamic communication that was left in the hands of the officially recognized ACIC encountered difficulties in adapting to the realities of deregulation characterized by the creation of competitive private FM radio stations. As a result, it failed to attract audiences, most of which can tune into the available interactive Islamic programs broadcast by private FM radios and hosted by charismatic young Muslim scholars from the large organization Cameroon Muslim Student Union (CAMSU). The marabouts who once produced Islamic communication over the radio went through the multiparty political system without apparently gaining any tangible experience sufficient to usher in innovations in the preparation, conception, and diffusion of messages about Islam. Almost all the hosts of the weekly Islamic show Connaissance de l'Islam (Knowledge of Islam) were "traditional" marabouts regularly officiating in nearby mosques, where, due to their deficiencies in the Arabic language, they were content with the rote recitation of previously selected Quranic verses instead of effectively preaching or offering explanations or sermons that were of practical use for listeners. Radio programs aired on Friday afternoons were often little more than the same readings of the Quran initiated a few hours earlier in the local mosques.

Until recently, this was the general perception of the (mass-)mediated Islamic communication in the Muslim community. But shortly before 1990, a newly founded Islamic organization, Jeunesse islamique du Cameroun (JIC, or Islamic Youth of Cameroon), came up with radically different approaches in terms of how the new media could be positively exploited to best serve the interests of Muslims and expose the Muslim community to a wider audience both at home and abroad. The JIC was created by Arabic-speaking young men who had returned home after graduating from Middle Eastern and Nigerian universities. Besides knowing Arabic and local languages (namely, Hausa and Fulfulde) widely spoken among the Sahelian Muslim community, they proved to be knowledgeable in biblical studies and fluent in French and English for those who were trained in Nigeria. Unemployed by the public administration that was reluctant to recognize their degrees, and ostracized by the state structures and apparatus, most of them sought private employment and initiated parallel ways to fend for themselves. They focused their efforts primarily on the educational system, which would later serve as a springboard to greener pastures. Financially supported by transnational Islamic organizations such as the World Association of Muslim Youth (WAMY), the Qadaffi-era Libyan Islamic Call Society (Da'wa al-Islamiyya) (Otayek 1993; Racius 2004), and other generous foreign donors, the new ulama (Coulon 1993) rapidly set up viable and reliable Arabic schools, which turned out to be popular and successful in various cities.

Benefiting from the success in promoting competitive private schools in urban areas, the JIC positioned itself at the avant-garde, as a group of competent Muslims and dedicated volunteers devoted to implementing new and useful knowledge to enlighten the *umma* "held hostage by illiterates and compromising religious leaders."[3] Of course, this narrative was in itself new not only within the diverse Muslim community but also in the general public as a whole. One important aspect to mention here is that the JIC was not exclusively composed of Arabic-speaking scholars nostalgic about implementing a new and purified religious order. A large number of Western-educated Muslim elites affiliated with the movement also played a prominent role in the decision-making process at the higher level of the JIC's administrative hierarchy.

Broadly speaking, while ACIC leaders were appointed to manage the educational crisis within the subsidized French and Arabic primary and secondary schools and broadcast their conservative discourses over regular programs on the public radio, the JIC members were committed, with the support of transnational organizations, to the reimplementation of what they considered a "purer" and "cleaner" Islam, devoid of local customs, rituals, and traditions. The JIC realized this commitment by creating distinctive private schools and entering pilgrimage networks, mosques, hospitals, prisons, and university campuses. Their individual and dedicated investment in the social sector proved effective and successful, so much so that caravans of Arab doctors were visiting the cities in the north yearly from 1995 to perform eye surgery and provide eyeglasses free of charge for those in need. This practical and altruistic approach of communication "from below" was highly successful and changed the general perception of Islam within the Muslim community and in the larger society as well.

Equally, over the radio, for instance, instead of following the pattern adopted by the "traditional" marabouts as regards the relationship to media, the scholars opted deliberately for lively exchanges of ideas, interfaith dialogue, discussions, and contradictory debates. Predictably, the introduction of these vocal and charismatic young men, subtly marginalized by the administrative apparatus but overtly popular with the masses, put forward questions about the legitimacy of those who could be judged as qualified to speak publicly for the entire Muslim community. As might be expected, Muslims were divided between those who favored continuity and respect for the elders (symbolized by the presence of marabouts) and the younger generation, avid for knowledge and poised to use the prestige conferred upon their scholarship by virtue of their mastery of Arabic and their ability to perform in front of a microphone or a camera. Beyond individual ambitions and doctrinal approaches, they presented it as a choice between the representatives of a localized Islam with some measure of conservatism (but discredited by their alliance with the state authorities) and the apologists for a standardized and global Islam (Roy 2002), heralding a new form of progressiveness that was still unclear to its potential supporters. Quite rapidly, the cleavage between the two antagonized camps took on a more passionate and radical form with the advent of private television networks.

While the ACIC leadership, given its privileged stance with the public authority, blacklisted those who professed a different vision of Islam from state media, the JIC, well aware of the academic competence and professionalism of its members, engaged in popular activities by expanding its area of intervention to health centers and offering assistance to Cameroonian pilgrims in Saudi Arabia during the Hajj. Once again, the prestige and respect gained "from below," for achievements recorded in the education and health service, ended up compelling the state to reconsider its initial position and to implicitly recognize the JIC by opening up the state radio and public television to some of its "moderate" members. When invited on live talk shows to give an opinion, conduct a discussion, or coordinate a debate, JIC members frequently outwitted their counterparts from ACIC in terms of language fluency, charisma, and knowledge. It was therefore those brief appearances on public radio and television that allowed the scholars to capture listeners' and viewers' attention and support both from within the Muslim community and beyond.

The squabble between "traditional" marabouts and Arabic-speaking intellectuals over privileged access to the state-controlled media was also shifted and transposed to the contents and the structure of programs. On television, the regular Islamic programs used to be furnished with mostly clandestine recordings of prayer sessions broadcast over digital Arab networks via the communications satellite operators, Arabsat or Nilesat, coupled with off-screen commentaries and pictures shot in local prayer places. Here again, opposition in criticism of the anachronism in connection with the local realities was raised by the scholars, who increasingly pushed the marabouts toward the exit by laying bare their ineptitude in using the new communications technology. The criticism was focused on the imbalance of knowledge in the programs and the factual level of Islamic education in the Muslim community. According to the scholars, radio and television could be immensely beneficial and highly productive in transforming society if they were to be employed in educating and training Muslims in practical issues such as performing prayers, Islamic ethics, and how to lead a "good" family life.

While claiming greater visibility on state radio and television programs, Muslim intellectuals literally occupied the private FM radios and satellite television stations, forums in which they professed a new form of Islam to the listeners and viewers. Parallel to the new digital media, religious songs in Arabic were translated into local languages (Fulfulde, Hausa), performed with the same lyrics and made available to the larger public through CDs and DVDs. Prominent association leaders wrote satirical and dramatic plays and staged them on screen to sensitize Muslims to adopting normative religious behaviors in society and in relationship with alterity (e.g., Souleymane 2001a, 2001b, 2001c; Adama 2007). In addition, blogs and listservs (Woylagroups, Shouragroups, Camsu, etc.) were launched and quickly developed to network members and stimulate the exchange of ideas and web discussions.[4]

To summarize, the second period was characterized by the setting up of a more democratic society. However, the controversy between the marabouts and the new scholars was to the disadvantage of the former. After having succeeded in marginalizing the marabouts from the mass media, the new ulama concentrated on both revising the contents of Islamic communication to make it more effective and expanding it in order to reach wider audiences, including prospective converts. In that respect, not only did the new media change and transform the Muslim community in Cameroon by providing consistency to the Islamic corpus, but the new media actually popularized and helped build self-esteem for the new-media Muslim pundits. One striking example of this situation is Doubla Avaly, the founder of the Islamic newspaper *An-Nour*, whose trajectory in the new media is both reflective and indicative of the relationship between Islam and media in Cameroon today.

The *An-Nour* Experience

As discussed earlier, radio and television were far from being the only illustrative cases in which mutual transformations in religion were engendered by the media. Without exactly replicating that history, the Islamic print medium initiated and developed shortly after 1990 appeared very different in its conception, tone, editorial line, and objectives when compared to Islamic communication carried out over radio and television. The direction taken by the Islamic newspaper in Cameroon, *An-Nour* (literally "light"), is illustrative and cannot be ignored, since it remains unchallenged. *An-Nour* was initially designed and developed by a group of Muslim scholars who were educated in Arabic, French, and English, besides being fluent in the national languages. From the very beginning, it represented a new challenge set up by the Muslim intellectual elite to introduce a different tone and voice in the communication landscape in public life.

By resorting to modern communication tools, materialized by the idea of establishing an Islamic newspaper, Doubla Avaly, a university professor in physics, assisted by an editorial board composed of his closest friends, succeeded in sensitizing the Muslim community to a new and contextualized form of Islamic proselytism over the course of a decade. With the assistance of a group of friends, all convinced of the need to reform the Islamic educational system—hitherto in the hands of individuals they portrayed as having "few scruples" and doomed to decrepitude—Doubla Avaly edited, in November 1993, an advance copy of what he explained was to become a monthly Islamic paper dedicated to expressing Muslim opinion on local and global issues. Its motto, proudly displayed in bold characters on the front page, clearly stated its orientation: "The truth must triumph."[5]

In an effort to justify the reason behind the choice of this concerted initiative, Moustapha Ramadan Nlend, one of the columnists of *An-Nour*, says the following:

> Communication rightly appears . . . as the spearhead of any ideological system. And the triumph of any system of life appears to be intimately linked to the efficiency of its communications policy. Hence, Islam, which is an entire life system should make use of this means of this century to combat ignorance,

the source of prejudice, therefore, of evil, and cause truth and the light [*An-Nour*] to triumph and deliver humankind from heedlessness as well as from moral and spiritual torpor, all heralding certain and inevitable decadence.[6]

To clear all doubts regarding the real intentions of *An-Nour,* Nlend came up with the essentials and added the following:

> In a chaotic world in which the value systems are crumbling, in a world where the mass media seems to have renounced its mission for egoistic and partisan reasons and in which communications appear henceforth militate in favour of alienation and pernicious propaganda . . . , it was imperative that a ray of light [*An-Nour*] illuminate our hearts and cause in us the emergence of community awareness, tolerance, mutual understanding, and justice, for without these, the ruin of the community is imminent.[7]

These two statements clearly indicate and arguably justify the necessity of creating an Islamic newspaper entirely dedicated to the service of the Muslim community at large. More significantly, *An-Nour* was initially established with the objective of providing a different tone, view, vision, and perspective of the Cameroonian Muslim community. The materialization of this project was presented as a salvage gesture, a refusal to helplessly watch the Muslim community sink into political and economic marginalization because of poor Western education. What was presented can therefore be seen and described as a communication substitution and a bearer of hope heralded by dedicated Muslim intellectuals acting as volunteers who were committed to promoting their own vision of Islamic faith in an era of modern technology and active communication.

Physically, *An-Nour* was presented in a tabloid format and contained several columns with the most regular ones being "Teachings and Predications," "Events," "Culture and Society," and an entertaining "Magazine Corner" or "Reader's Tribune." Its 12 pages included articles on various themes ranging from religious to social, political, economic, doctrinal, ethical, moral, and gender issues such as forced marriages, contraception, youth marriage, the marginalization of girls, and female illiteracy. The majority of the articles published, often illustrated with black-and-white photographs, strove to reveal the "Islamic" point of view not in relation to global Islam—that is, ideas brought in from abroad—but by relying on an intelligible harmony of the universally admitted Islamic sources contained in the Quran and the Sunna, which remain the basis for consensus between Muslims the world over. In addition, *An-Nour* combined this with positive interpretations of local customs and cultural heritage. The tone, mostly borrowed from comics, was willfully alert and harsh in some sensitive articles dealing with religious issues or education, but it deliberately targeted traditional forms of Islamic practices popularized by peripheral and ostracized

Islamic movements qualified by the *An-Nour* columnists as "enemies of Islam" (*bida, shirk, fitna*, etc.) within the Muslim community in clear and lucid French. The front page is boldly highlighted by enlarged captions, willingly provoking debate and questioning the need for an efficient and practical Islamic education meant to foster and stimulate exemplary spiritual life both in public and private. These were, though rapidly examined, some of the features and main characteristics of this monthly bilingual—French (80 percent) and English (20 percent)—tabloid paper chaired and edited by Doubla Avaly.

Above all the issues regularly discussed, however, it was unquestionably the scourge of illiteracy, with respect to Western-style education within the Muslim community, which rapidly became a special subject of concern to the editorial board of *An-Nour*—a natural development, since most of the writers were teachers by profession—and to the entire community. Judging from the headlines regularly published in almost all the subsequent issues, it was possible to detect a surreptitious strategy designed to purposely articulate Islamic communication in a friendlier manner in line with the ambitious, newly self-proclaimed spokesmen of the Muslim community.

Actually, Doubla Avaly and his team did succeed, through the print media, in raising awareness among Muslims and sensitizing the state about the need for private Islamic education. Their efforts were rewarded in 2000 when the Minister of National Education appointed Doubla Avaly chairman of the newly created Islamic Private Education Authority. He was instructed to deeply reform, renovate, and restructure Islamic education, widely thought to be in decline, throughout the nation.

Whether by chance or deliberately, after Doubla's administrative promotion, *An-Nour* started ailing and ended up disappearing completely from the press stalls. Indeed, financial problems, the lack of a reliable distribution network, and difficulties related to the 50 percent devaluation of the currency (CFA franc) in 1993 all combined to offer reasonable explanations of this sudden disappearance of *An-Nour*. It would also be dishonest, however, to ignore the relationship between the media campaign launched by *An-Nour* on education issues, the appointment of Doubla Avaly, and the closure of the only Islamic monthly newspaper in Cameroon. Opposite justifications abound, and manipulations as well as the instrumentalization of the media are certainly not the least of these.

Since then, though, many individuals have toyed with the idea of creating an Islamic newspaper, a magazine, or a journal that might recapture the passion of the early days. The vacuum left by *An-Nour* is still unfilled, and partners of the early days have become disillusioned. *An-Nour* is remembered as an Islamic mass medium that played an important role in sensitizing national public opinion to the poor literacy rate of North Cameroon with regards to Western education. It was through this press organ and its nonprofessional but charismatic and highly talented writers that the state and the civil society came to appreciate the job done by Doubla Avaly, who eventually became a role model for the younger and Western-educated generation in a context of religious competition and Islamic stigmatization both nationally and globally. The appreciation and popular enthusiasm generated by Doubla Avaly and his team of writers were also—and largely but not exclusively—dependent on a functional ethno-regional representation of the members constituting the editorial board of *An-Nour*. Drawing from the heterogeneity, diversity, and complexity of the Cameroonian Muslim community, Doubla Avaly judiciously exploited the concern for complementarity and interrelationship that admittedly governs regional balance and equilibrium between Arabic-speaking and "Europhone" Muslim intellectuals in his composition of the executive board of *An-Nour*. Such decision making, stemming from a blend of common sense and national sociological realism, remains the sole guarantor of stability, longevity, and success in any national and lasting undertaking in Cameroon.

By and large, experiences from the *An-Nour* newspaper show that media participation by religious actors can bear fruit and bring change by transforming desperate situations and established images and opinions. Conversely, increased media exposure of religious actors or organizations can also generate suspicion, resistance, and new patterns of exclusion. All things considered, one might be tempted to wonder about the effectiveness of the (mass-)mediated Islamic communication in molding a specific public opinion so as to encourage cooperation within and between religions.

(Mass-)Mediated Islamic Communication and Public Opinion

One way of defining public opinion would be to admit that it is a collective will of the people, a summation of public expression regarding a specific issue or event. Once such an instrumentalist definition is admitted, the difficulty remains of articulating Islamic communication in its relationship to general or "Muslim" public opinion in an environment characterized by a rapidly increasing media influence.

Beyond the mutual impact between mass-mediated Islamic communication and public opinion, the main preoccupation, expressed otherwise, is to determine whether there can be a distinct and/or specific Muslim public opinion, molded by constant Islamic communication; conceived, carried out, and articulated through the new media within Cameroon; and independent, in all its forms and kinds, from any foreign influence or trusteeship. Scrutiny of such a question warrants beforehand an assessment of the relationship that exists between mass-mediated Islamic communication and Cameroonian society. Official or formal communication has always lagged behind the transformations of Cameroonian

society as a whole both under the one-party system and the era of political pluralism. Since the colonial era, increased Middle Eastern religious influences and
openness to Hausa-Fulani cultural ties with Nigeria have played active roles
among Cameroonian Muslims.

To escape from the repetitive Islamic communication diffused in the state-
controlled media and its rather uninteresting nature in terms of both form and
content under the one-party system, Muslims learned to turn to alternative
sources of information. During the Ahidjo regime (1960–1982), the advent of cassette recorders and VCRs meant that lively sermons by charismatic clerics could
easily be found in the local weekly markets. This development led to the popular-
ization of such media. Thus, faced with the boredom of formal mediated Islamic
communication, the Muslim audience, which to some extent also constituted the
most targeted group in the northern provinces, favored alternative solutions. New
ways of Islamic communication, which gradually were substituted for the monologue of state mass-mediated narration, translated, in practical terms, the urge to
get viable and reliable information through other means. Similarly, the massive
marketing of audio- and videocassettes by some charismatic religious leaders,
notably Moddibo Abdoulaye in Garoua and Modibbo Beka in Ngaoundere, was
only the tip of the iceberg. In any case, it widely and indirectly expressed a silent
contestation of political interference in the conception, orientation, and exploitation of Islamic communication carried out in the mass media.

The tendency, inherited from the colonial administration, of the political
authority to control the mass media is not a new occurrence in Cameroon under the Biya regime (1982 to the present). It was simply accentuated and became
widespread in the early 1990s, right after the setting up of the multi-party political process in the country. But, this time around, the socio-political environment
had changed. Consequently, the communications on offer had more than ever
been democratized and the audience—listeners, readers, or viewers, let alone internet and telephone users—henceforth had more than one alternative in case
of dissatisfaction or unavailability. Moreover, this diversity in communications
on offer did not at all mean that the multiplicity of choices was either accessible
or affordable to the ordinary citizen. That was very much the reality, and it is
still the case. If we limit our observation to what we can see in urban areas, we
notice that the formal (mass-)mediated Islamic communication on offer did not
necessarily meet the expectations of the growing number of educated Muslims
living in a cosmopolitan and increasingly secularized environment. Radio programs, for instance, even though some were broadcast in the national languages,
continuously reproduced moralizing monologues, which in most cases did not
give any room for insightful debate and expression of pluralism. By mixing content and form, it also happened that television programs, instead of the expected
weekly Islamic productions, showed duplicate documentaries on the lives of Arab

communities that were completely disconnected from awareness about Islam. Since the off-screen commentaries of these borrowed or pirated documentaries were in Arabic, which is actually the liturgical language of Islam, the resulting confusion that occurred between the secular and the sacred was significant.

In any case, the related experience reveals a number of facts. One of them leads to the conclusion that official and formal (mass-)mediated Islamic communication is largely out of step with its audience. This discord could be partially explained by the control brought to bear on it by the state supervisory authority that, from all evidence, was not in any way, after independence, willing to encourage, through the media, the emergence of a supplementary pole of opposition to its totalitarianism and lack of popular legitimacy. This precautionary measure that was raised to government policy possibly underlines the almost irresistible reflex of the political authority to regulate the media and specifically the (mass-)mediated Islamic communication in public life.

As a result, the token alliance sealed between the political authority and guardians of "traditional" Islamic orthodoxy also falls in line with this logic of partnership between the two rather conservative bastions. From the state's point of view, regulating the mass media has always been a matter of safeguarding the legal rights of controlling all aspects of public life (a sort of established tradition inherited from colonization) by imposing full respect of its authority, while on the other hand, the concern was to preserve the localized Islamic practices that some referred to as "backward-looking" but that, all things considered, promoted social harmony with the cultural heritage and loyalty to the chief while rejecting insurgency and rebellion (*fitna, bida*) against political authority.

Conversely, informal (mass-)mediated Islamic communications have always had trouble getting their message across to the people, due to the state monopoly on a wide range of public radio and television, and found their only real outlet in the private press or alternative ways of communication such as plays and sketches. But even though unofficial mass-mediated Islamic communication was somehow constrained to use alternative means of communication to reach a wider audience, it remained under public authority monitoring through the Press Act (1966) and the Social Communication Act (1991), which in both cases required editors to give advance copies of final proofs to the office of the Minister for Territorial Administration (MINAT) and the subdivisional officer hours before publication and distribution. MINAT had therefore the right to censor or suspend any material of a seditious nature or anything that was considered contrary to accepted standards of morality. Violation of the 1991 act was punishable by fine, imprisonment, and/or seizure of printed copies.

With some restrictions, private (mass-)mediated Islamic communication was tolerated, just like many other press organs, provided that "this liberty is exercised within the limits of the provisions of the laws" (Mani 1987). This *modus vivendi* sealed by mutual interests was also symptomatic of a shaky relationship between Islam and the state in Cameroon. Paradoxically, these conflicts and debates provided a never-ending source of inspiration for writers of the private press, including the Islamic press—inspiration but not necessarily information— as the raw material for this press is usually opinion instead of facts. The majority of articles published in 2000 can be summarized as attempts at persuasion on various issues, condemnation of government actions, interviews with opposition leaders, and so on. The ideal article in that case was not the one that claimed to provide a comprehensive survey of a specific event in an unbiased manner. Instead, the ideal paper was one that conveyed its message effectively.

Since the final objective in the case of mass-mediated Islamic communication, be it formal or informal, private or public, was to persuade, to convince, and to rally, while simultaneously informing, entertaining, and educating, what then could possibly be its contribution to the social development of the Muslim community? Expressed otherwise, in what way does (mass-)mediated Islamic communication impact the Cameroonian Muslim community?

Under one-party politics, we have seen that (mass-)mediated Islamic communication remained out of sync with the social transformations of the Muslim community. Its allegiance and subordination to state authority might partly explain the reason for Muslim disillusionment. In that respect, its impact was decreasing to an almost complete loss of credibility. By adopting as principal objective the satisfaction of its powerful and omnipresent trusteeship—to the detriment of its audience—(mass-)mediated Islamic communication failed to consider the social development of the Muslim community as its main priority, let alone keep pace with the emerging trend. But for the return of many Arabic-speaking Cameroonians trained in Middle Eastern universities, who were to influence the content and orientation of the new (mass-)mediated Islamic communication at the turn of the 1980s, no tangible social development could have been recorded. These young Muslims contributed a great deal in sensitizing public opinion to various aspects of Muslim life, both socially and politically.

On the social level, for instance, they participated in setting up health services, training female workers, and building Islamic schools in rural and urban areas. The fruits of these philanthropic and altruistic efforts could only be measured in two or three decades. Politically as well, Muslims became aware of the active role they could play to help develop their regions, influence state decisions, and channel funding for socio-economic development projects. Registration campaigns for prospective participation in local and general elections were popularized and became successful among the Muslim community.

Mass-mediated Islamic communication did contribute to the molding of a distinct public opinion in the civil society of contemporary Cameroon. Directly and indirectly, willingly or unwillingly, it accompanied some irreversible social changes, motivated a few, and stimulated many others. The fact that professional politicians integrated so-called Islamic opinion into their campaign strategies to gain the endorsement of Muslim voters is a palpable indicator of the (mass-) mediated Islamic communication impact on the civil society. How Muslims would exploit this increasing influence to help combat illiteracy, alleviate plagues that are still devastating their historical strongholds in northern Cameroon, and positively transform their environment constitutes the greatest challenge in the future.

An analysis of (mass-)mediated Islamic communication in Cameroon clearly leads us to one important remark. Despite government support and structures, formal and public (mass-)mediated Islamic communication carried out through the state-controlled media strain to reach its audience due to its rather anachronistic approaches, incompatible knowledge, and contested relationship with the state, and this has handicapped its efficiency and pertinence and considerably reduced its scope. On the other hand, informal but well-structured and private (mass-)mediated Islamic communication has progressively gained ground by resorting to its intelligibility and its adequately articulating viable approaches into a realistic *modus vivendi* with the state authority. In a constantly changing context with endlessly renewable information technology and patterns, this adjustable pragmatism, carried out with professionalism, would not only generate tangible results but would also prove more successful than its state media counterpart.

Notes

1. National Institute of Statistics. 2002. *Cameroon in Figures 2001*. Yaoundé: 12.
2. In French ACIC stands for Association Culturelle Islamique du Cameroun.
3. Interview: Modibbo Aboubakar, Yaounde, 2003.
4. The Shoura is to this date the most visited and influential Islamic website and listserv among Cameroonian students. It was created in 2000 by Bana Barka, who was then a teacher at a government high school in Nkongsamba.
5. In French it is "Pour le triomphe de la vérité."
6. *An-Nour*, no. 1 issue of November 1993 / *Jamadi (al-Awwal al-Arkhir)* 1414. This monthly newspaper, published in French and English, is officially registered and legalized in keeping with the Cameroonian law on the private press.
7. Ibid.

References

Adama, H. 1999. "L'enseignement privé islamique dans le Nord-Cameroun." *Islam et Sociétés au sud du Sahara, Revue de la Maison des Sciences de l'Homme* (13): 7–40.
———. 2007. "Islamic Associations in Cameroon: Between the Umma and the State." In *Islam and Muslim Politics in Africa,* edited by Benjamin F. Soares and René Otayek, 227–241. New York: Palgrave Macmillan.

Coulon, C. 1993. "Les itinéraires politiques de l'islam au Nord-Nigéria." In *Religion et modernité politique en Afrique noire,* edited by Jean-François Bayart, 19–22. Paris: Karthala.

Kane, O. 2003. *Intellectuels non europhones.* Dakar: CODESRIA.

Launay, R. 1997. "Spirit Media: The Electronic Media and Islam among the Dyula of Northern Côte d'Ivoire." *Africa* 67(3):441–452.

Mani E. F. M. 1987. "Presse privée et déséquilibre de l'information au Cameroun." PhD thesis, University of Yaoundé.

National Institute of Statistics. 2002. *Cameroon in Figures 2001.* Yaoundé: INS Press.

Njeuma, M. Z. 1978. *Fulani Hegemony in Yola (Old Adamawa):1809–1902.* Yaoundé: Ceper.

Otayek, R., ed. 1993. *Le radicalisme islamique au sud du Sahara.* Paris: Karthala.

Racius, E. 2004. "The Multiple Nature of the Islamic Da'wa." PhD thesis, University of Helsinki.

Roy, O. 2002. *L'islam mondialisé.* Paris: Seuil.

Souleymane. 2001a. *Islam: notre choix.* Yaounde: Dâr el-Hikma.

———. 2001b. *Le cheikh et le DG.* Yaoundé: Dâr el-Hikma.

———. 2001c. *Scie-Da.* Yaoundé: Dâr el-Hikma.

Tremblay, G. 1974. "Radio et éducation au Cameroun." *Canadian Journal of African Studies* 8: 575–587.

8 "We Are on the Internet"

Contemporary Pentecostalism in Africa and the New Culture of Online Religion

J. Kwabena Asamoah-Gyadu

THE WORLD WIDE WEB has undoubtedly become an important location for religious activity in the world today.[1] This chapter examines media usage among contemporary Pentecostals in Africa, focusing on their uses of the internet.[2] Contemporary Pentecostalism consciously presents itself as a "globalizing religious project" and therefore deliberately cuts a very international outlook in terms of public image (Meyer 2010). We will look at how the Christian movements concerned mediate religious experiences online and the ways in which they have adapted to the reality of virtual culture as part of their mission. We are dealing with movements for which the Holy Spirit is a defining experience and by whose presence even the most profane of spaces, such as the internet, could be made sacred for God's use. The media in general and the internet in particular offer an important medium for the actualization of the globalizing Pentecostal project. It is with these global aspirations in mind that the contemporary African churches under consideration here usually incorporate the expressions "global," "international," "intercontinental," or "worldwide" in their names.

The use of the internet adds status to a religious organization and affirms an entity's international relevance, offering opportunities to stay connected with the world. The World Wide Web or cyberspace presence, Jeffrey Hadden and Douglas Cowan (2000) note, "has established itself as one of the leading emblems of progressive engagement with culture." Cyberspace is where anybody who is somebody is represented, and it offers these Christian communities the opportunity to express and practice their religion in ways that bridge the gap between online and offline presence. Thus, this study is important for three reasons. First, although studies on religion and the internet have been ongoing for at least a decade now, not much has been done on developments in Africa.[3] Second, contemporary Pentecostalism has within the last 30 years blossomed into the most important development within Christianity in Africa. Third, the use of the media has become part and parcel of the self-definition of this new stream of Pentecostal Christianity. Africa's contemporary religious communities, especially the newer-generation Pentecostals, have been quicker and more savvy than most mainline churches in taking advantage of the potentialities of the media as channels and sites for religious activities. Generally, the Pentecostal perception of the media as empowered by God for the task of world evangelization could not have been otherwise for a stream of Christianity that has its foundations in the promise of Jesus to pour out his Spirit on all flesh to facilitate the task of worldwide mission.

The advent of electronic communication, for such evangelically minded Christians as Pentecostals, is a paramount event in human history that offers the ability to transmit the voice and visual image of the preacher in fulfillment of the mandate to reach the farthest parts of the world with the gospel. Thus, these contemporary Pentecostals regularly use radio and television; they circulate their sermons and programs through the wide distribution of CDs, DVDs, and publications. In recent years, some Pentecostal leaders like Ghana's Mensa Otabil of the International Central Gospel Church have even developed their own daily Bible reading notes, which are sold by street hawkers, fuel-filling station shops, and shopping malls in urban centers. The point is that the leadership of contemporary Pentecostals extensively uses modern media, and the internet has been embraced as a divinely inspired breakthrough in contemporary mission endeavors. It has become common for their leaders to sign off radio, television, or even actual church services and revival meetings with direct appeals to patrons, requesting them to stay connected through the internet. The usual catchphrase is "We are on the internet," followed by a reference to the internet address.

The churches we are concerned with in this chapter belong to a new stream of global Pentecostalism that shares the following features:

A charismatic and often well-educated, gifted, articulate, and professional leadership;

Mostly urban-centered mega-size congregations that appeal to an upwardly mobile youth and, linked to this, fashion-conscious and relaxed dress codes for members;

Worship styles that use contemporary music and musical instruments and that are pneumatic, exuberant, affective, emotionally laden, expressive, and dynamic;

An internationalism that is evident in the names, the choice of religious symbolism, the worldwide missionary peregrinations of the leadership, and the establishment of transnational networks, including the formation of foreign branches;

The preaching of a Christian message that directly addresses contemporary concerns of upward mobility; seizing social, political, and economic opportunities; and the application of certain social and biblical principles for the realization of success in this life;

Active evangelism and a theology of dominion in which the Christian is taught
  to take authority in Christ to dominate and influence his or her environment; and
Innovative uses of modern media technologies such as interactive internet
  websites and the use of PowerPoint in preaching and, related to that, extensive and evangelistic uses of media for advertising religious programs
  and mediating religious services and supernatural power.

The level of sophistication in these movements, as far as internet usage is
concerned, includes procedures for the born-again and Holy Spirit baptism experiences, healing, and payment of tithes and offerings. The work of the Spirit is
important in Pentecostal definitions of faith and understandings of community.
It is the shared experiences of the Spirit that give Pentecostalism its unique character. So this is a "movement of the Spirit," and when spirits move, they need to be
embodied in the process of religious communication. This need for embodiment
explains the importance of the media to Pentecostal religion. Thus, Pentecostals
realized the potential of media early and quickly seized the opportunities they
offer for mediating supernatural experiences. Today, even the cardinal Pentecostal phenomenon of "speaking in tongues" is used for purposes other than prayer,
such as in recorded gospel music, cell phone ringtones, and prayers delivered and
appropriated over internet sources.

Spirit, Mission, and Media

Television transformed the media landscape when it was launched in the early
1960s but the internet has been revolutionary. The interactive potential of
computer-mediated communication, Lorne D. Dawson (2005) has pointed out,
gives it an advantage in mediating religious experience over conventional broadcast media. Indeed, there is no medium that has promoted religious communication, globalization, and pluralism more than the World Wide Web has done since
its inception in the early 1990s. Its added resources of social media such as Facebook and Twitter, as well as blogs, have widened the scope of usage, reach, and
excitement of the internet. The internet had by the beginning of the new millennium facilitated the use of related mobile devices such as cell phones, Sidekicks,
and IP phones. John Palfrey and Urs Gasser (2008) draw attention to how these
electronic technological devices do not just make phone calls but also send text
messages, surf the net, and download music. We are living in a technological age
in which individuals, companies, corporations, religious figures, and religious
communities and their activities have to be represented on the internet for them
to count as important.

In relation to our present task, the internet, it has to be noted, has transformed religion to the extent where priests, pastors, imams, rabbis, gurus, and

other religious functionaries now reach their faithful through blogs (Palfrey and Gasser 2008). Because spirits and spiritual resources are now mediated through the internet, African charismatic pastors tell those who attend church, "We are on the internet." Pastors who write are wont to add, "My books and sermons are there, too, and so if you need counseling, you know where to go." This use of the media, especially for religious purposes, has proved to be particularly significant as the public face of contemporary Pentecostal Christianity. There exists some affinity between Pentecostalism as a Spirit-inspired religion and media because spirits do not usually operate in a vacuum. Pentecostals belong to ecclesial communities in which experiences of the Holy Spirit are valued, cultivated, and very actively promoted as normative in worship and religious behavior. Thus, it is not uncommon for the Holy Spirit to take hold of somebody in Pentecostal worship and mediate through that individual "graces" such as prophecies, visions, or revelations.

Negotiating one's way through the internet is called "surfing." Elena Larsen (2004) notes that for "religion surfers"—many of whom may also be religious—the internet could be useful as a supplemental tool for the enhancement of faith, but it is also helpful for those who feel outside of mainstream religious groups. The internet has redistributed the sources of religious authority and power, and Pentecostalism in particular is a religion that appeals greatly to people who have lost their sense of denominational loyalty to historic traditions. Thus, in their quest to appeal to both insiders and outsiders, Pentecostals have taken control of cyberspace to stay in touch with not only their members but also those looking for new religious spaces to anchor their souls. They simultaneously mediate their brand of open spirituality for the consumption of denominationally disenchanted persons outside their weekly captive constituencies. All this is based on their simple desire "to make disciples of all nations," and there are a lot of potential disciples available on the internet. It does not mean that the historic mission denominations cannot be found on the internet. They are, but in the case of Africa, it is the Holy Spirit–driven movements that have taken full advantage of the potentials of computer-mediated communication as a non-negotiable part of religious faith and practice.

Religion Online and Online Religion

The speed and extent to which the internet has been embraced by a wide diversity of people within the relatively short period of its existence are unparalleled in human history (Dawson and Cowan 2004). Christopher Helland (2004) notes how when the World Wide Web was still relatively new and uncharted, organized religion was encouraged to secure a presence on the internet or risk losing the chance of keeping in constant touch with its followers. Some use the internet for ignoble purposes, and already the world of clinical psychology has to deal with situations in which people are addicted to the internet in the same way that others may be hooked on alcohol or hard drugs. Critics have therefore denounced the internet as a "de-humanizing medium" and a threat to "real" community and communication. The information superhighway, they warn, "isolate[s] individuals from real life," from themselves, and from their families (Dawson and Cowan 2004). Christian advocates of internet use for religious purposes, on the other hand, promote it as media brought into being by God for the expansion of his work and the influence of the church (Campbell 2003). In the words of one African pastor, "All over the world, the Spirit has been moving, and today he is online."

In the study of computer-mediated communication, scholars propose that we distinguish between religion online and online religion. Religion online describes the provision of information about religious groups. This information may usually be placed on the internet by persons or organizations that have something to say about religion, although they themselves may not be practitioners. Those who put religion online have no obligation to promote or defend religious values. Religion may therefore appear on the internet simply as another news item. Online religion, on the other hand, invites surfers to actually participate in religious activities. Here, religious organizations or their representatives deliberately put religious information online and invite interested members of the public to visit designated websites for all kinds of religious encounters. Glen Young (2004) explains the distinction as follows:

> Because it provides information about religion, religion online makes primary reference to offline, pre-existing religious traditions and institutions. Online religion, which involves participation in religious activity, refers to the online environment itself as the primary context of that activity.

Most of what we describe regarding contemporary Pentecostals and their use of the internet amounts to "online religion" because they use the internet to serve their own purposes. For example, on the websites of the major African churches here, there are not only live church services but provision for donations, tithes, and offerings. The lines of demarcation between religion online and online religion could be very thin indeed. Hence, religion on the internet, Young explains, "includes a multiplicity of activities that fall at various places along the spectrum that extends between information and participation." He continues:

> If religion online and online religion are treated as two theoretical end points, then the issues of information provision versus religious participation and primary reference to offline verses online activity can be understood as two axes which extend between them.

Throughout his essay referenced here, Young adduces evidence, albeit from the Western context, to indicate that religion online and online religion can be seen to coexist within Christianity on the internet. In Africa, as I have noted elsewhere, the contemporary Pentecostals are clearly in the lead when it comes to online religious activities (Asamoah-Gyadu 2007). The websites of Pentecostal "big men," as Rosalind Hackett (2009) designates the leadership of contemporary Pentecostal churches, "are designed to convey to the world that their religion is empowered and empowering, enriched and enriching, healed and healing, protected and protecting, connected and connecting." The website, she continues, "can situate the Pentecostal CEO squarely at the heart of a huge religious empire, whose multilayered complexity he apparently masterminds with ease."

Through internet resources, which are combinations of online Pentecostalism and Pentecostalism online activities, the churches in this study attempt to "sacralize" cyberspace by using it as a medium for the work of the Spirit. They do so in the power of the Spirit and thereby help turn the hearts, minds, and energies of their youthful patrons and members away from dangerous and demonic sites toward those sites where Christ and the power of his Spirit may be encountered. "We are on the internet" is how the presence of these Spirit-inspired churches invite people for internet-based spiritual encounters. Typically, the theological idea is that nothing that God has created must be considered unclean, as Peter was reminded through a vision in the Acts of the Apostles (Acts 10: 9ff.). So, although some may be using the internet for evil and morally reprehensible purposes—such as the so-called *sakawa* phenomenon in Ghana, in which foreigners are lured into shady contract deals and marriages—the Pentecostals think that that ephemeral space could be "baptized" to serve the purposes of the God who is believed to have created it.

Pentecostalism, Media, and Dominion

Contemporary Pentecostals in particular, we have noted, are guided by a dominion religious orientation in which the media are expected to be reclaimed for the purposes of religion. The internet is one of such media that needs "deliverance" from the custody of those believed to be representing the Devil on it. Viewers and listeners are invited to visit websites where they can listen to or follow live services, download motivational messages, read church newsletters, request for special prayers, or fulfill tithing obligations. Following Peter Horsfield (2008), "media" are understood here not simply as instruments for carrying fixed messages but as "sites where construction, negotiation, and reconstruction of cultural meaning takes place in an ongoing process of maintenance and change of cultural structures, relationships, meanings, and values." Many of these interactions take place through the different communication and interactive options available on the internet.

For the contemporary Pentecostal movement, the media offer something much more than just serving as an instrument for evangelization or mission. This is a movement that believes it has been called to literally dominate or occupy global space. One contemporary Pentecostal pastor in Ghana, for example, identifies completely with the slogan of the sports manufacturing giant Adidas, "Impossible Is Nothing," which has been adopted by his church. In the words of this pastor:

> Impossibility should be ruled out of your vocabulary.... We have the mandate to change our environment by speaking the word of faith. . . . We have the mandate to set the oppressed free and our boldness in the exercise of authority is crucial to the blessing of humanity. (Eastwood 2004)

In keeping with this dominion theology, Pastor Matthew Ashimolowo's Kingsway International Christian Church advertises itself on the internet as a church that is "Raising Champions and Taking Territories;" Otabil's ICGC says it is "Raising Leaders, Shaping Vision and Influencing Society through Christ." The theology of dominion is therefore important for understanding the extensive appropriation of modern media technologies such as the internet by the movements under study here. The matter of their religious emphasis is succinctly articulated by André Corten and Ruth Marshall-Fratani (2001) as they compare the religious orientation of contemporary Pentecostals and their conservative evangelical compatriots of the early to mid-twentieth century:

> [Believers] no longer retreat among themselves in order to maintain the purity of their beliefs and their moral rigor. . . . Salvation is now resolutely this-worldly, and the evidence of new life has become as much material as spiritual. . . . [The] notion of transformation has been broadened to include the possibility of material change in everyday life. . . . Biblical verses mixed with popular self-help discourses exhort converts to identity the sources of their frustration and suffering and embark on a process of continual self-overcoming. The image of salvation at the heart of this process increasingly means upward mobility and personal success.

Contemporary Pentecostal theology, as pointed out in this quotation, is oriented toward physical and spiritual dominance of public space, influence of society, modernity, globalization, and prosperity in both its spiritual and physical senses. Spiritually, every power is expected to be brought under the control of the one Holy Spirit of Christ, and physically, Pentecostal presence is expected to be felt in education, sports, banking and finance, politics, recreation, and international relations. This is a religion that promotes upward mobility, sometimes even doing so unashamedly in secular tones and categories. Its prosperity theology has a very materialistic dimension in addition to whatever may be defined as spiritual prosperity. To that end, the media, especially the internet, which is now available even on cell phones and other devices, offer the means by which these aims and deliberate search for global relevance, material success, upward mobility, and religious empire-building may be realized.

This is well evidenced by an electronic mail message that I received in March 2010 from the General Secretary of the Royalhouse Chapel International. Royalhouse, popularly *Ahenfie* (palace of kings), is one of the mega-size contemporary Pentecostal churches in Ghana. The email was about the redesigning of the church's website, which had been redundant for quite some time. The exciting tone of the message was indicative of the central role that the internet has come to play in contemporary Pentecostal religion. The relevant portion of the message read:

> Praise God! I write to inform you of a new website for Royalhouse Chapel (RCI Missions) in the UK. It also has links to all our sister churches which have websites, and so you will find it quite useful indeed as a one-stop place where the Royalhouse Chapel family can be accessed. We are at present slowly but steadfastly updating the website, so do not worry if you do not get all the information you expect to see. Though not a sophisticated website, but rather a simply constructed one, the aim is to deliver a user-friendly, informative, and exciting website employing cutting-edge 21st-century ministry technology with enhanced consumer friendliness. We aim to have useful features such as live video and audio podcasts, possibly online marriage and general counseling with the possibility of a virtual cyber church once we are through with it!

The references to "user-friendly information," an "informative . . . and exciting website employing cutting-edge 21st-century ministry technology with enhanced consumer friendliness," and the offer of "live video and audio podcasts," including online marriage counseling services, are very intriguing. They serve to outline the very innovative ways in which the new churches may be using internet resources as tools for ministry. These are churches that have proven exceptionally attractive to Africa's upwardly mobile youth, partly on account of the ways in which they have come to terms with modern technology. Major aspects of the social and religious lives of these young people are mediated by digital technologies. It must therefore not surprise us that the new churches have been keener to use the internet for religious purposes than their historic mission compatriots.

On the extensive use of the internet by the new churches, consider the case of the Lighthouse Chapel International, which is representative of what could be gleaned from the web pages of these Pentecostals. Bishop Dr. Dag Heward-Mills, founder and Presiding Bishop of the Lighthouse Chapel International, uses the media extensively, and the internet constitutes one of the church's major media resources (Sam 2010). He has one of the largest new Pentecostal churches in Ghana, with an auditorium that can hold 5,000 people, and about four other chapels in the same location in Accra. In addition, Dag Heward-Mills has opened branches in many African, European, and North American countries. Unlike other churches of this type, Bishop Heward-Mills is gradually building a denomination in which all local and foreign branches are centrally administered from the headquarters in Accra known as *Quodesh,* meaning "the hill of the Lord." LCI has different websites, including one called the *Good Shepherd,* which was created to enable pastors and lay leaders to access information from the headquarters in Accra.

The daghewardmills.org website provides up-to-date information on the daily activities of the Presiding Bishop and access to all his messages. This includes live presentations of messages. He is also on Facebook where his books—consisting almost entirely of his sermons—are advertised. A number of LCI member churches also run their own websites, and so the very thriving Tema church has set up the website www.temacathedral.lighthousechapel.org. There is also a special website for Bishop Heward-Mills' wife Adelaide: www.firstlady.lighthousechapel.org. Here, members and supporters can follow the activities of the "first lady" of the church. Additionally, there is a separate one for youth: www.iamsaved.org.

KICC, ICGC, and LCI, together with the Nigerian-led God Embassy in the Ukraine, all host very flashy and informative websites with lots of moving graphics and tabs across the top that easily bring surfers up to date with all that is happening in any particular ministry. In almost all the cases, there is information on branches, intergenerational ministries focusing on children and youth, as well as gender-based or profession-based communities, and past and upcoming conferences and summits. Talking about current happenings within particular ministries, Otabil's ICGC has information and a slide show of its extra-religious activities, including an annual "Walk for Life" event used to raise funds for charitable causes. The annual walk goes through designated streets in Accra led by the General Overseer, Pastor Mensa Otabil himself. In some years, including 2011, he was joined by Matthew Ashimolowo and other leading charismatic pastors. Figures are hard to come by, but these are health walks that attract up to 5,000 persons and more who are either members of ICGC or some other church of Pentecostal persuasion.

The internet has therefore emerged as nothing less than a technological revolution, with Africa's contemporary Pentecostals seeing it as a "technological miracle" for the evangelization of the world. Thus, the Nigerian charismatic pastor and healing-miracle televangelist Chris Oyakhilome, of Christ Embassy Ministries based in South Africa, speaks of how Jesus Christ instructed him to "get on the internet" if he wanted to make the desired impact in ministry. Important items available at the websites of these mega-size contemporary Pentecostal churches, as I noted above, are the messages preached by the leaders. Whether it is Sunday Adelaja of God Embassy, Heward-Mills of Lighthouse, Otabil of Central Gospel, or Ashimolowo of KICC, it is possible not only to access previously preached sermons but also to tune in and listen to live messages during services. Bishop Agyin-Asare of the Word Miracle Church International (WMCI) in Ghana specializes in the ministry of miracles and travels around Africa and beyond as a modern-day Morris Cerullo or Reinhard Bonnke. WMCI proclaimed 2011 as the "Year of Divine Performance." Not only was this announced on the website (as most of the others also announce their annual themes), most importantly, there are messages that deal with the theme on the website. Additionally, there are also video recordings of some of the miracles accompanying Bishop Agyin-Asare's open-air crusades, including some from the largely Muslim city of Maduguri in Nigeria and Pakistan. For those who are unable to attend offline services, Bishop Agyin-Asare offers the benefit of receiving supernatural interventions mediated through the internet.

Social Media and Community

Cyberspace opportunities seized by contemporary Pentecostals include the more sophisticated social aspects that the younger generation has embraced with ease. Mensa Otabil uses Facebook and has a "public figure" page in which he provides inspirational messages to readers. Information from the site indicates that more than 20,000 people have commented on how helpful these devotional messages have been to them. Otabil updates this page regularly, and he offers similar devotional thoughts on Twitter, on which he has more than 1,500 followers. His popularity as a Christian charismatic figure is attested to by the fact that he has more than 4,000 friends on his Facebook page, with a backlog of friends who are unable to join because of the numbers seeking to do so! The same is true of Otabil's charismatic compatriot Matthew Ashimolowo, who is also not just on Facebook but uses Twitter as well; he has nearly 1,000 followers.

Rosalind Hackett (2009) has noted how increasing numbers of African Pentecostal ministries are developing websites as a major new interface for interacting not just with their membership but also with potential converts. Her observation on the relationship between these charismatic personalities and their web pages is an important one. This is what Hackett says with reference to Otabil in particular but that also is true of the rest:

> Just as the church and its various are centered on his charisma and popular sermons and broadcasts, so too is the website. Much more elaborate in its multi-media capabilities than its earlier incarnation, the images and themes convey a progressive religious organization.

The followers of these two charismatic personalities on Facebook and Twitter are representative of the pulling power that the charisma of these contemporary Pentecostal leaders gives them. Hackett (2009) concludes that the new media platform allows the Pentecostal leader to authenticate his authority through the use of testimonies, histories, and biblical passages that then "become both expressive and constitutive of his power." In addition to whatever else these new media have achieved for contemporary Pentecostals and their sophisticated charismatic leaders, new online and offline communities have been generated. This has helped the new churches to claim even more ground from the older historic mission churches in terms of influence and relevance.

Contemporary Pentecostalism and the Impact of the Internet

One way to appreciate the interface between contemporary Pentecostalism and the media is to consider the relationship from the perspective of African migrant Christian communities in Europe and the United States in particular. Heidi Campbell (2005) talks about how, through the internet, people seek to build social groups that challenge traditional ideas of community. Cyberspace presents enormous potential for the dissemination of religious ideas and the formation of new virtual religious communities. The element of "communing" is implied in the process and end of communication. The goal of communication, therefore, is partly the call to community. Most diasporic charismatic communities are of the contemporary Pentecostal type, and they rely on modern media resources to stay connected to events and their charismatic pastors in Africa.

Those who make up these new charismatic communities are people whose lives may be full of uncertainties due to immigration, health, marriage, and employment problems. Against the backdrop of an African worldview within which misfortune is often traced to the work of negative supernatural forces, such persons easily resort to religion for the diagnosis and resolution of their difficulties. Pentecostal religion, with its interventionist approach to Christianity, is thus a major source of hope and stability for many Africans living abroad. Hope is kept alive through the availability of internet sermons and other means of interaction in cyberspace. Cyberspace gives access to power, improves networking, and generates new following, and all these feed very much into the dominion theology of contemporary Pentecostalism.

To possess the powers that cyberspace offers, one must be able to go there. Such access springs in turn from the notion that there is power to be gained through cyberspace, making access to those powers for religious purposes fundamental to success (Jordan 1999). To properly appreciate Pentecostalism's love of technology, we must look beyond technology as something that has simply become part of modern ways of life. Contemporary Pentecostalism functions within a theology of dominion, as we have noted, and this translates into developing transnational networks for the churches and upward mobility and personal success for the membership. None of these is possible without access to the wider world of religion and business facilitated by the internet and available through computers, cell phones, and related equipment.

In my earlier study cited at the beginning of this chapter, for example, it was interesting and fascinating to see that whereas the historic mission churches used the internet in a limited way to talk about the historical importance and legacy of their churches, contemporary Pentecostals use the same medium in very evangelistic ways. At the website of Mensa Otabil's ICGC, for example, one can learn how to be born-again and, depending on your location, how to find a place of worship. At the time of my study, most historic mission church websites were either nonexistent, out of date, or simply filled with history, lengthy lists of bishops, and pictures of cathedrals and projects. If you contrast this approach with the fact that it is possible to listen to every single sermon preached by Heward-Mills of Lighthouse Chapel or Sunday Adelaja of God Embassy on their websites, then it tells you how slow the older churches have been to realize that media could serve as a powerful instrument of mission.

In the world of globalization, the media are a source of empowerment, and this comes from their primary function of communication. The power of communication is also linked to the power of control. What this means is that the more people read a charismatic pastor's publications or listen to his or her sermons, the more their life is shaped by the information received. In his book *Communication Power,* Manuel Castells (2009) argues that power is based on the control of communication and information, and communication power is at the heart of the structure and dynamics of society. The point is that by seizing the opportunities offered by the media, the new Pentecostal-Charismatic churches have been able to take control and exercise the power of religion in public spaces. The following observation by Marleen de Witte (2005) constitutes an apt summary of the overall influence and impact of charismatic religion on African public space because of the use of modern media:

> Having access to the means of representation, charismatic churches also influence the dominant modes of representation, the formats, styles and ways of framing in the public sphere. Charismatic styles of discourse and of worship have a large impact not only on other religions, but beyond institutionalized religion, on popular culture, entertainment, on public debate and opinion, and on politics. The emphasis on emotional expression, personal spiritual experience, and charismatic leadership links up easily with the formats of celebrity, show, and spectacle popular with the new, commercial media.

The new charismatic churches have indeed taken territories and raised champions—as KICC advertises itself—and are set to dominate the religious life of Africa for the foreseeable future. The media, which they use extensively, provide communication power—and "the most fundamental form of power lies in the ability to shape the human mind" (Castells 2009). The internet is perhaps the most audacious, fascinating, and exciting of the new forms of media available to the world today. Contemporary Pentecostals have acted to appropriate its benefits. Being on the internet is an indication that a person or institution "exists" and that they must be taken seriously. Thus, in African Christianity, the internet, as a modern communication medium, places the contemporary Pentecostal on the frontlines of religious expansion and influence.

Notes

1. For important studies, see Campbell 2005; Dawson and Cowan 2004; Mitchell and Marriage 2003: part 6, chapters 19–23.
2. For some studies, see Asamoah-Gyadu 2007; Hackett 2009.
3. For a useful collection of essays and some of the most important works on religion on the internet, see Højsgaard and Warburg 2005 and the bibliography accompanying the essays in the book.

References

Asamoah-Gyadu, J. Kwabena, 2007. "'Get on the Internet' Says the Lord: Religion, Cyberspace and Christianity in Contemporary Africa." *Studies in World Christianity* 13(3): 225–242.

Campbell, H. 2003. "Approaches to Religious Research in Computer-Mediated Communication." In *Mediating Religion: Conversations in Media, Religion and Culture,* edited by J. Mitchell and S. Marriage, 213–228. London: T & T Clark.

———. 2005. *Exploring Religious Communities Online: We Are on the Network.* New York: Peter Lang.

Castells, M. 2009. *Communication Power.* Oxford: Oxford University Press.

Corten, A., and R. Marshall-Fratani, eds. 2001. *Between Babel and Pentecost: Transnational Pentecostalism in Africa and Latin America.* Bloomington: Indiana University Press.

Dawson, L. L. 2005. "The Mediation of Religious Experience in Cyberspace." In *Religion and Cyberspace,* edited by M. T. Højsgaard and M. Warburg, 15–37. Abingdon, UK: Routledge.

Dawson, L. L., and D. Cowan, eds. 2004. *Religion Online. Finding Faith on the Internet.* New York. Routledge.

Eastwood, A. 2004. *The Workability of Faith.* Bolgatanga, Ghana: Desert Leaf Publications.

Hackett, R. I. J. 2009. "The New Virtual (Inter) Face of African Pentecostalism." *Society* 46: 496–503.

Hadden, J. K., and D. Cowan. 2000. "The Promised Land or Electronic Chaos?: Toward Understanding Religion on the Internet." In *Religion on the Internet: Research Prospects and Promises,* edited by J. K. Hadden and D. E. Cowan, 3–21 Amsterdam: Elsevier Science.

Helland, C. 2004. "Popular Religion and the World Wide Web: A Match Made in (Cyber) Heaven." In *Religion Online: Finding Faith on the Internet,* edited by L. L. Dawson and D. E. Cowan, 23–36. New York: Routledge.

Højsgaard, M. T., and M. Warburg, eds. 2005. *Religion and Cyberspace.* Abingdon, UK: Routledge.

Horsfield, P. 2008. "Media." In *Key Words in Religion, Media and Culture,* edited by D. Morgan, 111–122. New York: Routledge.

Jordan, T. 1999. *Cyberpower: The Culture and Politics of Cyberspace and the Internet.* London: Routledge.

Larsen, E. 2004. "Cyberfaith: How Americans Pursue Religion Online." In *Religion Online: Finding Faith on the Internet,* edited by L. L. Dawson and D. E. Cowan, 17–22. New York: Routledge.

Meyer, B. 2010. "Pentecostalism and Globalization" In *Studying Global Pentecostalism: Theories and Methods,* edited by A. Anderson, M. Bergunder, A. Droogers, and C. van der Laan, 113–130. Berkeley: University of California Press.

Mitchell, J., and S. Marriage, eds. 2003. *Mediating Religion: Conversations in Media, Religion and Culture.* London: T & T Clark.

Palfrey, J., and U. Gasser. 2008. *Born Digital: Understanding the First Generation of Digital Natives.* New York: Basic Books.

Sam, I. F. 2010. "Pentecostalism and Media in Ghana: The Media Ministry of the Lighthouse Chapel International." Unpublished Master of Theology thesis, Trinity Theological Seminary, Legon, Ghana.

Young, G. 2004. "Reading and Praying Online: The Continuity of Religion Online and Online Religion in Internet Christianity." In *Religion Online: Finding Faith on the Internet,* edited by L. L. Dawson and D. E. Cowan, 93–106. New York: Routledge.

9 Conveying Islam

Arab Islamic Satellite Channels as New Players

Ehab Galal

WITH THE LAUNCHING of Iqraa as the first Arab Islamic satellite channel in 1998, Islamic satellite channels were introduced as a new phenomenon in the North African and Arab media landscape. Since then, a range of Islamic satellite channels have been introduced by Arab businesspeople. The most well-known channels in the Arab North African countries include Iqraa, Al Majd and Alresalah, Al Nas, Al Rahma, and Azhari. These channels represent well-established business elites who, along with other new media actors, challenge the former media monopoly of the state. Although several of them are Saudi owned, like Iqraa, they reach the widespread Arab and North African audiences due to their transnational transmission and their use of standard Arabic. Because of this transnational reach and their Islamic ideological platform, these channels are a potential challenge to the North African Arab countries' state-controlled and secular public-service media. In this way, they seem to openly challenge national channels' priorities of religious issues and interpretations of religion's role in society by presenting Islam as the platform for all programs that are broadcast. In comparison, for Arab African countries, religion has had from the beginning an isolated place and limited time on national TV (Abu-Lughod 2005). Thus, satellite television, together with other new, border-crossing media such as the internet and the cell phone, has been part of bringing religion into the public sphere in the Arab world (Eickelman and Anderson 1999). Consequently, the Islamic channels do potentially contest the traditional players within the religious field by promoting an Islamic discourse and religious authorities that are not necessarily sanctioned or appreciated by the state or the traditional religious institutions.

Despite this possible undermining of the state as a media and religious actor, the new Islamic channels seem to be largely accepted by Arab African states. This raises questions of how these new Islamic channels relate to Arab African state(s) and what lies behind this seeming acceptance. In order to answer this question, I emphasize five aspects that I find crucial for understanding the relationship between Arab African states and the Islamic channels. First, the Islamic channels are, like other Arab satellite channels, the result of new developments within the political landscape based on close relations among economically, politically, and religiously new elites. Second, Arab African states, as well as the rest of the Arab world, are still institutionalizing new instruments to maintain control with new media, including Islamic channels. Third, the Islamic channels promote a seemingly apolitical and nonsectarian understanding of Islam. Fourth, the Islamic channels are to some degree in line with the religious establishment and/or with neo-liberal ideas about religious lifestyle and individualization rather than being revolutionary. Fifth, the Islamic channels offer a space for interpreting, negotiating, and coping with global conflicts and consequently contested relations with Western countries. Before elaborating on each of these five aspects, I present a short account of other key premises for understanding the field of Islamic channels in Arab African countries.

The Media Landscape of Arab Islamic Channels

The media landscape within Arab African countries has changed considerably during the last 20 years due to satellite technology. Not only has today's access to more than 730 Arab satellite channels increased the supply massively, but it has also created a media landscape characterized by multitude, diversity, specialization, and fragmentation. Thus, it is no longer sufficient to include just the TV production or broadcasting of the country or region in question, if one wants to understand the influence of television. Rather, the Islamic channels reaching across national and regional borders seem to structure their own mediated field of Islam. From interviews with television audiences in Egypt,[1] it has become clear that they do not choose Islamic television because of its national embeddedness. Instead, audiences generally combine national and transnational broadcasting, and when it comes to Islamic TV, this seems even more predominant. This may be explained in part by the development within Islamic satellite television and in part by the nature of Islamic TV, which I shall return to in later sections. Not only was the Saudi-owned Iqraa the first and only Arab Islamic satellite channel for several years, but it also won widespread popularity due to the use of well-known former Egyptian actresses. They embodied the pious Muslim after having exchanged the fame and glamour of popular film for the hijab or headscarf, indexing their piety (Galal 2010). At the same time, the studios of Iqraa were placed in different Arab countries, involving more Arab nationalities in production. Not least by using Egyptians, the channel was capitalizing on the general idea that Egyptian Arabic and their use of modern standard Arabic is easily understood and digestible by all Arabs—and so is their relatively moderate interpretation of Islam. Likewise, while the Al Majd group of channels was established in 2002, in 2011 around 45 percent of the channels' production was produced by

Egyptians in Egypt. Despite the channel's being owned by a Saudi businessperson, almost half of the production and staff are Egyptian.[2] The same goes for other Islamic channels such as Huda and Iqraa International (in English), where most programs are produced by Egyptians in Egypt. It was not until eight years after the launching of Iqraa (in Arabic) that an almost 100 percent national production of a privately owned Islamic satellite channel was born. Hence, channels like Al Nas, Azhari, and Al Rahma are Egyptian companies. However, they are also dependent on foreign investors, many of whom are Gulf Arabs. In general, the Islamic channels are transmitted via different satellites such as Intelsat 10 to African countries, Intelsat 9 to North America, and Hotbird to Europe. In other words, the Islamic satellite channels are characterized by being produced by a majority of Egyptians and financed by businesspeople with a dominant influence of Saudis, while the target group consists of Muslims all over the world who understand Arabic.

To understand the development within the Islamic media landscape, it is also important to understand that during the last 30 to 40 years, Arab states and countries have undergone processes of the Islamization of national identity discourses, educational systems, and several other state branches (Eickelman and Anderson 1999). Also, the media audiences have changed both in relation to expectations for media supply and in relation to an increasing individualization of religious identity (Hoover and Clark 2002). Finally, the media are not only an instrument in local, national, or regional politics, but they have become an instrument in global geopolitics, too.

Having stressed these premises, I now turn to the five factors that explain the relatively uncontroversial relationship between Arab African states and the new Islamic channels.

Media as an Instrument of the New Elites

To understand the relationship between the state and the Islamic channels, I believe we need to explore the Arab African media landscape as something that reflects the changes caused by division and reorganization among the ruling elites, rather than looking at media content as something to trigger political change. Hence, I suggest a research perspective in which political life is changing media as opposed to understanding media as changing politics (cf. Wolfsfeld 1997). I do not deny that the media can help to put pressure on those who are in power and force them to change their policy. However, what I want to emphasize here is how the ruling Arab elites' political and economic alliances and priorities influence the shape and orientation of Arab media. Within this perspective, the program content is the result of political interests and agendas that reflect patterns of elite ownership and control. Television is an instrument of the elite for negotiating political power and change. Political actors who want a change of policy can use the critical media coverage to achieve space for negotiations in relation to other members of the elite. The widespread elite divisions and the political uncertainty within several Arab governments provide an argument for understanding the Arab media as a tool for competing political forces (Sakr 2001). This is mainly due to the intense internal and external pressures on the governments to adopt new policies. Such pressures come respectively from the national populations and from Western countries, international financial institutions such as the World Bank, global conflicts, and so forth. Consequently, the change of policy is not the result of an apparently liberal public sphere, just as there are only a few signs of a positive development of liberal institutions and no facilitation of lifting the control over free opinion formation in Arab countries (Sakr 2001). The media's critique of state politics is still subject to strong political control.

The consequence of this perspective is that satellite television does not only count as a potential threat to the state, since it might be more difficult to control, but becomes an opportunity and instrument for new elites to participate in the struggle for power. Also, the Islamic satellite channels, which have increased considerably in numbers since 1998, are players within this political field. As an overall rule, the Islamic satellite channels are funded and launched by Arab businesspeople, business consortia, or finance companies. The channels are a result of wealthy interests, which also means that they are expected to provide some form of economic returns. Let me give a short introduction to the most important players:

Iqraa was the first Islamic Arabic satellite channel, and it started in 1998. As part of the channels bouquet of ART (Arab Radio and Television Network), it is owned by the Saudi billionaire Sheikh Saleh Kamel. ART was established in 1993 with its headquarters in Italy. ART set off with a few thematic channels, including a movie channel, a music channel, and a sports channel. The idea of establishing a religious channel in 1998 held on to the thematic concept to which ART was already accustomed and had the expertise.

The second Islamic channel, Al Majd, was launched in May 2002 and later extended with a package of channels under the general name Al Majd. Al Majd channels are based in the free media centers in Dubai, Egypt, and Saudi Arabia, and the owner is a Saudi consortium that also owns, for instance, Meridian Hotel in Mecca.

Alresalah (The Message), launched in March 2006, is owned by the Saudi Prince al-Walid ben Talal, who is the executive director of Kingdom Holding Company; that company owns Rotana Media Group, which has investments in media, music, hotels, and travel. In November 2013, 20th Century Fox, with Rupert Murdoch as chairman and CEO, purchased a 19 percent stake in Rotana.[3]

In these three cases, the owners are Saudi, but we can find the same tendency in other Arab countries where businesspeople have established Islamic satellite

TV channels, such as Al Rahma TV and Azhari TV in Egypt. Al Afsi was established by the businessman and the Kuwaiti religious scholar Mshari ibn Rashid al-Afsi and was launched in 2005. Tiba TV was initiated by a Kuwaiti investor in 2007. Al Najah started in 2006 as an investment consulting TV channel, and after a short while it switched to a religious TV channel. The channel is owned by the company Al-Najah, whose owner is a Jordanian businessman, Ghazi Mahfuz. Al Nas TV, Al Hafez TV, Al Khalijia TV, and Al Siha wa al-Jamal TV are all owned by the international company Al-Baraheen, which has offices in both Riyadh in Saudi Arabia and in Cairo. The company is owned by Ali Sad and Ben Kadasa, who are both Saudi businessmen. All four channels are Islamic. While Al Khalijia in the beginning broadcast music videos and golf, it changed in 2007 into a family based, social-religious channel to share pain and hope with all Muslims, as it is written on the channel's website.

The four channels Iqraa, Alresalah, Al Majd, and Al Nas are often referred to as the most popular among the Islamic satellite channels (al-Dagher 2007; Amin 2007; Salem 2007). All four were, as stated, launched by Saudi business empires or billionaires as part of larger business empires that also house several media and other forms of investment. Hence, the Islamic channels can be seen as a business, among other business interests. To invest in an Islamic channel is to invest in yet another audience. Supporting this argument is the fact that the Islamic channel is often only one among other non-Islamic channels within a media empire. For example, in the summer of 2008, ART—which launched Iqraa—had 21 thematic channels before they sold all their sports channels to Al Jazeera.[4] Thus, a satellite bouquet might hold several movie channels, sports channels, cartoon channels, and news channels in addition to Islamic channels.

The inclusion of the religious channels among these different thematic channels emphasizes the strategic element of launching the religious channels. As the establishment of satellite television in general (Sakr 2001, 2006, 2007), they are the result of both political and economic interests. For the business part, the channels can be seen as a tool for business empires to advertise other products and to advertise themselves.[5] At the same time, by launching a satellite channel, they portray themselves as reliable business partners. This self-promotion is no less powerful if the channel is Islamic. Second, the satellite channels are an element in the interaction between economic and political elites in Arab countries (Sakr 2007: 6–7). Thus, the owners of Iqraa, Alresalah, and Al Majd all have good relations with the Saudi royal family. Also, the channels might be used by the owner to try to establish himself as not only a reliable business partner but as a potential political player on the national political scene.

Motives behind launching a satellite channel therefore involve both making money and obtaining political influence. To launch a satellite channel is to place oneself within the established economic and political field. One might add that the launch of Islamic channels may also be linked to the owners' own religious values that they wish to promote.

Maintaining Control within a Changed Arab Media Landscape

The development of transnational Arab television does not prevent Arab African states from trying to keep up their traditional control with the media. Thus, at a meeting in Cairo in February 2008, Arab information ministers adopted a new charter entitled "Suggested Guidelines and Principles for Organizing Satellite TV in the Arab World." It contains a number of requirements for satellite TV channels:

> [They should] not offend the leaders or national and religious symbols in the Arab world;
>
> [They should] not damage social harmony, national unity, public order, or traditional values;
>
> [They should] conform with the religious and ethical values of Arab society and take account of its family structure;
>
> [They should] refrain from broadcasting anything which calls into question God, the monotheistic religions, the prophets, sects, or symbols of the various religious communities; and
>
> [They should] protect Arab identity from the harmful effects of globalization. (cf. al-Tahhawi 2008a)

The Charter can be seen as the Arab states' attempt to maintain or regain influence on a media development that they have not had the same ability to control as they had with national media. Since satellite technology makes it possible to broadcast from other countries over long distances and with relatively simple technology (a satellite dish and a receiver), satellite television is much more difficult to control than national TV. However, Arab states have engaged various strategies in an effort to control satellite TV. One strategy was to ban private ownership of satellite dishes, which was a previous Saudi strategy (Sakr 2001). Another strategy was to enable a liberalization of the Arab media market and thus invite Arab satellite channels to establish themselves in an Arab country instead of in Europe, from where they were broadcasting. One tool was the "free media cities,"[6] which provided shelter and certain economic and technological advantages for the satellite companies but at the same time also created the basis for some government control over the transmission by the channels placed within these media cities (Sakr 2001).

The abovementioned Charter confirms a third strategy, which particularly affects the channels established within the Arab world but also might affect channels that broadcast via an Arab satellite. According to the Charter, the violations of the above rules will gradually lead to sanctions. First, the channel will get a warning, then equipment will be confiscated, and finally, the station's

broadcasting license will be terminated (al-Tahhawi 2008a). Regarding the channels that are transmitting via an Arab-owned satellite, Arabsat or Nilesat, their
license can be revoked by the owner of the satellite. That means Egypt can with-
draw the permission to broadcast via the Nilesat satellite owned by Egypt. Soon
after the adoption of the Charter, this became reality. Thus, on April 1, 2008,
Egypt revoked the license of the Arab news channel Al-Hiwar (Dialogue) that
transmitted from London. The blocking of Al-Hiwar followed the repeal of
two other channels' broadcasting licenses on Nilesat satellite in February 2008:
the Iraqi channel Al-Zawraa and the religious channel Al Baraka (al-Tahhawi
2008b). In May 2010, Al Rahma, another privately owned religious channel in
Egypt, had its license revoked as well. According to observers, the revocations of
these four satellite channels' broadcasting licenses was a direct result of the new
charter (al-Tahhawi 2008b). According to Al-Hiwar, Al-Zawraa, and Al Baraka,
they have not been given any official explanation by Nilesat of why precisely these
channels were stripped of their broadcasting licenses. However, Al Rahma got
an official explanation. The channel's license was lifted due to a French protest
against one of Al Rahma's programs that France considered anti-Semitic. According to my interviewees in Egypt, Al Rahma later regained its license and
was one of the most popular channels among viewers of Islamic channels in
Egypt. As a result of the Arab Spring and since the military-backed protests that
ousted former Muslim Brotherhood–affiliated president Mohamed Morsi on
June 30, 2013, four of the most popular religious channels in Egypt and North
Africa were suspended on July 3, 2013, for their alleged association with the former Egyptian president Morsi's government. The four channels were Al Hafez,
Al Nas, Al Rahma, and the Muslim Brotherhood channel Misr 25. A few days
later, two other news and talk show channels, Al Jazeera Egypt and Al Fareen,
were closed as well, and Al Jazeera Egypt was forced to broadcast from Qatar.
Although Al Fareen had been transmitting anti–Muslim Brotherhood programming for months, it had also criticized the leaders of the new government.
Al Fareen was closed down during Morsi's tenure on June 27 2013.[7]

 The point is that Arab states still use the resources available to limit or control the media stream, and with the Charter, the grounds for a common Arab
policy have been formulated trying to avoid internal rivalry within Arab countries (al-Tahhawi 2008a). So the Charter reflects media political realities in the
Arab world. This reality has contributed to setting the framework for the Arab
religious media landscape. Both Arab and Western critics suggest that the above-
mentioned guidelines and principles violate freedom of speech and freedom of
information and that they primarily serve the purpose of limiting the political
opposition (see, e.g., al-Tahhawi 2008a). In my view, another important point is
that Arab information ministers in this way promote and restrict specific cultural resources and identities on Arabic satellite TV. Thus, the Charter shows

how Arab states promote the protection of religious and family values. But how should we understand this focus on religion, when, for instance, Egypt, until recently, refused to broadcast Christian Coptic Orthodox religious channels on Nilesat, arguing that religious channels encourage sectarian strife? The Egyptian government has generally tackled this threat by virtually eliminating the Coptic Church and Coptic religious programs from national television (Abu-Lughod 2005).

Thus, religious values are protected, whereas religious channels are forbidden and Islamic channels are accepted. This apparent paradox is related to Islam representing the majority religion and to the Islamization of Arab countries where Islam has become embedded in a generalized national and regional identity discourse. Islam is presented as more than "just" religion. This brings us to further characteristics of the Islamic channels.

What Characterizes the Islamic Channels?

What makes a satellite channel Islamic? There are several reasons to take this issue seriously. It is not only a question of defining an analytical concept that makes it possible to analyze the topic at hand. The definition of Islamic satellite television is a political and religious question that both those persons behind the channels and the state may have and share an interest in defining.

Let me stress two points here. First, the defined goals of the channels are indeed broad and generalized to a degree that they hardly differ from the above-mentioned requirements of the state. Second, the channels try to legitimate themselves by doing everything "the Islamic way" without being sectarian.

THE GOALS OF THE CHANNELS

If we look at the channels' defined goals as they present themselves on their websites or in their programming, it is clear that the TV programs are produced with *an Islamic frame of reference.*

Like other popular Islamic channels, such as Al Nas, Al Rahma, Alresalah, and Al Majd, they define their purpose with very general statements about Islam as a universal value that unites all Muslims. The channels consider themselves facilitators of knowledge about religious, cultural, social, educational, economic, and political issues based on the Quran and the Prophet Muhammad's Sunna. Their goal is to strengthen Muslims' belonging to "the Arabo-Islamic nation and culture." Thus, they refer to an idea of an imagined Arab community defined by a common Arab culture and a common religious identity as Muslims. With the intention of strengthening this identity, the channel wants to convey knowledge of the Arabic language and the Arabo-Islamic civilization's contribution to history.

By highlighting terms like *tolerance, moderate Islam, positive interaction, nationally,* and *internationally,* Iqraa also expresses a desire to correct the Western image of Muslims. While building bridges between different Muslim countries and other cultures, the channel supports the idea of a moderate course (*al-wasatiyya*) of Islam.

Al Nas writes on its website that it wants to serve the Muslim *umma* (global community of Muslims) and pass on knowledge about religion and life. The goal is to cultivate the Muslim and Arab *umma* in religion, in society, and in health without broadcasting anything that is contrary to the principles of Islam and Islamic behavior. On Alresalah's website, it is stressed that the channel is addressing

> all the Arab Muslims who are moderate in their Islamic beliefs, and those who are always proud of their religion. It is not targeting the extremists, who also might find interesting programs. It is not targeting those who don't believe in moral ethics. [The linguistic uncertainty is quoted with loyalty to the original.][8]

Again, moderate and nonextremist aspects are highlighted in full conformity with what is written in the Arabic version of the website. At the same time, all the channels emphasize that they produce and transmit quality programs to the entire family. None of these channels thus address a specific belonging to a direction or Islamic school; on the contrary, they stress that they address all Muslims—"the Islamic community."

"THE ISLAMIC WAY"

To come closer to this representation of a universal "Islamic way of being," it is important to be aware of the relationship between the owners and the content of the channels. Being funded and launched by Arab businesspeople, business consortia, or finance companies, the Islamic satellite channels have not been initiated directly by religious groups or organizations. This is otherwise the case for many websites and various forms of Islamic pamphlet literature with more explicit ties to various religious groups. While many Arab Christian channels are launched by churches or religious groups, the Islamic channels do not proclaim belonging to a specific interpretation of Islam or school of thought.

However, this does not mean that the channels do not differ in religious interpretation and ideology, and they might also have hidden political as well as religious goals. Most of the channels are Sunni Muslim, some of whom have connections to Sufism. Others are Salafi with close ties to the Saudi religious establishment. A minority of the channels are Shi'ite (i.e., Al Kawthar TV, Al Anwar TV, and Ahlulbayt TV). However, they formulate a similar strategy as those of the Sunni Muslim channels. For instance, the channel Ahlulbayt TV explains that its purpose is to deliver

> the true voice of Islam through the teachings of the Holy Quran, the Holy Prophet, and his immaculate Household. While maintaining neutrality and not subscribing to any political, governmental, or special interest group, our only pursuit is the education of our viewers and the acceptance of our Lord.[9]

By presenting such generalized goals without specifying any ideology or interpretation, the channels construct or support an idea of universal Islamic ideas and values. While the interpretations vary—even among different programs on the same channel—the channels stress a view that there exists an Islamic perspective on all aspects of life. As Tash (2004) argues in an article about Islamic media, they are "a comprehensive and total system" (3). As such they cannot be reduced to representing one religious moral order among others (for instance, Christianity). They are the majority norm.

In Line with the Religious Establishment and/or with Neo-Liberal Ideas

Being business-minded, having close contacts with the political and religious establishment, and supporting a nonideological but individualized and all-comprehensive Islamic identity seem to place the Islamic channels in the center of and in full agreement with developments in the Arab world. There seems to be no opposition between the generalized values promoted by the channels and the requirements formulated by the information ministers. And if there are some, the states now have the possibility to restrict their transmission, as was the case with Al-Hiwar, which was closed down because it broadcast an interview with a prominent member of the Muslim Brotherhood.

At least three characteristics of the Islamic channels can be seen as the precondition for the friendly relationship between the channels and the states: *compartmentalized, commoditized,* and *state-promoted Islam.*

The channels are *compartmentalized* because they represent a specialized set of channels among other channels. As such, it is possible to argue that the Islamic channels, despite their claim of being all-comprehensive, reproduce secular ideas of different spheres in society. They might be easier to accept by the state, since watching them is a personal choice of the audience members who can choose among many nonreligious channels.

This is further supported by the *commoditization* of Islam, which the channels promote. Though religion is a somewhat different topic than those of the previous, purely entertainment-based channels—for example, those ART had operated for some years—the choice of promoting a religious channel can be understood as an expression of an increasing trend that presents religion, including Islam, as a consumer and entertainment product, which it pays to produce.

Religion can be brilliant entertainment while complying with the need for iden-tity among people in a globalizing world (Clark 2007). Looking into the pro-grams available on Islamic TV, one will find that many programs are using global models of popular entertainment.

Last, but not least, this individualized and commoditized Islam goes hand in hand with a *state-promoted Islam.* For instance, the Saudi government wants to promote a conservative re-Islamization that goes well with the individualized Is-lam promoted by private and economically liberal media houses (Roy 2004). On the one hand, we have a political-religious approach to Islamic mission (da'wa) dominated by a Saudi Salafi tradition, and on the other hand, we have the priva-tization of religion through economic liberalism, which emphasizes individual re-Islamization and various social dignitaries as a model. These two tendencies of Islamization find common ground around their opposition to political and radi-cal Islam. This is illustrated by Al Majd's proclaimed wish to get young people away from extremism.

Where some channels, like Al Majd, lean toward a state loyalist, regional (Gulf States), conservative re-Islamization, others, like Iqraa and Alresalah, to a higher degree lean toward promoting the privatization of Islamization through their focus on social dignitaries and prominent Muslim celebrities. This becomes obvious from their websites, where programs are promoted by idolizing the pro-gram host and by promoting the owners as prominent Muslims, because of their economic standing and the way they use that standing. The channels reflect in this way the development of Islamization toward a more universalist and less political Islamic interpretation.

A Space for Positive Religious Identity

The last aspect influencing the relationship between the Islamic channels and the Arab states, I want to emphasize, is their role in situations of political conflict. As I have already argued, the channels present themselves as mainly apolitical in relation to internal political affairs. Obviously, they are *not* the media being praised for channeling the emotions and mobilization of the Arab Spring. How-ever, they do play a political role as implicated in the first section. Not only are they, as mentioned, the tools of the political and economic elite, but they may also be seen as accepted by the state, because they offer the population a space for channeling emotions due to political conflicts in specific directions away from the state. The reactions that followed from the Danish Muhammad car-toons controversy that culminated in the beginning of 2006 serve as an illustra-tive example. Also, the new Egyptian regime's suspension of the abovementioned Islamic channels after the fall of Morsi shows that the awareness of and reactions to the potential political role of the Islamic channels are embedded in ongoing political changes.

After 9/11, the number of Islamic channels increased from only one to five. After the cartoon controversy became an international crisis in January 2006, the number of Islamic satellite channels nearly exploded in one year to at least 21 channels. Among them are the channels Al Majd (The Praising/Brilliant), Alresalah (The Message), Al Haqiqa (The Truth), and al Fajr (The Dawn). While it may be difficult to prove a directly causal relation between international crises and the numbers, I suppose the Muhammad Channel, introduced shortly after the cartoon controversy and praising the Prophet, can be explained as such. Also, it is possible to argue that the rhetoric of the channels and especially within the so-called *fatwa* programs is influenced by international developments.

During the 1990s, the main Western discourse on "Islam" increasingly became one of a dichotomy between "Islamism" (or "fundamentalism") on the one hand and "moderate" or "liberal" Islam on the other. This dichotomy was further strengthened due to global events like 9/11 and the Muhammad cartoon controversy. The Islamic channels and programming can be analyzed as an instrument of Muslims to try to challenge and contest Western interpretations of Islamic positions, reaching out for viewers all over the world by offering a transnational position on which to reframe Muslim identity. There is, of course, no one answer from Muslims on Western representations of Islam and Muslims. Instead, the satellite programs present different rhetorical strategies among the religious reasoning of various TV preachers, TV hosts, and TV viewers. However, on a very general level, it is possible to identify changes in rhetorical strategies by analyzing the development within the preaching and teaching of specific well-known Muslim figures.

BEFORE 9/11

Before 9/11, the religious rhetoric on Iqraa and in other conventional channels' religious programs was first and foremost stressing the necessity for Muslims to learn about and engage in their religion. It was a primarily dogmatic, text-interpretative, and history-telling rhetoric used to communicate an authoritative interpretation of Islamic knowledge. The authorities, who communicated this knowledge on TV, were primarily religious scholars from Islamic universities but also the so-called new missionaries, who, as partly self-taught authorities by virtue of their media appearances combined with personal charisma, have become strong competitors to "traditional" Islamic scholars or the ulama. These TV preachers appear as both religious experts, either as guests or as the general figure in religious talk shows and other programs, and as hosts of their own programs. The programs and TV preachers vary considerably, but I will give two rather different examples: Yusuf al-Qaradawi and Amr Khaled. Qaradawi is a traditional scholar, and Amr Khaled is a new-style missionary. Despite their differences, they share Islamic rhetorical trends.

Qaradawi is one of the most famous and most discussed TV preachers, who became well known in all the Arab countries through his appearance on Al Jazeera with his program Al-Shari'a wa al-Hayat (Shari'a and Life). Al-Shari'a wa al-Hayat originated in the concept of the fatwa program and is the only religious program on Al Jazeera. It has the same role as religious programs on national television stations. In Al-Shari'a wa al-Hayat, Qaradawi has put the focus on the central concepts and dogmatic elements of Islam. In general, Qaradawi, albeit taking a dogmatic basis, attempts to include a practical perspective. When he discusses an issue like *zakat* (obligatory alms), he relates it to the situation of the society where Muslims are living. For instance, what if Muslims lived in a country where they had to pay taxes that were used to cover some of the expenses zakat was meant for? Qaradawi is not content with just interpreting the dogmatic in an abstract, timeless, and noncontextual way, as is typical for many "traditional" Islamic scholars (cf. Gaffney 1994). He is insisting on making the point relevant for the life of Muslims today, not only in Muslim countries but all over the world. The combination of realism, a global perspective, and the middle course is in this respect obvious. But he has at the same time an Islamically legitimate answer to all questions and thereby constructs Islam as a universal practice. In spite of his realistic approach and focus on context, Qaradawi does highlight universalism in regard to religious practice and traditions as well. He argues that Islam *is* life, and therefore one can find answers about everything in Islam. The road to becoming Muslim and being a righteous Muslim is to follow the shari'a.

Another kind of preacher is the so-called new missionary. Such new-style missionaries differ from traditional preachers like Qaradawi and have had success due to, among other things, their skills in adapting their rhetorical reasoning to a modern TV audience. One relevant example is the Egyptian TV preacher Amr Khaled, who in his own programs has with great success addressed his way of argumentation to the educated middle and upper classes, using examples picked from a middle-class lifestyle—referring, for instance, to getting new cell phones or cars. Compared to the often abstract and universalistic answers of "traditional" scholars on the religious dilemmas of the individual Muslim, Amr Khaled has tried to make Islamic history relevant to and readily identifiable by his viewers. Before 9/11, his strategy was like Qaradawi's: to communicate knowledge. The aim was to convert Muslims into "real" Muslims. One could call it a revival movement, where the individual Muslim was expected to return to Islam, and what others have called re-verting (instead of con-verting), or to use another metaphor, "born-again" Muslims. A strategy for this process is to place God in the center of every action taken by the believer. Submission to God is the way to become a true believer. You may act, but if you do not act for God, your actions are worth nothing. This approach was further elaborated in a series of ten episodes called *Hedaya* (Guidance), broadcast in 2000. The series was released as audio lectures in 2001 on Iqraa.[10] In the episode "Rida" (Satisfaction), he talks about *'ibadah al-gawarih* (worship of testimony) and *'ibadah al-qalb* (worship of the heart). While *'ibadah al-gawarih* in the shape of prayer, fast, or pilgrimage, for example, gives points only as long as the Muslim practices these, the *'ibadah al-qalb* gives points all the time, because if you love God in your heart, the heart will be full and active even when you are sleeping or going about your daily affairs. A Muslim is, in Amr Khaled's interpretation, a person who by redirecting his or her entire daily troubles into the love of God will feel satisfied and therefore become a happier person.

In the first period of religious Islamic satellite television, it seems that it was Muslims' relation to God that should be strengthened and from which the rhetoric borrowed its fuel. Despite the differences between the two preachers—the traditional scholar on the one hand and the self-made TV missionary on the other—they both agree on Islam's all-embracing power and that becoming Muslim means to submit to God. Either by rule, as Qaradawi would argue, or by individual choice of interest, as Amr Khaled would argue, piety seems to be the aim.

AFTER 9/11

After the events of 9/11, a new variant of the religious rhetoric was strengthened. There seemed to be an increasing tendency among TV preachers to use a defensive rhetoric. By defending Muslims and Islam, they rejected the accusations of the West about a direct connection between Islam and the terrorist attacks in United States. The way to legitimate the argument was typically by comparison with the time of the Prophet. One example is from 2002 from the program *Amr Khaled wa nalqa al-ahiba* (*Let's Meet the Beloved Ones*) on Iqraa. Amr Khaled argues for the necessity of setting a good example. He says, "A Muslim should aim at becoming sublime in his own field." Amr Khaled uses the story of the later grand Muslim army commander Khaled ibn al-Walid, who became a Muslim not because he saw Muslims praying but because he himself had been defeated by the Prophet Muhammad in a military battle. It was the cleverness of the Prophet that converted al-Walid, not his piety, if we believe the story as told by Amr Khaled. He uses the story to tell Muslims that it is cleverness and high morality, not superficial piety, that convinces opponents about the justice of Islam.

Compared to the previous approach of Amr Khaled, where he focused on the individual's mental state of psychological well-being, after 9/11, he seems to emphasize that Muslims should work hard to become role models and prove the superiority of Islam. After 9/11, the rhetoric of the programs seems increasingly to target reestablishing the reputation of Islam and the relationship with non-Muslims, through Muslims' demonstration of personal skills and upstanding morals. The way to become Muslim is no longer mainly a question of living up to God's law; it is to demonstrate and implement personal as well as collective skills to prove the credibility of the Muslim *umma* vis-à-vis Western countries. While new missionaries like Amr Khaled are focusing on the responsibility of the individual and striving toward perfection, Qaradawi is focusing on the responsibility of the Muslim *umma* to prove its worth.

AFTER THE CARTOON CONTROVERSY

After January 2006, the defensive tone of the rhetoric was aggravated, putting the Prophet Muhammad and Islam in the forefront. Praise of Muhammad was given a predominant position. The focus was on how Muhammad was kind, patient, tolerant, merciful, and dialogue seeking. Several programs about his life were produced, which among others were broadcast on the Islamic satellite channels Iqraa and Al Majd in 2006. As a direct reaction to what Muslims considered slander about Muhammad, they began to instead paint a flattering picture of Muhammad, even as they were distancing themselves from more radical elements among Muslims.

The launching of new religious satellite channels following the caricature crisis supports my argument. One example is Alresalah, a "24-hour family channel" (as the channel presents itself), that started airing programs on March 1, 2006. The owner, Prince al-Waleed, said at the press conference announcing the channel, "We are offering the world an Islamic Arabic language channel to present true Islam." And he continued, "Islam is being hijacked and defamed by a group of deviants who operate in the name of religion in several parts of the world." He also said the channel would

> seek to project the true message of Islam and its teachings, and it would provide a platform for a dialogue on a range of religious, social, and economic issues that affect everyday life. *But more important its priority would be to counteract the misconceptions of Islam in other societies.* [my italics][11]

As the quotation indicates, the greatest change of the rhetoric after the caricature crisis was the strengthening of the defense strategy with a renewed focus on Muslims as victims of Western persecution or distortions of Islam. At the same time it wants to present another picture of Islam. From its inception, the channel broadcast a weekly program each Sunday with the channel's director, Tarik al-Suidan, called "al-Rasoul an-Insaan" (The Human Prophet). The program stressed that Muhammad was a human being and described his daily life as a human being—how he loved and how he hated, how he laughed and how he felt pain. Al-Suidan argues that by knowing the life of Muhammad and his responses as a human being, the viewer will come closer to the Prophet and follow his ways.

Stressing the unjust pursuit is not a new position, but it has been introduced frequently in relation to international conflicts such as those in Chechnya,

Palestine, Bosnia, Somalia, Afghanistan, and Iraq. Even before 9/11, Qaradawi had already given Friday sermons on these issues, pointing at the Western enemies of Islam (Galal 2003). But the cartoon controversy has obtained a special meaning because it has explicitly linked present conflicts with the religion, Islam. It has, so to speak, given Muslims final proof of Western countries' persecution of Muslims and Muslim countries exactly *because* they are Muslim. The argument is that it is no longer a question of the West being under some kind of delusion; now it is interpreted as a deliberate pursuit. This slandering of Islam per se has further pushed the rhetorical strategy into direct reference to the superiority of Islam.

The rhetorical discourse about being a victim of persecution is implemented in different strategies. One is confrontational and radical, and another is encouraging of dialogue. The latter one has been predominant on religious satellite television. Dialogue is presented as a natural part of Islam; Islam is the true civilization, while the West is to blame for all the troubles of the world.

In Amr Khaled's Ramadan series from 2005, *On the Path of the Beloved,* he presented and discussed the life of the Prophet Muhammad. The focus was Muhammad's personal side and how he dealt with difficult situations. Ramadan started in October 2005, shortly after the cartoons of Muhammad were published in the Danish newspaper, *Jyllandsposten,* on September 30, 2005. The program's theme had likely been chosen before the caricatures, but it gave Amr Khaled the best opportunity to put forward his message about "the beloved" Prophet Muhammad. It is possible to decode his messages as direct and indirect references to the wrongful representation of the Prophet. Episode 11, called "The Siege," is an example. The topic is the Quraysh tribe's blockade imposed on Muslims and unbelievers of the Banu Hashim. The Quraysh were during Muhammad's life the most powerful and strongest tribe on the peninsula, but despite the Muslims' military weakness, they always succeeded. According to Amr Khaled, this is because the Quraysh didn't have a real cause to defend, which made them resort to violence. Of the seven to nine assassination attempts on Muhammad, not one succeeded. Khaled continues:

> Also, when Futhalah had a dagger in his cloak and followed the Prophet [Muhammad] (SAWS) with the intent of killing him. The Prophet sensed it, turned around, and asked him, "What has your spirit tempted you to do, Futhalah?" The Prophet (SAWS) smiled, asked him to watch for God [Allah] and patted Futhalah's chest. Futhalah later said that before the touch, the Prophet was the most hideous person on earth to him, but after that, he became the dearest to his heart.

One of the repeated messages of the episode is that the Prophet's enemies do not have the power to kill him. He was steady in his belief, and he met his enemies with dialogue. Khaled is in this way stressing the greatness of Islam, which has been suffering during this period but now has the chance to regain its previous strength. What follows is not a rejection of any non-Muslim; on the contrary, a repeated point throughout the program is that the unbelievers stood as steady as believers, side by side with Muhammad during three years of siege with all its hardships.

In March 2007, another program was broadcast with Amr Khaled with the title *A Call for Coexistence.* In the first episode, he not only conveys the message of coexistence, but he also speaks of the superiority of the Islamic civilization—for instance, by connecting the message of coexistence with Islam:

> I'm challenging all of the constitutions of the Western world to state a single phrase included in them that encourages their people to go and get acquainted with others. The only constitution that has such a phrase is the Quran. The West should not look upon us condescendingly, saying that it was them who invented coexistence, because this is not true.

The rhetorical strategy seems to be to present Islam as a misunderstood and underrated civilization—a combination of taking on the role of the victim while emphasizing the truth of Islam as being the true civilization. It implies at the same time that Muslims are encouraged to live up to the true behavior of a Muslim as civilized and dialogue seeking. The argument does involve a demand of action in relation to less-civilized people—in this context, the West. From this perspective the way to become Muslim is to go into dialogue proving by deeds that Islam is civilization and Muslims are wrongly accused. One might even argue that the preachers in this way are trying to patent liberal values as originally Islamic.

One may argue that the relation to the West, as deeply embedded in the rhetoric, makes the Islamic public a global counterpublic. If so, it is a rather powerful counterpublic that is trying to renegotiate the West's distinction between "good" (liberal) and "bad" (Islamist) Muslims. The rhetorical constructions seem to transpose the distinction, turning the dichotomy upside down. In the rhetoric, the liberal who is *Muslim* is the good and true liberal, while the liberal *from the West* is the bad and wrongful liberal. The Muslim is civilized, and the Western citizen is the noncivilized one who must be approached with the Islamic-defined liberal civilization.

The main question here is why the Islamic channels in general seem to be accepted by the Arab states, despite their potential threat against state ideology and the religious establishment. None of the so-called Islamic channels are explicitly or openly supporting any state or political movement that could further strengthen potential conflict. However, they highlight a pious and religious lifestyle and promote what I call an Islamic identity politics. The focus is on the individual Muslim's life and the moral and ethical ideals of the Muslim community. Further, being nonpolitical, the channels are more in accordance with the Islamization politics of several Arab states than in opposition to them. At the same time, Arab African states may also accept the channels because they offer the audiences a space wherein people can react to national and international conflicts while the channels lead the audiences in the direction of piety rather than national opposition politics. Also, it is better to let their populations be preoccupied with such distractions as the cartoon crisis and external enemies than with internal political affairs.

Notes

1. In the fall of 2012, I conducted interviews with television audiences in Egypt to learn about their viewing habits, particularly their use of religious TV. The interviews are part of a larger research project about audiences and Islamic television.

2. Interview: Al Majd TV's PR manager, Egypt, January 11, 2012.

3. Kingdom Press and Media. http://www.kingdom.com.sa/prince-alwaleed-meets-rupert-murdoch-in-new-york.

4. Al Jazeera. http://www.artonline.tv/home/.

5. This was also the case for the first private radio stations in Egypt in the beginning of the 1920s.

6. Since 2000, free media cities have been established in Egypt, Dubai, and Jordan in the form of state-established production centers with all modern technical facilities, where production companies and other stakeholders can become renters. They are organized differently from country to country and with different degrees of control and restrictions (Sakr 2001).

7. *Asharq Al-Awsat,* July 5, 2013, and September 16, 2013.

8. http://www.alresalah.net/whoarewe_en.htm.

9. http://ahlulbayt.webintrix.com.

10. According to his CV available at his official home page: http://www.amrkhaled.net/.

11. http://www.iccuk.org/media/reports/2006/launching_al_risalah_islamic_satellite_channel_in_saudi_arabia.htm.

References

Abu-Lughod, L. 2005. *Dramas of Nationhood: The Politics of Television in Egypt.* Cairo: American University in Cairo Press.

al-Dagher, M. M. 2007. "Itijāhāt al-Qanawāt al-Faḍāiya al-Islāmiya fi muɛālajit qaḍāya al-Aqaliyāt wa al-Jāliyāt al-Islāmiya fi al-ɛālam" (Satellite Television Attitudes towards Islamic Minorities in the World). Paper presented in Arabic at International Conference on Satellite Television and Cultural Identity. Visions for 21st Century Media, December 11–12, 2007. College of Communication, University of Sharjah.

al-Tahhawi, A. 2008a. "Arab Ministers Finally Agree—on Limiting Press Freedom." In *Menassat,* February 15, 2008. http://www.menassat.com/?q=en/news-articles/2968-arab-ministers-finally-agree-limiting-press-freedom.

Amin, R. A. W. 2007. "Attitudes of Religious Elite towards the Present and Future of the Islamic Satellite Channels: Field Study." Paper presented in Arabic at International Conference on Satellite Television and Cultural Identity. Visions for 21st Century Media, December 11–12, 2007. College of Communication, University of Sharjah.

Clark, L. S., ed. 2007. *Religion, Media, and the Marketplace*. London: Rutgers University Press.

Eickelman, D. F., and J. B. Anderson, eds. 1999. *New Media in the Muslim World: The Emerging Public Sphere*. Bloomington: Indiana University Press.

Gaffney, P. D. 1994. *The Prophet's Pulpit: Islamic Preaching in Contemporary Egypt*. Berkeley: University of California Press.

Galal, E. 2003. "Islam via Satellite." In *Being Muslim in Denmark* (in Danish), edited by L. P. Galal and I. Liengård. Copenhagen: Anis Press.

———. 2010. "The Muslim Woman as a Beauty Queen." *Journal of Arab and Muslim Media Research* 3(3): 159–175.

Hoover, S. M., and L. S. Clark, eds. 2002. *Practicing Religion in the Age of the Media: Explorations in Media, Religion, and Culture*. New York: Columbia University Press.

Roy, O. 2004. *Globalized Islam: The Search for a New Ummah*. London: Hurst.

Sakr, N. 2001. *Satellite Realms: Transnational Television, Globalization and the Middle East*. London: I. B. Tauris.

———. 2006. "The Impact of Commercial Interests on Arab Media Content." In *Arab Media in the Information Age*, 61–85. Abu-Dhabi: Emirates Center for Strategic Studies and Research.

———. 2007. "Approaches to Exploring Media-Politics Connections in the Arab World." In *Arab Media and Political Renewal: Community, Legitimacy and Public Life*, edited by N. Sakr, 1–12. London: I. B. Tauris.

Salem, R. M. 2007. "Arab Islamic Culture on Satellite Television." Paper presented in Arabic at International Conference on Satellite Television and Cultural Identity: Visions for 21st Century Media, December 11–12, 2007. College of Communication, University of Sharjah.

———. 2008b. "Al-Baraka TV, First Victim of the Arab Charter?" In *Menassat*, February 27, 2008. http://www.menassat.com/?q=en/news-articles/3054-al-baraka-tv-first-victim-arab-charter.

Tash, A. Q. 2004. "Islamic Satellite Channels and their Impact on Arab Societies: Iqraa Channel— A Case Study." *TBS*, 13. http://www.tbsjournal.com/Archives/Fall04/tash.html.

Wolfsfeld, G. 1997. *Media and Political Conflict: News from the Middle East*. Cambridge: Cambridge University Press.

10 Religious Discourse in the New Media

A Case Study of Pentecostal Discourse Communities of SMS Users in Southwestern Nigeria

'Rotimi Taiwo

IN THE AGE OF GLOBALIZATION the importance of telecommunication to the economy of nations has been stressed. In this vein, the Nigerian government deregulated the telecommunication sector in 2001. This led to the introduction of the Global System for Mobile Communication (GSM) into the country.[1] Since then, the growth in mobile phone use has been tremendous. Ernest Ndukwe, the executive vice chairman of the Nigerian Communications Commission, outlined the benefits of GSM to the nation as foreign capital flow, stimulation of foreign investment, increased access to telephone services, job creation, indigenous skills acquisition and technology transfer, economic empowerment of the local population, and increased tax revenue for the government (Ndukwe 2003: 6). Since the introduction of mobile telecommunication in Nigeria, the use of short message service (SMS) has grown rapidly, especially among young people. SMS offers a cheaper means of communications for many mobile phone users. Today in Nigeria, SMS is used for a variety of purposes, such as interpersonal communication, invitations for interviews, electioneering, banking transactions, seasonal greetings, and so forth.[2] This chapter examines its use among Nigerian Pentecostal Christians in southwestern Nigeria, with a focus on its use for communal bonding, proselytization, and fulfillment of Christian social responsibilities.

Text Messaging as a Social Interactive Technology

SMS is one of the social interactive technologies that are becoming very popular as a means of global communication. It is also commonly referred to as "text messaging," or simply as "texting." With the surge in the use of SMS all over the world, especially among the younger generation, a new form of writing has emerged to help users cope with the limitations of the small keypads (Thurlow 2003; Bush 2005). This new form of writing, which can basically be described as shorthand, helps users save a great deal of time and also manage the limited space available for their messages (mobile phones allow up to 160 characters).

Research findings have shown that there is interplay among relationship formation, reinforcing, and texting (Parks and Floyd 1996; Thurlow 2003; Roman 2006; Ling 2008). In fact, Fischer (1998) describes mobile phone technology as a "technology of sociality." Ellwood-Clayton (2003: 253) observes what she calls cell discourse and how it has infiltrated Filipino social life as a powerful and far-reaching communication device. According to her, SMS acts to enrich and nurture relationships, keep people feeling socially connected, and abate loneliness and social alienation (259). Thurlow (forthcoming) also observes that texting has the communicative intent of maximizing sociality.

Mobile telephones open up a whole new world of opportunity for users as SMS enables them to organize and coordinate their social activities with relative ease. SMS also lends itself as an outlet for use by civil society organizations. Due to its communicative potential, it has been used for various socio-political activities in the past in Nigeria. For instance, it was used to mobilize the people against President Olusegun Obasanjo's desire for another political term after spending the constitutionally required period as president.[3] It was also used in 2003 by the National Association of GSM Subscribers of Nigeria and the Consumers Rights Project to organize mobile phone subscribers for a one-day boycott against their unreasonably high tariffs. The campaign was successful; about 80 percent of mobile phone users switched off their phones on September 19, 2003, and this led to a reduction in the tariffs (Obadare 2006; Taiwo 2008a). It was also used at different times to raise awareness of the AIDS campaign by the National Agency for the Control of AIDS (NACA).

Background: The Advent and Use of Text Messaging in Nigeria

Before 2001, the telecommunication system in Nigeria consisted of a congested landline system, which was only available for the privileged few, and the functionality was very erratic. The telecommunication industry was opened up by the Olusegun Obasanjo civilian regime when it licensed two private and one government-run GSM operators—the South African–based MTN and the Econet Wireless (later changed to Vodacom, V-mobile, Celtel, Zain, and now Airtel) and the state-run M-Tel—to provide mobile telephone services in the country. The fourth operator, Globacom, was licensed in August 2003. Currently, there are 11 major mobile phone service providers in the country.

The use of SMS text messaging started in Nigeria after the licensing of the operators to provide telecommunication services. Initially, because of the high cost of obtaining mobile phones and the SIM card, very few Nigerians were able to own mobile phones. However, within a few years, with the reduction in mobile phone tariffs and the prices of cell phones and SIM cards dropping sharply, mobile phone starter packs could be purchased for very little. Together with the inflow of large quantities of mobile phones and accessories (mostly inexpensive, new and secondhand), more Nigerians now have access to mobile telephony (Osibanjo and Nnorom 2006).

Text messaging is one of the features of mobile telephony that many Nigerians have adopted as a regular means of communication. Its use in Nigeria covers a wide range of communicative activities, such as interpersonal communication among friends, acquaintances, and colleagues; official communication, such as summoning people for a meeting or inviting them for an interview; banking services; group communication, such as raising prayer requests and alerts among religious groups; and mass communication, such as news and politics.

Perspectives on Text Messaging

Text messaging is a relatively new text-based way of communicating, within the broader context of technology-mediated communication. Text messaging as a means of communication went public in the mid-1990s and has attracted the attention of scholars from different disciplines. Some of their studies include the social perspective (Harper, Palen, and Taylor 2005); the use of text messaging in business and commerce (Hsu, Wang, and Wen 2006); and text messaging in medicine (Downer et al. 2006; Robinson et al. 2006; Koshy, Car, and Majeeb 2008). In the last decade, there has been a growing interest among linguists in the language of text messaging. Most linguistic researchers focus on the socio-linguistics of text messaging, specifically on such issues as gender, age, and status. On gender differences, Ling (2005) observed that female teens and young adults use text most frequently in Norway. He also found that young women send longer and more complex messages. Kasesniemi (2003) also looked at gendered differences in text messaging in Finland, reporting that teenage girls are heavier texters than boys, and while the former place emphasis on emotional exchanges, the latter do so on speed.

SMS has been identified as a creolizing blend of written and spoken discourse (Thurlow 2003). This was earlier noted by Baron (1998) as a typical characteristic of the language of email. Thurlow (2003) observes that the language of SMS appears to be underpinned by the three key socio-linguistic "maxims" of brevity and speed, paralinguistic restitution, and phonological approximation. Several scholars have observed the distinct register of text messaging, which users create in order to manage their text communication through mobile phones. Bush (2005) discussed the experimentation of text messagers with written English and the development of stylistic shorthand, such as grapheme abbreviation (e.g., *c* for *see*), numeric characters replacing homophones (e.g., *l8r* for *later*), vowel dropping (e.g., *rcvd* for *received*), and so forth.

Ellwood-Clayton (2003) described the use of text messaging among Filipino Christians.[4] She observed how religious text communication created an independent form of community religiosity that was more or less autonomous from the Catholic Church (255). In a related work, Roman (2006) discussed how cell phones are used for straightforward evangelizing purposes and how the use of text messages in the form of chain texts and prayer requests among Filipino Christians strengthens individual beliefs and communal ties.

A few Nigerian linguists have studied different aspects of the text messaging phenomenon, such as its various forms and functions (Taiwo 2008a), its use for fulfilling the function of social responsibilities (Taiwo 2008b), its use in constructing values and sentiments in religious discourse (Chiluwa 2008), text multilingualism in Nigerian text messages (Awonusi 2004), and socio-linguistic relevance of the indigenous languages in the context of SMS texts (Ofulue 2004). Chiluwa (2008) particularly shares a similar thematic focus with the present work, as he discusses how SMS is used to communicate faith-based messages, prayer, admonition, and assurance, and how this medium is beneficial to church communities. While Chiluwa identifies some text message types and how they are used to construct sentiments among the Pentecostals, this study goes beyond these to underscore the roles the growing text messaging culture plays in spiritual bonding among Pentecostal Christians.

Many religious traditions have embraced the use of the internet and computer-mediated communication (CMC) as their means of communication. This migration of religious communication into cyberspace was the focus of a study by Ess (2007). Another group of scholars in a special issue of the *Journal of Computer-Mediated Communication* discussed the use of cyberspace by a wide range of religious communities, such as Buddhism (Fukamisu 2007) and Islam (Abdulah 2007), using quantitative and qualitative methods. Among other issues, they discussed religious counseling, religious authority, terrorism, and cyber-rituals (Campbell 2007; Jacobs 2007; Kwabata and Tamura 2007).

There have been reports on how SMS has found relevance in different religious settings. Pope Benedict was reported to have sent SMS to thousands of young pilgrims in Australia during the World Youth Day in Sydney, urging them to renew their faith. Likewise, the Church of England during the 2007 Lenten season launched a website and invited communicants to share Lenten jokes. The website had a text-messaging service, which sent subscribers daily suggestions on how to spread generosity and neighborliness, with the exhortation to make someone laugh.[5] *PRLog Press Release* also reported how Christians across the United Kingdom are getting daily Bible verse SMS text messages on their mobile phones through pray4u.co.uk.[6]

The wide use of SMS has also been reported among young Pakistanis by Rollier (2010). In an ethnographic study carried out in Lahore, the author reported that the growing importance of texting has led to a greater visibility of Islam, mediating religious and aesthetic sensations in the most unexpected corners of everyday life in the country. *Islam in Action* also reported how Islam allows men in Saudi Arabia to divorce their wives via SMS.[7] In a related development, BBC News reported that a Malaysia court had ruled in favor of a man who served divorce papers to his wife via a text message.[8]

Methodology

The data for this study were sourced from 500 text messages collected from mobile phone users in southwestern Nigeria. In collecting the data, I focused on both interactional and transactional text messages exchanged among Pentecostal Christians. Such messages were obtained either directly from respondents' phones or from a stock of messages usually sent by a circle of text messagers to which I belonged. The overall goal was to establish the linguistic and sociolinguistic patterns in the messages and how these relate to social interactions and spiritual bonding within the Pentecostal fold in southwestern Nigeria.

Critical Discourse Analysis (CDA) was chosen as the framework for analyzing the jokes because it is appropriate for the interpretation of the diverse social issues in the text messages. CDA sees a relationship between a particular discursive event and the situation(s), institution(s), and social structure(s) that frame it. CDA, according to van Dijk (1988), represents a means of unraveling the discursive sources of power, dominance, inequality, and bias and how these are initiated, maintained, reproduced, and transformed in language within specific social, economic, political, and historical contexts. In addition, CDA examines the significance of language as a tool in the production, maintenance, and change of social relations of power, especially in relation to how language contributes to the domination of some people by others by explicating the rich and complex interrelationships of language and power. Since text messages are products of the social process, this study demonstrates how they reveal through their discursive nature the ideology, power, hierarchy, and biases among Nigerian Pentecostal communities in southwestern Nigeria.

Findings and Discussion

The existence of a community of Pentecostal SMS users in southwestern Nigeria has been established by this study. Though the term *community* means different things to different people, here we mean a group that shares common beliefs, practices, and interests distinct from those of the larger society. This community is a digital or virtual one, which Porter (2004) defines as "an aggregation of individuals or business partners who interact around a shared interest, where the interaction is at least partially supported and/or mediated by technology."[9] This community is motivated by the need to communicate the basics of Christianity, and they have developed a functional genre in order to accomplish their communicative purpose. Their communication hinges on a culture of speed, brevity, and the use of nonstandard orthography. Jaffe (2000: 498) captures the use of SMS succinctly, describing it as a powerful expressive resource that can graphically capture the authenticity and flavor of the spoken word. For members of this community, the cell phone is a lifestyle accessory that they use to fulfill their social roles within and outside their church communities.

A noticeable feature of this community is the circulation of messages within the group of users at regular intervals—almost on a daily basis, but typically at the beginning of a new day, month, or year, and during festive periods. Creativity is one of the hallmarks of their messages, which are woven around Christian topics, and they are aimed at admonishing members and helping them to build up their faith. Sometimes, such texts are in the form of prayer and good wishes for the addressee (see Chiluwa 2008 and Taiwo 2008b). In the sections that follow, we examine some of the uses of SMS within this community.

To properly report on the features in the text messages and describe them accurately, I classified the text messages in the data, as shown in table 10.1. The original source of a typical text message is not always clear. It may be composed by the sender or just copied from a pool of messages in the sender's inbox and forwarded to others within the discourse circle. A new day/month/year message typically comes at the beginning of such periods, and members may receive several such messages from different users. Ellwood-Clayton (2003: 256) also identifies these two types of text messages in the Philippines and refers to forwarded messages as "hallmarks," named after Hallmark cards, the world's largest social expression company. The focus of the new day, month, or year messages is typically encouragement, hope, and prayers. They are meant to encourage the addressees to embark on a new month or year with fresh hopes. They engage extensive figurative language in order to create the appropriate tone for the messages and communicate the emotion of the writer. The lexicon is carefully chosen to paint clearly the picture of the writer's purpose, which could, for instance, be humorous as well as instructive, as found in T5 and T6 in table 10.1. Most humorous text messages are not just intended to make the receiver laugh. Rather, they are meant to help the receiver to develop Christian virtues, such as experiencing joy when faced with adversity. The informative nature of the first two clauses of T5 may make them initially appear to the average addressee to be three real visitors waiting at the door, especially with the message coming possibly from a person well known in face-to-face discourse to the addressee within the Pentecostal fold. A deeper reflection on the message brings out the true communicative intent of the sender: humor. The second text message uses a combination of irony, imagery, and personification. These messages draw from the experiential knowledge

Table 10.1. SMS classifications

Type of text message	SN	Examples
New day/month/ year SMS	T1	Can you cope with all these in April? Surprises! Elevation! Favour! Breakthru! Joy! Luv! Success! Prosperity? God is able to work it out.
	T2	As u drive in to 2008, may u experience God's mercy & blessing.
	T3	As u run the last lap of the race to the new year, may u & ur fml not be erased from the race God'll keep, guide, & protect u. Welcome to the month of December!!!
	T4	As u go in2 new mth, Eyes will turn; Heads will shift; Breaths will seize; Mouths will open; ears will itch; Hearts will melt in admiration of God's glory in ur family. Have a wonderful 2008.
Playful and humorous SMS	T5	There are three visitors waiting at the door; they have knocked and there was no response. They are Joy, Peace, and Love. Please open the door for them. I have sent them to stay with you tonight and bless you.
	T6	The pastor must hear this; yesterday, you were with Peace, and today again I saw you going out with Favour. It is an open secret to brethren that Joy is your regular companion.
Prayer alert SMS	T7	Pls pray for us. The next training is tomorrow. PRAY FOR THE HEALTH OF THE FAMILY.
	T8	Praise God, proliferation of malignant epithelia cells found. All I have left is prayer.
	T9	Pls pray for M. He has convulsions today; he is currently on admission. He is our last-born. Thanks Bro F.
	T10	Emergency: pls pray for Pastor Fredic lores, missionary in East Timor. He's going to be executed today by beating. Pls 4wd 2 all Christians.
Prayer SMS	T11	May God give u a rainbow 4 every storm, a smile 4 every fear, a blesn 4 every trial, a sweet song 4 every sigh, and an answer 4 every prayr.
	T12	God's favour, mercy, blessing, grace . . . shall abide in ur life even byond ur wildest imagination. Blv it u've been markd 4 monumental success.

Table 10.1. (*continued*)

Type of text message	SN	Examples
	T13	Dear son, as u proceed on ur journey for higher qualification, I wish u God's journey mercy, message, and blessing. Psa. 121:7–8
	T14	Surely, hardship & difficulties shall follow all ur enemies, every seconds of their lives, & dey will receive 10,000 bullets each in their foreheads, which will result 2 their death forever, Amen. Gd morni.
	T15	Have u ever seen a heavenly bulldozer? Very mighty, bigger than ur imagination! I saw it last night breaking the heads of all ur enemies, destroying the house of failure & killing poverty to permanent silence in ur life.
Seasonal greetings SMS	T16	Jesus is GOD spelling Himself out in language dat man can understand, celebrate his birth, share luv like he did. MERRY XMAS!
	T17	Christ is d reason 4 dis season n by d reason of d season u shall be seasoned 4 gr8tness& success. Wishing u d very best dis season n beyond.
	T18	Happy Easter. May the power of resurrection revive us did season n set us aglow in God's love in Jesus name.
Creative inspirational SMS	T19	God is going to reply ur prayer with full text message and not a flash.
	T20	U re cr8td without simpack. God preserve u without voucher. He energise u without charger; surely ur validity is eternal and ur access days will b forever.
	T21	God's love 4 u is nt proud like GLO. It does not change ownership like CELTEL. It is nt expensive as MTN and does nt av NAFDAC no, so it cant expire.
Message of salvation	T22	Join God's Family Today By Becoming a Born Again. However, if you are already a Born Again, continue to seek God's Kingdom and Righteousness. John 3:3 Mat 6:33.
	T23	Stop playing with HELL FIRE, join The Lord's Army today. Give your life to JESUS CHRIST TODAY!!!!

that some contemporary Pentecostal Christians in Nigeria adopt these virtues as personal names (see Akínnásò 1980; Ikotun 2013).

Also worthy of note is the metaphorical structuring of the message. Metaphor can generally be seen as a device for rhetorical flourish. The conceptual mappings of the whole idea of moving toward another year as a JOURNEY in which the receiver is DRIVING is a reflection of how abstract categories can be organized cognitively by structures borrowed from more concrete categories (Bednarek 2005: 7). This is also reflected in T3, where going through the months of the year is seen as a RACE.

The use of rhetorical questions (T1 and T15) is also significant. They are meant to help the receiver to reflect on the issues highlighted in the messages. They provoke and engage the imagination of the receiver to help them look ahead in their lives for hope and succor. In T3 there is a rhyme in the expression "erased from the race" with the repetition of the sound syllable /e□z/ in the two words.

The domain of raising prayer alerts is no longer limited to the four walls of any church. The virtual community has further strengthened Christian belief in God's omnipresence and agreement in prayer (Matt. 8:19). The use of text messages to request prayers is becoming a common phenomenon among Pentecostal communities. The messagers' faith may be strengthened when they know that a good number of people are praying for them. Personal prayer requests can cover several aspects of the life of the messager, such as health (T8 and T9) and deliverance (T10). The style of prayer requests differs from one composer to the other. While some simply make direct requests, others make a request indirectly, as in T8. The composer first expressed faith in God through praise before making a disclosure of being diagnosed with cancer, followed by a declarative sentence, "All I have left is prayer," which should be understood as a request for prayer. This clearly follows Christian principles of giving thanks to God in all things and faith in our prayer as enjoined in the Bible in 1 Thessalonians 5:18 and John 5:14. This can also be likened to what Chiluwa (2008: 16) referred to as "faith-based pronouncements." T9 is a direct personal prayer request for the composer's son.

Raising prayer alerts is not limited to personal prayers. Sometimes, issues that are perceived to constitute a threat to Christianity are forwarded to members of the community to pray on. T10 is a message that addressed one of such issues. Many members of the Pentecostal SMS community received this text in 2006, and it was the focus of individual and corporate prayers until another text circulated to announce that the pastor had been released. Text messages like this present a common and unifying ground for all believers to pray on issues that threaten their faith.

SMS is not only used to request prayer; it is also used to pray for people. Prayer SMS is directed toward the purpose of social bonding. When Christians pray for one another, it signals love and concern for one another's welfare, and this further binds them together. Prayer SMS can also be as creative as other kinds of SMS. One of the commonest kinds of prayers used in SMS is imprecation. An imprecation is a prayer for evil or misfortune upon others, who may be perceived or real enemies. Imprecations construct imagined weapons aimed at destroying the enemy, as in "10,000 bullets" (T14) or "heavenly bulldozer" (T15). Imprecations, according to Taiwo (2010), give a feeling of victory to the person using them because they provide a sense of the ability to diffuse the power of one's enemies, which is a major source of fear and anxiety in the African consciousness.[10]

The SMS culture is rapidly changing many cultural symbols affiliated to certain Christian traditions, such as the use of seasonal greeting cards. Many members of the SMS community find this to be a cheaper alternative to using customized greeting cards, which are usually mass-produced. SMS gives users the opportunity to express themselves by creating their own texts that have their individual linguistic and literary flavor. T16 through T18 are some seasonal greetings from our data collection. The overall goal of seasonal SMS greetings is to wish the receivers well and sometimes to let them know that somebody, somewhere was thinking about them during this period. The service providers in Nigeria help mobile phone subscribers in fulfilling this social function of SMS by sometimes providing free services during some of the major Christian holidays, such as Christmas and Easter.

Mobile phones offer users a unique opportunity to demonstrate their creative abilities in the context of SMS text messaging. Users can capitalize on their shared symbolic and cultural values with other users. Two kinds of creativity can be identified in the use of text messages: experimenting with language through the use of immediate socio-cultural elements and through the use of nonconventional (typically short forms) linguistic symbols. The latter are inspired by the limited space, while the former draw inspiration from the immediate socio-cultural context of the language being engaged. T21 engages the names of three telecommunications service providers—GLO, CELTEL, and MTN—as well as a government agency, National Agency for Food, Drug Administration and Control (NAFDAC), to drive home a message on "what God's love is not."

These text messages are targeted at inspiring the receiver, mainly by playing on words, giving them new meaning in the context of the messages. In T19, a prayer is conceptualized as a message sent through a mobile phone, while a full text message can be seen as an appropriate answer to a prayer and a "flash as inappropriate." This refers to a cultural practice in mobile phone use in Nigeria that is commonly referred to as "flashing."[11] In other contexts, particularly in Asia, it is referred to as "beeping" (Donner 2007). Flashing is the act of dialing a number, letting it ring, and then hanging up before the receiver answers. Flashing is believed by many Nigerians to have some communicative values. Some of the reasons people flash may be to remind the receiver about something, to make the receiver call the flasher, to tell the receiver that the flasher is thinking about him or her, and so forth. Flashing for some people is considered to be distractive, even impolite.

T20 uses words associated with mobile telephony, such as *SIM pack, voucher, charger, validity,* and *access days.* A *SIM pack* is the starter pack that a subscriber gets when he signs up for phone service. It contains a card, the SIM (subscriber identification module), with a chip with the necessary information to operate the phone. A voucher is the card the mobile phone user uses to load money onto the phone. A charger is used to charge the battery. Validity and access days are terms used to indicate how long subscribers can have access to the services after activating their phones or account. The creativity in this text message can be found in the conceptual usages the composer made of the terminologies selected. Institutional names and what typically characterize them were played on in T21. The institutional brands GLO, CELTEL, MTN, and NAFDAC are typically associated with pride, constant change of ownership, being expensive, and expiration, respectively.[12] The figurative language includes simile with these names and what is typically associated with them to illustrate what God's love is not.

Implications for Proselytization and Christian Social Responsibilities

The use of SMS, as already observed, is helping to maintain and strengthen social relationships among members of the Pentecostal community. The regular circulation of text messages helps to promote cohesive relationships. In addition, since the gospel is concerned with the spiritual as well as the physical condition of believers, this particular use of text messages among southwestern Nigerian Pentecostals blends both social and evangelistic responsibilities. Text messaging is not limited to just in-group socialization among Pentecostals. Its use is sometimes extended to the public, thereby making it available to people outside the group, who may not necessarily share their beliefs (see T22 and T23). According to Hackett (2003), Nigeria has a virulent and diverse media scene that is arguably one of the most lively and developed on the African continent. The preaching of the gospel is being maximized through the various mass media in the country (see Taiwo 2007: 81).

The use of SMS for religious purposes has been extended to the dynamic context of Nigeria's mass media, where most preachers on the radio and television solicit feedback through either voice calls or SMS from their audiences. This is also true of newspaper preaching columns, where preachers display their mobile numbers for readers to contact them through SMS. It is also common for Pentecostal Christians to use SMS to invite people to programs. This popular use of SMS among the Pentecostal communities provides forums for expressing the fundamental beliefs in the Christian faith. An innovative approach to counseling, called SMS counseling, is also developing in the country. People can send text messages to Christian counselors, who can send advice to them periodically or refer them to counselors.

The use of SMS also promotes a paperless religious community, where major communications in churches, such as invitations, reminders, short notices, prayer requests, and so forth, are conducted through this new medium. This reduces wastage as well as the stress of information distribution associated with conventional methods. The communication is immediate, as well as being convenient and cost effective. Service providers in Nigeria are not oblivious to the growth in the use of SMS in the Christian context. Pentecostalism is growing so powerful in Nigeria that its influence cannot be ignored by media and telecommunications practitioners. Service providers offer opportunities to subscribers to express themselves through customized ringtones. For instance, most of the telecommunications service providers allow subscribers to download ringtones of popular gospel music songs and even provide access to spoken expressions, such as the prayers of popular Pentecostal preachers (Dr. Enoch Adeboye,[13] the General Overseer of the Redeemed Christian Church of God, for example) as ringtones.

The use of text messaging as a force for shaping social relationships in the age of globalization is a noticeable feature of every modern society. In this study, I examined how SMS usage has brought about the formation of a community of users within the Pentecostal Christian fold in Nigeria. We observed the different ways SMS users in this virtual community use text messages to express their faith through seasonal greetings, playful and humorous compositions, prayer and prayer alerts, and creative inspirational SMS. We concluded by noting the implications of embracing the new media, especially the rapid and inexpensive SMS, to help spread the gospel, and we noted that taking the Christian message into the virtual realm of SMS may not only offer succor to individual Christians but also build religious community among friends and church members. The use of SMS is also a subtle way of popularizing the Christian message in a nonconfrontational way, even among non-Christians. Further research will be needed to ascertain to what extent the dissemination and consumption of these messages might lead to a standardization, or even a Pentecostalization, of Christian belief and practice in the Nigerian context and beyond.

Notes

1. The introduction of GSM into Nigeria is generally referred to by Nigerians as the "GSM Revolution."

2. See Taiwo (2010). http://hss.fullerton.edu/linguistics/cln/W10PDF/Taiwo-ThumbTribe .pdf.

3. Shortly before the end of President Olusegun Obasanjo's second term, some members of his party and loyalists moved to engineer a constitutional change that would allow him to run for the third term in the office. The rejection of a bill sent to Parliament stopped the move.

4. The Philippines is generally referred to as "the SMS capital of the world." According to the country's National Telecommunications Commission, reported in *The Hindu Business Line* on October 6, 2006, Filipinos send an average of 250 million text messages a day (www .thehindubusinessline.com/todays).

5. Times Online. http://www.textually.org/textually/archives/cat_sms_and_religion.htm?p=2.

6. http://www.prlog.org/10009629-new-technology-used-for-god-at-last-sms-bible -texts-and-internet-praying.html.

7. http://islaminaction08.blogspot.com/2009/04/sharia-court-approves-text-message .html.

8. http://news.bbc.co.uk/2/hi/asia-pacific/3100143.stm.

9. *Journal of Computer-Mediated Communication* (10)1. http://jcmc.indiana.edu/vol10 /issue1/porter.html.

10. Though Nigerian Christians differ in their attitudes toward imprecatory prayers, it is a common feature in many contemporary Pentecostal gatherings in the country. Its use in text messaging is a reflection of its widespread use in Pentecostal prayers.

11. Flashing is also referred to in some literature as "beeping," "pranking," or "missed calling" (Donner 2007). The practice is more common among African and Asian mobile phone users.

12. GloMobile has the slogan "Glo with Pride"; CELTEL started as Econet Wireless and changed to VMobile, Zain, and now Airtel; MTN then was reputed to offer the most expensive service.

13. Dr. Enoch Adejare Adeboye is the general overseer of the Redeemed Christian Church of God, one of the fastest-growing Pentecostal churches in Nigeria and Africa. He was listed as one of the 2008/2009 50 global power elites by *Newsweek*. The first Holy Ghost Congress organized by the church in 1998 was reputed to have drawn together the largest number of Christians (over 6 million) in Africa.

References

Abdulah, R. 2007. "Islam, Jihad, and Terrorism in Post-9/11 Arabic Discussion Boards." *Journal of Computer-Mediated Communication* 12(3): article 15. http://jcmc.indiana.edu/vol12/issue3 /abdulla.html.

Akínnásò, Fúnṣọ N. (1980): "The Sociolinguistic Basis of Yorùbá Personal Names." *Anthropological Linguistics* 22(7): 275–304.

Awonusi, S. 2004. "'Little Englishes' and the Law of Energetics: A Sociolinguistic Study of SMS Text Messages as Register and Discourse." In *The Domestication of English in Nigeria,* edited by S. Awonusi and E. A. Babalola, 45–62. Lagos: University of Lagos Press.

Baron, S. 1998. "Letters by Phone or Speech by other Means: The Linguistics of Email." *Language and Communication* 18: 133–170.

Bednarek, M. A. 2005. "Construing the World: Conceptual Metaphors and Event-Construal in News Stories." *Metaphoric.de* 09/2005. http://www.metaphorik.de/sites/www.metaphorik .de/files/journal-pdf/09_2005_bednarek.pdf.

Bush, C. 2005. "Language Beyond the Text: Txt Msgs 4 a New Gnr8n." *Journal of New Media and Culture* 3(2). http://www.ibiblio.org/nmediac/summer2005/text.html.

Campbell, H. 2007. "Who's Got the Power? Religious Authority and the Internet." *Journal of Computer-Mediated Communication* 12(3): article 14. http://jcmc.indiana.edu/vol12/issue3/campbell.html.

Chiluwa, I. 2008. "SMS Text-Messaging and the Nigerian Christian Context: Constructing Values and Sentiments." *International Journal of Language Society and Culture* 24: 11–20.

Donner, J. 2007. "The Rules of Beeping: Exchanging Messages via Intentional 'Missed Calls' on Mobile Phones." *Journal of Computer-Mediated Communication* 13(1): article 1. http://jcmc.indiana.edu/vol13/issue1/donner.html.

Downer, S. R., J. G. A. Meara, A. C. Da Costa, and K. Sethuraman. 2006. "SMS Text Messaging Improves Outpatient Attendance." *Australian Health Review* 30(3): 389–396.

Ellwood-Clayton, B. 2003. "Texting and God: The Lord Is My Textmate, Folk Catholicism in the Cyber Philippines." In *A Sense of Place*, edited by K. Nyiri, 91–106 Vienna: Passanger Verlag.

Ess, C. 2007. "Cross-Cultural Perspectives on Religion and Computer-Mediated Communication." *Journal of Computer-Mediated Communication* 12(3): article 9. http://jcmc.indiana.edu/vol12/issue3/ess.html.

Fischer, C. 1998. "Gender and the Residential Telephone, 1890–1940: Technologies of Sociability." *Sociology Forum* 3(2): 211–233.

Fukamisu, K. 2007. "Internet Use among Religious Followers: Religious Postmodernism in Japanese Buddhism." *Journal of Computer-Mediated Communication* 12(3): article 11. http://jcmc.indiana.edu/vol12/issue3/fukamizu.html.

Hackett, R. I. J. 2003. "Managing or Manipulating Religious Conflict in Nigerian Media." In *Conversations in Media, Religion and Culture,* edited by Jolyon Mitchell and Sophia Marriage, 47–64. Edinburgh: T & T Clark.

Harper, R., L. Palen, and A. Taylor. 2005. *The Inside Text: Social Perspectives on SMS.* Amsterdam: Springer.

Hsu, T., Y. Wang, and S. Wen. 2006. "Using the Decomposed Theory of Planned Behaviour to Analyse Consumer Behavioural Intention towards Mobile Text Message Coupons." *Journal of Targeting, Measurement and Analysis for Marketing* 14(4): 309–324.

Ikotun, R. O. 2013. "New Trends in Yorùbá Personal Names among Yorùbá Christians." *Linguistik Online* 50(2): 67–85.

Jacobs, S. 2007. "Virtually Sacred: The Performance of Asynchronous Cyber-Rituals in Online Spaces." *Journal of Computer-Mediated Communication* 12(3): article 17. http://jcmc.indiana.edu/vol12/issue3/jacobs.html.

Jaffe, A. 2000. "Introduction: Non-Standard Orthography and Non-Standard Speech." *Journal of Sociolinguistics* 4(4): 497–513.

Kasesniemi, E. 2003. *Mobile Messages: Young People and a New Communication Culture.* Tampere, Finland: Tampere University Press.

Koshy, E., J. Car, and A. Majeeb. 2008. "Effectiveness of Mobile-Phone Short Message Service (SMS) Reminders for Ophthalmology Outpatient Appointments: Observational Study." *BMC Ophthalmology* 8(9): 2415–2419. http://www.biomedcentral.com/1471-2415/8/9#IDAoW3AO.

Kwabata, A., and T. Tamura. 2007. "Online-Religion in Japan: Websites and Religious Counseling from a Comparative Cross-Cultural Perspective." *Journal of Computer-Mediated Communication* 12(3): article 12. http://jcmc.indiana.edu/Vol12/Issue3/kawabata.html.

Ling, R. 2005. "The Sociolinguistics of SMS: An Analysis of SMS Use by a Random Sample of Norwegians." In *Mobile Communications: Re-Negotiation of the Social Sphere,* edited by R. S. Ling and P. E. Pedersen, 335–350. London: Springer.

———. 2008. *New Tech, New Ties: How Mobile Communication Is Reshaping Social Cohesion.* Cambridge, MA: MIT Press.

Ndukwe E. 2003. "Three Years of GSM Revolution in Nigeria." http://www.ncc.gov.ng/archive /speeches_presentations/EVC's%20Presentation/GSM%20REVOLUTION%20IN%20NIGE RIA%20%20-140504.pdf.

Obadare, E. 2006. "Playing Politics with the Mobile Phone: Civil Society, Big Business and the State in Nigeria." *Review of African Political Economy* 107: 93–111.

Ofulue, C. I. 2004, October. "Interconnexity in Other Tongues: A Sociolinguistic Study of SMS Texts in Yoruba." *Paper presented at the 18th Annual Conference of Linguistics Association of Nigeria*, University of Port Harcourt.

Osibanjo, O., and C. Nnorom. 2006. "Material Flows of Mobile Phones and Accessories in Nigeria: Environmental Implications and Sound End-of-Life Management Options." *Environmental Impact Assessment Review* 28(2–3): 198–213.

Parks, M. R., and K. Floyd. 1996. "Making Friends in Cyberspace." *Journal of Computer-Mediated Communication* 1(4): 80–97. http://onemvweb.com/sources/sources/making_friends_cyber space.pdf.

Porter, C. S. (2004). "A Typology of Virtual Communities: A Multidisciplinary Foundation for Future Research." *Journal of Computer-Mediated Communication* 10(1): article 3. http://jcmc .indiana.edu/vol10/issue1/porter.html.

Robinson, S., S. Perkins, S. Bauer, N. Hammond, J. Treasure, and U. Schmidt. 2006. "Aftercare Intervention through Text Messaging in the Treatment of Bulimia Nervosa—Feasibility Pilot." *International Journal of Eating Disorders* 39(8): 633–638.

Rollier, P. 2010. "Texting Islam: Text Messages and Religiosity among Young Pakistanis." *Contemporary South Asia* 18(4): 413–426.

Roman, A. 2006. "Texting God: SMS and Religion in the Philippines." Paper presented at the 5th International Conference on Media, Religion and Culture, Stockholm, July 2006.

Taiwo, R. 2007. "Tenor in Electronic Media Christian Discourse." *Nordic Journal of African Studies* 16(1): 75–89.

———. 2008a. "Linguistic Forms and Functions of SMS Text Messages in Nigeria." In *Handbook of Research on Computer Mediated Communication,* edited by S. Kelsey and K. St. Armant, 1:969–982. Hershey, PA: Information Science Reference.

———. 2008b. "Interpersonal Social Responsibility in the Context of SMS Messaging in South-Western Nigeria." In *Culture and Society in Nigeria: Popular Culture, Language and Intergroup Relations,* edited by T. Babawale and O. Ogen, 165–179. Lagos: Centre for Black and African Arts and Civilization (CBAAC).

———. 2010. "The Thumb Tribe": Creativity and Social Change through SMS in Nigeria, *California Linguistic Notes* 35(1). https://www.uni-leipzig.de/~ecas2009/.

Thurlow, C. 2003. "Generatn Txt? The Sociolinguistics of Young People's Text-Messaging." *Discourse Analysis Online.* http://extra.shu.ac.uk/daol/articles/v1/n1/a3/thurlow2002003.html.

van Dijk, T. 1988. *News as Discourse.* Hillsdale, NJ: Lawrence Erlbaum.

PART III

ARENAS OF EXCHANGE, COMPETITION, AND CONFLICT

11 Media Afrikania

Styles and Strategies of Representing "Afrikan Traditional Religion" in Ghana

Marleen de Witte

RELIGION IN AFRICA, as all over the world, is closely bound up with the field of modern media. This is not new as such. Modern media have been integral to the presence of Christianity in Africa ever since the first missionaries brought printing presses with them. But since the 1990s, processes of media deregulation in many African countries have greatly enhanced the public manifestation of religion in mass-mediated forms. Groups and individuals of various religious backgrounds eagerly use the new possibilities for asserting public presence and attracting new audiences offered by electronic and digital media. Scholars of religion have become increasingly aware of these developments and over the past decade have established a burgeoning study field of religion and media (for edited collections and review articles, see, for instance, de Vries and Weber 2001; Stolow 2005; Meyer and Moors 2006; Morgan 2008; Meyer 2009; Engelke 2010; Morgan 2013; Lundby 2013).

In this field, the importance of mass media is well recognized for global religions, such as Christianity and Islam. The global movement of Charismatic-Pentecostalism in particular has been fruitfully analyzed as a media-driven phenomenon (e.g., Marshall-Fratani 1998; Coleman 2000; Robbins 2004).[1] A focus on the global spread of Pentecostalism alone, however, may fail to reveal interactions and tensions in local religious and media landscapes. In Ghana, the focus of this chapter, the fervent media activities of Charismatic-Pentecostal churches have resulted in a heightened public presence of a particular, exclusionary type of Christianity and a rise in interreligious tensions in the public sphere, especially between charismatic Christians and "traditionalists." Confronted with the media presence and popularity of charismatic preachers who display a marked hostility toward indigenous religious traditions, neo-traditionalist groups increasingly feel the need to also enter the media and compete for public presence and followers. In the literature, however, African traditional religion is generally thought of outside the context of modern mass media and the public sphere. Partly, this may be due to the rural bias of most literature on traditional religions in Africa, and partly to the mutually reinforcing tendencies of African media institutions and practitioners to censor traditional religion out of the media and of traditional religious practitioners to be wary of accommodating modern media.

This chapter explores the media activities of a neo-traditional religious movement, the Afrikania Mission, in Ghana's Christian-dominated public sphere. Afrikania presents an interesting case of a religious movement that aims at reforming traditional religion and putting it on the national and even world map with a radical ideology of Africanness and cultural-religious identity. Analyzing Afrikania's changing position in and interactions with the public sphere in relation to shifts in Ghana's political, religious, and media landscape, I show how new constraints and opportunities have pushed Afrikania to adapt its strategies of accessing the media and its styles of representation.

By calling attention to strategies and styles, I suggest moving away from a sole preoccupation with meaning in the study of religion. To understand the dynamics of religion in an era of rapid media development, we cannot limit ourselves to the study of doctrine, beliefs, and rituals but must take into account matters of power and form associated with public representation. As Ghana's formerly state-controlled media scene has developed into a plural, liberalized, and commercialized field of interaction, religion has increasingly become an arena for struggle and competition between different societal groups and a matter of conscious choice and contestation rather than an automatically received heritage. Media have become crucial to this struggle. The question then is how changes in the institutions, economics, technologies, and practices of media have changed access to the public sphere and inform strategies of representation, exclusion, and inclusion. Closely connected to this question is the question of style and form. Mass media are never just a technology; they entail specific formats, styles, and modes of address. Style and form are also at the core of religion, as religious content only comes available via particular aesthetic forms that shape religious subjectivity, community, and authority (Meyer 2009). This raises the question of who controls the forms and styles of media representation and how these media forms relate to religious forms and aesthetics.

As this chapter shows, Afrikania's politics of representation is complicated by its awkward position between the dominant, Christian formats and styles of representing religion and the shrine priests and priestesses that it claims to represent but who are often more concerned with concealing than with revealing. Founded in 1982 by a former Roman Catholic priest, Afrikania's mission was to reaffirm an "African" religious culture and create a new "African" self-consciousness.[2] Ever since the movement's birth at a press conference, media have been central to Afrikania's identity politics of justification and defense against other groups. To frame and justify a common cultural and religious identity, the movement has created new and refashioned old symbols, traditions, and rituals and has rewritten African history. Paradoxically, in this process of reforming

"African traditional religion" for nationalist purposes and bringing it into the public sphere as an alternative "world religion" in its own right, Christianity, in its changing dominant forms, has provided the template for Afrikania at the same time as being its major opponent. The irony of Afrikania's project, then, is that in presenting itself as the public face of all traditional religions in Ghana, the movement has become removed from traditional religious practice on the ground. This tension between Afrikania's reform movement and the often contradictory concerns with spiritual power and the secrecy of traditional religious specialists has existed throughout Afrikania's history. And although the current leaders have tried to bridge this gap through the greater involvement of shrine priests and priestesses, conflicts of interest are often exacerbated during media activities, when Afrikania finds itself caught between those it aims to represent and the available means and modes of representation.

Religion in Ghanaian Media

Over the past two decades, the representation of religion in Ghanaian media has drastically changed. Until the mid-1990s, media in Ghana have been largely controlled by the state. After independence, in the euphoria of freedom and national pride and progress, radio was celebrated as a means for social and political reform. The new state inherited the Ghana Broadcasting Corporation (GBC) from the colonial government and employed radio—and from 1965 also TV—to enhance national education, integration, and development. In line with Nkrumah's nationalist discourse and anti-colonial critique, media production aimed at the promotion of national culture and "African traditional religion" was presented as part of the "African Heritage" in which people took pride. Much later, when Jerry Rawlings came to power in 1981, he revived this interest in the nation's cultural roots and implemented a cultural policy of *Sankofa* ("go back and take it"). Accordingly, the neo-traditional Afrikania Mission was the only religious group granted airspace on state radio and soon came to be perceived as the religious branch of the revolution. For a long time the airwaves remained inaccessible to any other religious group.

This situation changed when Ghana returned to democratic rule in 1992. As part of democratic reforms, the Ghanaian state gradually loosened its control over the media and from 1995 gave way to a rapidly evolving privatized media scene. Local newspapers, tabloids, FM and TV stations, cable television providers, video producers (Meyer 1999b), and internet cafes started mushrooming and are omnipresent today. The commercial formula of the new radio and TV stations has been very successful, forcing GBC to start selling airtime, too. The most eager consumers of this new "merchandise" are Charismatic-Pentecostal churches (de Witte 2011), which have successfully used the new media freedom to claim public presence and to spread their messages across the nation and abroad. They thus dodge Ghana's media law that disallows religious organizations to set up broadcast stations but allows them to buy airtime or appear on programs. Contrary to other religious organizations, many of these highly popular churches have the financial resources to produce their own programs and pay for airtime on radio and television, as they attract many upwardly mobile professionals and demand a tenth of members' income through tithing (Gifford 2004). Moreover, because of their popularity, these churches can fairly easily obtain sponsorship for their media programs from large companies such as soft-drink producers (who see a market in the Pentecostal ban on alcohol), transport companies, or furniture manufacturers. Finally, many media owners and practitioners are convinced born-again Christians themselves. As a result, the new media scene is dominated by Charismatic-Pentecostalism to the extent that, as radio pastor Reverend Cephas Amartey of Joy FM put it, "religious broadcast has become the bedrock of the media industry in the country."[3] Religious TV broadcasts, radio sermons, phone-in talk shows, religiously oriented video movies, audiotaped sermons, popular gospel music, and Christian printed materials now inundate public and private space. Tuning into the radio at any time of the day or surfing through the TV channels on weekday mornings or on the weekends, one cannot miss the energetic, charismatic pastors who, as professional media entertainers, preach about their convictions and communicate their spiritual powers and miracles to a widespread audience through the airwaves.

A new mass-mediated form of Christian religiosity has thus emerged that makes the specific ways of worshipping in Charismatic-Pentecostal churches available to the eyes and ears of a large audience, and it has been widely appropriated (de Witte 2003). This also has implications for the representation of traditional religion, since these churches use the media not only to advertise their own success and morality but to circulate a counter-image of the non-Christian "Other." In particular, their hostile stance toward African traditional religion and their use of media to represent it as the evil enemy make for a particular result in increasing interreligious tensions and intolerance (Hackett 2012). Contrary to mission Christianity, African Pentecostalism acknowledges the existence of local gods, spirits, witches, and other spiritual beings that characterize African traditional beliefs. Whereas Catholic and Protestant mission-related churches disregarded such agents as "superstitious beliefs," Pentecostalism integrates them into Christian doctrine as demons and offers people ways to fight these evil forces with the power of Jesus Christ and the Holy Spirit (Meyer 1999a). This demonization of African traditional religion nurtures a widespread fear of and animosity toward traditional religion. The media play an important role in sustaining and reinforcing such popular fears with sensational stories and images of "juju" priests and shrines. At the same time, people are fascinated by such visualizations of evil, and video movies, tabloids, posters, and calendars depicting traditional religion as the dark and evil Other are a commercial success.

A case in point is Dr. Beckley, a famous Ghanaian "occultist" and medical doctor who was arrested and saw his house and shrine destroyed by a mob in April 2002, after he was accused of abducting a tomato seller and binding her to a tree on his compound. Following the incident, a media scandal evolved and created considerable negative publicity for traditional religious practices in general. But rather than reporting on the court proceedings and on what had actually happened—it turned out there was no evidence, and eventually Dr. Beckley was released from custody—all the tabloids carried front-page stories about Beckley's occult practices and allegations of the sale of human blood and the ritual use of human body parts. Clever entrepreneurs printed poster-calendars titled "Beckley's Juju: Seeing Is Believing" or "Beckley's Evil Deeds Exposed," with pictures showing all kinds of "fetishes," statues of the gods in his shrine, his "flying coffin," a "victim's skull," and other frightening things allegedly used in his spiritual practices. On the street corners where they were for sale, people gathered to look at the images as a source of news. The pictures confirmed people's belief in the power of traditional priests and "occultists" and of Dr. Beckley in particular. As he said to me in an interview, "The media are just interested in sensation, not in reporting or even discovering the truth. The media are trying to destroy me, but they have rather made me even more popular. They have made me a popular and well-known personality in Ghana and abroad."[4] Not long after the media scandal (and I return to this below), Afrikania welcomed Dr. Beckley into their midst, albeit reluctantly. These kinds of stories dominate public representation of traditional religion and link up with widely broadcast Pentecostal views of traditional religion as Satanic, and as such exacerbate people's fear of and hostility toward traditional religion and its adherents. To counter such negative, stereotypical representations, Afrikania tries to present an alternative image.

The Afrikania Mission: Representing "Afrikan Traditional Religion"

In response to the (charismatic) Christian dominance in the public sphere, the Afrikania Mission aims to reconstruct and represent "Afrikan Traditional Religion" (ATR)[5] as a modern pan-African religion to serve as a source of African pride and strength and a religious base for political nationalism and pan-Africanism. Despite its explicit non-Christian stance, the reformation and public representation of ATR involved the appropriation of Christian forms. Over the course of the movement's 30-year history, however, the specific styles and representational strategies employed have changed in relation to wider religious and political developments.

In several studies of the Afrikania Mission (Boogaard 1993; Opoku 1993; Gyanfosu 1995, 2002; Schirripa 2000), two aspects emerge as central to the foundation of the movement in 1982: the connection with flight-lieutenant Jerry Rawlings's "31st December Revolution" in 1981 and the Roman Catholic background of founder Kwabena Damuah. Both have shaped Afrikania's representations of ATR. A few years after Damuah's return from a 12-year period of study in the United States (1964–1976), where he was inspired by the American civil rights movement and issues of black experience, Black Power, identity, and dignity, Rawlings invited him to take part in his Provisional National Defence Council. Damuah accepted, but he left the government not long afterward to focus on the spiritual, cultural, religious, and moral aspects of nation-building. On December 26, 1982, he resigned from the Roman Catholic Church and founded the Afrikania Mission. Rawlings supported Damuah with a car, a public address system, a press conference, and airtime on state radio. Afrikania was an explicitly nationalist movement with a strong political vision on African identity and national development. According to Damuah, "Religion and nation-building should always go together. Our national duty is a religious duty" (cited in Boogaard 1993: 148).

Afrikania's "origin myth," as it circulates among members and is taught to prospective priests, recounts that the mission was conceived on a global religious platform, the World Religions Conference, a multifaith conference held annually in various parts of the world. Damuah, who at that time had been a Catholic priest for 25 years and was about to be ordained a bishop, was sent as the Ghanaian representative for the Catholic Church. At the conference he noticed that all parts of the world had representatives for their own religion—Islam, Christianity, Judaism, Buddhism, Hinduism, Confucianism—but there was not a single representative for African religion. Thus, he got the idea to form Afrikania to represent Afrikan Traditional Religion as a world religion in itself. Conceived in a global context of world religions as different, but structurally comparable, varieties of "religion," it may thus not be surprising that the reformulation of African traditional religion implied the adoption of a universalized, yet originally Western Christian concept of religion as belief. To create a "systematic and coherent doctrine for Ghanaians and Africans in the diaspora," Afrikania has picked elements from traditional religious belief—such as belief in multiple gods and spirits, the power of ancestors as manifested in dreams, and spirit possession—and reformed and brought these together in an intellectualist, Christian-modeled doctrine, including Holy Scriptures; the *Divine Acts* (Ameve 2002b) (also referred to as the "Afrikania Bible"); prophets; a list of commandments; and a standardized liturgy, prayers, and slogans. So while Afrikania consciously posits itself as non-Christian and calls for a revolution in the meaning of "religion," it precisely subscribes to a universalist, modern definition of religion by recasting traditional religion in terms of belief, teaching, and symbols (cf. Asad 1993). Local religious traditions are rather organized around practices of communicating with and influencing the spirit world.

Damuah's Catholic background further provided the practice of and model for Afrikania's newly invented Sunday worship. The whole sequence of prayers, greetings, slogans, songs, rituals, "bible" readings, preaching, communion, offertory prayers, and benediction is modeled after Catholic liturgy. All these structural elements have been given "traditional" content and symbolism. Clearly, all ingredients—the symbols, the texts, the rituals, the songs, the sequence of events—are carefully selected, recreated, and arranged in a way that has very little to do with what goes on in shrines. Afrikania's justification of this is that to unite all traditional religion, which includes so many different cults that all have their own practices and ways of worship, one has to "find a form where everybody can feel at home."[6] Sunday mass provided this form.

Damuah's revolutionary background, moreover, provided the intellectual, political, nationalist orientation and the rhetorical styles. Afrikania shared the anti-Western and anti-Christian ideology of the Revolution and radically rewrote the history of civilization, inspired by black emancipatory literature (e.g., James 1992 [1954]; Williams 1992 [1971]). This version of history teaches that civilization was born and developed in ancient Egypt, which was, contrary to what the colonialists have encouraged Africans to believe, inhabited and ruled by blacks. This ancient black civilization spread across the continent after the Romans invaded Egypt and formed the basis of all African culture and religions. For Afrikania, recourse to ancient Egyptian religion and civilization was also a solution to the problem of how to unite a variety of ethnically and territorially specific local religious traditions with one pan-African religious ideology and form. Because the various local deities and their cults are often incompatible and even competing with one another, Afrikania had to look for a common, universal object of worship elsewhere. This was found in the supposed common religious source of all these cults: ancient Egypt. Damuah, influenced by the popularity of ancient Egyptian spirituality among American pan-Africanists, appropriated the Sun God Amen-Ra, or Ra, into Afrikania's doctrine as "our supreme Creator and universal almighty God." During Sunday service, this divine creator is endlessly addressed with the phrase "Amen-Ra!—Amen!" and called upon as "Father" (just like the Christian God) in prayers and formulas. When I talked about Ra with some Afrikanians, however, it appeared that Ra had very little personal significance for them. In contrast to various local deities and spirits, Ra was generally not believed to have any impact on one's life. Likewise, the *Egyptian Book of Life and Death* is accepted as one of the written Revelations on which ATR is built, and King Mena of Ethiopia, King Akhnaton of Egypt, and Akhnaton's wife, Queen Nefertiti, feature together with the famous Asante priest Akomfo Anokye, King Shaka Zulu, Marcus Garvey, W.E.B. DuBois, and Kwame Nkrumah as its prophets. In his book *The Origin of the Bible* (Ameve 2002a) Afrikania's second leader Kofi Ameve traces the concept of monotheism, the

Bible, the Ten Commandments, and other central elements of Christianity to black African religion. Wrapped in a revolutionary discourse of African emancipation and liberation of mental slavery, Afrikan Traditional Religion became an ideological resource. Afrikania engaged very little with the actual practices of shrine priests and priestesses and traditional healers. Damuah's main strategies of mobilizing people were giving speeches and organizing rallies, as well as a weekly radio broadcast (see below) that was also replete with revolutionary rhetoric.

Two events in 1992 had great implications for Afrikania's link to national politics and for the directions Afrikania took over the subsequent decade. First, the turn to a democratic constitution in Ghanaian national politics eventually implied the break of Afrikania's ties with the government. Although the democratic elections kept Rawlings in power, relations between the state and Afrikania became weaker, as the government now had to compete for popular support. It especially could not do without the increasingly popular Pentecostal and charismatic churches, which gained a strong public influence as the 1990s progressed (de Witte 2003; Gifford 2004). Rawlings gradually embraced Christianity and even—according to Afrikania under the influence of his wife, Nana Konadu—Pentecostalism. Pentecostal influence and rhetoric started penetrating the government on several levels and pushed the state's cultural policy of Sankofa to the background. Moreover, Rawlings relinquished his radical anti-Western rhetoric of his early years in power and adopted a more Western-oriented strategy in order to receive international loans and foreign assistance. In the 2000 elections, Rawlings's National Democratic Congress government lost power to the liberal opposition party, the New Patriotic Party, resulting in a further loss of state support for traditional culture. The increasing encroachment of Charismatic-Pentecostalism upon Ghana's public and political life has entered a new phase with the election in 2008 of president John Atta Mills, a born-again Christian, who expressed the wish to turn Ghana into a "prayer camp." With this gradual "Pentecostalization" of the state, Afrikania became increasingly critical of the government and its cultural policy and fiercely raises its voice in defense of tradition.

The second event that changed the course of Afrikania as an organization was the death of its founder, Damuah, in August 1992. After an internal succession conflict, Osofo Kofi Ameve, a building contractor by profession, became Afrikania's new leader. He died in June 2003. A successor has been chosen in the person of Osofo Atsu Kove, who—unlike his two predecessors—is not an ex-Christian who "converted" to ATR out of intellectual conviction but is a born traditionalist. The future of the mission remains uncertain, however, especially since a conflict with Ameve's children over property led to Afrikania's eviction from the headquarters building.

Ameve led Afrikania to much greater public presence and its establishment as a religious organization:

> It is only now that Afrikania is getting established. There were many difficulties in the past. We had government support, both morally and in the form of a loudspeaker system, vehicles and other equipment, from Rawlings's revolution, but no popular support. People thought it was only revolutionary. We have been doing our thing quietly, so not many people knew us. Recently we came out. In 1997 we organized a big convention at the Independence Square that shocked the world. Thousands of traditionalists came from all over the country. Those Christians tried to block the road and prevent us from reaching the square, but in the end we got there. Now we are not doing propaganda, but really establishing something.[7]

Apart from the public conventions mentioned by Ameve, "establishing something" meant building huge new headquarters (which after his death, however, turned out to be owned by Ameve's construction company), founding a "mission school for Afrikan Traditional Religion," publicly ordaining 60 newly trained priests and priestesses, and adopting an "evangelization" program of mobilizing traditionalists and establishing branches (shrines) throughout the country and abroad, linking up with local chiefs, traditional priests and healers, and building a network of traditionalist associations. Due to the severing of ties with the government, competition with other religious groups has grown. Afrikania increasingly needs to present itself in the public sphere and has during Ameve's time established a strong public presence in its own right.

In this struggle to enhance its public profile, Afrikania has appropriated many symbols of ecclesiastical establishment: a conspicuous building, head offices with a spacious office for the leader, a signboard indicating times of worship, a "ministry" school, a printed cloth with its name and emblem, official registration,[8] a constitution, membership cards, and branches in Ghana and abroad. In addition, the terminology Afrikania uses points to this borrowing from a Christian idea of religion: church, headquarters and branches, bible, liturgy, preaching, communion. With the rapid rise and public appearance of charismatic churches, Afrikania now increasingly adopts practices like public conventions, evangelization, camp meeting, all-night prayer, sharing of testimonies, and a preoccupation with public visibility and audibility. With the expansion of television culture in general and religious television in particular, Afrikania is more than ever concerned with public image, with beautification, and with making their religion *look* attractive. This is not to the neglect of sound, however. Competing with what is known as "Pentecostal noise-making," Afrikania has readily embraced the use of a public address system. This serves not so much for reaching the few dozens of people who attend services but for establishing a sonic presence in Sunday's battlefield of religious sound (de Witte 2008).

Not surprisingly, Afrikania's creation of a new, Christian-derived common form of religion and worship for all cults and shrines is not undisputed. In fact, a constant tension exists between this "modern" reformulation and the interests of the "traditional" shrine priests, priestesses, and adherents that Afrikania tries to mobilize and claims to represent. Elsewhere (de Witte 2004), I have explained that many of these adherents contest Afrikania's leaders, most of whom are ex-Christians; its "easy" initiation of anyone, even foreigners, into priesthood; and its concern with orderliness, cleanliness, and beauty that goes against the "messiness" of dealing with spiritual power. The question of how to relate to traditional priests has always been a matter of dissent within Afrikania (Boogaard 1993). Whereas Damuah was extremely reluctant to involve them at all, Ameve has during his time done much to mobilize and engage them.[9] Still, there is a tension that is particularly exacerbated, as we shall see, in Afrikania's engagements with the mass media. Afrikania's leaders are aware of this, but they also know that in order to gain recognition and compete with Christian churches, they have to create a clean and beautiful image and make this image public through the various media channels. Yet, they are also highly suspicious of the media because of the media's Christian bias and their "wrong" portrayal of traditional religion as filthy, ugly, and backward or, worse, as evil and demonic.

Afrikania and Mass Media

From its very beginnings, Afrikania has used the media to proclaim its message. In fact, the movement was born through a press conference. In Damuah's time, its constant media presence was sustained by its friendly rapport and the convergence of interests with the government, serving to make the movement and its leader widely known. Afrikania was the only religious group granted airtime on state radio, which was the only radio available. Its weekly radio broadcast, in which Damuah explained the objectives and doctrines of the mission, thus reached a large audience throughout the nation. Every Tuesday evening, Afrikania voiced its ideology to the nation:

> This is Afrikania Mission, the religion of those who have freed themselves from foreign religions and have the courage to serve God according to their conscience and the holy traditions of Africa. Yes, Afrikania is a way of life and more especially a spiritual revolution that tells the African to be himself. (opening Afrikania radio broadcast, October 3, 1989, quoted in Boogaard 1993: 86)

Moreover, Afrikania was regularly invited on state television to express its ideas and vision in all public debates concerning traditional culture and religion. Finally, Damuah's repeated presence at all kinds of official ceremonies greatly enhanced his appearance in the TV and radio news and the newspapers.

After the deregulation of the media in the mid-1990s, Afrikania's relation with and access to the media have become increasingly difficult. Afrikania no longer receives free radio time but instead has to pay for it and compete with others in a now Christian-dominated media scene. The major setback for Afrikania vis-à-vis the charismatic churches is its lack of financial resources. Afrikania has never been money-minded, and in this time of commercial media this makes it difficult to be heard. Half an hour of radio airtime may cost about US$50, excluding registration fees and "chop money" (a "tip" in the form of money to buy food) for the workers involved. For 30 minutes on TV one pays US$600. That is too costly for Afrikania, where members pay monthly dues of 1,000 cedis (US$0.12), if they pay at all, and contribute coins rather than banknotes to the Sunday collection.[10] Afrikania's major source of money was Ameve's private capital, until he died in 2003. He used this to pay for airtime on GBC radio for some time, but he stopped his regular radio preaching when he thought it was more effective to invest in the new building and the establishment of the school. Another disadvantage Afrikania faces, compared to Christian churches, is the lack of traditionalists working in the media field. Almost all professionals working with the various media houses are Christians, and often committed born-again Christians, and this does influence media content (de Witte 2011). The few traditionalists working in the media, like a young Afrikanian who works with GBC radio, always have to face the majoritarian attitude, and by extension the discrimination, of their colleagues.

Afrikania's lack of money and connections in the media sector thus makes it very difficult to counter the strong Christian dominance and public opinion about African traditional religion. It cannot make and broadcast—and thus control—its own programs as charismatic churches do. Afrikania thus tries to find other ways into the media, but they do not control the media formats that they are forced into nor the message carried into the public sphere. Like Damuah did in the past, Ameve features in radio and sometimes TV talk shows, taking the opportunity to make Afrikania's political-religious voice heard in public debates, create awareness among the people, and get recognition for African religion. Yet, it is always the talk show hosts who direct the interviews and more or less control what can be said by the questions they ask and their interruptions to the answers. Afrikania also invites (and pays) the press to attend traditional festivals where Afrikania plays a major role, Afrikania events (e.g., the opening of the new headquarters), and press conferences on specific topics. Here too, Afrikania can only wait and see what the journalists make of it, as the following three examples make clear.

After Afrikania's twentieth anniversary, a TV3 journalist proposed making a TV documentary about Afrikania. Because in Ghana the subjects of such documentaries often ask to be documented and pay for it themselves, Ameve was quite pleased with this proposal, as it meant TV3 was to bear the cost. He thus agreed despite his bad experiences with "misrepresentation" of traditional religion by TV3. But of course interests differed, and control over the images to be broadcast was negotiated between the different parties involved.[11] Ameve organized worship services at the Accra branch and a rural branch and a trip to a "neat" shrine in Accra for the TV crew. The priestess whose shrine Ameve selected did not really see the benefit of the documentary and had to be convinced. Beforehand Ameve told me that "we will not go and shoot what we want, but ask her what she wants the world to see, whether healing, prayer, sacrifice."[12] The priestess, however, did not want the world to see any of these and only allowed the crew to take static shots in the neat waiting room outside the shrine. This greatly disappointed the producer, who afterward commented to me that "it was nothing much after all, the shrine was very neat, nothing like the images we see on TV and in films. They didn't perform anything."[13] The producer, herself a Catholic, wanted to give an "objective" impression of Afrikania's survival in these times of Christian dominance and thus to show what was going on, but her imagination of shrines was certainly influenced by the dominant images on TV and by her own religious background. And although she did not mind visiting a shrine for this documentary, she did pray to Jesus about it and hoped that she did nothing that insulted the divinities.

For TV3's visit to one of the rural branches, a crowd of people had been mobilized. In front of the camera, Ameve was spectacularly welcomed like a big chief, followed by a drumming group and hundreds of cheering and singing people. Unfortunately, no shots of this were included in the documentary. In his speech to the worshippers, in English for the purpose of television and translated into Ewe, he said:

> I am happy TV3 is here to cover the activities of the shrine. I thank them for that. They for some time have not been our friends. Because when they cover our things, they don't show them well. But today they are here to cover our activities for the purpose of a documentary on our religion. I am very happy about it. They are welcome.

Soon, however, trouble arose about what was to be filmed and what not. As soon as the ceremony started with the taking of some bowls and objects from the altar and the calling of the deity Apetorku with "special prayers" and rituals, the shrine keepers told the cameraman, to his anger, not to film from this point onward until they told him it was all right to continue. When the animal sacrifice started, he could film again, but only from one position and in one direction so as not to film the holiest shrine at the back and disturb Apetorku. The shrine keepers were thus constantly busy preventing the camera from capturing the deity's dwelling place. Ameve's concern was first of all to present to the public a nice, clean picture of Afrikania and traditional religion and thus did not want bloody images of animal sacrifice included. His disappointment was acute when the documentary came out with abundant shots of just that. This, he said, would only confirm people's prejudices about traditional religion as dirty and cruel. But he did not have a say in the end product anymore. With TV3 being a commercial station, the audience's satisfaction in seeing stereotypes confirmed counted for more in the long run.

The third event to be filmed, a Sunday service at the Accra headquarters, caused another problem. The TV crew planned the visit during the annual "ban on drumming and noisemaking" preceding the traditional Ga *Homowo* festival. The "ban on drumming" is a 30-day period of ritual silence meant to give the local deities the peace to look after the growth of the ritually sown corn before it is harvested and prepared into a ceremonial dish (*kpokpoi*) to "hoot at hunger" (as *homowo* translates) during the harvest festival (de Witte 2008). This meant drumming and libation, both crucial to Afrikania worship, would not be allowed by the traditional religious authorities in Accra. Afrikania could not influence the date, and the result was a rather dull service without any drumming and with "dry libation"—that is, a calabash without any alcohol and, thus, devoid of spiritual meaning. The whole making of the documentary involved the negotiation between Afrikania's interest in presenting a positive image of traditional religion, the traditional priests' concerns with not showing certain things, and the objectives of the TV crew and the station as a whole. The resulting frictions were also clear during two other media events, a press conference and a talk show.

When, in September 2002, a government minister called for the abolition of libation at state functions and a heated media debate followed, Afrikania organized a press conference to speak its mind. The Sunday before, Ameve encouraged all members to show up "so that at least our numerical strength will be shown and these people will not shoot and show empty seats,"[14] and funds were raised from among the members and leaders because "they won't talk unless you pay them." The organizer explained:

> All the newsmen coming should be paid some "transport money," about 100,000 cedis each [about US$12], which is for them personally, not for the station. We call that public relations. If you don't recognize somebody as PRO [by giving some money], they will not carry your message. If you give them only Coke, they will not talk. If you call journalists to come and take your message outside, even for a short news item, you always have to pay them.[15]

Counting the reporters, cameramen, lighting crew, and soundmen from the various radio stations, plus the additional costs, he estimated the total cost of the press conference at about 6 million cedis (over US$700), the bulk of which had to come from Ameve's pocket. Journalists from two TV stations, four radio stations, and four newspapers attended the press conference; filmed, taped, and listened to Ameve's speech; and then asked questions. But when afterward they discovered that Dr. Beckley, who had after his court case joined Afrikania and was made a prominent member, was present and ready to talk to the press, they flocked around him with their microphones, cameras, recorders, and notebooks to record his words and ask questions. Ameve received little attention. The press was more interested in Beckley's sensational story than in the more political and much less scandalous debate about libation. And indeed, Dr. Beckley made the headlines in the newspapers in the following days with the statement that he would demand reparation from the government. The issue of libation at public functions disappeared in the background, and some newspapers and radio stations failed to even mention it at all, much to the anger of Ameve, who had spent so much on the press conference. It is clear that Ameve's attempt to exploit Dr. Beckley's celebrity and reputation as a powerful occultist by welcoming him and granting him prominence, albeit reluctantly, had backfired. Due to Beckley's presence, Ameve could not escape the very sensationalist media representation of African traditional religion that he tried to counter.

That same day, Ameve was invited to the TV3 talk show *Hot Issues* to talk about "the religion of the African." During this interview, which was recorded for a later broadcast, the host addressed Ameve as an exotic Other, the representative of a religion that believes in all kinds of strange things and spirits. Ameve, pushed into this role, but also feeling quite comfortable in it, talked in a very intellectual way about the Egyptian origin of African religion, the various spiritual beings "the African" believes in, and the significance of libation. When the conversation reached the "wrong" Christian use of the words "fetish" and "primitive," it turned into a verbal fight between the Christian and the non-Christian. Here is part of the argument:

> HOST: So when we describe [your way of worship] as primitive, why do you want to contest it? You use stones and blood and other related materials to worship. What is nice about that?
>
> AMEVE: What is fetish about it?
>
> HOST: Why stones?
>
> AMEVE: What has that got to do with you? Do we not have freedom of worship?
>
> HOST: We do, but how you do it. . . .
>
> AMEVE: If I decide to sit by a stone, and slaughter a fowl on it, and get the result of what I want, how does it affect you? I have carried my own stone to my house, or to a selected place, and slaughtered a fowl on it, because I want something, and I got that something, and I am satisfied.

HOST: So to you, the end justifies the means. How you get there should not be anybody's concern.

AMEVE: It should not be your concern at all. I have the freedom to do what I am doing. When you sit in your chapel, praying, speaking tongues, shouting, do I come to condemn you?

HOST: Don't you find anything wrong with it?

AMEVE: Do I come to condemn you?

HOST: No, but if you find something wrong with it, you have to condemn it.

AMEVE: Why do I condemn somebody's worship? Unless that worship affects me. If it does not affect me, nothing is wrong with it.

(*Hot Issues*, September 10, 2002)

As much as the host was posing his questions from a Christian viewpoint, Ameve was also opposing a Christian Other, almost to the point of personally accusing the host of what he had accused the whole Christian society of. At a certain point the interviewer rightly commented that he hoped Ameve was not targeting him personally. This antagonistic tendency was also very clear during the press conference, when all Afrikanians addressed the press as the Christian Other, as if they assumed that all the press was on the Christian side. This assumption is not unfounded, of course, but the tendency was more to oppose the press as almost an enemy than to manipulate and use the press. To them, the reporters were Christians in the first place and professional journalists only in the second.

Afrikania's interactions with the media are thus characterized by an ambiguous relationship. Afrikania is very much aware that it needs the media to achieve its goals, but at the same time, it adopts a highly distrustful, sometimes almost hostile, attitude toward the media, which are, for obvious reasons, perceived as belonging to the field of the Christian enemy. Afrikania's media interactions, then, often take the form of a battle of "the Christians against the traditionalists." Moreover, since Afrikania does not have the means to produce its own programs in the way that the rich Christian churches do, it is always dependent on the goodwill and concerns of the media practitioners and has hardly any control over the images and messages eventually produced and broadcast. Finally, the media formats that Afrikania is forced to use allow mainly for statements *about* traditional religion and leave hardly any room for the mediation of spiritual power itself, which is the case of Charismatic-Pentecostal broadcasts (see de Witte 2003, 2005a). This works in tandem with Afrikania's intellectualist approach and its efforts at keeping supposedly dirty and disorderly practices out of public view. The mass-mediated face of traditional religion thus remains far removed from what occupies the traditional religious specialists that Afrikania tries to mobilize.

Conclusion: Styles and Strategies of Representation

This chapter addresses the ways in which a neo-traditionalist political-religious movement in Ghana seeks to access the public sphere in the context of shifting relations among the state, religion, and the media. From its very birth, the Afrikania Mission has used mass media. Its styles and strategies of representation, however, have changed over the course of its development in relation to transformations in Ghana's religious, political, and media landscape.

In Ghana's religious field, the balance of power has shifted from the older mission churches to the new type of independent Charismatic-Pentecostal churches. Starting in the late 1970s and thriving during the 1990s, the phenomenal rise and spread, high popularity, and public dominance of this exclusionist type of Christianity have greatly impacted interreligious relations and tensions in the country, sometimes leading to outright clashes. Over the same period, Ghana's political scene has been greatly transformed. Where the 1980s were marked by Rawlings's revolution, his subsequent military rule, and his anti-Western ideals of political and cultural self-consciousness, the 1990s saw a return to democratic rule, a growing leaning toward the West, and a gradual "Pentecostalization" of the state. As a result of these two developments, Ghana's public sphere has also seen a shift from a state monopoly on the media, which were employed to voice the nationalist state ideology, to a liberalized media scene, which is characterized by the mushrooming of a myriad of private, commercial radio and TV stations and other media channels and an upsurge of religion, especially Charismatic-Pentecostalism. Negative stereotyping of African traditional religion in public has intensified tensions between Christians and traditionalists. Sensationalist representations of "juju" priests and practices flourish in the media and reinforce Pentecostal conceptions of traditional religion as demonic and feed both popular fear of and fascination for this evil Other.

In this nexus of politics, religion, and the public sphere, the Afrikania Mission has seen a history of growing public presence and establishment, severing ties with the government, and intensifying competition with other religious groups. This history is reflected by the movement's changing styles and strategies of representation. In line with Rawlings's revolution and with its pan-Africanist inspiration, Afrikania at first developed a radical anti-Western political-religious discourse, directed against cultural and mental domination by the West and propagating African pride and self-consciousness. In its early years of state support, Afrikania's public representation was characterized by political rhetoric and slogans—"propaganda," as Ameve said—combined with traditional drumming. Now, in response to the rise and public dominance of an exclusionist form of Christianity embodied by Africans themselves, Afrikania's media strategies are in the first place directed at "our own brothers and sisters" in the

Charismatic-Pentecostal churches and, with the "Pentecostalization" of the state, at the government. Paradoxically, in the project of reforming traditional religion and making it a public religion, Afrikania has adopted a Christian-derived form and concept of religion. Both its coherent doctrine and form of worship are a purposely created "invention of tradition," modeled after Christianity. And it is the same charismatic type of Christianity that has pushed Afrikania to take on a more anti-Christian attitude that now also provides the model for what religion is and forces Afrikania, if it wants to survive in the competitive religious field, to take over many of its practices and styles of representation. The revolutionary rhetorical styles of Damuah's time have made room for emphasis on visual attraction, beautification, and spectacular public performances.

In its efforts to counter the Charismatic-Pentecostal stereotypes and bring its own, positive image of traditional religion into the media, Afrikania constantly has to negotiate between the media and the shrines. Because it depends on the media for publicity, it tries to attract media attention, but it often has to give the media what pleases them and depends on media formats that do not allow it much control over the message and image produced. Afrikania thus finds it hard to escape the stereotypical representations of traditional religion that it tries to counter. This has so often led to disappointments that in many of Afrikania's media encounters, they approach the media (which are dominated by Christians and Christian views and attitudes) as an opponent rather than a strategic means to public representation. But in representing traditional religion in the media, Afrikania also has to negotiate with the traditional priests and priestesses, who are often reluctant to come on TV. Afrikania's aims and project and the ways in which it has been able to enter the media, but also the idea of looking for publicity as such, conflict with the practically oriented ways of working with spiritual power that characterize African traditional religion and that are closely linked to secrecy and concealment. The process of bringing traditional religion into the media, then, implies a constant struggle about revealing and concealing, about what can and cannot be shown.[16] In the public face of traditional religion, what really matters for many practitioners and adherents—namely, its spiritual power—seems to be absent. The result is a major gap between the intellectualist and sanitized version of traditional religion that Afrikania brings to the attention of the general public and the practices and concerns of traditional religious practitioners on the ground.

Some new developments, however, suggest that traditional religious specialists may in fact be very successful in using the opportunities of audiovisual and digital media. A case in point is that of Nana Kwaku Bonsam (see also de Witte 2009), a famous "fetish priest" who in 2008 fought—and won—a media battle with a Charismatic-Pentecostal pastor after he had proclaimed in the media that many pastors secretly got "juju" powers from him so as to ensure success for their churches and threatened to publicize their names. While Afrikania has made similar claims, what is new in the case of Kwaku Bonsam is his effective employment of various media (radio, television, website) to establish himself as a powerful "fetish priest." He organized a spectacular TV show full of sensational miracles, has appeared on many radio shows, and has his own website, where he advertises himself in the world as "a powerful fetish priest from Ghana" (www.kwakubonsam.com) and offers his healing practices via the internet. So whereas the traditional shrine priests that Afrikania claims to represent used to be wary of modern media and thus are unable to counter the audiovisual hostility of Charismatic-Pentecostal churches, the mediagenic priest Kwaku Bonsam now turns this struggle in new digital and global directions—and he does so to his advantage. What is particularly striking is that he, just like the charismatic churches, succeeds in employing media as effective public relations. Unlike his colleagues whose power thrives on secrecy and seclusion, Kwaku Bonsam derives his persuasiveness from spectacular media shows. The appearance in cyberspace of traditional African religious specialists (see also Chidester 2008 and chapter 15 in this volume) suggests that indigenous religious resources may become extra powerful and compelling when cast in global formats of commercialized spirituality in the new religious spaces opened up by the internet.

Acknowledgment

The research on which this chapter is based was carried out within the frameworks of the PIONIER research program "Modern Mass Media, Religion and the Imagination of Communities" and the research program "Heritage Dynamics," both sponsored by The Netherlands Organization for Scientific Research NWO.

Notes

1. I use the term "Charismatic-Pentecostal" to refer to the new wave of independent Pentecostal groups and churches that emerged in Africa from the late 1970s and are also known as neo-Pentecostal churches or charismatic ministries.

2. The terms "African" and "African traditional religion" are problematic because they suggest bounded, unchanging entities that do not correspond with ever-changing realities, and moreover, they are themselves historical constructions. I use the terms to indicate people's own constructions of "Africa" and "tradition," be they Afrikania's, the state's, the media's, Christians', or any other.

3. Interview: Reverend Cephas Amartey of Joy FM in Radio and TV Review, 28 (2001): 57.

4. Interview: Dr. Beckley, Accra, December 5, 2002.

5. Afrikania officially spells Afrikan Traditional Religion with a "k" as a protest against being misrepresented on outsiders' terms and as a claim to self-representation, and with capitals in analogy to other world religions.

6. Interview: Kofi Ameve, July 16, 2001.

7. Interview: Kofi Ameve, July 16, 2001.

8. PNDC law 221, passed in 1989 and repealed in 1994, was meant to control the mushrooming of new religious groups and required all religious groups in the country to register. Like many new, independent churches, Afrikania saw this as an opportunity to gain legitimacy. It was the only traditional religious group that registered.

9. The present leader's non-Christian background may make a considerable difference for Afrikania's relationship with traditional shrines. To what extent, however, remains to be seen.

10. In July 2007, Ghana introduced a new unit of currency, the Ghana cedi, that equaled 10,000 old cedis. All figures and conversion rates given in this chapter refer to the situation in 2002.

11. A more elaborate account of the making of this documentary and the struggles involved is given in de Witte 2005b.

12. Talk with Kofi Ameve, Accra, April 30, 2002.

13. Talk with Kafui Nyaku, Accra, May 5, 2002.

14. Kofi Ameve, Sunday service, Afrikania Headquarters, Accra, May 5, 2002.

15. Interview: Osofo Boakye, Accra, September 9, 2002.

16. As I have argued elsewhere (de Witte 2005a), this struggle about revealing and concealing is not particular to African traditional religion alone. Although at first glance African traditional religion might seem a religion of secrecy and charismatic Christianity one of publicity, charismatic churches' media strategies also involve considerable concealment.

References

Ameve, Osofo Kofi. 2001. Interview by author, July 16. Accra.

———. 2002a. *The Origin of the Bible and Pertinent Issues.* New edition. Accra: African Renaissance Books.

———. 2002b. *The Divine Acts: Holy Scriptures for the Sankofa Faith (Afrikanism).* Accra: Afrikan Renaissance Mission.

Asad, Talal. 1993. *Genealogies of Religion: Discipline and Reasons of Power in Christianity and Islam.* Baltimore: Johns Hopkins University Press.

Bediako, Kwame. 1995. *Christianity and Africa: The Renewal of a Non-Western Religion.* Edinburgh: Edinburgh University Press.

Boogaard, Paulien. 1993. "Afrikania of: Hervormde Traditionele Religie. Een Politiek-Religieuze Beweging in Ghana." MA thesis, University of Amsterdam.

Chidester, David. 2008. "Zulu Dreamscapes: Senses, Media, and Authentication in Contemporary Neo-Shamanism." *Material Religion* 4(2): 136–159.

Coleman, Simon. 2000. *The Globalisation of Charismatic Christianity: Spreading the Gospel of Prosperity.* Cambridge: Cambridge University Press.

de Vries, Hent, and Samuel Weber, eds. 2001. *Religion and Media.* Stanford, CA: Stanford University Press.

de Witte, Marleen. 2003. "Altar Media's *Living Word*: Televised Charismatic Christianity in Ghana." *Journal of Religion in Africa* 33(2): 172–202.

———. 2004. "Afrikania's Dilemma: Reframing African Authenticity in a Christian Public Sphere." *Etnofoor* 17(1/2): 133–155.

———. 2005a. "The Spectacular and the Spirits. Charismatics and Neo-Traditionalists on Ghanaian Television." *Material Religion* 1(3): 314–335.

———. 2005b. "Insight, Secrecy, Beasts, and Beauty: Struggles over the Making of a Ghanaian Documentary on 'African Traditional Religion.'" *Postscripts* 1(2/3): 277–300.

———. 2008. "Accra's Sounds and Sacred Spaces." *International Journal of Urban and Regional Research* 32(2): 690–709.

———. 2009. "Eigen ogen en levende lijven. Antropologie, media en de fetisj van het face-to-face." In *Antropologie in een zee van verhalen*, edited by Thijl Sunier, 111–135. Amsterdam: Aksant.

———. 2011. "Business of the Spirit. Ghanaian Broadcast Media and the Commercial Exploitation of Pentecostalism." *Journal of African Media Studies* 3(2): 189–205.

Engelke, Matthew. 2010. "Religion and the Media Turn: A Review Essay." *American Ethnologist* 37(2): 371–379.

Gifford, Paul. 2004. *Ghana's New Christianity: Pentecostalism in a Globalising African Economy.* Bloomington: Indiana University Press.

Gyanfosu, Samuel. 1995. "The Development of Christian-Related Independent Religious Movements in Ghana, with Special Reference to the Afrikania Movement." PhD thesis, University of Leeds.

———. 2002. "A Traditional Religion Reformed: Vincent Kwabena Damuah and the Afrikania Movement, 1982–2000." In *Christianity and the African Imagination: Essays in Honour of Adrian Hastings*, edited by David Maxwell and Ingrid Lawrie, 271–294. Leiden: Brill.

Hackett, Rosalind. 2012. "Devil Bustin' Satellites: How Media Liberalization in Africa Generates Religious Intolerance and Conflict." In *Displacing the State: Religion and Conflict in Neoliberal Africa*, edited by James H. Smith and Rosalind I. J. Hackett, 153–208. South Bend, IN: University of Notre Dame Press.

James, George M. 1992 (1954). *Stolen Legacy.* Trenton, NJ: Africa World Press.

Lundby, Knut, ed. 2013. *Religion across Media: From Early Antiquity to Late Modernity.* New York: Peter Lang.

Marshall-Fratani, Ruth. 1998. "Mediating the Global and the Local in Nigerian Pentecostalism." *Journal of Religion in Africa* 28(3): 278–315.

Meyer, Birgit. 1999a. *Translating the Devil: Religion and Modernity among the Ewe in Ghana.* Edinburgh: Edinburgh University Press.

———. 1999b. "Popular Ghanaian Cinema and 'African Heritage.'" *Africa Today* 46(2): 93–114.

———, ed. 2009. *Aesthetic Formations. Media, Religion, and the Senses.* New York: Palgrave.

Meyer, Birgit, and Annelies Moors, eds. 2006. *Religion, Media, and the Public Sphere.* Bloomington: Indiana University Press.

Morgan, David, ed. 2008. *Key Words in Religion, Media, and Culture.* New York: Routledge.

———. 2013. "Religion and Media: A Critical Review of Recent Developments." *Critical Research on Religion* 1(3): 347–356.

Opoku, Kofi Asare. 1993. "Damuah and the Afrikania Mission: The Man and His Message: Some Preliminary Considerations." *Trinity Journal of Church and Theology* 3(1): 39–60.

Robbins, Joel. 2004. "The Globalization of Pentecostal and Charismatic Christianity." *Annual Review of Anthropology* 33: 117–143.

Schirripa, Pino. 2000. "Afrikania: une église afrocentriste du Ghana." In *Afrocentrismes: L'histoire des Africains entre Egypte et Amérique*, edited by François-Xavier Fauvelle-Aymar, Jean-Pierre Chrétien, and Claude-Hélène Perrot, 341–352. Paris: Karthala.

Stolow, Jeremy. 2005. "Religion and/as Media." *Theory, Culture, and Society* 22(4): 119–145.

Williams, Chancellor. 1992 (1971). *The Destruction of the Black Civilization: Great Issues of a Race from 4500 B.C. to 2000 A.D.* Trenton, NJ: Africa World Press.

12 Ṣenwele Jesu

Gospel Music and Religious Publics in Nigeria

Vicki L. Brennan

IT WAS LATE IN THE AFTERNOON when Funmi finally returned home. She had left the flat in Surulere early that morning in May 2002 to go to Tinubu Square on Lagos Island to buy lace cloth for a new party dress. Kicking off her stained shoes at the door, Funmi collapsed on the sofa and began fanning herself with a magazine. As we admired her purchases, she proceeded to tell us the story of her morning: how she bargained with the Alhaja selling lace, how crowded the buses were, how she had to pick her way through large puddles of water that had been left by yesterday's downpour. She described the new lace styles that the vendors were selling, how she was hungry but she didn't want to eat sausage roll or any of the food in the market, so she hadn't eaten since morning. And finally she described the reason why she was so delayed: as she was on the bus headed back toward Obalende, the central bus stop in Surulere, she jumped off when she heard some music blasting from the speakers of a music vendor. "The sound of this music grabbed me," she explained. "I had to go and buy this cassette." She pulled it from the nylon bag, handed it to me, and said "Vicki, you will be interested; it is a new gospel." I looked at the cover of the cassette, which featured a picture of a woman wearing a large church hat, smiling at the camera. The album's name was *Beautiful Testimonies,* and the musician was Rachael Bukola Bolarinwa.[1]

Before I describe in detail the recording that "grabbed" my friend away from her purpose that day in 2002, let me first consider that very act. Such a calling is made possible by the city itself. People, items, and sounds move through the city and inhabit its public spaces. Even setting aside the sounds of engines, car horns, generators, and other machinery, Lagos is saturated by a number of humanly produced sounds that hail its inhabitants as they circulate through its neighborhoods. The sounds of the city—the calls of bus touts announcing the destination and route of buses as they traverse the city, those of hawkers describing their wares, the call to prayer broadcast over loudspeakers across the city five times a day, distorted blasts of noise from amplifiers set outside of music sellers' shops—these sounds call out to various audiences: consumers, religious subjects, people in transit. The sound of this cassette called Funmi—grabbing her while the boys selling sausage rolls had not—and made her branch from her intended route to investigate its source.

While the city itself, as a hub of commercial and social exchange, makes this particular hailing of a hearer possible, so also does the technology used to amplify this call. The use of electronic media in this case—from the recording technology that led to the production of the cassette to the loudspeakers blasting the music to passersby—enables this sound to be detached from the contexts of its immediate performance and to be commodified and circulated. Mediated sounds call to people as they move about the city on their way to work, to school, and to shop. Electronic media thus enable and enhance the circulation of discursive forms in urban public spaces and the possibilities for people to be grabbed by those forms—and in doing so, to recognize themselves as belonging to a public: a set of anonymous, individual, yet equivalent persons who are bound together by virtue of their being called by circulating discursive forms (Warner 2002).

While the initial concept of the public as defined by Habermas assumed that publics were secular, religious movements have increasingly come to rely on the public sphere to promote themselves (Taylor 2007). As many scholars have noted, many religious publics have been constituted as such through the use of electronic media (Meyer 2004; Hirschkind 2006; Meyer and Moors 2006: 3; Larkin 2008a). These scholars have productively examined how the proliferation of electronic media in urban contexts contributes to the increasingly public character of religion, which has in turn profoundly shaped people's lifeworlds. The use of mass-mediated forms by religious groups generates new forms of religious publics at the same time that older publics are reproduced and reconfigured. In urban contexts in West Africa, Pentecostal Christianity has begun to saturate urban public spaces through the use of mass-mediated, electronic forms (Hackett 1998; Marshall-Fratani 1998; Meyer 2004; Ukah 2005). This is particularly true in Lagos, where Christian popular media are readily available in commoditized forms ranging from gospel music recordings to Pentecostal video films, from Christian radio broadcasts to stacks of inspirational literature and pamphlets.

Gospel music plays a key part in the circulation of Christian media throughout the city. Music vendors in the market who specialize in selling Christian recordings set up elaborate kiosks with racks containing hundreds of different cassette recordings, compact discs, and video discs of musical performances.[2] A loudspeaker is always situated outside of such stalls, blaring out the latest gospel hit recording and grabbing potential listeners, such as my friend Funmi, to come and purchase their wares. Alternately, vendors set up displays of recordings along the side of the road near busy intersections or on the pedestrian bridges that cross Lagos's highways. These vendors will employ three or more "boys" who carry a selection of the inventory on their heads or in a backpack, displaying the best-selling titles in their hands to motorists as they drive by and thrusting them into open windows of cars that have slowed to a crawl in one of Lagos's infamous "go-slows" in an attempt to win customers. Many church musicians dream of entering the recording studio to produce what they hope will become a best-selling gospel recording. As a result, a dizzying number of new recordings are released into the market. I asked one marketer of Christian music in Ibadan to make a list of the recordings he had released in the prior month, and two days later he returned with a list of over 60 albums. All this makes clear that gospel music is a central part of how Pentecostal Christianity has "gone public" in Nigeria. However, the specificity of music in producing religious publics has thus far gone unexamined.

As exemplified in the recording discussed in this essay, gospel music is both religious music and popular music, and as such it entails a shift in the nature and meaning of religion and popular culture in urban Nigeria. Understanding electronically mediated sounds such as the gospel recording that grabbed my friend requires that scholars think about how media help to construct and reconstruct overlapping publics. At the same time that media construct publics, they also allow members of certain publics to negotiate and contest public space in cities such as Lagos. In this light, we can understand Nigerian gospel music as a genre produced by and in relation to the intersections between urban infrastructure and electronic media—not just in Lagos but also in other cities in southern Nigeria such as Ibadan and Port Harcourt.[3]

Commercially recorded and distributed gospel music recordings allow Christian songs to circulate outside of the contexts of Christian worship. These recordings circulate according to a particular logic that is in some part related to the medium through which they circulate. In other words, the medium of sound recordings itself is connected to forms of popular and secular entertainment. This connection informs but does not determine the way in which one hears the message of the recording. Hirschkind (2006) found something similar in his analysis of the "ethical soundscape" of Islamic cassette sermons in Cairo. He describes how listeners of cassette sermons cultivate modes of hearing that enable them to acquire religious knowledge and sensibilities in accordance with changing urban contexts. However, the medium of the cassette tape is also linked to other modes of listening—particularly to forms of popular entertainment—that differ from the pious listening practices encouraged by religious leaders. As we will see, the production and circulation of commercially recorded gospel music that draws on a diverse array of musical genres produces new conceptions of Christian practice in urban Nigeria. In addition, gospel music also has an impact on what it means to be a member of a particular religious public, including enabling one to become grabbed by certain sounds, as my friend Funmi was that day in the market.

In this chapter, I examine the case of Bukola's gospel recording in order to consider tensions that animate and transform the nature of religious traditions in urban spaces such as Lagos. As we will see, the space of the city, combined with forms of electronic mediation, produces mutual tensions between religious traditions in contemporary urban spaces. These tensions are between forms of worship and forms of entertainment such as those described by Hirschkind, but also tensions between musical forms belonging to distinct religious traditions. My analysis details how musicians associated with particular religious traditions borrow from each other at the same time as they define themselves against one another. This is particularly true in Lagos, where Christianity, Islam, and "traditional religions"[4] often uneasily coexist and are claimed by distinct publics who draw on these traditions in order to construct ethically informed subjectivities that shape the stances taken by members of one religious public toward another.

I explore the dynamic relationships between religious publics in Lagos and the tensions that animate these relations from the perspective of genre conventions as an aspect of musical style. Drawing on insights developed by ethnomusicologists and linguistic anthropologists into the relationships between genre, intertextuality, and audience, I analyze how gospel musicians use a diverse array of musical genres that are designed to grab certain listeners in order to circulate their Christian message in Nigeria's urban spaces. In doing so I elaborate the implications of the use of musical styles and genres for the kinds of religious audiences and publics produced through the circulation of their music and the impact this circulation has on the nature of religious practice in urban Nigeria.

Şenwele Style

To return to the example with which this essay opened: Before I could turn the cassette over to examine the songs listed, Lola grabbed it out of my hand. "Auntie Funmi! I know this music—I've seen her music video. Are you sure you like it?" It seemed that the cassette that had "grabbed" Funmi that morning was controversial. The album featured songs in a variety of musical genres—those popular with Yoruba Christian audiences such as highlife and *jùjú* but also styles of popular music typically linked with Yoruba Muslim listeners such as *àpàlà* and *fújì*. The associations between Christian and Muslim listeners and these musical genres are not absolute—many jùjú musicians are Muslims, and fújì musicians may also be Christian, though this is less common. What is similar about all four of these genres is that they are all musical styles used in mainly nonreligious contexts: at parties, in nightclubs, as forms of popular entertainment. Jùjú, àpàlà, and fújì are Yoruba musical styles; in other words, the rhythms and melodic qualities of these styles are marked and heard as distinctly Yoruba, feature Yoruba drums— including the talking drum, which is a distinctive marker of Yoruba identity (Euba 1990; Waterman 1990)—and include lyrics written primarily in the Yoruba language. Highlife, in contrast, is a West African musical genre that is not solely the province of the Yoruba but is performed by other ethnic groups in West

Africa. Many songs in the highlife style feature lyrics sung in English or pidgin English, though some are sung in Yoruba or other local languages as well (Collins 1989; Waterman 1990). Like many other Nigerian gospel artists, Bukola had adopted these musical genres and styles associated with non-Christian publics and nonreligious contexts for Christian purposes. But as I soon discovered through conversations with gospel music listeners, it was Bukola's use of the ṣenwele style in particular that distinguished her and made this recording so controversial.

A conversation between Funmi and Lola about Bukola's use of the ṣenwele style of music ensued. Funmi asserted that what had drawn her was the combination of compelling rhythms with "Godly" lyrics and "strong prayers." "But is it enough to change the words, Auntie?" countered Lola, "The music is nice, but the people who listen to it are not Christian." She then noted that she thought Bukola sang really well and that she enjoyed the highlife track on the album. Funmi insisted that Bukola's use of ṣenwele style was good and that if people who were not Christians would listen to Bukola because they like the rhythms, then they might listen to the words and be drawn to hear the Christian message of the music and "come to Christ." Lola conceded that this was a possibility, and that Bukola's music must be acceptable because she had performed with the German evangelist Reinhard Bonnke when he led a series of popular revivals in Nigeria earlier that year.

This conversation was typical of most comments I heard from Yoruba Christians about Bukola's music: most agreed that she sang well, wrote "prayerful" lyrics, and was a good Christian, but some observed that her use of the ṣenwele style wasn't immediately acceptable. Thus, even though Bukola was able to compose lyrics that helped her to "grab" Christian listeners, it wasn't a sufficient mode of producing a Christian public. For some listeners, such as my friend Lola, approval by authority figures, such as the international evangelist Bonnke, helped to cement the acceptability of Bukola's music and its ability to be recognized as Christian by Christian audiences.

What is ṣenwele music and why would it be controversial for a gospel musician to use it? As one of Bukola's fans explained to me, ṣenwele is a "style of music for the Ilorin people of Kwara state." A predominantly Yoruba city, Ilorin is the capital of Kwara state, geographically located at the northernmost boundary of the Yoruba region of Nigeria. Originally founded as a military outpost of the Oyo Empire, in the early nineteenth century Ilorin became an emirate of the Sokoto Caliphate, and since that time Islam has played a defining role in Ilorin's social and political life. Ṣenwele is thus linked not only to a particular Yoruba city and sub-ethnicity but also to a predominantly Muslim Yoruba community. As such, it is linked to a longer history of inter-religious encounter among the Yoruba, as well as to the development and recognition of Yoruba-ness itself (Peel 2000).[5] This history in part makes possible Bukola's and Funmi's abilities to recognize şenwele as a Yoruba style, as well as the possibility for Christian listeners to Bu-kola's music to be grabbed by this style even though it has connections to differ-ent religious traditions.

Şenwele is a style of music also generally associated with a particular per-former: Iyaladuke Alalake. Mosobalaje (2008: 109) observes that şenwele is "a vocal and percussion sort of song-poetry" and that it is "one of the oral forms of Ilorin metropolis." According to Mosobalaje, there are varying accounts of the origins of şenwele, though most of his informants identified the style as an Is-lamicized musical form derived from *egúngún* chants (109).[6] He also suggests that şenwele may be a gendered musical style, one associated with women, with a par-allel genre associated with men called *dadakuada*.[7] Both şenwele and dadakuada are widely performed by Muslims in Ilorin and "often engage Yoruba-Islamic socio-cultural issues" (109). Mosobalaje also links şenwele to another genre of Yoruba sung poetry: that of *efe,* abuse songs, which engage in satire and wordplay often involving lewd or obscene materials. Mosobalaje and his informants thus cite varieties of traditional Yoruba sung poetry, including those associated with certain aspects of traditional religion as well as with Islam, as antecedents to the genre that has come to be known as şenwele.

But as Mosobalaje notes, the original performer who made a name for her-self by singing şenwele also makes her own claims to the origination of the genre. According to Iyaladuke, she began by singing *waka* songs, which are often sung to welcome back pilgrims who have returned from Hajj, but she added her own secular texts to entertain her customers. Iyaladuke claims that şenwele is about name calling, and her lyrics often include explicit or lewd references to both male and female genitalia, as well as other forms of joking and sarcasm. She developed her style of singing as a way to attract people to purchase food she sold out of her canteen in Ilorin's main market. Her singing attracted large crowds in Ilorin, who began to spontaneously "take over the chorus from her" (Mosobalaje 2008: 110), solidifying the call-and-response aspect of şenwele performance. These sing-ers, mostly women, began to invite her to perform at parties, including naming ceremonies, housewarmings, and other social gatherings. They also organized a social club around her performances that would travel around Ilorin to perform at various social occasions. By 1990 their performances had been standardized, and Iyaladuke and a group of musicians went into the studio to make their first recording. This recording enabled şenwele, a musical style associated with a par-ticular urban space and experience, to become available to audiences outside of Ilorin. According to Mosobalaje, the recording "finally made [Iyaladuke] a na-tional celebrity" (110).

As we can see from this discussion, şenwele itself is a genre made possible by urban space and the circulation of people and sounds that urban space en-ables. In this case, the city of Ilorin provided a context that allowed Iyaladuke to bring together a number of musical genres and styles. In doing so she produced a new genre, one which she claims to have named herself. Mosobalaje describes three modes through which ṣẹnwele circulated in Ilorin: the first enabled by Iyaladuke's performances in the city's main market in order to attract passersby so they would come to purchase her food; the second via the organization of the women who frequented Iyaladuke's food canteen, who began to hire her to perform at parties; and the third through the audio recording, made available on cassette, which allowed the sound to circulate within and outside of the city of Ilorin. All of these media forms allowed audiences in Ilorin to be grabbed by Iyaladuke's music and had the potential to produce certain kinds of social contexts and modes of interaction in urban space: from the passersby who became listeners and customers of Iyaladuke's canteen to the women who began to "take up her chorus" and then to hire her for social occasions. These social contexts and interactions produced new communities and identities, particularly in the formation of a women's social club organized around her performances (Mosobalaje 2008: 110). The production of a cassette recording of Iyaladuke's music also had the potential to expand the audience for this musical genre beyond the particular urban spaces in which her songs originated, making it possible to listen to ṣẹnwele in one's home, car, or place of work. The cassette recording also helped to circulate ṣẹnwele from the particular urban space in which it originated, Ilorin, to very different and exponentially larger urban spaces, making it available to the cosmopolitan, multi-ethnic, and multi-religious audiences who inhabit the urban space of Lagos.

Gospel Ṣẹnwele

The story of how ṣẹnwele, a genre associated with particular places, peoples, contexts, and modes of performance, came to be adapted by Bukola as a form of Christian music parallels in many ways Iyaladuke's story of how she came to sing ṣẹnwele. According to Bukola, she first heard Iyaladuke's music on a visit to Lagos: "I was in Lagos visiting the Local Government Administration Offices and noticed men near the garage dancing. They were really enjoying the music, so I went to ask them, 'What is that?' I liked the rhythm, but the words were not Godly. I knew that people were ready to listen to this music in a Godly way. So I asked God for the grace to do that. I developed this music with wording from the Bible."[8] Much as Bukola's music grabbed my friend Funmi, Iyaladuke's music grabbed Bukola. The sound of it called her as she was traveling through Lagos and demanded her attention. She was drawn to the sound of the music—the rhythm in particular—but knew from the words of the songs that she was not the intended audience for these songs; as she explained to me, "The words were not Godly."

Bukola was "born and bred," as she put it, in Ibadan, not Ilorin, and although her mother was a Muslim, Bukola converted to Christianity while in primary school. She began attending the Christ Apostolic Church and soon joined the choir.[9] Her pastor had encouraged her to pursue a career singing gospel music, and her soon-to-be husband was an accomplished musical performer and arranger. These interests—Christian evangelicism, musical aspirations, and life circumstances—shaped the way she heard the recording of Iyaladuke's music that day. Bukola's use of ṣenwele style, and her overall musical career, can thus also be understood as made possible by electronic mediation and circulation in urban spaces.

In adapting ṣenwele to gospel music, Bukola created a signature sound that would help to distinguish her recordings in a competitive gospel music market. This was necessary because, due to piracy issues in Nigeria, recordings aren't the primary income generator for gospel musicians but rather a means by which their name becomes known. The recording allows their music to be played on the radio and the videos to be broadcast on television, with the hope that the name of the musician will become known so that she will be hired to perform at parties and revivals. For these reasons, many Nigerian gospel musicians try to create a niche for themselves in order to distinguish their names and the "sound" associated with their names. Bukola's use of ṣenwele to sing gospel songs can be understood in part as making use of such a strategy. Indeed, that she names herself with this genre—by calling herself Ṣenwele Jesu on the recordings—may be understood as an attempt to ensure that listeners will remember her.

However, the style of music that Bukola uses on her recordings is not limited to ṣenwele. As noted earlier, she also includes songs sung in jùjú, highlife, and fújì styles, among others. Thus, Bukola's appropriation of ṣenwele, as well as her use of a variety of musical genres on her recordings, may also be understood in part as an attempt to "grab" various audiences under the umbrella of gospel so that both her audience and the gospel music–listening public may be as broad as possible. As she explained to me, she uses a variety of genres on her albums because "if you are not interested in the àpàlà, you will be interested in the fújì style. If you are not interested in the fújì, you will like the afro; if you don't like the afro, you will like the highlife; you don't like the highlife, there's the mixed one, with the minor and the reggae. They will like it." As this suggests, the audience for gospel music is understood to be diverse, made up of multiple sub-audiences whose musical tastes run in a number of generic directions. By recording gospel songs in multiple genres, Bukola tries to maximize her influence with these audiences. And in doing so, she also produces a newly formed singular audience: those who listen to Ṣenwele Jesu.

How is Bukola able to link these audiences together? And further, how does she create an audience that is willing to listen to gospel ṣenwele? As she explained, "And all the likeness [sic] and whatever enjoyment [people get] will derive with the wordings. The message. The whole album was based on the second coming of Christ. If you check it out, it was based on the second coming of Christ." As this comment makes clear, the words of the songs—the "message" in Bukola's terms and indeed in the terms that many Nigerian gospel musicians and listeners use to describe what is particularly Christian about popular forms of music like gospel—are able to overcome the ways in which a musical style like ṣenwele indexes non-Christian contexts.

A brief example will demonstrate how Bukola repurposes a style of music associated with Muslim audiences and non-Christian contexts by inserting a Christian "message" and appropriate "wordings." The song "Orísun Ayọ̀" ("Source of Joy" [lit. wellspring of joy]) from her first album uses the ṣenwele musical style, bringing together the rhythms and call-and-response patterns typical of this style with Christian-themed lyrics. The song opens with a short formulaic statement sung by Bukola that directly addresses the listener and asks them to patronize her by buying her album. This is followed by a series of statements that praise Jesus Christ, sung in a call-and-response pattern with Bukola singing the lead and a chorus of male and female voices echoing her:

Mo júbà Jesu ọba (2xs)	I acknowledge Christ the King (2xs)
ọba dá ni w'aye	The King who created us
Adáni ma gbagbe	The Creator who never forgets his creations
Oun lo bá mi ṣe	He did it for me

The song continues to thank God for creating life, for his mercy, and for sacrificing his son to redeem humans from sin.

The lyrics of "Orísun Ayọ̀" also emphasize the importance of giving thanks to God through praise. Bukola points to her own observance by singing this song and asks her listeners to help her proclaim the goodness of Jesus to the world. She also draws attention to her use of the ṣenwele style to praise God, by directly engaging the listener to join in her transformation of the genre for the purposes of Christian praise:

Ẹma bá mi k'a lo	Come along with me
Ẹma bọ lẸhìn mi ni	Follow me
B'o ṣe ni ṣenwele	If it is ṣenwele
A fi yin Jesu ọba	We use it to praise Jesus!

This example makes clear that Bukola intends to use the ṣenwele style for Christian purposes. Yet, as the conversation between my friends Funmi and Lola made clear, this shift of linkages from Yoruba Muslim communities, "traditional religion," and secular contexts to Christian contexts isn't complete—the traces of prior linkages still remain. "Is it enough to change the words?" Lola asked about Bukola's ṣenwele gospel. For many Christians who purchase Bukola's recordings or hire her to perform at parties and revivals, it clearly is. Yet, doubts still linger for some listeners and may even contribute to their attraction to the music.

Promiscuous Forms

The social interactions and communities that emerge out of the example of Iyaladuke's and Bukola's ṣenwele are both produced by and involved in producing new understandings of musical styles and the relationships between them. Urban infrastructure and electronic mediation allow differing and potentially new publics to be grabbed by the style. But what does it mean to be grabbed by a musical style, as my friend Funmi was? How are musical styles linked to groups of people? What makes a musical form "Muslim" or "Christian"? Further, what is at stake when these musical styles are linked to religious publics? Answering these questions goes a long way toward connecting the ethnographic example of ṣenwele back to the questions asked at the beginning of this essay about the effects that electronic media and urban infrastructure have on the articulation of relationships between religious traditions and the production of religious publics. It also helps to make sense of the impact that the traces of linkages to other religious forms present in the adaptation of a musical style associated with Yoruba Muslim communities and nonreligious social contexts to sing Christian gospel has on the interrelationships between religious publics in urban spaces.

Brian Larkin's (2008b) idea of "promiscuous forms" provides an analytical insight into the potential effects that Bukola's appropriation of a style such as ṣenwele, with its links to secular and Muslim contexts and audiences, has on Yoruba Christian experience in urban Nigeria. Larkin identifies "promiscuous forms" as those that emerge "when one public takes the discursive forms used to constitute another public" (105). The idea of "promiscuous forms" problematizes assumptions underlying scholarly discussions of how publics are formed via the circulation of discursive forms and that publics exist as such primarily through discursive circulation (e.g., Warner 2002; Taylor 2007). As Larkin notes, in Warner's and Taylor's discussions of publics, "there is an implicit assumption that different publics each have their own circulatory modes, their own discursive forms, so that one can neatly be separated from the other. A single person might inhabit multiple publics, but each of those publics is united (and thus separable) through its own specific genres, types of speech, and modes of address" (104).

Larkin explores the example of how South African Muslim cleric Ahmed Deedat responds to Christian evangelism by adopting non-Islamic, identifiably Christian forms of discourse such as biblical hermeneutics and secular criticism. According to Larkin, Deedat uses the reflexive capacity of language and performative events to comment on and undermine Christian rhetorical forms and Christian claims to divine revelation and religious superiority. By doing so, Deedat reinforces and reenergizes Muslim religious identity. But, as Larkin argues, such reflexivity also brings with it complicity in that "to comment upon Christianity Deedat also must inhabit it and his polemic necessitates entanglement" (118–119). As Larkin demonstrates, "Deedat's da'wa [call or invitation to Islam] raises issues of reference and presence, the boundaries of religious practice and their transgression, and how religious identity is formed through the hostile and tactile engagement with competing religious practices." (119). In other words, in drawing on Christian forms, Deedat also risks reinforcing them. Deedat makes biblical forms of exegesis real and legitimate by inhabiting them, even as he does so in order to argue against them.

Larkin's analysis makes clear how the circulation of discursive forms between differing religious publics has the potential to shape the nature of those religious publics themselves, as well as the practices and identities central to being a part of a religious public. This discursive circulation is central to how ṣenwele grabs listeners and produces particular kinds of publics in Nigeria's urban spaces. It is clear that Bukola's use of ṣenwele to sing gospel music draws attention to the relationship between Muslim and Christian publics in cities such as Lagos, much as Deedat's use of Christian rhetorical forms in his Islamic sermons does. This helps to account for Lola's question, "Is it enough to change the words?" For many Christian listeners, and despite Bukola's claims to the contrary, her music can't just be reduced to the message transmitted via her Christian lyrics. Bukola's Christian message does not simply overwrite or erase any linkages between the genre of ṣenwele and its origins in a particular place and orientation toward non-Christian audiences or nonreligious contexts of performance; those references remain. Furthermore, these references to non-Christian contexts and origins—particularly to the predominantly Muslim Yoruba metropole of Ilorin—help to reinforce the difference between Christian and Muslim publics in Nigeria.

However, the similarity between the case of Bukola's ṣenwele gospel and Deedat's da'wa only goes so far. For example, for many listeners Bukola's use of the ṣenwele style to sing gospel is more controversial than her use of musical forms associated with entertainment rather than religious contexts, such as highlife or jùjú. This suggests that in some cases there may be little to no tension felt when one public borrows the discursive forms of another public, as is clearly the case when Yoruba and other Nigerian gospel musicians use a highlife style of music to sing their Christian lyrics. The case of gospel music sung in the style of jùjú is more ambivalent. For example, a reader once corrected me when I said the songs Yoruba Christians sing sound like jùjú music. "Jùjú music is not Christian," she stated emphatically. "It is performed in nightclubs, and it is not appropriate for Christians to sing such songs." However, most listeners I spoke with easily identified as unquestionably Christian gospel songs featuring Christian lyrics and sung in a jùjú style. This ambivalence points to how publics themselves are constituted in relationship to formal promiscuity: for some jùjú gospel is a form belonging to one public, and for others it is seen as pointing to two separate publics, one explicitly Christian and the other linked to forms of secular entertainment enjoyed by middle- and upper-class educated colonial and postcolonial populations (Waterman 1990).

At the other extreme, the promiscuity of discursive forms is difficult if not impossible. One well-known example of the impossibility of promiscuity is that of the Danish cartoons of the Prophet Muhammad and the ensuing controversy that followed their publication in 2006. While there are a number of discursive forms in which members of either Muslim or secular publics may write about the Prophet, for certain Muslim publics using the secular form of satire to represent the Prophet is particularly charged (see Asad 2009). Indeed, this event precipitated riots and violence between Christians and Muslims in the Nigerian city of Maiduguri. Such moments bring out the stakes of Larkin's argument about the formation of religious identity via a sometimes hostile, though often benign, engagement with the forms of other publics.

Bukola's use of ṣenwele style in her gospel music lies somewhere between these examples. Indeed, even referring to ṣenwele as a Muslim musical genre is ambiguous. Though it was developed in a primarily Muslim city by Muslim musicians and is understood by listeners to draw on particularly Islamic genres such as waka songs, it is performed primarily in nonreligious contexts and its lyrics use language and images not appropriate in religious contexts, whether Muslim or Christian. As noted earlier, there are a variety of claims to conflicting and competing religious groups made by various informants and writers as to the origins of ṣenwele. Thus, claims that ṣenwele is derived from egúngún chants based on Iyaladuke's use of call-and-response forms are not so much about an absolute origin of the genre in traditional religious musical forms but rather point to tensions between traditional religion and Islam in Ilorin. Claims of a link to traditional religion in the emergence of ṣenwele may also point to tensions within Islam in Ilorin. Mosobalaje discusses how musical styles and genres in Ilorin were shaped by Islamic reform in the nineteenth century, which resulted in a curtailing of many forms of sung poetry, particularly those associated with traditional religion. Mosobalaje argues that this, together with the shift in gender relations as a result of Islamic influences in Ilorin, worked to shape Iyaladuke's ṣenwele style as a practice that signifies her disaffection with current gender relations in Ilorin.

The ambiguous relationship between religious and secular publics in Iyaladuke's ṣenwele is further exacerbated by Bukola's transformation of ṣenwele for Christian purposes. This ambiguity may be due in part to the nature of musical forms themselves. The way in which musical forms in particular move between different religious publics and between religious and secular publics, as well as the nature of the communities and identities produced via this circulation, must be more clearly addressed.

Musical Styles and Generic Intertextuality

Comments such as Lola's question about whether it was enough for Bukola to change the words in order to make ṣenwele an acceptably Christian style draw attention to the forms of address that are understood to be appropriate for Christian and Muslim publics and their relationship to the moral practices and orientations central to being a member of a particular public. Yet, the effects that Bukola's ṣenwele has on the production of a Yoruba Christian public does more than reinforce and reify norms of Christian practice and belonging in urban Nigeria. Indeed, as noted earlier, there is a certain value placed on using the discursive forms of other publics to sing gospel music in Nigeria, because it can maximize a performer's commercial potential. Such formal promiscuity may increase the potential for the singer to grab audiences, expanding the possibilities for circulating a Christian message via her music to an ever-expanding public. Yet, in doing so, the nature of a Christian public and the practices that are central to being a member of that public—which includes being grabbed by certain sounds—are potentially transformed and reconfigured.

One way to account for the effect that this particular discursive circulation has on the production of religious publics in Nigeria is to pay attention to how music works in relation to the intertextuality of genres. Linguistic anthropologists, following Bakhtin and colleagues (1986), have noted that genre conventions help to shape how a given text is produced and received, and further that connecting a particular utterance to a genre necessarily invokes the relationship of that text to prior texts (Bauman 2001: 79). However, while these generic conventions shape the production and reception of a given text, the intertextual relationship to prior texts does not overdetermine meaning. As Briggs and Bauman (1992) note, "When genre is viewed in intertextual terms, its complex and contradictory relationship to discourse becomes evident. [They] suggest that the creation of intertextual relationships through genre simultaneously renders texts ordered, unified, and bounded, on the one hand, and fragmented, heterogeneous, and open-ended, on the other" (147). Briggs and Bauman also note that "the process of linking particular utterances to generic models thus necessarily produces an intertextual *gap*" (149). This gap emerges out of the more or less imperfect fit between a particular text and the generic model the text is connected to. In other words, genres have both synchronic and diachronic dimensions. In performance, they may have the effect of unifying discourse, constructing boundedness and wholeness, and adding to authority. At the same time, using a particular genre also potentially draws attention to the constructedness of discourse and to how authority is constituted through such practices rather than merely given.

Following from this, the promiscuity of religious forms, including musical genres, must be understood in relationship to the dynamics of intertextuality and the interpretive gap produced by connecting particular texts to formal models. For example, Jane Goodman (1998, 2005) has drawn on a model of intertextuality in order to show how musicians involved in the creation of a genre of Berber world music manipulate an intertextual gap as they transform Kabyle village poetry into songs appropriate for a world stage that can circulate through global music markets. As Goodman convincingly argues, this intertextual gap allows Berber artists and audiences to make broad and often divergent social and political claims about Berber culture and postcolonial identity. Connecting such studies to the discussion of promiscuity at hand, we might note that musical genres may be more promiscuous than text-based genres because music can be used to suppress such generic intertextual gaps and at the same time to foreground them (Briggs and Bauman 1992: 158).

In the case under consideration here, Bukola draws attention to the gap by using a genre that is distinctly marked, one that indexes specifically non-Christian contexts, including Muslim communities and nonreligious forms of sociality. Further, ṣenwele, through the use of obscene and hyper-sexualized forms of humorous banter, indexes contexts and forms of discourse that are counter to the middle-class moral values and ideal practices articulated by Bukola in her lyrics, which often emphasize prayer and correct behavior as necessary to ensure God's blessings in the form of financial security, health, and children.

To what end would a Christian musician put such a musical genre? Bukola's musical promiscuity may be understood as working to shape the overwhelming public character of Christianity and the transformation of a Christian public in Nigeria into one that is decidedly Pentecostal in nature (Ojo 2006; Ukah 2008; Marshall 2009). Ṣenwele gospel may thus be understood as part of an ongoing shift in Christian sensibilities and orientations toward the world in contemporary Nigeria. In her study of Pentecostalism in Nigeria, Ruth Marshall (2009: 138–165) argues that Pentecostal use of electronic media creates "communities of sentiment" that "entail articulations and discussion not only of models of 'correct' behavior and new regimes of personal and collective discipline, but also new attitudes toward consumption, dress styles, aesthetics, and ways of speaking and moving" (138). In this sense, Bukola's use of ṣenwele helps to articulate a perceived difference between Christian and non-Christian moralities. A Christian listening to Bukola's songs is bound to think, even if only for a moment, about the distinction between the image of a good Christian, projected in Bukola's lyrics, versus the image of Muslims who engage in obscene and explicit bantering in public spaces, pointed to by the musical genre. The values that Bukola emphasizes in her lyrics are visually reinforced in her music videos which emphasize a particularly Yoruba vision of a good life, one that is built on hard work and adherence to Christian moral codes. Most videos feature Bukola with a chorus of female singers and male instrumentalists dressed in Yoruba traditional clothing styles dancing in a variety of urban public spaces—at a church revival, in the lobby of a hotel, in front of a swimming pool, and in one video, in a room filled with exercise equipment. The appearance of modern urban public spaces in gospel music videos helps to create a link between these spaces and Christianity, asserting the naturalness of their connection. These images of public space stand in contrast to an imagining of gritty market sellers trading lewd jokes with each other in public spaces, associated with the audiences for Iyaladuke's ṣenwele.[10]

By using musical sounds that index non-Christian contexts and actors, Bukola also reaffirms a Christian ideology of evangelism, demonstrating through her performance that those non-Christian elements can be converted through careful attention to the message over the form. Bukola's listeners admit this as a possibility, and it is central to how they assess Bukola's use of ṣenwele. As Funmi noted, many of Bukola's fans suggest that her use of ṣenwele may encourage the original audience for the style, those who were grabbed by the sound intended for Muslim market-goers, to "come to Christ." The potential of ṣenwele gospel to remake listeners who are grabbed by the ṣenwele sound into proper members of a Christian public articulates a key modality of contemporary Christianity in Nigeria: that of conversion and redemption. This foregrounding of the interpretive gap between genre and message allows for a staging of what Marshall calls the "born again program of conversion" that "self-consciously and critically engages with local cultural practices, moral codes, modes of sociability, rituals, forms of authority, and techniques of power, subjecting them to a normative reevaluation, which renders possible and legitimates new practices" (2009: 6–7; see also Meyer 1998). Ṣenwele gospel points to a desired break with the forms associated with local publics—those associated with Islam or traditional religion, as well as publics produced in certain urban spaces such as markets or the predominantly Muslim Yoruba town of Ilorin—at the same time as it works to rehabilitate these local forms and the publics that are grabbed by them through their connection to Christian messages and practices.

By articulating her Christian message through genres and forms that index non-Christian identities, modes of acting, and social contexts, Bukola's music also contributes to an ongoing reconfiguration of what it means to be a good Christian in urban contexts such as Lagos. Bukola's remotivation and recirculation of ṣenwele as part of a repertoire of forms belonging to Christian listeners contributes to the reorganization of selfhood and subjectivity that Pentecostal Christianity works to produce. Genres such as gospel ṣenwele help to construct and reinforce a Pentecostal conception of Christian practice as a matter of inward reflection and personal devotion, a notion that links up with its moral program that emphasizes individuality and interiority. As one fan of Bukola's music affirmed, "*Wa ṣere ọmọ*, keep on the music, it's good to praise God in different kind of ways, God accept any kind of ways we praise HIM, what matters is our heart." In other words, what makes it possible for a Christian to be grabbed by the sound of gospel ṣenwele depends on being able to overcome the intertextual gap produced by using non-Christian musical forms to sing Christian songs through recourse to one's own self-knowledge and self-production as a true Christian.

Conclusion

The case discussed in this chapter contributes to the way in which scholars of media and religion in Africa understand how the circulation of religious forms via electronic media in urban contexts makes genres available for new intertextual possibilities and new possibilities of entextualization. As I have shown, this circulation has the potential to redefine religious publics not only from within but also in relation to other publics. My examination of how Yoruba gospel music circulates in Nigerian urban spaces to produce and transform a Christian religious public allows scholars to better understand the processes of transformation and differentiation of religious practices and communities through their representation in and use of mass-mediated musical forms.

Acknowledgments

I am grateful to the Wenner-Gren Foundation, the National Science Foundation, and the University of Vermont for their financial support of my research and writing. I want to thank Rosalind Hackett and Benjamin Soares for inviting me to be a part of this project from the conference in Abuja to the production of this volume. An earlier version of this article was presented at the 2010 Cadbury Conference: Tuning in to African Cities: Popular Culture and Urban Experience in sub-Saharan Africa" held at the Centre of West African Studies, Birmingham, and I am grateful to the participants for their comments on this material. I also appreciate the valuable comments and suggestions provided by Benjamin Eastman, Kelda Jamison, Emily Manetta, Danilyn Rutherford, Jesse Shipley, Jonah Steinberg, Kabir Tambar, and Andrea Voyer.

Notes

1. Since that time, Bukola has married and now uses her married name: Rachael Bukola Akinade. She is also popularly known as Ṣenwele Jesu. For the sake of clarity in this essay, I refer to her as Bukola.

2. The media technology for gospel music has changed rapidly since the afternoon in 2002 when Bukola's recordings were first brought to my attention by Funmi. More research on the

changing use of media technology in Nigeria's gospel music industry, from cassette to CD to digital files, remains to be done.

3. Southern Nigeria is the primary site for the production and consumption of gospel music, given that the majority of Christians who live in Nigeria are located there. Brian Larkin (2008a) explores the interrelationships between electronic media and urban infrastructure in the predominantly Muslim Nigerian city of Kano.

4. While referring to African indigenous religious practices as "traditional religion" is problematic (see Shaw 1990), I use it here because it is the term used most frequently by Nigerian Christians to talk about such practices.

5. Christian missionaries during the colonial period encountered both "traditional" religion and Islam in their attempts to convert the Yoruba. There has been a long history of both borrowing and competition between Islam and Christianity among the Yoruba, as Yoruba Christians drew on already established Islamic concepts and practices in order to translate Christianity into Yoruba terms but also took care to distinguish the two monotheistic traditions in order to support the assumed link between Christianity and modernity (see Peel 2000: 187–214).

6. Egúngún is the Yoruba ancestral masquerade and is understood to be part of a ritual form belonging to traditional religion. The evidence of the link to egúngún chants cited by Mosobalaje's informants is the use of call-and-response forms in ṣenwele performances.

7. For more on dadakuada, see Na'Allah 1992, 1994.

8. Author interview: Rachael Bolarinwa Bukola, Ibadan, Nigeria, June 8, 2002.

9. It is worth noting here that Bukola's church, the Christ Apostolic Church (CAC), is an independent Yoruba church that was established as part of a series of Christian revivals among the Yoruba in the 1920s and 1930s. They are collectively referred to as Aladura churches (*Aladura* literally means "owner of prayer"). Charismatic Christian practices, including prayer healing and speaking in tongues, are central to most Aladura practices. See Peel 1968 for more on the Aladura movement. The CAC is unique among the Aladura churches in that its members do not wear a white prayer gown while worshipping. Notably, a large majority of Yoruba gospel musicians are connected to the CAC.

10. Iyaladuke's ṣenwele may reinforce boundaries between Muslim and secular publics in Ilorin. As Mosobalaje notes, Muslim authorities there have their own reaction to Iyaladuke's appropriation of musical styles associated with Muslim contexts for more secularized purposes and their linking to such imaginings of public audiences.

References

Asad, Talal. 2009. "Free Speech, Blasphemy, and Secular Criticism." In *Is Critique Secular?: Blasphemy, Injury, and Free Speech,* edited by W. Brown, J. Butler, and S. Mahmood. Berkeley: University of California Press.

Bakhtin, Mikhail. 1981. *The Dialogic Imagination: Four Essays.* Austin: University of Texas Press.

Bakhtin, Mikhail, Michael Holquist, and Caryl Emerson. 1986. *Speech Genres and Other Late Essays.* Austin: University of Texas Press.

Bauman, Richard. 2001. Genre. In *Key Terms in Language and Culture,* edited by Alessandro Duranti, 79–82. Malden, MA: Wiley-Blackwell.

Briggs, Charles L., and Richard Bauman. 1992. "Genre, Intertextuality, and Social Power." *Journal of Linguistic Anthropology* 2(2): 131–172.

Collins, John. 1989. "The Early History of West African Highlife Music." *Popular Music* 8(3): 221–230.

Euba, Akin. 1990. *Yoruba Drumming: The Dùndún Tradition.* Bayreuth: E. Breitinger.

Goodman, Jane. 1998. "Singers, Saints, and the Construction of Postcolonial Subjectivities in Algeria." *Ethos* 26(2): 204–228.

———. 2005. *Berber Culture on the World Stage: From Village to Video.* Bloomington: Indiana University Press.

Hackett, Rosalind I. J. 1998. "Charismatic/Pentecostal Appropriation of Media Technologies in Nigeria and Ghana." *Journal of Religion in Africa* 28(3): 258–277.

Hirschkind, Charles. 2006. *The Ethical Soundscape.* New York: Columbia University Press.

Larkin, Brian. 2008a. *Signal and Noise: Media, Infrastructure, and Urban Culture in Nigeria.* Durham, NC: Duke University Press.

———. 2008b. "Ahmed Deedat and the Form of Islamic Evangelism." *Social Text* 26(3): 101–121.

Marshall-Fratani, Ruth. 1998. "Mediating the Global and Local in Nigerian Pentecostalism." *Journal of Religion in Africa* 28(3): 278–315.

Marshall, Ruth. 2009. *Political Spiritualities: The Pentecostal Revolution in Nigeria.* Chicago: University of Chicago Press.

Meyer, Birgit. 1998. "Commodities and the Power of Prayer. Pentecostalist Attitudes Towards Consumption in Contemporary Ghana." In *Globalization and Identity. Dialectics of Flow and Closure, Development and Change,* edited by Birgit Meyer and Peter Geschiere. Malden, MA: Blackwell.

———. 2004. "'Praise the Lord': Popular Cinema and Pentecostalite Style in Ghana's New Public Sphere." *American Ethnologist* 31(1): 92–110.

Meyer, Birgit, and Annelies Moors, eds. 2006. *Religion, Media, and the Public Sphere.* Bloomington: Indiana University Press.

Mosobalaje, Adebayo. 2008. "The Return of the Landowner: Islamic Strictures and the Emergence of a Female Art." *The African Symposium: An On Line Journal of African Educational Research Network* 8(1): 109–117.

Na'Allah, A. 1992. "Dadakuada: The Crisis of a Traditional Oral Genre in a Modern Islamic Setting." *Journal of Religion in Africa* 22(4): 318–330.

———. 1994. "Oral Tradition, Islamic Culture, and Topicality in the Songs of Mamman Shata Katsina and Omoekee Amao Ilorin." *Canadian Journal of African Studies* 28(3): 500–515.

Ojo, Matthews A. 2006. *The End-Time Army: Charismatic Movements in Modern Nigeria.* Trenton, NJ: Africa World Press.

Peel, J. D. Y. 1968. *Aládúrà: A Religious Movement among the Yoruba.* London: Oxford University Press.

———. 2000. *Religious Encounter and the Making of the Yoruba.* Bloomington: Indiana University Press.

Shaw, Rosalind. 1990. "The Invention of African Traditional Religion." *Religion* 20: 339–353.

Taylor, Charles. 2007. *A Secular Age.* Cambridge, MA: Harvard University Press.

Ukah, Asonzeh. 2005. "The Local and the Global in the Media and Material Culture of Nigerian Pentecostalism." *Entreprises religieuses transnationales en Afrique de l'Ouest (Transnational Religious Enterprises in West Africa).* Paris: IFRA, 285–313.

———. 2008. *A New Paradigm of Pentecostal Power: The Redeemed Christian Church of God in Nigeria.* Trenton, NJ: Africa World Press / Red Sea Press.

Warner, Michael. 2002. *Publics and Counterpublics.* Cambridge, MA: Zone Books.

Waterman, Christopher A. 1990. *Juju: A Social History and Ethnography of an African Popular Music.* Chicago: University of Chicago Press.

13 Managing Miracles

Law, Authority, and the Regulation of Religious Broadcasting in Nigeria

Asonzeh Ukah

The modern citizen is regulated by the state and entertained by a powerful mixture of secular culture and popular religion.

> Bryan S. Turner, *Religion and Modern Societies: Citizenship, Secularisation and State*

Father Andrew Kiernan (Gabriel Byrne) to Father Gianni Delmonico (Dick Latessa): "I travel around the world investigating miracles. Then I disprove them. Real miracle is anybody believes anything."

Father Gianni Delmonico: "We live in a very competitive world, Andrew. The Church is no exception."

> *Stigmata* (MGM Studios Inc. 1999)

ON APRIL 1, 2004, the National Broadcasting Commission (the NBC), Nigeria's official broadcast regulator, started policing the Nigerian airwaves to ensure that what it termed "unverified miracles" marketed by entrepreneurial Pentecostal pastors were no longer broadcast on national television stations. The NBC was perturbed by the inundation of half-truths and untruths by fraudulent, business-driven Pentecostal pastors who use the broadcast media to deceive unsuspecting Nigerians. More importantly, the NBC wanted its Code of Broadcasting to be respected and adhered to by all broadcasting practitioners and their clients. The agency had announced its intention to prohibit the airing of dubious and fake miracles six weeks earlier to give the television stations time to adjust to the new regime of "miracle-free" programming. The action of the NBC was openly supported by the Pentecostal Fellowship of Nigeria (PFN), an umbrella organization of many but by no means all Pentecostal churches, fellowships, and ministries in Nigeria. Although this type of "miracle broadcast" had been (and still is) a huge source of revenue for broadcast stations, the NBC was now acting as a moral/spiritual police officer holding the powerful Pentecostal elite responsible and accountable and enforcing doctrinal orthodoxy in order to protect the less-powerful public. Some prominent individuals and (Pentecostal) church leaders disagreed with the NBC's action, claiming it was an infringement of the religious freedom of Christians. What was more worrisome to many scholars and commentators, however, was the apparent lack of guidelines by the NBC to determine what qualified as a genuine miracle or the processes to follow to verify a miracle claim, and for whom or to whom such a verification would be directed. One of the critics of the NBC's ban claims that by abolishing miracles on television, "the government becomes God."[1] How can a secular state agency—which lacks any ecclesiastical authority or knowledge—be in a position to certify an event or claim as a miracle other than saying it is an event with unsatisfactory (scientific) explanation?

Central to the arguments and counter-arguments emanating from the NBC's apparent proscription of miracle broadcasts is the place of technologically mediated religious communication in a secular—albeit multi-religious—democracy such as Nigeria where in theory religion is constitutionally disestablished but in practice is central to the state's self-(re)presentation. When the state agency proscribed what it termed an "unverified miracle" broadcast, it demonstrated its anxiety not just about the power of religions to inspire action but also the tremendous influence of the media on public behavior, and more importantly, the propensity of the media to be manipulated and abused by powerful individuals such as politicians, businesspersons, and superstar, miracle-vending pastors. In a recent attempt at analyzing the issues brought to the fore by the actions of the NBC, Ukah (2011a) argues that one way to look at what is happening in the Nigeria media marketplace is to regard both the government and the PFN as cartels with important interests in the market for loyalties who are ready to, and do, use media regulation to control access and activities within the media market. In this chapter, the argument is that regulations have never been the reason for the messy character of the Nigerian broadcast market, but rather the problems stem from the selective enforcement (even manipulation) of these laws to satisfy sectional interests, often couched as "national interests." This argument is articulated and contextualized by examining the laws regarding the broadcast of religion generally, and miracles specifically, as laid out in the NBC's *Nigeria Broadcasting Code* and *The Nigerian Code of Advertising Practice* published by the Advertising Practitioners Council of Nigeria (APCON).

The remainder of this chapter is divided into five segments, the first of which contextualizes the current broadcasting regulation regime in the political economy of media liberalization championed by the Babangida regime (1984–1993). The next section examines the provisions of laws designed to both deregulate and regulate religious programming. The third section provides empirical data on the practices and politics of broadcasting religion in the government-owned Nigeria Television Authority (NTA), which is the largest television network in Africa. The fourth section discusses some factors ignored in the NBC's selective enforcement of its rules on religious broadcasting, such as equal access and the doctrine of fairness. The last section is a short conclusion advocating for a more stable regulatory regime that would enhance robust media practices relating to religious broadcasting in Nigeria.

The Political Economy of Media Liberalization in Nigeria

In recent decades, the media landscape in Nigeria has been deregulated and diversified, making it one of the most vibrant media marketplaces in Africa. The liberalization of the media industry brought in new industry players and actors, intensified competition, and created complex sets of interactions between media producers, regulators, and consumers. The tension between increased deregulation and the enforcement of regulatory functions has meant that the state as the sole regulator of the industry plays a more forceful role in controlling the content and quality of media programs. This contradictory tendency is nowhere more evident than in the broadcast media, particularly the television industry. The state focus on the television industry is partly because of the power of modern technology that makes it possible to disseminate both sound and moving pictures in color and partly because of the role the medium has played in the history of popular mobilization around the world (Hoover and Kaneva 2009; Meyer 2009: 114–123).

The introduction of the electronic media (radio and television) in the 1930s and 1950s was directly connected to the dissemination of colonial (and later, postcolonial) governments' propaganda needs as well as the entertainment of the governed. The expanding media arena soon went beyond the traditional functions ascribed to the media: the provision of education, entertainment, and information. The media became instruments of governmental control, wealth accumulation for entrepreneurs, and the maintenance of influence and soft power, sidelining their constitutional duties as stipulated in Article 22 of the 1999 Constitution: "The press, radio, television and other agencies of the mass media shall at all times be free to . . . uphold the responsibility and accountability of the Government to the people." An important aspect of the responsibility of the government to its people, it would seem, has been judged to be the management of the quality of media programs available to its citizens. Some scholars interpret the government's action—through its agency, the NBC—to banish the broadcast of miracles on national television stations starting from April 2004 as a fulfillment of the duty of the state to ensure and manage quality media programs for the benefit of its citizens (Magbadelo 2004; Nihinlola 2008; Ukah 2008a: 170–171; Dairo 2010).

The constitutional guarantees of religious freedom and practices also fore-ground religious speech and communication. Article 38 (1) of the 1999 Constitution states explicitly, "Every person shall be entitled to freedom of thought, conscience and religion, including freedom to change his religion or belief, and freedom (either alone or in community with others, and in public or in private) to manifest and propagate his religion or belief in worship, teaching, practice and observance." This is almost the same wording as Article 18 of the International Covenant on Civil and Political Rights (ICCPR). Religious communication is an integral right and an aspect of manifesting and propagating one's religious beliefs and practices; viewed in the light of the ICCPR, it is also a political right of citizens. Article 17 (b) of the Constitution requires that the state provide "adequate facilities for leisure and for social, religious and cultural life." The establishment of communication facilities such as radio, television, and the press has initially functioned as structures of governance. Before 1992, the growth of the broadcast industry in general was primarily driven by the desire of specific governments (federal and state) to erect an overarching propaganda network for societal control and manipulation. Although there might have been other supporting arguments or reasons for the establishment of television and radio by different governments—such as education, entertainment, prestige, and the dissemination of information—politics and the need for the control of popular loyalty rank uppermost. The authoritarian control of the stations by government officials, nepotistic recruitment of staff, and the quality of program content all point to the overriding political function to which broadcasting stations in Nigeria were directed (Esan 2009: 111). Furthermore, the refusal of the NBC to issue licenses for community radio stations in spite of protracted clamor reinforces the view that broadcast stations function more as political than social instruments (Alumuku 2006; Moemeka 2009: 31–57).

Liberalizing or Regulating Religious Broadcasting?

As Chuka Onwumechili and Donatus Uzomah (2005: 109) argue, "The role of the broadcast regulator is crucial in ensuring the country's liberalization success." The creation of the NBC by Decree 38 of 1992 (in the current dispensation regarded as Act 38 of the National Assembly and further amended by Act 55 of 1999) was the singular most important structure in deregulating the broadcasting industry (Ukah 2008a: 170). This involves the elimination of government monopoly of the broadcast market and, more effectively, the expansion of the broadcast frontier, as well as the expansion of public freedoms such as free speech and expression, dissemination of ideas, and associations. The "regulatory" function of the agency includes the determination of broadcast content, the setting of standards, quality control of programming, and the exercise of oversight function on the industry and its rules. Some of these functions are in tension with one another.

How far the agency has achieved its organizational objectives may be assessed by considering how it has created an enabling and free environment where broadcast journalists and stakeholders perform to their optimum. The NBC's neoliberal philosophy presupposes that competition is good for business and that enhancing broadcast competition would not only improve the media market but also provide quality programs for consumers. By April 1992, there were fewer than 30 broadcasting stations in Nigeria, almost all of them urban-based and all of them government owned and controlled. By the middle of 2011, the number of broadcasting stations in Nigeria had increased to 394. Included in this figure are 55 privately owned and operated radio stations; 45 government owned and operated radio stations; 145 television stations (25 of these privately owned and operated); 35 wireless cable (MMDS) companies; and 5 direct-to-home (DTH) satellite television platforms.[2] These statistics illustrate the tremendous transformation of the media market within a period of two decades. The diversity in the media market would ordinarily generate competition among the operators and the need to create niches. However, competition for patronage and resources among the television stations has, rather than improve quality, compromised standards, particularly among government-controlled stations where, according to Ojebode (2009: 70–76), "the sale of the sacred" and "the reign of junk" soon became the culture of programming among broadcast stations in Nigeria in the era of liberalization.

The expansion of the broadcast market effectively marginalized a large segment of the community—namely, religious organizations. The military dictators who framed the original NBC law of 1992 included two exclusionary elements under section 10: "The Commission shall not grant a license to (a) a religious organisation or (b) a political party." The law did not specify reasons for prohibiting religious organizations (or political parties) from obtaining broadcast licenses. That religious organizations and political parties are lumped together in one section of the law suggests that both types of organizations are thought of as sharing significant characteristics—for example, extreme divisiveness, intolerance, and aggressive competition. But in what ways could political parties be likened to religious organizations? In Nigeria, when a political party controls a state government or the federal government, it monopolizes all public broadcasting stations and converts them to party organs to the exclusion of opposition parties and their views. In other words, political parties are as exclusionary as competitive religious organizations.

Bala Musa (2000: 107) points out that "the volatile religious atmosphere in the country, the abuse of religious speech in the past, the excessive politicization of religion, and the constant use of the mass media to heighten religious tensions" in Nigeria have necessitated the state's institutionalization of a policy of "prior restraint" on Christians and Muslims in relation to religious broadcasting.

"Religious broadcasting" here means the technological mediation of religious speech or communication, specifically via radio and television. A critical perspective on the history of the NBC laws vis-à-vis the wider political practices of the individuals and groups in control of state power in Nigeria would demonstrate that the doctrine of "prior restraint" is nothing but a myth. It is doubtful why, on the one hand, a government would want to censor religious views and communication before they are expressed, while on the other hand, the same government heavily and unabashedly expends public funds on explicitly religious programs such as pilgrimages (in 2010 Nigeria spent N1.54 billion on pilgrimages [Ukah 2014: 93f]), festivals, holidays, and so forth.[3] A government that deliberately, relentlessly, and consistently saturates public discourse and political practice with religiously motivated practices cannot without contradiction logically institutionalize and defend a doctrine of "prior restraint" as a rationale for prohibiting the religious ownership of broadcast licenses. It also contravenes the constitutional guarantees in respect of fundamental human freedoms, particularly those concerning freedom of expression and of the press. Prior restraint is an unconstitutional restraint on free speech and press freedom.

Furthermore, the doctrine of "prior restraint" fails to account for the role of the state as a principal player in the media market; the state and its organs and representatives play a not-insignificant part in the equivocations and tensions evident in state policies and politics of deregulation and regulation of the media marketplace, particularly in respect to religious broadcasting. More importantly, excluding religious organizations from owning broadcast media construes religious communication as more problematic than integrative of the society. Explicitly, it construes religious communication as in conflict with political communication. According to Monroe Price (2007: 85), in the twenty-first-century modern society, "religious or explicitly religious speech is inflected with new power, as if it were a form of violence itself." Even when Nigeria is an evolving liberal democracy, religion is an integral feature of the country's identity and self-definition. Considering the doctrine of prior restraint, religion features prominently in the country's definition of threats to national security and integration.

Part of the NBC's responsibilities is to determine the standard and quality of broadcasts in the country. This it does through the crafting of a Broadcasting Code, the latest of which is the *Nigeria Broadcasting Code* (4th edition, 2006, hereafter, the Code). Such a document has the force of law and, like the law establishing the NBC itself, may be judged as undemocratically drafted by a select group to preserve the self-interests of some persons or sections of the country. In order to assuage this public anxiety, NBC officials make spirited attempts to justify the reasonableness and therefore legitimacy of the contents of the Code. Its purported goal is to create a credible, ethical, constructive, and responsible broadcasting industry in a rapidly changing media arena.

The NBC Code devotes two sections to religion—namely, Religious Programming (§4.4.1a–i) and Religious [Advertisement] (§7.5.1a–c). The Code situates the justification of the regulation of religious programs in the multireligious character of the Nigerian society: Nigeria is a multireligious society where religious "beliefs and practices are central to people's lives and are capable of evoking strong passions and emotions." As a result of this pragmatic reason of respecting people's religions and avoiding any offense to the religious sensibilities and sensitivities of Nigeria's diverse communities, broadcasting stations in the country are to give "equal opportunities and equitable airtime, not less than 90 minutes" of weekly airtime to "all religious groups" as "a civil responsibility without charge" (The Code, §4.4.1a). The Code cautions that religious broadcasts of any station shall not exceed 10 percent of its weekly airtime. This ceiling is to prevent the religious takeover of the airwaves and to create diversity in programming. Further specifications include the responsible and accurate presentation of religious programs, and where possible by "responsible representatives of the given religion"; the prohibition of attacks on, or ridicule of, another religion or sect; and the avoidance of the casual use of names, words, and symbols regarded as sacred by believers. The Code specifies that a religious broadcast "shall restrict itself to the content of its creed and shall not be presented in a manner as to mislead the public" (The Code, §4.4.1f). This element in the Code sets up the NBC as the arbiter of orthodoxy even though it does not state who determines when a particular religious doctrine is *not* misleading or deceptively motivated. The presentation of rites and rituals that border on obscenity are generally prohibited except where these are to teach the beliefs of a religion. Here, too, it is difficult to understand the intention of the framers of the Code, since "obscenity" is not defined and no examples of such rituals are given.

The other section of the Code, which deals with the presentation of religion in the broadcast media, revolves around how to advertise religion. Containing only three items, it is an elaboration or repetition of the earlier section (§4.4.1a–i) dealing with the content of religious programs or the requisites for religious programming:

> ªAn advertisement promoting religion in any form shall present its claims, especially those relating to miracles, in such a manner that is verifiable, provable and believable; ᵇnot use the peculiarities of broadcast technology to mislead the viewer/listener; ᶜnot cast aspersions on any other religion or sect; and shall not be seen to exploit the weakness, handicap(s), shortcomings or state of desperation of members of the public. (§7.5.1a–c)

A related piece of legislation concerning the advertisement of religion is found in *The Nigerian Code of Advertising Practice* (3rd ed., 2005) published by the Advertising Practitioners Council of Nigeria (APCON). Established by Act 55 of 1988 (and amended by Act 93 of 1992), APCON is the statutory regulator of all facets of advertising in Nigeria. The code of advertising specifies under section §4.16 the purpose of religious advertisement: "Advertisements of religious products and services, shall not go beyond an effort to encourage the social and psychological wellbeing of the adherents." Section §4.16.1 repeats verbatim section §7.5.1c of the NBC code: "No religious advertisement shall be seen to try to exploit the weaknesses, handicaps, shortcomings, or state of desperation of members of the public." Section 4.16.2, which has four distinct subsections (i–iv), is devoted entirely to "Miracles, Portents, Coercion, etc.": religious advertisement should avoid exaggeration in its claims concerning miracles and the use of "spurious testimonials likely to deceive the audience." Furthermore, religious advertisements should avoid the promise of financial prosperity, not "cast aspersion on any other sect or religion, and not coerce, cajole, or otherwise compel anyone to become an adherent of a particular sect or belief" (APCON Code of Advertising, §4.16:2iii–iv).

Like other core elements of religious belief, miracles by definition defy natural explanation or proof (but see Sogolo 1993: 91–116 for different explanatory models of miracles); however, a central item of the Code is that "a programme promoting religion in any form shall present its claims, especially those relating to miracles, in such a manner that is provable and believable" (The Code, §4.4.1g). At issue is not "believability" but rather the provability and the procedures that a claimant would engage to arrive at a conclusion that an occurrence or claim constitutes a "miracle." The Code does not provide a definition of "miracle" or who determines or certifies that a claim constitutes a miracle and could be broadcast. Perhaps the framers were using the concept of "miracle" in the same way it has been deployed in popular discourse and in popular media: a direct, beneficial intervention in the affairs of humans by a supra-human entity.

The Nigerian Pentecostal and charismatic communities have been at the forefront in popularizing miracles and, in the words of NBC officials, turning them into an "everyday occurrence." As the Nigerian state became more dysfunctional and approached the tipping point of a failed state or, in the apt words of John Campbell, "dancing on the brink" (2011), there was a discernible and heightened ascendancy, supremacy, and ubiquity of miracles as well as miracle-producing and -marketing entrepreneurs. In other words, there was an obvious deregulation of miracles as the state economy became more deregulated starting in the late 1980s. A variegated set of ministries and churches that emerged in the post–civil war Nigeria proliferated during the difficult decade of the 1980s, consolidated themselves in the 1990s, and eventually became a multi-billion-dollar industry in the first decade of the twenty-first century. These churches also soon became prominent players in the broadcast media (Ojo 2006; Ukah 2008b; Marshall 2009; Onoja 2009: 263–273).

A Nigerian born-again Christian is either a consumer or a producer of miracles—or both. In the history of religions, "miracle" as an analytical concept or attribute ascribed to certain occurrences by certain persons had always been controversial and contested (see, e.g., Nickell 1993; Sogolo 1993: 91ff.). The controversies surrounding the prohibition of miracles on the airwaves, fiercest among the Pentecostal communities, relate to the diverse interpretations given to the above sections of the NBC Code and the APCON Code by different interest groups in the broadcast market. Every religion deals with unverifiable, improvable, and hard-to-believe doctrines and practices, but the Pentecostal groups have special interest in marketing miracles as their "unique selling proposition/point." The "sovereignty of miracles" among Nigerian Pentecostals sets them apart from other religious communities. The core of the groups' self-understanding revolves around the staging of the miraculous and "the fundamentally democratic access to divine grace and miracles" (Marshall 2010: 209).

From its Latin etymology of *miraculum*, meaning "object of wonder, awe, or amazement," the root meaning of "miracle" is "to smile upon."[4] A miracle may be defined in many ways, but a general understanding is that it is "an event that appears to be contrary to the laws of nature and is regarded as an act of God."[5] This definition covers the core meaning that religious believers give to the word "miracle." This, too, is at the root of the NBC's complaint: a miracle as an act of God/ deity that apparently transgresses the laws of nature cannot be an everyday occurrence. The NBC's description of "miracle" corresponds with the central ideas of David Hume's (1711–1776) now classic definition of a miracle as "the violation of the laws of nature. . . . Nothing is esteemed a miracle, if it ever happens in the common course of nature" (Hume 1996 [1854]: 130). Hume provides arguments in support of his skeptical position that miracles are unprovable. The positive character of miracles is often neglected in academic discussions of miracles. Nigerian Pentecostal pastors insist a miracle of necessity benefits someone or other. Pastors insist the miracles they produce and disseminate on television benefit the believer who actively and financially supports their cause. Chris Oyakhilome, founder-owner of Believers' LoveWorld (better known as Christ Embassy) and a foremost performer/producer of miracles on pre-ban television, articulates the mindset of the Pentecostal community when he says, "A miracle is an inexplicable intervention by a supernatural power in the natural affairs of man. A miracle is something beyond the normal course of events. Usually a miracle is a positive event. It is not something that destroys."[6]

What worried the NBC was the apparent takeover of the broadcast industry by the miracle merchants, who have the funds to buy well over 50 percent of a station's airtime and by so doing marginalize other voices or public interest programs, such as those pertaining to education and development. The greatest beneficiaries of the miracle broadcast were assumed to be first the miracle merchants themselves, who enjoyed expanded market share and loyalty, and second the cash-strapped, government-owned broadcast stations, which rake in millions of dollars from the sale of airtime. The tension between public-service programming and self-sustainability is most evident in the practices of the Nigerian Television Authority (NTA). As a public-service institution that claims to be independent of and impartial toward any religion or ethnic group in Nigeria, it is expected that the NTA, more than any other station, would be able to interpret, translate, and exemplify in practice some of the ambiguities exhibited by government policies and practices relating to the broadcast of religion.

The NTA and Religious Broadcast

As stated earlier, an important item in the NBC Code contains what amounts to the "public strain" in the broadcasting industry: "Equal opportunity and equitable airtime, not less than 90 minutes of a station's weekly airtime, shall be made available to all religious groups in the community as a civil responsibility without charge" (§4.4.1a). Established by Decree 24 in May 1977—with retroactive effect from April 1, 1976—by the federal government, the Nigerian Television Authority (NTA) represents the largest publicly funded television network in Africa, with 97 stations, "more than 84 transmitters, and 19 satellite earth stations linked with three INSTELSAT transponders" airing more than 85,000 hours of programming with a daily viewership of well over 100 million—and many thousands outside the country as the organization has extended its programming reach to the Nigerian diaspora (Alozie 2003: 66). At its creation, the NTA had an exclusive television broadcast right that was abrogated by the 1979 Constitution, which gave rights of ownership of broadcast media to state governments, organizations, or individuals that the president of the country may so authorize.

How a public-service network like the NTA accommodates the public strain of the NBC Code is a pointer to the intricacy of the politics of religious broadcast policies in Nigeria. In the late 1970s and 1980s, NTA subsidized religious broadcasts (Lyons and Lyons 1991: 112). In the era of commercialization that followed the economic downturn of the mid-1980s and the privatization/liberalization that started in 1992, the organization started to aggressively seek revenues from advertising and sponsored programs. Soon, sponsored religious programs and advertising by conglomerates and multinationals, including mega-churches, became a steady source of funds, augmenting its dwindling subvention from the federal government. The huge revenues from competing churches soon asphyxiated whatever was left of the station's public-service programming. Walter Ihejirika (2006: 133) quotes an NTA manager as asserting that "TV evangelism is for those who pay. There is no space [in the NTA's schedule] for public service." In order to maintain its clientele of advertisers—and to the disregard of the Code of Broadcasting—programs of questionable character, including doctored news, were allowed to be broadcast insofar as someone was willing to pay for them

(Ojebode 2009: 69). Oluyinka Esan (2009: 157) aptly describes the state of broadcasting in the era of commercialized television in Nigeria:

> Commercialised [television] stations featured productions with a questionable mix of claims and values by traditional and spiritual healers, with little effort made to verify those claims. Religion (Christian and Islamic evangelists) became a brand . . . and personal celebrations of the privileged tended to dominate the screen. [Station general managers were] most unapologetic for this trend even when [they] found some of the programmes distasteful.

If this is the case, how does the NTA observe the provisions of the NBC Code in relation to (1) equal access for all religious groups; (2) 90 minutes weekly free airtime dedicated to religious broadcast; and (3) devoting no more than 10 percent of total weekly airtime to religious broadcast?

With respect to equal access for all religious groups, NTA demonstrates the strong bias which the state harbors for and against some religious organizations in some regions of the country. In southern Nigeria, for example, NTA stations are biased in favor of Christian groups and against Muslim groups. This is consistent with the conclusions of Walter Ihejirika (2009) on how Muslim and other religious minorities in the city of Port Harcourt are marginalized in terms of media access and their strategies for gaining media space. Evidently, this is because Christian groups, particularly Pentecostal churches, are favored clients doling out large sums for airtime. At NTA Ibadan, for example, during the first quarter of the programming schedule for 2008, virtually all the religious programs were Christian-sponsored. Without doubt this is a breach of the Code, but station officials insist this was so because Muslims and other religious groups were not ready to pay for airtime. One official avers that Muslims do not like using the services of the station "because of their belief that their religion [Islam] is not for sale."[7] Implied in this statement is the knowledge of the station managers that religious broadcasting now exists in a primarily commercialized format, and Christian groups are willing and ready to patronize the commercialized airwaves in order to sell their religion. Muslims depend on wealthy individuals to sponsor their media broadcasts, while Christians depend on church owner-founders to engage television stations in showcasing their charisma. During the second quarter of 2008, there were more than 15 Christian programs on air at NTA Jos but only 3 Muslim programs. African indigenous religions are almost completely absent from the airwaves except in a few cases of sponsored advertisements of traditional herbal products (see chapter 11). Even in these cases, the sponsors have to secure clearance from the Federal Ministry of Health and from the National Agency for Food, Drug Administration and Control before the programs are accepted for broadcast. In the core northern cities such as Kano and Maiduguri, NTA stations systematically and consistently exclude Christian programs from their broadcast schedule even when there are sponsors "who are ready to pay one million naira for a 30-minute slot," according to an NTA official in an interview in May 2008. The stations that indulge in this practice accept only a single network program, *Christian Half Hour.* In Kano, the situation is direr: "No Christian broadcasts are allowed under any circumstances, even at [Christian] festival time—which is a contravention of NTA guidelines" (Kukah 1992: 199; Hackett 1998: 269–270). Among other reasons, Pentecostal programs are particularly abhorred because they are perceived as more aggressively proselytizing and, therefore, in bad taste.

All over the NTA network, Islam is privileged in the north and Christianity in the south, but African indigenous religions and other minority religions are subjected to systematic exclusion. An NTA program manager in one of the Middle Belt states asked rhetorically during an interview, "Are there people who still practice African indigenous religions these days" to warrant allocating airtime to them?[8] Such sentiment characterizes the constitutional privileging of Semitic religions (Christianity and Islam) in most African states to the disenfranchisement of adherents of African religions and, in the words of Makau Mutua (1999: 170), "a repudiation . . . of the humanity of African culture."[9] The pattern evident in how the NTA politicizes religious broadcasts with respect to "equal access" reflects a broader pattern of the politicization of religion in Nigeria, particularly since the return to civilian rule in 1999 when former president Olusegun Obasanjo constructed a chapel at the seat of government in Abuja and some state governors, such as of Joshua Dariye of Plateau State, followed his example and built the "Chapel of Grace" at the Government House in Jos. The NTA network, therefore, glaringly fails to adhere to the NBC's equal or fair access to all religious communities as enshrined in the NBC Code. The situation in 2008 remains as it was a decade earlier, when Rosalind Hackett (1998: 274 [note 20]) said, "Despite the provisions for fair access to the media especially at festival time, it is clear that when Christianity or Islam dominate in a particular area, this type of access may be very restricted or non-existent" (see, also, Hackett 2012).

The NTA's official policy—which coincides with the NBC's official position regarding the 90 minutes of free airtime to be devoted to religious broadcast—is that each general manager of each television station has the discretion to allocate it as s/he deems fit. An investigation of two NTA stations, one in the south and the other in the north, reveals that in the era of full commercialization of broadcast media, the tyranny of profit has led to the breach of this provision. According to the NTA station in the north programs manager, "We cannot devote 90 minutes free of charge anymore to religious broadcast, but at least we have two 30-minute programs, one for Muslims, the other for Christians, broadcast each week free of charge."[10] The second NTA station does not even have any such religious program, as it claims that it devotes its entire "quota" for public service to sponsored religious programs that bring in much-needed revenue for the station. The philosophy behind the practice is termed "Let Them Pay" (LTP).[11]

Apart from what constitutes "religious news from the perspective of the stations," a sponsor pays for every other religious item on the air. Even some items broadcast as "news" or "news report" are in reality paid for by the group (companies or churches) that may be considered to gain from the airing of such an item. Because sponsored programs bring in large amounts of funds for NTA, "not-for-profit programmes are not treated as important conduits of change any longer" (Ojobode 2009: 74).

Before the enforcement of §4.4.1 of the NBC Code, many NTA stations were *de facto* quasi-religious stations, broadcasting a huge amount of religious programs, mainly Pentecostal programs for the stations located in the south and Muslim programs for those located in the north. As a result of the searchlight turned on them by the NBC and the general public, many of the stations claim they are not exceeding the 10 percent airtime specified in the NBC Code. NTA Ibadan, for example, claims that religious programs within its first quarter of 2008 constitute only 4.5 percent of its total weekly broadcast, and these programs were mainly Christian evangelical programs. Similarly, NTA Jos claims to be within the 10 percent ratio, since it devotes nearly 75 percent of its airtime to network programs. What has happened in the years since the "demiraculization" of the airwaves started is that NTA stations have come under increasing scrutiny and pressure to diversify their clientele by seeking corporate sponsors of events and programs rather than concentrating on the miracle Pentecostalism as their main revenue stream. Also, multi-millionaire preachers (for example, T. B. Joshua, Chris Oyakhilome, and Lazarus Mmuoka) have since moved to South Africa to host their satellite television stations.

The politics and policy of religious broadcasting in Nigeria have implications for religiously related conflict and violence (Hackett 2012). The privileging of Islam in the north and the consequent systematic exclusion of non-Muslim broadcasts creates information asymmetry and "a territorial psyche that gives [Muslim] communities [in the North] the audacity to deny others an equal right to exist in their enclaves" (Musa 2000: 106; Ukah 2013: 43-62). According to the secretary of Kaduna State Chapter of CAN, the Christian Association of Nigeria, Elder Saidu Dogo, the death of two Christians in Kaduna on October 12 and 13, 2007, was directly linked to the (re)broadcast on NTA Kaduna of the sermons of the late Sheikh Abubakar Gumi on September 21 and 22, during the *tafsir*—the reading and interpretation of the Quran during the month-long celebration of Ramadan (on Gumi see chapter 3). The CAN leader recounted how, in the broadcast, Gumi referenced the way the Prophet Muhammad captured the Arabian Peninsula and the British colonial forces captured northern Nigeria. Gumi thereafter called upon Muslims to carry out jihad against young Christians in order to retake that which was originally theirs.[12] Broadcasting such fiery sermons breached the NBC Code, but NTA Kaduna, which was responsible for this breach, was not sanctioned. This is an obvious pointer to selective enforcement of the Code by the NBC because of the politics of religion that has influenced both the formulation and implementation of the policy of religious broadcasting. The lack of autonomy as well as political correctness has compelled NTA stations in the north to be co-opted into the state apparatus as mouthpieces of state governments and the religious establishment; in this condition, they compromise their constitutional duties as spelled out under Article 22 of the 1999 Constitution—namely, to "uphold the responsibility and accountability of the government to the people." Leo Igwe, a scholar of religion and a Nigerian humanist critic of the religious establishment in Nigeria, observes, "Officially, religious minorities in Nigeria suffer systematic exclusion, discrimination, and violation of their rights [which] has caused a lot of tension, division, alienation, and conflict. In Northern Nigeria—especially in the Muslim majority states—religious minorities are systematically marginalized and disadvantaged."[13]

Manipulation Regulation / Managing Miracles

It may be argued that liberalizing the broadcast market would entail minimal regulation. The NBC's action regarding miracle broadcasts would amount, therefore, to an unwarranted interference in the logic of the free-market system. If the free media market dictated that miracle broadcasts were popular among the people and the producers of miracles paid the stations for the airtime, why should the government be bothered about this? Is the government truly "playing God," as Chris Oyakhilome accused it? The other side of the argument that the NBC and its allies espouse is that the media shape worldviews; as the airwaves belong to the people, it is the state's prerogative to intervene in issues that affect society as well as the protection of the weak.

So while the state cannot, and does not, dictate which religious group a citizen should join, the state ensures powerful individuals and cartels do not monopolize broadcast media as instruments of propaganda to disseminate biased views or disinformation to promote their own interests. The marketing of half-truths and lies with the purpose of making profit is an outright fraud. The state has a clear responsibility to intervene in order to control such activities. The government acknowledges in the preamble to the codes under discussion here, as well as in the distinct elements in the codes, that religion is vital to the social and personal self-understanding of citizens; as a result, the dissemination of religious ideas and information through the media cannot be left unchecked or in the hands of profiteering cartels such as big churches and religious entrepreneurs. What the NBC did was not the prohibition of miracles but the prohibition of the broadcast of "unverified miracles." This means that miracle claims that are authenticated through specific processes (pre-miracle, during-miracle, post-miracle videos together with medical evidence) can be broadcast without further ado. Aside from claiming to protect society from harmful, simplistic and distorted religious communications, the state can, and does, use regulation to control media market dynamics. Because the state is actively involved in the market for loyalties, it uses media regulation to control and further its own interest of securing a share of the audiences. Poignantly, however, miracles are a response to and a critique of a dysfunctional, failing state that is increasingly irrelevant in the life of citizens, and this point could be as irritating, as miracles are deemed offensive to some government officials.

To complicate the discussion further, some commentators argue—and with some justification—that the media landscape and media laws in Nigeria are biased not against religion but in favor of it. Even where it appears that the state is stifling religious communication—as in the miracle ban, for example—a critical examination of the content of broadcast media, as well as the controlling voices, demonstrate convincingly that pro-Muslim and pro-Christian views saturate the media to the exclusion of dissenting voices. This is what the examination of the NTA practices regarding the broadcast of religion demonstrates convincingly. Leo Igwe articulates this critical perspective thus: "Media agencies in Nigeria are biased. Many of what we have as national newspapers—both privately and state owned—are in fact religious—Christian or Islamic or 'chrislamic' dailies whose 'unwritten policy' is to further these religious interests."[14]

This sort of lamentation, correct as it is, points to another reason why an agency like the NBC needs to ensure that its guidelines are followed or interpreted in ways that reflect the broad spectrum of opinions (beliefs and unbeliefs) of majority and minority religious groups. Comprehensive enforcement of its regulations would safeguard the airwaves as a public resource rather than a resource for the rich and powerful, the religious, and the establishment. Again, there is an echo of a long-running controversy over whether or not Nigeria is a secular state. Some argue that the Constitution's stipulation that there should be a separation of state and religion does not make the country a secular state. According to a recent statement credited to the Sultan of Sokoto, Alhaji Muhammad Saad Abubakar III, "Anyone saying Nigeria is a secular nation does not understand the meaning of the word 'secular.' There is nothing secular about the Nigerian nation, since whatever we do will always put Islam and Christianity in the fore front [*sic*]."[15] The argument for the "unsecular" character of Nigeria has been forcefully put forward by Muslims. But Christians as individuals and groups have not acted as if the country is "secular" either; they have actively interpreted secularity of the country as "equal treatment of Christianity and Islam," which are now de facto "state religions." Christians who have gone into broadcasting have not failed to sacralize the airwaves by the overt display of their religiosity, even when they acquired their broadcast license by agreeing not to be religiously biased. The founder-owner and chairman of Inspiration FM, Erastus S. B. Akingbola—who was also the former CEO of the now defunct Intercontinental Bank[16]—is quoted as saying, "We want to use the power of the mass media to redress and reconstruct our national value system. We do not preach religion. We preach godliness, morals, ethics and sound value."[17] As Akingbola also doubles as a serving pastor of the Redeemed Christian Church of God, arguably the largest and wealthiest Pentecostal church in Nigeria, it is not clear on what platform his radio station would preach "godliness without religion" when part of the mission statement and philosophy of the station is to provide the public with "live Christian music" and "up-to-date discretionary time information."[18] As broadcast license-holders manipulate broadcast regulations to sustain profitability, so the state would increasingly intervene in the media market to manage religion, even when this means manipulating media regulations to achieve its goals.

The practice of religious broadcasting as exemplified by the NTA demonstrates a high degree of selective interpretation of broadcast rules and government manipulation of regulation to manage religion. The NTA practices regarding the broadcast of religion create isolated "enclaves" with fairly uniform religious viewpoints rather than a robust environment that nourishes the discussion of divergent perspectives and debates about important social issues. "Enclave broadcasting" may be construed by its practitioners as being in the "public interest," but it in practice denies the public "cultural recognition and diversity" as well as a reasonable opportunity for a robust discussion of complex perspectives and views on issues of public significance (Chibita 2011: 269; see, also, Hackett 2012). This is the point Leo Igwe decries in his comments cited above. If the airwaves are public property, it is only proper that those who are licensed to use portions of it do so in the interest of the public, at least by covering divergent views—religious or otherwise—of the population. The NBC Code and APCON's Advertising Code, in differing degrees, try to articulate what may roughly approximate to "the Fairness Doctrine" of the United States Federal Communications Commission: that broadcast license-holders devote quality airtime to discuss issues of public interest and importance and to do this in such a way that covers diverse, contrasting perspectives (for details, see Hazlett and Sosa 1997). Under "Fairness," the NBC Code (§4.6.1) states, "No individual or organization shall be treated in an unjust or unfair manner in any programme," and §4.6.4 reinforces the fairness aspiration by stating, "Broadcasters shall always ensure that all parties to a programme are offered the chance to contribute so as to achieve fairness." To protect the views and interests of persons and groups, the Code cautioned, "When the views of a person or organisation that is not participating in a programme are being represented, they shall be done in a fair and just manner" (§4.6.5).

Two levels of difficulties regarding the Code are specificity and enforcement: many of its stipulations are not just abstract but ambiguous and can be translated into different types of practices or completely ignored. Failure in exercising its oversight function in enforcing its rules and regulations is a more troubling feature of the agency. The NBC knows and acknowledges that its regulations are consistently flouted by television stations but justifies its inaction by claiming that it has "elected to be more preventive and corrective rather than punitive. This is to encourage the growth of the broadcast industry."[19] In its enforcement of miracle-free broadcasts, the NBC has presented itself as a neutral enforcer of fairness, program standards, and quality. However, it is only in implementing its own version of the fairness doctrine, particularly in government-owned broadcast networks such as the NTA, that the NBC can be seen to be a neutral broadcast industry watchdog and enforcer of broadcast regulations. What the agency is doing at the moment may at best be described as helping the state to manage religion by manipulating (and ignoring) in a selective way its own regulations concerning the broadcast of religion.

Conclusion

In the twenty-first century—and due partly to the events of 9/11 and partly to the unfolding processes of globalization, particularly of the media—monitoring, managing, and regulating religion, especially religious communication, are important aspects of state function almost everywhere. Hence, the Nigerian state considers it necessary to police the airwaves, not merely to protect vulnerable groups but to keep a tab on economically and politically powerful preachers and groups. The debates arising from the ban on miracle broadcast brought to the fore important issues concerning the limits of the power of the state to determine religious orthodoxy as well as the place of religious communication in a quasi-secular democracy.

The NBC needs to fiercely and fearlessly enforce its fairness doctrine. Failure in doing so may result in some sort of "yellow broadcasting" where the religious propaganda of millionaire pastors and imams holds sway with no regard for balance, truth, or attention to diversity. Furthermore, it is an integral aspect of the public-interest doctrine that diverse points of view and political and religious arguments representing all shades of opinion on public issues be available on public and private broadcast stations. No one opinion or the views of a religious (or political) group are to be advanced over others (as is the case in the NTA of 2011), but all arguments/opinions are to be represented and given a reasonable airing. This is all the more reason why "enclave broadcasting" needs to be replaced by a more inclusive programming.

The pressures of commercialization and profitability have pushed public interest broadcasting away from the priority agenda of both the NBC and broadcast licenses, creating a media scenario where fairness and quality programming are secondary to sustainability. The laws liberalizing the media used the phrases "national interest," "public interest," and "interest of the public" six times, but these concepts and their complex philosophical, legal, and social ramifications are not reflected in the oversight functions of the NBC (Ukah 2011a: 44). A more holistic approach to the regulations of religious broadcasting—one that guarantees that the NBC and APCON codes are adhered to—would be capable of creating a more robust broadcast environment that safeguards the interest of the people above the interests of broadcast license-holders. This is what is needed in the Nigerian media market at the moment. According to the law establishing the NBC, it is the right of the Nigerian public, and not the right or interest of the broadcasters—government or private—that is paramount. Selective manipulation of regulations—or rather the politicization of broadcast policies—directed toward the management of religion without enforcing fairness and diversity would only exacerbate the situation of religious intolerance and the hostilities which have marked inter- and intra-religious relations in Nigeria since the late 1970s. Evenhanded enforcement of laws and regulations regarding technologically mediated religious communications by an independent industry regulator

> can also play a role in revitalizing public deliberations and debate. While the liberal state cannot directly bring about the requisite change in mentality on the part of religious and secular citizens, it can . . . play an important role in developing the institutional and structural framework that can facilitate critical engagement, debate, and reflection. (Baumeister 2011: 238)

Notes

1. Chris Oyakhilome, published interview, *National Standard* (Abuja) 1, no. 2 (January 2005): 20.

2. http://www.nbc.gov.ng/broadcast.php?menu=1&submenu=4. Also see the "Frequently Asked Questions" section on the NBC website at http://www.nbc.gov.ng/faq.php.

3. See C. D. Nguvughen, "Nigerian Religious Pilgrimages: Piety or Economic Waste?" http://www.tcnn.org/articles/RB54_Chentu.pdf.

4. http://www.thefreedictionary.com/miracle.

5. *Bloomsbury English Dictionary*, 2nd ed. (London: Bloomsbury Publishers Plc., 2004): 1202.

6. Chris Oyakhilome, published interview, *National Standard* (Abuja) 1, no. 6 (December 2004): 25.

7. Interview with NTA Ibadan program manager, March 15, 2008.

8. Personal interview with Peter Ochigbo, NTA Jos Programs Manager, May 13, 2008.

9. Religious national holidays are culled from Christianity and Islam; during these periods public resources are deployed in distributing rams and bags of rice to civil servants, while indigenous religious festivals and feasts are marginalized and left to ethnic groups to celebrate.

10. Peter Ochigbo, interview. The station broadcasts *Christian Half Hour,* sourced through the Christian Association of Nigeria, and *Islam Calling,* sourced through Jamaatu Nasiru Islam (JNI).

11. Any individual or group that seeks the publicity of an event or even a news item (be it religious, economic, or social) is made to pay for such publicity. (Interview with program manager, NTA Ibadan, February 19, 2008.)

12. "Nigeria: Two Christians Murdered in Kaduna: Sword, Wooden Club Attacks Follow Calls for Violent Jihad by Muslim Leaders," *Compact Direct News,* October 22, 2007. http://compassdirect.org/en/display.php?page=news&lang=en&length=long&idelement=5090&backpage=summaries&critere=&countryname=&rowcur=.

13. Leo Igwe, "The Rights of Religious Minorities," *The Guardian* (Lagos), May 5, 2008. http://www.guardiannewsngr.com/editorial_opinion/article02/indexn2_html.

14. http://www.butterfliesandwheels.org/2011/media-and-religious-censorship-in-nigeria/.

15. Ahmed Oyerinde, "Nigeria Not a Secular State—Sultan," *The Sun* (Lagos), August 25, 2011. http://www.sunnewsonline.com/webpages/news/national/2011/aug/25/national-25-08-2011-007.html.

16. There is an irony here. Akingbola, who wants to instill "godliness without religion," was removed in 2009 as the CEO of Intercontinental Bank Plc. by the governor of Central Bank of Nigeria, Sanusi Lamido Sanusi, for manipulating bank records, stealing depositors' funds, and money-laundering (Ukah 2011b: 209–210).

17. "Nigerian Banker Sets Up Radio Station to Promote 'Godliness.'" http://www.christiantoday.com/article/nigerian.banker.sets.up.radio.station.to.promote.godliness/22789.htm.

18. http://inspiration-radio.com/site/.

19. http://www.nbc.gov.ng/faq.php.

References

Alozie, Emmanuel C. 2003. "Critical Analysis of Cultural Values Found in Nigerian Mass Media Advertisements." *SIMILE: Studies in Media and Information Literacy Education* 3(4): 1–12.

Alumuku, Tor Patrick. 2006. *Community Radio Development: The World and Africa.* Nairobi: Pauline Press.

APCON, 2005. *The Nigerian Code of Advertising Practice.* 3rd ed. Lagos: APCON.

Baumeister, Andrea. 2011. "The Use of 'Public Reason' by Religious and Secular Citizens: Limitations of Habermas' Conception of the Role of Religion in the Public Realm." *Constellations* 18(2): 223–243.

Campbell, John. 2011. *Nigeria: Dancing on the Brink.* Lanham, MD: Rowman and Littlefield.

Chibita, Monica B. 2011. "Policing Popular Media in Africa." In *Popular Media, Democracy and Development in Africa,* edited by Herman Wasserman, 269–281. London: Routledge.

Dairo, Olalekan A. 2010. "Privatization and Commercialization of Christian Message." In *Creativity and Change in Nigerian Christianity,* edited by David O. Ogungbile and Akintunde E. Akinade, 193–197. Lagos: Malthouse Press.

Esan, Oluyinka. 2009. *Nigerian Television: Fifty Years of Television in Africa.* Princeton, NJ: AMV Publishing.

Hackett, Rosalind I. J. 1998. "Charismatic/Pentecostal Appropriation of Media Technologies in Nigeria and Ghana." *Journal of Religion in Africa* 28(3): 258–277.

———. 2012. "Devil Bustin' Satellites: How Media Liberalization in Africa Generates Religious Intolerance and Conflict." In *Displacing the State: Religion and Conflict in Neoliberal Africa,* edited by James H. Smith and Rosalind I. J. Hackett, 153–208. South Bend, IN: University of Notre Dame Press.

Hazlett, Thomas W., and David W. Sosa. 1997. "Was the Fairness Doctrine a 'Chilling Effect'? Evidence from the Postderegulation Radio Market." *Journal of Legal Studies* 26: 279–301.

Hoover, Stewart, and Nadia Kaneva, eds. 2009. *Fundamentalisms and the Media.* London: Continuum.

Hume, David. 1996 [1854]. *The Philosophical Works of David Hume.* Vol. 4. Bristol: Thoemmes Press.

Ihejirika, Walter C. 2006. "Religious Broadcasting and the Nigerian Media Laws." *Journal of Religion and Culture* 7(1): 127–141.

———. 2009. "Muslim Minorities and Media Access in a Predominantly Christian City: The Case of Port Harcourt, Nigeria." *Journal of African Media Studies* 1(3): 469–492.

Kukah, Matthew Hassan. 1992. "The Politicisation of Fundamentalism in Nigeria." In *New Dimensions in African Christianity,* edited by Paul Gifford, 183–206. Ibadan: Sefer Publications.

Lyons, P. Andrew, and Harriet D. Lyons. 1991. "Religion and the Mass Media." In *Religion and Society in Nigeria: Historical and Sociological Perspectives,* edited by Jacob K. Olupona and Toyin Falola, 97–128. Ibadan: Spectrum Books.

Magbadelo, John Olushola. 2004. "Pentecostalism in Nigeria: Exploiting or Edifying the Masses." *African Sociological Review* 8(2): 15–29.

Marshall, Ruth. 2009. *Political Spiritualities: The Pentecostal Revolution in Nigeria.* Chicago: University of Chicago Press.

———. 2010. "The Sovereignty of Miracles: Pentecostal Political Theology in Nigeria." *Constellations* 17(2): 197–223.

Meyer, Birgit. 2009. "Pentecostalism and Modern Audiovisual Media." In *Media and Identity in Africa,* edited by Kimani Njogu and John Middleton, 114–123. Bloomington: Indiana University Press.

Moemeka, Andrew A. 2009. "Community Radio Broadcasting for Rural Community Education." In *Media and Communications Industries in Nigeria: Impact of Neoliberal Reforms between 1999 and 2007,* edited by Anthony A. Olorunnisola, 31–57. Lewiston, NY: Edwin Mellen Press.

Musa, Bala. 2000. "Pluralism and Prior Restraint on Religious Communication in Nigeria: Policy versus Praxis." In *Religion, Law, and Freedom: A Global Perspective,* edited by Joel Thierstein and Yahya R. Kamalipour, 98–111. London: Praeger.

Mutua, Makau.1999. "Returning to My Roots: African 'Religions' and the State." In *Proselytization and Communal Self-Determination in Africa,* edited by Abdullahi Ahmed An-Na'im, 169–190. Maryknoll, NY: Orbis Books.

National Broadcasting Commission. 2007. *Nigeria Broadcasting Code,* 4th ed. Abuja: National Broadcasting Commission.

Nickell, Joe. 1993. *Looking for Miracle: Weeping Icons, Relics, Stigmata, Visions and Healing Cures.* Amherst, NY: Prometheus Books.

Nihinlola, Emiola. 2008. "'What Does This Mean?' A Theological Approach to the Bewilderment, Amazement and Perplexity of Pentecostalism." *Ogbomosho Journal of Theology* 13(1): 134–143.

Ojebode, Ayobami. 2009. "Public Service versus Profit-Making: The Nigerian Broadcast Sector in a Neoliberal Economy." In *Media and Communications Industries in Nigeria: Impact of Neoliberal Reforms between 1999 and 2007,* edited by Anthony A. Olorunnisola, 59–80. Lewiston, NY: Edwin Mellen Press.

Ojo, Matthews A. 2006. *The End-Time Army: Charismatic Movements in Modern Nigeria.* Trenton, NJ: Africa World Press.

Onoja, Adoyi. 2009. "The Pentecostal Churches: Spiritual Deregulation since the 1980s." In *Religion in Politics: Secularism and National Integration in Modern Nigeria,* edited by Julius O. Adekunle, 262–273. Trenton, NJ: Africa World Press.

Onwumechili, Chuka, and Donatus Anaelechi Uzomah. 2005. "Nigeria's Broadcast Commission and Regulatory Challenges: Questions Asked and Answers Provided." *International Journal of the Humanities* 5(6): 109–118.

Price, Monroe E. 2007. "Religious Communication and Its Relation to the State: Comparative Perspectives." In *Censorial Sensitivities: Free Speech and Religion in a Fundamentalist World,* edited by A. Sajó, 85–106. Utrecht: Eleven International Publishing.

Sogolo, Godwin. 1993. *Foundations of African Philosophy: A Definitive Analysis of Conceptual Issues in Africa Thought.* Ibadan: Ibadan University Press.

Turner, Bryan S. 2011. *Religion and Modern Societies: Citizenship, Secularisation and State.* Cambridge: Cambridge University Press.

Ukah, Asonzeh. 2008a. "Seeing Is More Than Believing: Posters and Proselytization in Nigeria." *Proselytization Revisited: Rights Talk, Free Markets and Culture Wars,* edited by Rosalind I. J. Hackett, 167–198. London: Equinox.

———. 2008b. *A New Paradigm of Pentecostal Power: A Study of the Redeemed Christian Church of God in Nigeria.* Trenton, NJ: Africa World Press.

———. 2011a. "Banishing Miracles: The Policies and Politics of Religious Broadcasting in Nigeria." *Politics and Religion Journal* 5(1): 39–60.

———. 2011b. "God Unlimited: Economic Transformations of Contemporary Nigerian Pentecostalism." In *Economics of Religion: Anthropological Approaches*, edited by Lionel Obadia and Donald C. Wood, 187–216. Bingley, UK: Emerald Group.

———. 2013. "Born-Again Muslims: The Ambivalence of Pentecostal Response to Islam in Nigeria." In *Fractured Spectrum: Perspectives in Christian-Muslim Relations in Nigeria,* edited by Akintunde E. Akinade, 43–62. New York: Peter Lang.

———. 2014. "The Midwife or the Handmaid? Religion in Political Advertising in Nigeria." In *Religion and Society in the 21st Century*, edited by Joachim Küpper, Klaus W. Hempfer, and Erika Fischer-Lichte, 87–144. Berlin: De Gruyter.

14 Living across Digital Landscapes

Muslims, Orthodox Christians, and an Indian Guru in Ethiopia

Samson A. Bezabeh

> *We have abolished the real world: what world is left? The apparent world per-*
> *haps? But no! With the real world we have also abolished the apparent world!*
>
> Friedrich Nietzsche, *Twilight of the Idols*

THE ROLE OF MEDIA in social life has recently received considerable attention by social scientists. But until recently little attention has been devoted to the interface between religion and media on the one hand and the public sphere on the other hand (see Meyer and Moors 2006). In fact, the traditional dictum has been to look at the public sphere as a secular entity devoid of religion. However, as several recent studies have shown, religion has, indeed, been a part of the public sphere, and media have become intertwined with religion (de Vries and Weber 2001; Hackett 2003; Meyer and Moors 2006). Media are also recognized as a component that leads to the emergence of a new form of the public sphere (Meyer and Moors 2006).

Using these insights, this chapter explores the interface between religion and media in Ethiopia. Although the use of modern electronic media began at the end of the nineteenth century, its use by religious groups has been rather limited. This changed dramatically in the post–Cold War period with the downfall of the Derg socialist regime in Ethiopia, which had ruled the country since 1974. Following the fall of the Derg, the party that came to power, the Ethiopian People's Revolutionary Front (EPRDF), permitted the liberalization of electronic and print media. In the new environment, a number of Muslims and newly formed Islamic organizations started to publish on Islam, the Muslim community in Ethiopia, and Muslims around the world. Muslims also opened privately owned studios with the intention of producing audio and video materials about Islam. Since the government has also allowed satellite television broadcasting, such as

Arab Satellite Television (ARAB SAT), the private Islamic studios have engaged in extensive copying, translation, and distribution of sermons broadcast on satellite television. In Ethiopia, the distribution of such media has been a factor in the deterioration of the relations between Muslim and Christians. As Jon Abbink (2011) has recently shown, polemical discourses focusing on Muslims' and Christians' competing claims to power have been increasingly hegemonic. Tensions between Muslims and Orthodox Christians followed on from the wider distribution and availability of such electronic media.

To explain the complex dynamics between Muslims and Orthodox Christians, I analyze the distribution, use, and reception of the sermons of Dr. Zakir Naik, a Mumbai-based preacher, that are broadcast on Arab Satellite Television. In Ethiopia, Naik's sermons have clearly been the most popular sermons, and they have been widely translated into Amharic and distributed by local Islamic studios.[1] For this reason, they offer a unique opportunity for understanding the relationship between media and religion in Ethiopia. After discussing the broader context for understanding Naik's sermons, I analyze the sermons and the effects of their broadcasting and distribution.

Hyper-Reality, Meanings, and Media/Islam: Theoretical Departure Points

I want to examine Naik's sermons by looking primarily at media-based discourses as constructions rather than as representations of the social world. In recent studies of media and new public spheres, discourses in the media are often regarded as *representations* of the social world. Given such assumptions, these studies have been embedded in a realist project that focuses on showing *what media do* rather than *how media might conceal and produce reality*. This is especially true for studies that have focused on Islam and media, most notably research that has explored how media have been instrumental in shaping belief, authority, and community in the Muslim world (Eickelman and Anderson 2003); the role of media in the shifting public significance of Islam (Schulz 2003); the deployment of media for popular mobilization within Muslim settings (Mohammadi and Mohammadi 1994); the "packaging" and construction of specific forms of Islam (Oncu 1995); and the role of media in the interpretation of Islamic legal systems (Messick 1993).

Such realist depictions have featured in studies that have analyzed Islamic sermons. For example, Bruce Borthwick (1967) described the political nature of such sermons; Charles Hirschkind (2001) traced the role of audiocassettes in the redefinition of public piety within a context of so-called Islamic revival; Richard Antoun (1989) identified the entrepreneurialism of Muslim preachers; David Westerlund (2003) described the polemical features of Ahmed Deedat's sermons;

and Brian Larkin (2008) analyzed the role of mediation and circulation in Ahmed Deedat's sermons. In most of these studies, there is relatively little attention devoted to the performative aspects of these media. In the past, the term *performance* has been employed by scholars who were interested in Islamic sermons. For instance, Hirschkind discussed the role of performance in his analysis. Seeing cassette sermons as disciplinary mechanisms, Hirschkind (2001) used the term *ethical performance*; in using this term, he seems to be interested in analyzing the "particular affective volitional responsiveness of the listeners" (624). In addition, Brian Larkin (2008) also talked about performance in sermons, or what he has referred to as *polemical performance*. By using the term, Larkin focuses on how the seemingly different public sphere of Muslims and Christians was brought together through the reenactment of Christian proselytization and meta-reflexive commentaries. Considering performance in this way, these two authors have, however, ignored how sermons, as staged dramatic events with scenographic elements, continually create social reality. Following Judith Butler's (1993) definition of the performative as a "discursive practice that enacts or produces that which it names" (13), I see sermons as forming the listeners' or consumers' reality in an a priori manner. Viewed in this sense, sermons are acts that create illusionary social realities. In employing the term *performance* in this way, I am proposing that we refocus attention away from the sermon listener and to the giver and, in doing so, not only consider the polemical aspects of such sermons but also their power to produce the listeners' and consumers' reality.

In addition to the performative element, I believe we should also investigate how sermons as media products operate at the level of the hyper-real—that is, a world without a real origin—or, in other words, one conditioned in an a priori simulation activity. In addition to exploring media effects, I also discuss how Muslims have lived and are living within a hyper-real world. Moreover, I show how the sermons to which Ethiopians are exposed are constructions rather than representations of social reality. Rather than being grounded *in the present*, I posit that these sermons affect the events or the spectator *from the future, from a yet undetermined point, which is, however, bound to have an effect.*

To understand the constructedness of media and its performative aspects, I turn to the work of Jean Baudrillard (1983), especially his concept of *third-order simulation and hyper-real*—that is, "the generation by models of a real without origin or reality." Baudrillard attempted to understand the contemporary world by making a distinction between first-, second-, and third-order simulations. In first-order simulation, the real world is represented—albeit that this representation is artificial—for example, in novels. In second-order simulation, reality and representation are blurred. As an example, Baudrillard points to Borges's short story where a map-drawing exercise resulted in the actual covering of the territory, thus making the map as real as the actual territory. In third-order sim-ulation, the sequence between reality and representation is reversed. Rather than preceding it, reality follows models.

In examples ranging from the US Watergate scandal and Disneyland to more recent events such as the Gulf War, Baudrillard tried to explain the dif-ference between third-order reality, which produces a hyper-real situation, and other simulation processes that either represent or blur reality. In his discussion of Disneyland, Baudrillard (1983) asserts that it is not a fantasmic representation of reality. Rather, he argues, "Disneyland is there to conceal the fact that it is the real country, all of real America, which is Disneyland. Disneyland is present as imaginary in order to make us believe that the rest is real, when in fact all of Los Angeles and the America surrounding it are no longer real, but of the order of the hyper-real and of simulation" (25). In this way, Baudrillard is trying to show how the capitalist-driven system of the United States, which in reality is chaotic and irrational, is portrayed as rational by actually creating a seemingly fantas-mic world. In other words, Disneyland constructs our reality prior to our actual experience. According to Baudrillard (1995), the process of creating a hyper-real situation is, however, not limited to institutions such as Disneyland but is the very essence of modern media. News and other media outlets produce the reality we experience, including the reality of war.

The Ethiopian case exhibits conditions similar to what Baudrillard de-scribed. In the media-saturated context of Ethiopia, the relationship between Muslims and Christians is embedded within a third-order simulation process where their relations are not represented by media but rather constructed a priori through the spread of sermons such as those of Dr. Zakir Naik.

In addition to exploring how Muslims have been embedded in a hyper-real situation, I also examine Muslims' and Orthodox Christians' different and often divergent interpretations of Naik's videos, which nevertheless exist in the hyper-real. As they are taken as being real and not hyper-real by Muslims and Ortho-dox Christians who are increasingly living in digital landscapes, the videos of Dr. Naik have generated a range of interpretations. To ascertain these interpreta-tions, I rely upon the theoretical assumptions of Stuart Hall (1980) and Valentine Voloshinov (1973 [1930]). Hall points to the faultiness of ascribing a transmittive task to media. Rather than being a mirror of the social world, he tells us that me-dia languages are encoded entities that are intended to mean something. At the receptive end, these encoded media languages are decoded rather than accepted automatically by viewers. By presenting media as an encoded entity, Hall's argu-ment therefore transfers media messages from being viewed as raw reality to a perspective that treats them as stories. It is these encoded messages or stories that are, therefore, appropriated by viewers. When appropriated, such stories are not, however, appropriated as an effect but as meaningful discourses. Rather than *preceding,* the effect *succeeds* the decoding process. Ultimately, it is, therefore, this decoded meaning "which will have effect, influence, entertain, instruct, persuade, with very complex perceptual cognitive emotional ideological behavioral consequence" (Hall 1980: 130). The decoding process, however, is not unitary, but as a language phenomenon it is, to use Valentin Voloshinov's term, susceptible to "multiple accentuality."[2] If this "multiple accentuality" is a throwback to the social world, as Voloshinov (1973 [1930]) argues, we must also see how media messages become part and parcel of ongoing and historical social struggles. By combining Jean Baudrillard's perspective with Hall's and Voloshinov's, I want to explore Muslim-Christian relations in a world increasingly infused with media. Before doing so, let me briefly describe the historical and social contexts that have made the events that we are trying to understand possible.

Dr. Zakir Naik in Context

The sensational Islamic VCD/DVDs, which are popular among Muslims in Ethiopia, derive mainly from the International Islamic Research Foundation. The foundation is a Mumbai-based Islamic institution that aims to present Islam to the world through the use of modern mass media. As part of its attempt to propagate Islam, the institution operates the satellite television network Peace Television, which broadcasts its programs in English and Urdu to more than 125 countries. Peace TV was founded because of the alleged inability of Muslims to influence international media and the general misunderstanding of Islam and anti-Muslim propaganda propagated by Western media. Using the latest modern technology, the foundation aims to rectify such perceived injustices.[3]

Peace TV features a number of preachers as part of its programs. However, its founder, Dr. Zakir Naik, attracts most of the attention. A Muslim born in Konkan at the coastal edge of Maharashtra in Mumbai, Naik studied medicine at the Mumbai Nair Hospital. In the 1980s, after meeting the late Ahmed Deedat (d. 2005), the Durban, South Africa–based Muslim cleric, Naik turned his attention to the preaching of Islam through modern mass media. According to his autobiography on the Peace TV website, Naik has given 1,200 public talks in more than 20 countries. In a list of the 100 most influential Indians developed by the *Indian Express,* Naik ranked as number 82. In the list of the top-10 spiritual gurus of India developed by the *Daily Express,* Naik was number 3, following Baba Ramdev and Sri Sri Ravi Shankar, who are both Hindus.[4]

Looked at historically, the general emergence of Dr. Naik is related to the condition of Muslims on the Indian subcontinent, especially the city of Mumbai. If one looks at the historical context of Mumbai, it readily emerges that the work of Dr. Naik needs to be seen in relation to that particular socio-cultural context. The first historical context for Dr. Naik's work was a religious debate carried out in 1854 in Agra, northern India, between a Christian missionary, Reverend Carl Pfander, and a Muslim scholar called Mulana Rahmat Allah (Powell 1993: 226–262; Lewis 2011: 211). This event came to be a landmark due to its departure from "traditional" Islamic preaching that avoided active confrontation with non-Muslims, as well as its use of modern publications, such as tracts and books, that were at the time within the domain of Christian missionaries. The event also became an inspiration for the generation of twentieth-century preachers, notably Ahmed Deedat, who in turn inspired Dr. Naik (Sadouni 1999: 89–108).

Ahmed Deedat, a South African Indian with a Gujarati background, met Dr. Naik while he was a second-year medical student. However, even more influential than the personalized encounter with Deedat was the change in the knowledge structure he suggested. By challenging the "traditional" knowledge structure within Islam, Deedat paved the way for the emergence of people like Dr. Naik. Indeed, Deedat helped to nullify the need to wait for the alim, ulama, or imam to understand Islam or defend the Muslim community (Sadouni 1999: 155). He directly contributed to the establishment of institutions composed of ordinary Muslim preachers with little or no Islamic theological training who had more secular backgrounds, like Dr. Naik with his medical degree.

The political and religious tensions in Mumbai, particularly among its Muslim community, were also important for the emergence of Dr. Naik. Mumbai is a city marked by a history of religious conflicts such as the 1992 and 2002 Hindu-Muslim conflicts. Traditionally, the Muslims of Mumbai exhibited various differences, divided as it is between Bohras and Khojas, who are Shi'ites; Memons, with an Ahl al-Sunna wa'l-Jamā'at or "Wahhabi" background; and Marāthhī-speaking Muslims from Konka. In addition, there is a strong sectarian division between north Indian–based Deobandis and Barelwis. Apart from such theological debates, these divisions have resulted in violent antagonisms, including a community-based conflict in 1998 that resulted from a disagreement over the beginning of Ramadan (Blom Hansen 2000: 260–265, 2011: 171–178).

A number of Islamic organizations sought to unify Muslims within the Mumbai political environment, which had been dominated by the Bharatiya Janata Party (BJP), the Hindu nationalist party widely blamed for the 1992 violence against Muslims. Such organizations include Tablighi-e-Jamaat; Ulemma Council; All India Tabligh-e-Seerat; Student Islamic Movement; and Jamaat-i-Islami (Blom Hansen 2000: 260–265). The Islamic Research Foundation of Dr. Naik is another, albeit modernized, attempt at unifying Muslims in Mumbai and bridging sectarian differences (Blom Hansen 2011: 177). His organization directly addresses the issue of unity, and, as we have seen, portrays itself as an institution free from sectarian differences. Although there are numerous rumors circulating about Dr. Naik's sectarian allegiances, such as his alleged membership of the Barlewi sect and his affinities with Salafism, Dr. Naik has indeed always presented himself as neutral in relation to such differences.

Virtual "Islamic" Performances

As an electronic device, Dr. Naik's VCD/DVDs are media products that are deliberately produced for purposes of consumption. In other words, they are performances that try to construct reality. In view of this, I analyze these VCD/DVDs both in terms of the techniques employed in delivering messages as well as in terms of their content as narrative structures. The VCD/DVDs are presented in two formats that differ in content: the introductory part and the main body of the VCD/DVDs where the message is delivered.

The introductory part of the VCD/DVDs mainly advertises the International Islamic Research Foundation using techniques commonly employed in music videos. This includes the alteration of images at a rapid pace with the intention of speeding up the tension and sensation among the audiences. By using such techniques, the introductory segments try to entice audiences, mainly young viewers, who are very familiar with the production of fast-streaming images whose purpose is to capture one's attention rather than transmit messages. Unlike the introductory segments, the main body differs significantly as it tends to emphasize the transmission of messages. Marked with slow-moving images, the main body also consists of on-screen writing that emphasizes the main points made during the lecture.[5]

In both the introductory and main segments of the VCD/DVDs, major emphasis is devoted to authority building through the glorification of Dr. Naik and his stature and power. This is achieved by employing a number of rudimentary mass-media techniques that are often effective among audiences. The first of such techniques is the way the camera has been used in shooting the moving images. Most of the time, Dr. Naik is shot from a low angle. As a result, viewers do not see Dr. Naik from the same level but from a subordinate position. In other words, the viewer is made to reach out for Naik and his messages not only through the narratives but also virtually. The glorification of Naik is also made possible by employing the opposite techniques when shooting the audiences who are actually listening to him. These audiences are shot using a high camera angle. The camera looks down upon the audience, therefore making them look like insignificant, vulnerable beings who are ready to listen to Dr. Naik's message.

In addition to these techniques, Naik's authority is also reinforced by presenting his message as part of a natural and global message emanating from Allah. The main technique employed here is the use of images of a moving globe while statements about the goal of the Islamic Research Foundation are articulated. The naturalization of the message is also achieved by associating Naik's picture with a moving or still image of the globe. As a background clip, the VCD/

DVDs use nondiegetic sounds to naturalize the message, thereby making it seem to be part of the natural order.[6]

Aside from the camera and sound techniques, Dr. Naik's VCD/DVDs also project an image of Islam embedded in modernity. In his media appearances, Naik always wears a suit and tie, albeit worn with an Islamic cap. The location he uses for conveying his message is also an ordinary convention center rather than a "traditional" center associated with Islam, such as a mosque or a madrasa. Interestingly, the settings he uses are devoid of any possible Islamic symbols, such as the star and crescent. Taken in and of themselves, these VCD/DVDs are also expressions not of "traditional" Islam but of modernity. They flout some Muslims' "traditional" prohibition of the use of images, as well as self-glorification. Unlike some "traditional" Muslim religious leaders or shaykhs, who are usually reluctant to take photographs even for such basic and essential matters as passports and identity cards, Dr. Naik actively embraces the use of images. The slickly produced VCD/DVDs show that those involved in their production are well versed in modern techniques of mass-media communications. Although acknowledged and accepted in the electronic landscape as Islamic, Naik's VCD/DVDs are more akin to Hollywood movies.

In terms of narrative, Dr. Naik often employs binary oppositions as part of the overall message delivery. At its core the binary constructions include difference and opposition between the West and the Muslim community around the world, as well as difference between Islam and other religions—mainly Christianity and Hinduism. In this narrative structure, he portrays Islam as a coherent whole, albeit with internal differences. Despite mentioning differences between Muslims, he consistently presents Christianity as a homogenous entity. Within the narrative structure, Muslims are accorded the role of victims, while Christians and the West have the position of villain.

Attacks on Muslims in the world are emphasized virtually by writing key statements, which have just been made by Dr. Naik, across the screen. While images are streaming, the audience sees pop-ups such as "International media is bombarding misinformation about Islam"; "International media is projecting Islam as if it is a religion of terror"; and so forth. Insofar as Dr. Naik's VCD/DVDs feed purposefully on the vulnerability of Muslims, these VCD/DVDs can be said to have an element of demagoguery at their core. In addition, Dr. Naik also uses comparative strategies through which the vulnerability of Islam and Muslims is presented—for example, by contrasting Muslims and Christians, or comparing the West to the Muslim rest. One example is Naik's discussion of the vulnerability of Muslims in the media world:

> We have many Muslim magazines in the world for da'wa [propagation of Islam] purposes. What is the number printed in India? How much? Four thousand? Five thousand? Eight thousand? Number one English da'wa magazine

Islamic Voice [is] 15,000. I was in America a few years back. I did a survey. The maximum number of printed da'wa magazine is 50,000. Do you know there is a small cult in Christianity called Jehovah Witnesses which print a magazine by the name of *Watch Tower*? Do you know how much do they print? Monthly how much do they print? Can anyone guess? How much do they print? You won't lose any money? Any guesses? Did you know that they print 20.83 million copies? Leave aside the Muslims. We can not print; we can not even think. Leave aside printing, we can't even think.[7]

Comparing Islam and Christianity, however, is not only employed to show Muslims' vulnerability. Dr. Naik also adopts a so-called comparative perspective, popularized by Ahmed Deedat, in order to show the superiority of Islam and the Muslim community. In this regard, verses from the scriptures are quoted especially to prove the authenticity of the Quran or the superiority of Dr. Naik's arguments in favor of Islam.

Rhetoric is also a core strategy of Naik narratives. The rhetoric is mainly employed to cast away perceived attacks on Muslims. They are also employed as devices to mock supposedly serious statements made by the villains whom the narrative-plot intends to dismiss. Some of the rhetoric employed in his video *Media and Islam: War or Peace?* includes the following:

International Media are saying war for peace. Actually what they are doing is not war for peace (but) war on peace. In other words, war on the religion of peace, on Islam.

All of us know today that the international media say that the Islamic madrasas should be banned. Why? Because they produce human beings who cause terror. Who disrupt the peace of this world? Alhamdulillah [praise be to God] I know thousand human beings who have passed through Islamic madrasas. I don't know a single that encourage and propagate the destruction of peace. History tells us today about the human being that has killed the maximum number of people in this world. Who is he? Who is the man who has killed the maximum number of human beings in this world? Who is that person? Who is he? Hitler! It is a common knowledge! Which madrasa did Hitler learn in? From which madrasa did Hitler graduate?

Muslims today are labelled as terrorists. I say every Muslim should be a terrorist! What is the meaning of the world terrorist? Terrorist by definition means a person who can cause terror. When a robber sees a policeman, he is terrified. For the robber the policeman is a terrorist (laughter). So in this case whenever a robber, a rapist, and anti-social elements see a Muslim he should be terrified. The Muslim should terrify the anti-social element. That is what the Quran say in Surah al-Anfal verse 60: cause terror in the heart of the anti-social element.[8]

When looked at from various angles, one cannot help but see the constructed nature of Dr. Naik's VCD/DVDs. Indeed, Naik's videos are designed in such a way that they are meant to have an effect on the people watching them. Insofar as they are constructions, Dr. Naik's videos resemble what Baudrillard has called third-order simulation—that is, a model that generates a hyper-reality, a world or a condition without a real origin (Baudrillard 1983).

The Power of Performance: The Shaping and Construction of Muslim-Christian Relations

Having been born and raised in Ethiopia, my own religious affiliation during research for this article was not only questioned by my Muslim informants but also by acquaintances from the Orthodox Christian community. Although dealing with the multiple presences of both informants and friends in the field has been challenging, it has, however, led to a mine of information. One of the techniques I employed was to listen and pay attention to information that kept popping up in a seemingly fieldwork-free context. During my field visit in 2009, the gossip and information I heard centered around, among other things, Christian-Muslim relations.

Given my own background in the Orthodox Christian community, I was constantly informed about "Muslim Others" who are increasingly becoming fundamentalist and the action taken by Orthodox Christians to assert their own position. In my discussion with friends and informants, the distribution of a T-shirt from the "Orthodox camp" in 2009 has been much discussed. These T-shirts, which apparently were made by anonymous Orthodox Christians during the Ethiopian Epiphany of that year, read, "Ethiopia is an island of Christianity." This phrase, which has historically been used by Ethiopian emperors, seems to have been used to assert the position of Orthodox Christians. It was also deployed to oppose Muslims, since the phrase was historically used to indicate the vulnerability of the Orthodox-led Ethiopian empire, which has existed as a Christian sovereign state since the fourth century, to "pagan" and Muslim elements.

Among the Muslims, the slogan "Ethiopia is a Christian island" has naturally resulted in strong negative reactions. During the heyday of the tensions over the Epiphany T-shirt and slogan, Muslims went on a number of occasions to Orthodox Christian churches and pronounced the *takbir*—that is, they pronounced "Allahu Akbar" or "God Is Great." By saying the takbir, it seems that Muslims were talking back to the Orthodox community and opposing the claim that Ethiopia was a Christian island. During my stay in the field, on a number of occasions I have encountered discourses that tried to nullify some of the Orthodox Christian claims. One such discourse is that made by Mohamed, a Muslim whom I have known for the last several years. In his opinion, saying Ethiopia is a Christian island was a strong statement. Here is what he has to say:

> It is something that activates the jihād which is within you. Do you know the small shops near the post office? There you can find the T-shirts. However,

they are not the only T-shirts. There are T-shirts with the name of Ethiopia, and then they put the pictures of Christian emperors such as Haile Sellassie, Yohannes, and Menelik. These do not represent the Muslims. Do you know what Muslims said when the Orthodox claimed that Ethiopia is a Christian island? They said if Ethiopia is an island we are its creators. An island cannot be an island without the surrounding water, can it?

The polemical question posed by Mohamed and the argument mentioned by other Muslims that I encountered during fieldwork was similarly matched by questions and arguments in the "Orthodox camp." Eyob, a man in his seventies, explained to me how the slogan was a correct depiction of Ethiopia in the following way:

> Saying that Ethiopia is a Christian island does not mean anything. For me, it is an advertisement. What does an island mean? It means a small land surrounded by water. Ethiopia was like that. This is a historical truth. Before any African country became Christian, Ethiopia was a Christian nation. Before the coming of Muslims, Ethiopia was a Christian state. So the slogan shows the priority of Christianity in Ethiopia. Now it has passed from the stage of being an island to a stage of being a sea, but that is another issue. Now look at England. When England was a superpower, people used to say that the sun will not set on the British Empire. Now when its superiority has declined, it is still called Great Britain. Saying that Ethiopia is a Christian island is exactly like that. Muslim fundamentalists give a political meaning to it, and they talk nonsense. These are fanatics. In fact, Ethiopia was a Christian island even if there were other religions, including those who believe in natural phenomenon. Before all [these] religions arrived, Ethiopia was Christian. This is a historical fact. Muslims have the money, the manpower, and they want to dominate Ethiopia. This is not something that they only want to do in Ethiopia but also all over the world.

The argument over the printed T-shirts seems to be an uncompromising position. The production of the T-shirts may seem to be an isolated incident, but such T-shirts are, in fact, reactions to earlier publications that came from the "Muslim camp." To be precise, they are reactions to the distribution of Dr. Naik's VCD/DVDs and other materials distributed through satellite television by the International Islamic Research Foundation. To put it in the language of Stuart Hall (1980), they are different ways of decoding the message presented by Naik. In a bid to understand the event, let us look closely at the different decoding processes in both camps.

As Stuart Hall has shown, messages presented through mass media are translated in a variegated manner. This is clearly borne out when it comes to the VCD/DVDs of Dr. Naik. For the majority of Muslims I have met during my research, Dr. Naik's DVDs were truly inspirational. His words were authoritative and points of reference for many of them. The production of these VCD/DVDs was taken as part and parcel of their newly achieved constitutional rights, which came after the fall of the socialist regime. The VCD/DVDs have, in fact, become an important symbol of showing how Muslims have been attacked all over the world, in general, and in Ethiopia in particular.

On the other hand, among the Orthodox Christian community, the VCD/DVDs are received as bearing messages of hate, and Naik is portrayed as an evil personality from India. The overall presence of these VCD/DVDs is also regarded as an indication of the proliferation of radical Islam. Ironically, in the decoding by the Orthodox Christian community, we find a similarity between their reaction and the reaction of Muslims to the Danish cartoons depicting the Prophet Muhammad. As Faisal Devji (2006) argued about the cartoons, Muslims reacted not to their content as such but to the "apparent injury done to the Muslim feeling by report of their circulation." When it comes to the Orthodox Christians' reactions, this also holds true. Orthodox Christians who have not even seen the VCD/DVDs have been offended by their production, mere presence, and the extent of their dissemination. The widespread circulation, which has been achieved through the media, has been regarded as all-engulfing. The actual contents of the VCD/DVDs only added fuel to the fire.

The making of the T-shirts was, therefore, a part of the decoding of Naik's message by Orthodox Christians. After seeing the production of these VCD/DVDs for a number of years, Orthodox youth, particularly those organized under the Sunday School Department Mahbere Kedusan, started to teach in a similar way against Islam by comparing the Quran and the Bible. Such presentations were especially made in evening classes held after 5:00 P.M. The reaction to the Islamic publications, which developed in this way, also took root in the more informal associations that celebrate saints' days once each month, such as Tsewa Mahbere. Eventually, such efforts of resistance led to the production and circulation of the T-shirts as well as a number of polemical Christian books.

The publications that emerged directly attacked Islam, employing a methodology similar to Dr. Naik's. The first major publication was an article in the journal published by the Sunday School Department, *Hamere Tewehado*. Written by Afework Atnatewos (2001) and entitled "Allah Yemilew Semena Ye kuran Mesehaf Tarikawi Ametattchew Sifetesh" ("Enquiry into the Name of Allah and to the Origin of the Quran"), the article traced the pagan roots of Islam by drawing on Western sources and tried to label the Quran as an ordinary—that is, nondivine—book. This was followed by two books by Aba Samuel (2007) and Ephrem Eshete (2008) that explained the proliferation of international Muslim radicalism in the world and in Ethiopia, as well as attacks on the Orthodox Christian Church.

Significantly, the first of these two books was published by a high-ranking cleric in the Orthodox Church, Aba Samuel (2007), who at the time of publication was vice patriarch and bishop of the Addis Ababa Synod. At some point banned for its sensitivity, his book was provocatively titled *Ewen be Ethiopia Ye Haymanot Mechachal Alene? (Is There Religious Tolerance in Ethiopia?)*. Composed of seven chapters, the book described the history of Islam in Ethiopia and the rise of radicalism internationally and in Ethiopia, while it also pointed to the relationship between democratic principles and religious tolerance. The book directly attacked and responded to the VCD/DVDs circulated by the International Islamic Research Foundation. In this regard, Aba Samuel's (2007) book devoted a whole chapter to refuting Ahmed Deedat's attack on Christianity by trying to explain his arguments through a comparative methodology. What made Aba Samuel's publication provocative in the eyes of Muslims and, for our case, interesting were his explicit approaches to the matter at hand. Through the statement made in the first few pages of his book, the vice patriarch laid bare the current situation:

> Religious tolerance means allowing religion and religious rituals to be practiced in a free social environment. It mean supporting it, to stand in peace and for peace. . . . Our country Ethiopia is a country which guaranties the equality for all religions according to its constitution or government administration. For example, during the Imperial era, Ethiopia was a country with a national religion. Today its right to national religion is also ensured. Allowing freedom and not persecuting believers of other religions is something that emanates from accepting religious tolerance and democracy. . . . In many states, violations of the supremacy of law and human rights are apparent. For example, some individuals who say that they are the follower of Islam are violating the rights of our Christian religion. We thought that this will be improved as time passed, but it has worsened. For example:
>
> 1. The publication of Ahmed Deedat which says: "Is Jesus Christ a Creator?"
> 2. Is the Bible the word of God? What the Bible said about Mohamed? (Written by Ahmed Hussein Deedat and translated by Zekerya Abathun Werkeneh)
> 3. Let the Bible talk (Prepared by Abu Sumeya).
>
> We have found other cassettes VCD/DVDs that are attacking our religion and violating our rights. As a result we have written this [book] by using our democratic rights and by taking a limited publication [of the offending VCD/DVDs] so that they will know what we have tolerated. (i–iii)

The second major book by Ephrem Eshete (2008) was entitled *Akrari Eselemna be Etiyopia (Islamic Fundamentalism in Ethiopia)*, and it narrated the development of Islamic radicalism and the actual consequence of its spread in

Ethiopia. Ephrem Eshete seems to have had the same motives in writing the book as Aba Samuel:

> Our country, which was called a Christian island by the Portuguese who had been competing with the Ottoman Empire over the control of trade, is unlike any other time in history, now experiencing a religious revolution. In today's Ethiopia the previous practice of "forgetting the world while being forgotten by the world" has changed. Islam and Muslims are increasingly engaged in the economic, social and cultural life of the country. Ethiopian identity is changing under our own eyes. Although there are many reasons for publishing this book, the main reason is the increasing activities which might endanger our church while we are all drowsing. Although there were unrestrained books and audio-video material targeting the church, we can say that we have not thought of it as being something that is organized and rooted. Through time we have learned that the articles published in magazines such as *Bilal*[9] were not like rushing water which depends on momentary reactions. Rather it was an activity consciously undertaken with the involvement of foreigners. Even though we were late from yesterday, but we have now surpassed tomorrow. While we will walk over where we have reached we remember the past, and we want to indicate the good and bad for the coming years. (1–3)

As the above quotation indicates, the Orthodox Christians, like their Muslim counterparts, were adept at deploying modern values within the public sphere. The arguments were not just maintained as codes of meanings but were interpreted through a historical perspective. According to Orthodox Christians, Ethiopia has been linked to a national religion, which in this case is Ethiopian Orthodox Christianity, and the country is currently under attack by Muslims and their publications that violate constitutional rights and the principle of religious tolerance. As the slogan printed on the T-shirts, as well as the arguments presented by Aba Samuel, indicates, the messages of the media were situated not in the abstract but rather within the historical struggle for power where claims to dominance and superiority have become a bone of contention.

The attacks by Orthodox worshippers, as it might be expected, did not lead to a process of reflection in the "opposite" camp. Rather, it has in turn accentuated an already tense situation. Orthodox Christian discourse was, in fact, interpreted as stemming from jealousy and not truth. In response Muslim authors have also come up with writings that directly attack the Orthodox community, particularly the Sunday School Department Mahbere Kedusan. In this regard, Hassen Taju, who has translated a number of recent Islamic texts into Amharic, came out with a book-length denunciation of the Sunday School Department reflections on Islam. In his book entitled *Ye Hamere Tewahedo Ketfet Be Eslemena Ewnet* (*The Deception of Hamere Tewahedo in Light of Islamic Truth*), Hassen Taju (2002) describes the response made by Orthodox Christians as a deliberate lie

that stems from the very nature of Christianity. He also characterized the Orthodox community as a community devoid of rational thought and thus unworthy
of serious interreligious dialogue.

Making Sense of Dr. Zakir Naik: A Theoretical Conclusion

To conclude, Dr. Naik's VCD/DVDs entail the presence of viewers who often
share much in common, including the social and historical imagination. In fact,
they attest to the presence of what Appadurai (1996) has termed "communities
of sentiment." Naik's VCD/DVDs are also the consequence of the emergence of
media as a major mechanism of transmitting opinion within the public sphere in
Ethiopia. As the role of media in presenting public opinion is compromised, as
Habermas (1987 [1962]) tells us, due to the transformation from a media of "conviction" to one of "commerce," these VCD/DVDs are also part of an illusion that
is created by the process of embedding ideology within the public sphere. Their
effect is simultaneously the production of illusion through their own production
of ideologies by the deployment of rhetoric and other illusionary devices.

   Indeed, Dr. Naik's VCD/DVDs can be explained through semiotic and in-
terpretative analyses that recall the work of Hall (1980) and Voloshinov (1973
[1930]). As we have seen in the discussion above, these authors urge us to look
at media messages and languages in general as encoded stories that generate
meaningful discourse and that are differently interpreted by people with different backgrounds. If we interpret Naik's VCD/DVDs in light of this theoretical
framework, we can indeed find a semiotic game being played by the different actors. Rather than reflecting the raw outside world, they instead present encoded
meanings and stories that represent Islam in a specific way. The meanings encoded in such a way are, however, decoded in a multi-fractured manner. Played
out in the wider social field, or beyond viewer's homes, the decoding of Dr. Naik's
message reflects old positionalities that relate to historical domination and subordination between Muslims and Christians.

   As far as the encoding of messages given to Muslims being mere stories or
performances goes, our understanding of the messages and the events surrounding them should be conceptualized further in order to distance ourselves from
possible behaviorist interpretation. Other than being a story, the message presented to Muslims entails living in what Baudrillard (1983) has termed "hyper-
reality." Through Dr. Naik's VCD/DVDs, the world of Muslims in Ethiopia is
constructed by the media. Muslims are living not in a represented world but in
a constructed world that emanates from "Islamic media." Naik's videos produce
the supposed conflict Muslims are engaged in with Christians and with the West
through insistent discourse of war on Islam. And this already imagined war, this
war that has not yet happened but that exists in the electronic landscape and is

powerfully transmitted to Muslims in Ethiopia through various media messages, has generated new and increased tensions in the country and in the diaspora.

To conclude, emerging from an Indian context marred by recurrent Muslim-Hindu conflict and the subsequent attempts to overcome divisions between Muslims, Dr. Naik's VCD/DVDs have managed to generate a hyper-reality where the actual conflict is generated a priori to any actual or real conflict. Living in the twenty-first century, where existence is not limited by state boundaries but also affected by events in digital landscapes, Muslims in Ethiopia have been enmeshed in a hyper-real world where the real and the unreal, the simulated and the concrete are all blurred together. This affair, however, is not only affecting Muslims, since Ethiopian Orthodox Christians have also developed heightened sensitivity living across digital landscapes.

Notes

1. So far, Dr. Naik's sermons have been translated into Amharic, which is a language widely spoken in most urban areas of Ethiopia.

2. Voloshinov used the term "multiple accentuality" to describe the presence of multiple meanings in signs of language. Writing against Saussurean linguistics, he viewed language and signs as socially constructed entities susceptible to different interpretations and meanings. The meanings according to Voloshinov depend on and reflect already existing societal relationships such as class conflict. For a discussion of his ideas, see his book *Marxism and the Philosophy of Language*.

3. Islamic Research Foundation, "Dr. Zakir Naik; President IRF." http://www.irf.net.

4. Al-Qalam, "Dr. Naik Among 100 Most Powerful Indians." http://www.alqalam.co.za /index.php?option=com_content&view=article&id=297:dr-zakir-naik-among-the-100-most -powerful-indians&catid=54:international-news&Itemid=116.

5. Dr. Zakir Naik has a number of videos that employ these techniques. In this regard, see, for example, his video entitled "Media and Islam: War or Peace?"

6. Nondiegetic sounds are sounds that are exterior to the story spaces. They are usually nonhuman sounds that are used for producing an effect.

7. This and the subsequent quotes are taken from his video entitled "Media and Muslim: War or Peace?"

8. This quote is taken from Dr. Naik's video "Media and Islam: War or Peace?"

9. *Bilal* was one of the early Muslim magazines that emerged after the EPRDF takeover of power.

References

Abbink, J. 2011. "Religion in Public Spaces: Emerging Muslim-Christian Polemics in Ethiopia." *African Affairs* 110(439): 253–274.

Antoun, R. 1989. *Muslim Preacher in the Modern World: A Jordanian Case Study in Contemporary Perspective*. Princeton, NJ: Princeton University Press.

Appadurai, A. 1996. *Modernity at Large: Cultural Dimensions of Modernity.* Minneapolis: University of Minnesota Press.

Atnatewos, A. 2001. "Allah Yemilew Semena Ye kuran Mesehaf Tarikawi Ametattchew Sifetesh." *Hamere Tewahedo.* Addis Ababa: Amanuel Printing Press.

Baudrillard, J. 1983. *Simulations,* trans. P. Foss et al. New York: Semiotext(e).

———. 1995. *The Gulf War Did Not Take Place,* trans. P. Patton, P. Foss, and P. Beitchman. Sydney: Power.

Blom Hansen, T. 2000. "Predicament of Secularism: Muslim Identity in Mumbai." *Journal of Royal Anthropological Association* 6(2): 260–265.

———. 2011. *Wages of Violence: Naming and Identity in Post Colonial Bombay.* Princeton, NJ: Princeton University Press.

Borthwick, B. 1967. "Islamic Sermons as a Chanel of Political Communication." *Middle East Journal* 21(3): 299–313.

Butler, J. 1993. *Bodies That Matter: On the Discursive Element of Sex.* New York: Routledge.

Devji, F. 2006. "Back to the Future: The Cartoons, Liberalism, and Global Islam." *Open Democracy.* http://www.opendemocracy.net/faisal_devji_back_to_the_future_0.

de Vries, H., and S. Weber, eds. 2001. *Religion and Media.* Stanford, CA: Stanford University Press.

Eickelman, D., and J. W. Anderson. 2003. "Redefining Muslim Publics." In *New Media in the Muslim World: The Emerging Public Sphere,* edited by D. Eickelman and J. W. Anderson. Bloomington: Indiana University Press.

Eshete, E. 2008. *Akrari Eslemena Be Ethiopia.* Addis Ababa: Ethio Black Nile Printing Press.

Habermas, J. 1987 [1962]. *Structural Transformation of the Public Sphere: An Enquiry into a Bourgeois Society,* trans. T. Burger and F. Lawrence. Cambridge, MA: MIT Press.

Hackett, R. 2003. "Managing or Manipulating Religious Conflict in the Nigeria." In *Mediating Religion: Conversation in Media, Religion and Culture,* edited by Jolyon P. Mitchell and S. Marriage. London: T & T Clark International.

Hall, S. 1980. "Encoding/Decoding in Television Discourse." In *Culture, Media, Language,* edited by S. Hall, D. Hobson, A. Lowe, and P. Willis. London: Hutchinson.

Hirschkind, C. 2001. "The Ethics of Listening: Cassette-Sermon Audition in Contemporary Egypt." *American Ethnologist* 28(3): 623–649.

Larkin, B. 2008. "Ahmed Deedat and the Form of Islamic Evangelism." *Social Text* 26(3): 101–121.

Lewis, P. 2011. "Deceptions of 'Christianity' within British Islamic Institutions." In *Islamic Interpretations of Christianity,* edited by Lloyd Ridgeon. New York: St. Martin's Press.

Messick, B. 1993. *The Calligraphic State: Textual Domination and History in a Muslim Society.* Berkeley: University of California Press.

Meyer, B., and A. Moors. 2006. *Religion, Media, and the Public Sphere.* Bloomington: Indiana University Press.

Mohammadi, S., and A. Mohammadi. 1994. *Small Media, Big Revolution: Communication, Culture and the Iranian Revolution.* Minneapolis: University of Minnesota Press.

Nietzsche, F. 1990 [1888]. *Twilight of the Idols or: How to Philosophize with a Hammer,* trans. R. J. Hollingdale. London: Penguin Books.

Oncu, A. 1995. "Packaging Islam: Cultural Politics on the Landscape of Turkish Commercial Television." *Public Culture* 8: 51–71.

Powell, A. 1993. *Muslim and Missionaries in Pre Mutiny India.* London: Routledge Curzon.

Sadouni, S. 1999. "Le minoritaire sud-africain Ahmed Deedat, une figure originale de la da'wa." *Islam et Sociétés au Sud du Sahara* 12: 89–108.

Samuel, A. 2007. *Be Ethiopia Yehaymanot Mechachal Alene?* Addis Ababa: Mega Printing Press.

Schulz, D. 2003. "Charisma and Brotherhood Revisited: Mass Mediated Forms of Spirituality in Urban Mali." *Journal of Religion in Africa* 30(2): 146–171.

Taju, H. 2002. *Ye Hamere Tewahedo Ketfet Be Eslemena Ewnet.* Addis Ababa: Al Beyan Limited.

Voloshinov, V. 1973 [1930]. *Marxism and the Philosophy of Language.* New York: Seminar Press.

Westerlund, D. 2003. "Ahmed Deedat's Theology of Religion: Apologetics through Polemics." *Journal of Religion in Africa* 33(3): 263–278.

15 Zulu Dreamscapes

Senses, Media, and Authentication in Contemporary Neo-shamanism

David Chidester

DREAMS MUST SEEM the most insubstantial of media, nothing more than "subjective apparitions," as the Anglican missionary and ethnographer Henry Callaway described Zulu dreams in 1871—a medium of sensory experience, "brain-sight" and "brain-hearing," without any material referents (Callaway 1872). But the Zulu interpretation of dreams documented by Callaway showed that dreams were often understood as calls to action. Through the medium of dreams, ancestors called for sacrificial offerings (Callaway 1868–1870: 6), which would affirm ongoing relations of material exchange between the living and the dead, or an ancestor might call for the performance of homecoming rituals that would bring him "back from the open country to his home" (Callaway 1868–1870: 142). Dreams, therefore, were not merely sensory media to be interpreted. Although they were rendered meaningful through a hermeneutics of dreams, they were also given force through an energetics of dreams that demanded practical responses with material consequences. As a result, dreams were thoroughly integrated into the material relations of exchange and orientation in Zulu ancestral religion.

Now, under globalizing conditions, Zulu dreaming is undergoing transformation. Global claims are being made on Zulu dreams. Take, for example, Afrika Bambaataa, the African American godfather of Hip Hop, whose musical group, Zulu Nation, while not African, Zulu, or a nation, nevertheless moved symbolically into South African space to identify two kinds of religion: Afrika Bambaataa, which was identified as the "go to sleep slavery type of religion"—the religion of the dream, the religion of the oppressed that sealed their oppression— and the "spiritual wake up, revolutionary" religion, the religion of conscious, positive action, "like the prophets," in which "knowledge, wisdom, [and] understanding of self and others" inform a "do for self and others type of religion" (Chidester 2005: 230–231). At the same time, indigenous Zulu dreams are going global, as in the case of the Zulu witch doctor, sangoma, sanusi, and now shaman Credo Mutwa, the master of Zulu "dreams, prophecies, and mysteries" (Mutwa 2003), who has emerged in the global circuit of neo-shamanism (see Townsend 2004) as the bedrock of African indigenous authenticity to underwrite a variety of projects, including New Age spirituality, alternative healing, and encounters with aliens from outer space (Chidester 2002).

In this new globalizing terrain, electronic media have dramatically expanded the Zulu dreamscape. Zulu dreaming, along with religious or spiritual interpretations of Zulu dreams, visions, and mysteries, has been proliferating through film and video, musical CDs and DVDs, and the expanding global dreamscape of neo-shamanism on the internet. Nevertheless, in all of these media, we can find echoes of the nineteenth-century Zulu energetics of dreams that was based on sacrificial exchange and ancestral orientation.

First, we find echoes of sacrificial exchange, but now situated in the dilemmas posed by a global economy. Not only defined by the increased pace and scope of the flows of money, technology, and people, the global economy is also an arena for new mediated images and ideals of human possibility (Appadurai 1996), including the possibility that occult forces are both shadow and substance of global economic exchange (Comaroff and Comaroff 1999). In his own way, as we will see, Credo Mutwa has dealt with these dilemmas of the global economy by identifying aliens from outer space as the nexus of a sacrificial exchange into which he personally has entered by eating extraterrestrial beings in a sacramental meal and by being their sacrificial victim.

Second, addressing the demand for bringing ancestors home and reinforcing the sacred orientation revolving around the ancestral homestead, Credo Mutwa has tried for many years to establish a "Credo Mutwa village" in South Africa—in the township of Soweto during the 1970s, in the apartheid Bantustan of Bophuthatswana in the 1980s, and in the game reserve of Shamwari during the 1990s—but none of these homes turned out to be sustainable. On the internet, however, Credo Mutwa found a home. Mediated by the global network of neo-shamanism, he gained new credibility. While Credo Mutwa was going global, North American enthusiasts for New Age spirituality, including some white South African expatriates, found in this new global media an avenue for coming home to Africa by entering the "house of dreams" as a Zulu shaman.

In 1994, the American author James Hall described his initiation as a Zulu sangoma as "a journey to become the house of dreams" (Hall 1994: 202). In 2004, the South African expatriate David M. Cumes, who had established a medical practice in California, underwent his initiation as a Zulu sangoma, observing, "I had heard the term 'a house of dreams' applied to aspects of the *thwasa* [initiation] experience" (Cumes 2004: 84). How should we understand this new "house of dreams" that is emerging in a new, globalizing arena?

As an entry into this new Zulu dreamscape, I want to examine the role of the human sensorium and electronic media. Exploring Zulu neo-shamanism as material religion, I situate my analysis at the nexus of religious dreaming, sensory repertoires, and electronic mediation. Religion, as Jeremy Stolow (2005) observed, is "materialized in and through the most primary media of all, the human senses" (129). If embodied senses are media, then electronic media can also be understood as both extensions and limitations of the human sensorium. Dreams, our most intimate, embodied media, are also sensory, whether ordinary or extraordinary. Although dreaming has often been regarded as imaginary and immaterial, as nothing more than "subjective apparitions," dreams are material productions not only because they are generated by the neurobiology of the brain (see Lieberman 2000) but also because they have the capacity to elicit practical responses with material consequences. In the case of Zulu neo-shamanism, dreams entail material investments in sacrificial exchange and ancestral orientation that echo an earlier Zulu hermeneutics and energetics of dreams but now under rapidly changing global conditions. Within this new Zulu dreamscape, indigenous sensory repertoires for arranging (and deranging) the human sensorium merge with the limits (and potential) of electronic media.

By examining the work of a variety of contemporary Zulu shamans, including Credo Mutwa and P. H. Mtshali, as well as James Hall, David Cumes, Ann Mortifee, and other so-called white sangomas, we can discern basic strategies for engaging senses and media. In this new Zulu dreamscape, dreams are a sensory medium, involving "brain-sight" and "brain-hearing," as Henry Callaway suggested, but they also incorporate all of the senses, simultaneously, synesthetically, and expansively, perhaps even expanding to the 12 senses that Credo Mutwa will claim as the natural sensorium of human beings. All of this sensory experience, however, is thoroughly mediated through new electronic media. As I hope to show, Zulu neo-shamans have developed an ambivalent relationship to the very media that have made it possible for them to be shamans. Media, like sensory experience, are engaged in three ways—as limit, as potential, and as validation of the reality of this new Zulu shamanism. Within the dreamscapes of contemporary Zulu neo-shamanism, the human senses and electronic media are at play, and the question of authenticity is at stake, in the imaginative terrain that has opened between global exchanges and local homecomings.

Extraterrestrial Encounters

Vusamazulu Credo Mutwa has been described, internationally, as a Zulu shaman, the keeper of Zulu tradition, although he has often been characterized in South Africa as a fake, a fraud, and a charlatan (Friedman 1997; Johnson 1997). An extremely creative and imaginative author (Mutwa 1964, 1966), artist, and sculptor, Credo Mutwa has been celebrated within the global network of contemporary neo-shamanism as the High Sanusi of the Zulu nation, the highest grade of African shaman and the official historian of the Zulu people of South Africa.

Over his long career, Credo Mutwa has been adept at reinventing himself in relation to various alien appropriations of his authenticity. During the 1950s,

Credo Mutwa was used to authenticate African artifacts for a curio shop in Johannesburg. Through his writings in the 1960s, his tourist attraction in Soweto in the 1970s, and his cultural village in Bophuthatswana in the 1980s, he was used to authenticate the racial, cultural, and religious separations of apartheid. During the 1990s, as he acquired the label "shaman" through the interventions of Bradford Keeney (2001), Stephen Larsen (Mutwa 1996, 2003), and other exponents of New Age spirituality, Credo Mutwa's authority was invoked to authenticate a diverse array of enterprises in saving the world from human exploitation, environmental degradation, epidemic illness, endemic ignorance, organized crime, or extraterrestrial conspiracy. In all of these projects, the indigenous authenticity of Credo Mutwa added value, credibility, and force because he represented the "pure voice," untainted by modernity, of an unmediated access to primordial truth (Chidester 2005: 172–189).

One of Credo Mutwa's supporters, the New Age conspiracy theorist David Icke, produced a five-hour video, *The Reptilian Agenda,* based on interviews with the Zulu shaman. In this video, Icke explains, we are introduced to "a unique human being, the most incredible man it has been my honor to meet." Mutwa is "keeper of the ancient knowledge," the truth of history, as opposed to the "nonsensical version of history we get from universities." The true history confirmed by both Icke's recent research and Mutwa's ancient knowledge centered on a global conspiracy of aliens from outer space.

A former sports broadcaster in Britain, David Icke developed a distinctive blend of personal spirituality and political paranoia that he promoted through books, public lectures, and an elaborate website (Icke 1999, 2002, 2005). Although he seemed to embrace every conspiracy theory, David Icke identified the central, secret conspiracy ruling the world as the work of shape-shifting reptilians from outer space. According to Icke, these extraterrestrial reptiles interbred with human beings, establishing a lineage that could be traced through the pharaohs of ancient Egypt, the Merovingian dynasty of medieval Europe, the British royal family, and every president of the United States. Although they plotted behind the scenes in the secret society of the Illuminati, the aliens of these hybrid bloodlines were in prominent positions of royal, political, and economic power all over the world. Occasionally shifting into their lizard-like form, these aliens maintained a human appearance by regularly drinking human blood, which they acquired by performing rituals of human sacrifice.

David Icke invoked the indigenous African authority of Credo Mutwa to confirm this conspiracy theory about blood-drinking, shape-shifting reptiles from outer space. As Mutwa declared, "To know the Illuminati, Mr. David, you must study the reptile" (Icke 2002). In *The Reptilian Agenda,* Credo Mutwa confirms that extraterrestrials, the Chitauri, were a shape-shifting reptilian race that has controlled humanity for thousands of years. Subsequent to making this video, Icke and Mutwa appeared together on a popular American radio program, "Sightings," to explain the alien reptile conspiracy. They also reportedly joined forces on the eve of the new millennium to prevent an Illuminati ritual of human sacrifice at the Great Pyramid of Cheops. In his lectures, Icke insisted that Credo Mutwa provided proof for his conspiracy theory, as one observer noted, in the "pure voice of a primitive belief system" (Molloy 1999). In Credo Mutwa, therefore, David Icke found indigenous authentication for an alien conspiracy (see Icke 1999).

Authentication of the "truth" took different forms: First, this truth is a dangerous truth. Credo Mutwa is constantly subjected to death threats, including an attempt on his life just prior to filming, by those who want to prevent him from speaking the truth. The danger inherent in this truth is inherently validating. The conspiracy is not a "theory," Icke warns, because "theory does not kill people. The conspiracy is real."

Second, this truth is a "bizarre story," Icke admits, but it is confirmed by Credo Mutwa's "unique knowledge," which is drawn from secret traditions of, "Africa, this enormous and astonishing continent." Icke advises, "As bizarre . . . and as seemingly ridiculous as this story might seem," it is authenticated by the fact that Credo Mutwa "tells exactly the same story."

Third, this truth, in its African authentication, is a precarious tradition, since Credo Mutwa is one of only two Zulu sanusi left alive, but this truth, at risk of vanishing, will be preserved on video "for as long as the electronic medium exists." So while Credo Mutwa provides indigenous confirmation for Icke's "bizarre story," Icke, in return, promises permanence for Zulu tradition through modern electronic media.

In his video interviews for *The Reptilian Agenda,* Credo Mutwa describes his encounters with extraterrestrials with meticulous attention to the senses, creating a vivid impression of seeing, hearing, smelling, tasting, and touching aliens in two contexts: eating them and being violated by them.

According to Mutwa, African tradition provides wisdom on how to prepare, cook, and eat aliens from outer space. In 1958, he recalls, a UFO crashed in a mountainous area of Lesotho. A friend invited Mutwa over for a meal, promising him that they would be dining on "something holy," which turned out to be the meat of an extraterrestrial known as a Grey. Following African tradition, they had to eat this meal in a deep hole in the ground. As Mutwa reports, the meat of the alien was tough and dry, requiring much chewing, and it had the "same taste as a copper coin." After eating this "flesh of a god," Mutwa and his companion became deathly ill, suffering intense pain for a week, which seemed like a hundred years, blinded, deaf, and unable to breathe. After a week, they went "stark, raving, laughing mad." Then, suddenly, Mutwa recalls, he was "a person reborn." All of his senses were expanded. "I could see colours beyond colours," he recalls.

"I could hear a voice in my head." His taste buds were "souped up," so that ordinary water tasted extraordinary. In the ecstasy of this extraordinary sensory
experience, Mutwa recalls, "We were one with the entire universe." By eating the
alien, Mutwa had acquired an extraterrestrial sensorium. "Do you think those
senses you experienced are the senses of the Chitauri?" Icke asks. "Yes," Mutwa
responds. "Senses like no human being has."

By contrast to this extraterrestrial ecstasy, in 1959, Mutwa underwent the
alien agony of abduction. While looking for medicinal herbs in what is now Zim-
babwe, Mutwa was taken into a spaceship of the Chitauri, disappearing for a period of four days. Again, his account of alien abduction pays meticulous attention
to the senses, the "strange humming sound," the images of destroyed cities as
"pictures flooded my mind," and the horrible metallic, chemical smell of the Chitauri, the Greys, and other extraterrestrials. "I have seen the Chitauri," Mutwa
assures us. "I have smelled them. I have personal experience with them." But
that personal experience was entirely terrifying, an "eternity of pain" inflicted
upon him by aliens who tortured him, experimented upon him, and forced him
to have sexual intercourse with a female extraterrestrial. Throughout all of these
ordeals, Mutwa recounted, he felt like the victim at a sacrifice. Returning to earth
saturated with a "horrible non-human smell," and missing his trousers, Mutwa
was attacked by dogs but was saved by villagers who recognized by his odor that
he had been abducted by aliens. Although eating them had heightened his senses,
being abducted by aliens had confused his senses. "Since that time I have become
a very confused creature," he confides. "Since that time my mind does not seem
to be my own."

Transatlantic Exchanges

In a blurb on the back of the recent book by David M. Cumes (2004) *Africa in
My Bones: A Surgeon's Odyssey into the Spirit World of African Healing,* Credo
Mutwa praises the author, "who walks along two roads" as both Western medical
specialist and African ritual specialist, as both surgeon and sangoma, but also
as someone who has developed a kind of double vision. "The world needs such
people," Mutwa advises, "who see Africa through two eyes, the African eye and
the Western eye." Born in South Africa, Cumes relocated to the United States to
study medicine at Stanford and establish a successful practice as a urologist in
Santa Barbara, California. Although he often visited the place of his birth, Cumes
reported that he felt like an alien in Africa, which he described as a problem of
vision, noting that in Africa he "felt like an onlooker rather than a participant."
This problem of alienated vision, this subjectivity of the spectator, was resolved
for Cumes through dreams that led him to undergo initiation as a sangoma. "The
fact that my dreams were often quite prophetic," he recounted, "gave me reason to believe that I might be able to master this ancient discipline." In dreams,

he was "called" by the ancestors to enter into the ancient discipline of "seeing" (Cumes 2004: ix). Now, as a Zulu sangoma, he practices divination as a kind of dreamwork. As Cumes explains, "Reading the bones is a little like unraveling the metaphor of a dream. . . . Divining is like interpreting someone's dream" (Cumes 2004: 7, 18).

On his website, Cumes (2006) features a video of his life story, his initiation, and his plans for a healing village in South Africa. To the sounds of rhythmic African music, the video begins with an image of an African woman, traditionally attired, her eyes and mouth wide open. Moving through rural and urban scenes, Cumes, in voice-over, proceeds to use tactile metaphors to describe his early life in South Africa, weighted down under the "heaviness of the apartheid system," alienated from "connection with the native" and "connection with Africa." Following his dreams and the advice of author Susan Shuster Campbell (2000, 2002), he was led to an "old Zulu teacher in Swaziland," P. H. Mtshali. Undergoing a rigorous, although abbreviated, initiation, Cumes graduated as a Zulu sangoma. Now, running his life based on messages "from the dreamworld," Cumes reports, "I just head wherever the dreams and bones tell me." One place the dreams told him to head was the South African province of Limpopo, where he is establishing a healing center, Tshisimane, in which visitors can benefit from massage, yoga, Reiki, and consultations with sangomas. "I saw the place in a dream," Cumes reveals.

As a white sangoma, David Cumes represents a recently emerging trend in contemporary neo-shamanism in which aspiring Euro-American shamans are turning to African traditions as a source of authentic dreams, visions, and connections. The West African author Malidoma Patrice Somé has played an important role in this recent development (Somé 1993). John Hall, the American biographer of the great South African singer Miriam Makeba, was a pioneer in taking initiation as a Zulu sangoma (Hall 1994). But South Africans have also played a part. While Credo Mutwa has some white initiates, such as the "white Zulu" C. J. Hood, who has represented him at events in the United States, calling upon everyone to return to their ancestral traditions (Heart Healing Center 2001; Wellness eJournal 2001), P. H. Mtshali has shown a particular interest in training white sangomas who are currently practicing in South Africa, like Claudia Rauber in Cape Town (Anonymous 2000; Viall 2004), or in North America, like Gretchen McKay in Orange County, California (Mtshali 2004: 58–64).

In some cases, however, white sangomas in the United States have not required formal initiation to claim indigenous African authenticity. For example, Kenneth "Bear Hawk" Cohen, who claims to have been adopted by the Cree, studied with the Zulu shaman Ingwe, who was born in 1914 as M. Norman Powell in South Africa but moved to the United States to establish his Wilderness Awareness School. On his website, "Bear Hawk" announces that this association with Ingwe places him "in the lineage of the Holy Man, Vusamazulu Credo Mutwa" (Cohen 2006). Similarly, Tom "Blue Wolf" Goodman, who claims to be a Native American shaman, the "Faith Keeper of the Star Clan, Y'falla Band of the Lower Creek People," also claims to be heir to the spiritual lineage of Vusamazulu Credo Mutwa. "I am keeper of my grandfather's dream," he reveals. "My grandfather's medicine songs have been dreamed in South Africa by Sangoma spiritual leaders," spiritual leaders who are all led by "Vusamazulu Credo Mutwa, High Sanusi (High Priest) of the Zulu Nation" (Goodman 2004).

In North America, defenders of the integrity of indigenous traditions have labeled these white shamans as "plastic shamans" (Aldred 2000; Kehoe 1990). Websites identify them and scorn them (Anonymous 2003). Although these innovations in neo-shamanism might very well be "plastic," in the sense of invented or even fake, they nevertheless suggest real religious issues of location, dislocation, and relocation in the Atlantic world. Just as the South African David Cumes, who became a medical doctor in California, underwent initiation as a Zulu sangoma to establish "connection with the native" or "connection with Africa," other expatriates have entered the dreamscape of Zulu neo-shamanism as a way of coming home. In Canada, two South Africans, one black, one white, but both having established careers in the creative and performing arts, followed their dreams into Zulu shamanism.

Sibongile Nene describes herself as a singer, actor, and consultant for individuals, businesses, and community building. She also describes herself as a sangoma. As an actress, she appeared in the feature film *Jit* (1993). The plot of this film anticipated her later vocation as a ritual specialist in African ancestral religion: "Jokwa, a pesky ancestral spirit," wants the main character "to look after his aging parents, and keep her supplied with beer." Moving to Canada, Sibongile Nene continued acting and singing but also moved into business consultancy. Returning regularly to South Africa, she took initiation as a Zulu sangoma, a process she conveys through music on her musical CD, *Sangoma*. On her website, Sibongile Nene offers her services as an "African Spirituality Consultant in the Sangoma tradition of the Bantu people of southern Africa" (Nene 2006).

Ann Mortifee, described in the press as "one of Canada's most extraordinary vocalists, composers, and playwrights," but also as a "musical shaman" guided and inspired by Credo Mutwa, was born and raised on a sugarcane farm in Zululand. In 2005, she released a CD, *Into the Heart of the Sangoma*, dedicated to Credo Mutwa, which musically conveyed her journey from her experience of inauthenticity in exile to the authenticity of home. In her successful creative and performing career in Canada, as Mortifee revealed in an interview, "I had created a persona, but felt I had nothing authentic to give to the world." Here, once again, dreams intervened. "For two years," she recalled, "I had recurring dreams about a black woman and stars." Then she read Credo Mutwa's *Song of the Stars*.

"I discovered the Zulu 'Song of the Stars' and learned about the *sangoma*, shamen [*sic*] of the Zulu nation." She flew to South Africa, and her dreams eventually led her to Credo Mutwa (Weyler 2005).

Although she has told her story in interviews, Ann Mortifee's journey into Zulu shamanism is best conveyed by the music and commentary of her recording *Into the Heart of the Sangoma*. Opening with the song "Africa," she begins with her birthplace but also with her dreams. "Voices from my childhood linger in me still, voices that come from the dreamtime," she says. "It is the old Sangoma, Sikhowe, leading me deeper into the mystery." The next song, "I Dream," also evokes both Africa and the dreamtime. "One of my earliest recollections is of lying in my bed listening to the sounds of the African night," she says. "Something was out there beckoning to me, weaving a spell, which had the power, in some essential way, to mark my soul forever."

The next song, "The Stars Are Holes," finds her looking up into the night sky, but this song also directs her vision back home to South Africa. "Two years after writing this song," she says, "I found the very same story I had written in a book by Vusamazulu Credo Mutwa, the head Sangoma of the Zulu Nation. This strange occurrence caused me to go to South Africa and find him." Returning to South Africa, staying at a game reserve, she saw a herd of elephants that inspired the song "Indlovu" (the elephant), and that night, she recalls, "I dreamed . . . there walked a man whom I later knew to be Credo Mutwa. In the dream he said to me, 'Go to Shamwari tomorrow.'" Proceeding to this private game reserve in the Eastern Cape, where Credo Mutwa was employed for a while as a cultural advisor, she participated in "an ancient healing ceremony" at which she sang a song that she had just composed. "Who taught you this song?" the sangomas asked. When Mortifee replied that she had just made it up, the sangomas objected. "You did not make this up," they insisted. "This is the song we Sangomas sing when we go in search of spirit." Having established this connection in song and spirit, Mortifee's dreams were fulfilled by meeting Credo Mutwa. As musically represented in the song "For There Are Loved Ones," Mortifee learned from Mutwa that her dreams revealed that she was connected to his ancestral lineage. Ann Mortifee explains:

> When I finally met Credo Mutwa, he said: "Tell me about the Sangoma of your dreams. What is her name?" "Sikhowe," I answered. "And tell me, what do her eyes look like?" "Well, one is black and the other is completely white." "And which one is white?" "The right one," I said. "And tell me what do her legs look like?" "They look like the trunks of a tree," I replied. "That woman is my grandmother," Mutwa said. "She had a cataract in her right eye, which turned it completely white. And she had elephantitis, which made her legs look like the trunk of a tree. So you see, it is my grandmother that has brought you to me."

In this affirmation and connection, driven by dreams, Ann Mortifee could finally feel as if she were at home in Africa. She had been called by the maternal ancestor, herself a sangoma, of the highest shaman of the Zulu nation. But she could also return home to North America unburdened by any guilt. "I want you to listen to me," Credo Mutwa reportedly said to her. "Never again be ashamed of the privilege into which you have been born. And never, never be ashamed of the great gifts that the gods have given you."

Ann Mortifee's greatest gift, by her own account, is music that opens to the sacred, which provides both a zone of protection and a vehicle for entering the numinous. "Sacred music has been a way of my stopping the world and entering into a place of deep protection," she explains. "Music is a vehicle through which we've always been able to contact the numinous" (Frymire 2003).

Senses and Media

In his classic treatment of "the holy," Rudolf Otto (1923) disagreed with this proposition that music, or any artistic medium, could be a vehicle for direct contact with the numinous. Pointing to the mistake of "confounding in any way the non-rational of music and the non-rational of the numinous itself" (49), Otto insisted that music and other arts could only suggest the numinous indirectly, coming most closely to representing the numinous through two methods that "are in a noteworthy way *negative*, viz. *darkness* and *silence*" (68). According to Otto, therefore, not seeing and not hearing—or, better, seeing nothing, hearing nothing—were sensory experiences within the productions of artistic media that most closely approximated the numinous. Arguably, Otto's Protestant sensibility led him to engage aesthetic media through this negative theology of the senses.

By contrast, indigenous Zulu sensibility was actively engaged with sensory media of dreams and visions, exploring their potential as avenues for communicating with ancestors and responding to the energetics of exchange and orientation. In contemporary Zulu neo-shamanism, however, we find an ambivalent relationship to both the senses and electronic media, as vehicles for the numinous, which mirrors an understanding of the senses as limitation, as potential, and as validation for the extraordinary experiences of a shaman.

These three ways of dealing with senses and media are all registers of authenticity. By representing limits, senses and media stand as obstacles to authentic spiritual experience. But they also represent the boundary that is necessary to mark the transition from ordinary, everyday awareness to the extraordinary capacities of a shaman. In marking out limits, therefore, senses and media incorporate the classic ambivalence of liminality, as both wall and threshold, defining a boundary that simultaneously constrains and contains possibilities. Accordingly, senses and media also register as having transcendent potential, serving as means for achieving, modes for expanding, or metaphors for signaling shamanic awareness. Authenticity, in this respect, is marked by realizing the potential of the human sensorium and electronic media as meaning-making resources. Extraordinary sensory experience, including the intensification, rearrangement, and merger of the senses, is directly related to the capacity of electronic media to capture meaning like a camera and transmit meaning like film. In the process, shamanic authenticity is reinforced by activating the latent potential in senses and media for the production and reception of extraordinary meaning. Finally, human senses and electronic media provide validation, obviously, since "seeing is believing," in cognitive terms, but also in forensic terms when the testimony of intense sensory experiences or popular media representations provide confirmation for shamanic claims. By engaging senses and media in these three ways, as limit, potential, and validation, Zulu neo-shamans have sought to authenticate new Zulu dreamscapes.

Senses and Media as Limits

The five conventionally recognized human senses, according to Credo Mutwa, are limits, blocking awareness of spiritual realities. Seeing, hearing, smelling, tasting, and touching are inadequate for engaging this higher awareness. Fortunately, Mutwa assures us, these five senses are only part of a more expansive sensorium that extends to a total of twelve senses. As Mutwa insists, without explaining, "We in Africa know and please don't ask me to explain further—that the human being possesses twelve senses—not five senses as Western people believe. One day [it] will be accepted scientifically [that there are] twelve." These additional seven senses, whatever they might be, are part of the natural sensory capacity of human beings. Although they transcend the five senses, these additional senses are simply human nature. Accordingly, Mutwa maintains that "we must not call those as yet unknown senses, supernatural" (Mutwa 1996: 30).

Neo-shaman John Hall also finds that the five senses are limits. They cannot account for his intense encounters with the *lidloti*, the ancestors, which he experienced in dreams and visions during his initiation as a sangoma. Reflecting on ordinary sensory limits, Hall cites the authority of Augustine of Hippo, who observed, "I can run through all the organs of sense, which are the body's gateway to the mind, but I cannot find any by which some facts could have entered" (Hall 1994: 61). Although Augustine used this argument to posit an interior sense, or seminal reason, as a capacity for knowledge that was independent of ordinary perception, Hall concludes that this acknowledgment of the limits of the senses opens the possibility of extrasensory perception. Augustine, Hall found, "might have been describing my puzzlement following a lidloti experience" (61).

Like the five senses, electronic media can be regarded as placing limits on awareness. At one point, Credo Mutwa advises anyone who wants to be a sangoma, with prophetic vision, to stay away from electronic media. As Mutwa warns, "People who are aspiring to develop their gifts of prophesy should avoid exposing themselves over much to electronic devices such as television sets, radio sets, and other electronic gadgets of this day and age because, for some reason, these electronic devices emit an inaudible sound that blankets all psychic power." This unheard sound, as an undercurrent of electronic media, supposedly blocks the extrasensory perceptions of a sangoma. Accordingly, a sangoma should develop his or her psychic powers in a rural area not only to be closer to an ancestral home but also to be free of the limits to awareness generated by the modern network of electronic transmission and reception of media. "I have noticed over many years of close observation," Mutwa reports, "how difficult it becomes for a witch doctor from Soweto, for example, to foretell events in the future. This is unlike a witch doctor who has lived in an environment where these electronic devices do not exist. So there must be something in our electronic world that is destroying our Godgiven talents" (Mutwa 1996: 29).

John Hall (1994) also finds limits to electronic media. In a kind of allegory marking his independence from electronic media, he recalls that during his initiation he felt cut off from any news about the world outside. He acquired a radio, but it stopped working when its wiring was eaten by dozens of cockroaches. "They scrambled over my hands and arms and I dropped the radio in surprise and disgust," Hall recounts. "It smashed to pieces on the floor" (112). Television, as well, was an unnecessary medium, as Hall reflects, "not that I had seen a television image in over a year and a half. Nor had I needed to. Lidloti-vision had kept me enthralled" (196). The limits of television, therefore, had been transcended by a spiritual medium, ancestor-vision, which provided Hall with all of the information (and entertainment) he could desire.

Senses and Media as Potential

Although senses are limits, they also represent the potential for extraordinary experience. Eyes might be limited, but in distinguishing an authentic shaman, as P. H. Mtshali reveals, "the important thing is that they can 'see'" (Mtshali 2004: 22). Here the senses, as metaphors, represent the possibility of transcending the limits of ordinary perception. Credo Mutwa might have regarded the five conventional senses as limitations, but he also claimed to have entered an extraordinary trans-sensory ecstasy, an intense expansion of all the senses, after eating the meat of an extraterrestrial. Acquiring the sensory capacity of the reptilian extraterrestrials—"senses like no human being has"—Mutwa saw, heard, smelled, tasted, and touched beyond ordinary perception.

This intensification and expansion of all the senses recalls the role of synesthesia, the convergence, merger, or trans-modal transfer of the senses, in religious discourse and practice. In religious discourse, synesthesia can evoke perception that is intense, unifying, and extraordinary (Chidester 1992a, 1992b). In ritual synesthesia, ordinary perception is transcended in and through the senses, as when the persistent sound and visceral percussion of drumming induces shamanic "seeing" (Sullivan 1986).

During his initiation as a sangoma, John Hall experienced this synesthetic merger of visceral percussion, sound, and sight. "The loud drums had once more beaten my mind into myself," he recalls. But he immediately turns to media as metaphor, noting, "I had no more self-consciousness viewing these images than a person does watching an involving movie." The next day, when he related his experience to an elder sangoma, she observed, "Sometimes, it is like you are watching television. It's that way with me. Things come at you, like the *bhayi-skhobho.*" As Hall realized, this SiSwati term, *bhayiskhobho,* was derived from the antiquated term *bioscope,* which had been widely used in South Africa for the "motion picture process" (Hall 1994: 54).

Similarly, David M. Cumes represented the potential of shamanic perception as electronic media. Sangomas are connected to a communication network like the Western communication network of "satellite phones, fax machines and the internet." Since this sangoma communication network is based on a "sophisticated psychospiritual technology," Cumes advises, the "ancient African wisdom has a lot to teach us about communication" (6). Although Cumes contrasts modem Western and traditional African communication networks, sometimes it seems as if both share the same "cosmic field," since Cumes observes that "light, sound, radio, TV, electromagnetic pulses . . . are some of the knowable signals that travel through the cosmic field" (105).

During his initiation, Cumes also had dreams and visions that drew upon modern media technology as metaphors for ancient spiritual wisdom. "One night," he reports, "I dreamt that I was given a new shiny black Mamiya camera. I was told the lens I needed was 150 to 16—more powerful on the wide angle than on the telephoto side." Relating this dream to his teacher, P. H. Mtshali, Cumes asked if the ancestors were instructing him to buy this type of camera to keep a photographic record of his initiation. But Mtshali interpreted this dream not as request but as gift from the ancestors, revealing to Cumes that the camera was a sign that "you are being given tools to give you a broader vision" (Cumes 2004: 44).

Senses and Media as Validation

In his tales of encounters with aliens from outer space, Credo Mutwa pays meticulous attention to sensory perception, with particular emphasis on the sense of smell, as if "smelling is knowing," especially in knowing the foul odor of the Chitauri, Greys, and other extraterrestrials. As Mutwa claims, "They are tangible, they are smellable." By his own account, Mutwa was close enough to smell them; he was close enough to be infused by their odor; and he continued to bear that alien odor when he returned to earth, and villagers recognized the extraterrestrial stench. Such sensory details, we might assume, are cited to lend an aura of credibility to an unbelievable story. They provide a kind of visceral validation of the narrative.

Similarly, Hall, Cumes, and other white sangomas validate their accounts through vivid sensory detail, suggesting that their initiations revolve around a recovery of the senses. In their accounts, they see and hear extraordinary things, but they also smell fragrant herbs and foul concoctions, taste sour beer and disgusting medicines, and convulse in excruciating pain and induced vomiting in validating their initiations.

Electronic media also provide validation not only as metaphors for spiritual perception but also as enduring forms for transmitting indigenous spiritual wisdom. The relative permanence of video, as David Icke declared, promises to preserve the authentic Zulu wisdom of Credo Mutwa for "as long as this electronic medium lasts." Traditionally, according to Mutwa, this wisdom was kept secret, reserved for a small circle of initiates, and transmitted orally within a lineage of initiates from generation to generation. But now, as Mutwa declares, "Africa is dying," facing destruction from epidemic disease, endemic poverty, and global conspiracy. In this crisis, traditional ways of transmitting ancient wisdom are no longer viable. Urgently, everyone must know things that were previously known only by a few. Mass media, such as video, film, and the internet, are now necessary for broadcasting the truth and surviving this crisis. Accordingly, modern media become valid modes of disseminating ancient wisdom.

At the same time, mass media content can be invoked to validate ancient Zulu tradition. According to Credo Mutwa, the extraterrestrial reptilians, the Chitauri, will soon be returning to earth to exercise their oppressive domination and exploitation of humanity directly. The Chitauri have been content to exercise their power in disguise, operating through devious, shape-shifting reptilians such as George W. Bush, Tony Blair, and other Illuminati who maintain their human-like appearance through regular rituals of human sacrifice and blood drinking. Very soon, however, the alien Chitauri will appear on earth in their true, hideous forms. According to Credo Mutwa, an important feature of this global conspiracy of extraterrestrial domination of humanity can be found in Hollywood films.

Recent movies, beginning with *ET: The Extraterrestrial,* have been preparing humanity to accept the Chitauri and willingly submit to their authority. According to Mutwa, one *Star Wars* character, Darth Maul, "is exactly what the Chitauri look like," while *Stargate* depicts "a slimy, cream-colored creature" that Mutwa finds is the "speaking likeness of Mobaba, emperor of the Chitauri." Discovering the Chitauri and their evil emperor appearing in Hollywood films, Mutwa demands, "Where do filmmakers get their information?"

On the one hand, Hollywood filmmakers appropriate ancient African traditions. For example, *Men in Black,* according to Mutwa, has appropriated indigenous African traditions about how to deal with aliens and how to dispose of extraterrestrial rubbish. Through these popular films, Mutwa complains, the authentic traditions of African "Men in Black" have been stolen and Westernized by Hollywood.

On the other hand, filmmakers draw their information directly from the Chitauri, or indirectly through the hybrid Illuminati, because Hollywood is working on behalf of their global conspiracy by familiarizing audiences with the strange appearance of the aliens. By suspending disbelief, Hollywood films are preparing audiences all over the world to accept their imminent subjugation to reptilian extraterrestrials.

Going Global, Coming Home

Although Credo Mutwa is an acknowledged expert on aliens from outer space—acknowledged not only by New Age conspiracy theorist David Icke but also by Harvard researcher John E. Mack (1999)—this feature of his indigenous Zulu wisdom is not mentioned by white Zulu sangomas, such as John Hall and David M. Cumes, nor by the "musical shaman," Ann Mortifee, who has been guided and inspired by Credo Mutwa. As we have seen, while Credo Mutwa is going global, they are interested in coming home.

In developing a cultural and political analysis of Zulu popular music, Louise Meintjes (2003) has tracked mediations between the local and the global in which artists work in the studio on "performing Zuluness" while "imagining overseas." Similarly, Credo Mutwa has been situated in mediations between the local and the global by performing an indigenous Zulu vision of the world while looking overseas for a global audience. In the process, even if he displays a remarkable capacity for imaginative invention, Mutwa nevertheless suggests important features of a changing Zulu dreamscape.

During the nineteenth century, to tell a dream meant "to fetch" the dream, to go back to the place where the dream was originally experienced, its originating location, and carry it to the new place of telling. A dream, therefore, was portable, but it was situated in a specific landscape. It could be located and relocated, horizontally, within a terrain of human habitation. However, under colonial conditions of dispossession and dislocation, it became increasingly difficult "to fetch" dreams within an embattled terrain. As it became harder "to fetch" dreams, techniques for blocking dreams, including conversion to Christianity, were increasingly deployed. Credo Mutwa, I would like to suggest, has attempted to resolve this longstanding dilemma within the Zulu dreamscape by moving dreams, vertically, into the sky. The Zulu word *butongo,* which means "to sleep," according to Credo Mutwa means "the state of being one with the star gods." The Zulu word *ipupo,* which means "to dream," according to Credo Mutwa means "to fly." As Mutwa explains, "The verb 'pupa' refers to flight, therefore to say 'I dreamt' means 'I flew'" (Mutwa 1996: 173). These imaginative etymologies, whatever their validity, effectively shift the hermeneutics and energetics of Zulu dreaming from the land to the sky.

"We need to develop a relationship with the dream reality," urges Zulu sangoma David Cumes (Cumes 2004: 92). As a white South African expatriate, Cumes dreamed of coming home to South Africa. His initiation as a sangoma enabled him to establish "connection with the native" and "connection with Africa." In his dream reality, these connections entailed a fundamental reorientation in South African space. Although black South Africans had suffered under a long history of colonialism and apartheid, Cumes now saw that whites in South Africa had also suffered. "Without our knowing it," he observes, "the apartheid system had discriminated against us, too. As whites we had been forbidden access to another realm—we were not worthy and had been justifiably deprived. There were no signs to tell us, 'Whites not allowed,' but we were excluded all the same. We skirted around the authenticity of a magical continent thinking we were part of it when in fact we were not." Called by the ancestors to become a sangoma, Cumes was able to overcome the discrimination and alienation under which whites had suffered in South Africa. "Now the spirits had mandated and things had changed," he declared. "I was no longer underprivileged and would never be again" (Cumes 2004: 30).

Clearly, this testimony evokes a reorientation that is not of the sky but of the land. Locally, within South Africa, Cumes advances the argument that apartheid had disadvantaged white people by separating them from access to indigenous African spiritual traditions. Now, coming home, not as an observer but as a participant, he embraces the people and the land. Accordingly, Cumes represents his reorientation not as flying in the sky, expanding his global vision, but as a tactile connection, as being "blessed and touched by an unseen hand through a channel I did not even know" (Cumes 2004: 30). Here also, media, as a "channel," is evoked as metaphor, but the metaphor evokes the embodied reorientation established by a tactile connection with home.

In tracking Zulu dreamscapes, I have tried to show that dreams are not merely "subjective apparitions" or "brain sensation." Nor are dreams only "texts" to be interpreted. Involved in an energetics of sacrificial exchange and spatial orientation, dreaming can be a religious practice, a practice that can be dramatically altered by the shifting social fields in which dreams are situated. In response to economic dispossession and social dislocation during the nineteenth century, Zulu dreamers increasingly turned to ritual techniques, which arguably included conversion to Christianity, for blocking ancestral dreams, seeking to turn off this sensory media. By contrast, contemporary neo-shamanism cultivates a sensory extravagance, an overabundance of sensory engagements with things that are not there, from alien reptilians to ancestral spirits, which demand ritual response. Any apparitions that might appear, therefore, must be regarded as real and engaged accordingly.

Global in scope, this new Zulu dreamscape is saturated by media. Despite expressing occasional concerns that electronic media might block dreams and visions, neo-shamans dwell in a mediated world, a world shaped by media technology, possibility, and authentication. As both dreamscape and mediascape, Zulu neo-shamanism is emerging within a new energetics of global exchange and global orientation.

References

Aldred, Lisa. 2000. "Plastic Shamans and Astroturf Sundances: New Age Commercialization of Native American Spirituality." *American Indian Quarterly* 24(3): 329–352.

Anonymous. 2000. "Whites Embrace Traditional Healing in Swaziland." *Panafrican News Agency.* http://www.ancestralwisdom.com/whitethwasas.html.

———. 2003. "Native Religions and Plastic Medicine Men." http://www.williams.edu/go/native/natreligion.htm.

Appadurai, Arjun. 1996. "Disjuncture and Difference in the Global Cultural Economy." *Modernity at Large: Cultural Dimensions of Globalization,* 27–47. Minneapolis: University of Minnesota Press.

Callaway, Henry. 1868–1870. *The Religious System of the Amazulu.* Springvale: Springvale Mission; reprinted Cape Town: Struik, 1970.

———. 1872. "On Divination and Analogous Phenomena among the Natives of Natal." *Proceedings of the Anthropological Institute* 1: 163–183.

Campbell, Susan Schuster. 2000. *Called to Heal: African Shamanic Healers.* Twin Lakes, WI: Lotus Press.

———. 2002. *Spirit of the Ancestors.* Twin Lakes, WI: Lotus Press.

Chidester, David. 1992a. *Word and Light: Seeing, Hearing, and Religious Discourse.* Urbana: University of Illinois Press.

———. 1992b. *Religions of South Africa: Library of Religious Beliefs and Practices.* London: Routledge.

———. 2002. "Credo Mutwa, Zulu Shaman: The Invention and Appropriation of Indigenous Authenticity in African Folk Religion." *Journal for the Study of Religion* 15(2): 65–85.

———. 2005. *Authentic Fakes: Religion and American Popular Culture.* Berkeley: University of California Press.

Cohen, Kenneth. 2006. "About Kenneth 'Bear Hawk' Cohen." http://www.kennethcohen.com/sacred_earth/about.html.

Comaroff, Jean, and John L. Comaroff. 1999. "Occult Economies and the Violence of Abstraction: Notes from the South African Postcolony." *American Ethnologist* 26(2): 279–303.

Cumes, David M. 2004. *Africa in My Bones: A Surgeon's Odyssey into the Spirit World of African Healing.* Claremont, South Africa: Spearhead.

———. 2006. *Holistic Urology and Surgery, Psycho Spiritual Healing.* http://www.davidcumes.com.

Friedman, Hazel. 1997. "Of Culture and Visions." *Mail and Guardian* (March 27).

Frymire, Ange. 2003. "What's Sacred Got to Do with It?" *Common Ground* (November). http://commonground.ca/iss/0311148/music_festival.shtml.

Goodman, Tom "Blue Wolf." 2004. "Rekindling the Ancient Fires: Sacred Journey to South Africa." *Aquarius: A Sign of the Times.* http://www.aquarius-atlanta.com/aug04/balance.shtml.

Hall, James. 1994. *Sangoma: My Odyssey into the Spirit World of Africa.* New York: G. P. Putnam's Sons.

Heart Healing Center. 2001. "Heart Healing." http://www.hearthealingcenter.com/earthhealers.htm.

Icke, David. 1999. *The Biggest Secret.* London: Bridge of Love Publications.

———. 2002. "The Reptilian Brain." http://www.davidicke.com/icke/articles2/reptbrain.html.

———. 2005. *The Reptilian Agenda.* Venice, CA: UFO TV.

Johnson, Angela. 1997. "The Angela Johnson Interview." *Mail and Guardian* (July 18).

Keeney, Bradford, ed. 2001. *Vusamazulu Credo Mutwa: Zulu High Sanusi.* Stony Creek, CT: Leete's Island Books.

Kehoe, Alice. 1990. "Primal Gaia: Primitivists and Plastic Medicine Men." In *The Invented Indian: Cultural Reactions and Government Policies,* edited by James Clifton, 193–209. New Brunswick, NJ: Transaction.

Lieberman, Philip. 2000. *Human Language and Our Reptilian Brain: The Subcortical Bases of Speech, Syntax, and Thought.* Cambridge, MA: Harvard University Press.

Mack, John E. 1999. *Passport to the Cosmos: Human Transformation and Alien Encounters.* New York: Three Rivers Press.

Martin, Rick. 1999. "Great Zulu Shaman and Elder Credo Mutwa: A Rare, Astonishing Conversation." *The Spectrum Newspaper,* October. http://www.thespectrumnews.com/images/sb/1999/sb3-100599.gif.

Meintjes, Louise. 2003. *Sound of Africa! Making Music Zulu in a South African Studio.* Durham, NC: Duke University Press.

Molloy, Nicky. 1999. "David Icke's Lecture: The Biggest Secret." *Ufonet* (December 2). http://groups.yahoo.com/group/ufoneti message/3019.

Mortifee, Ann. 2005. *Into the Heart of the Sangoma.* Vancouver: Jabula Music.

Mtshali, P. H. 2004. *The Power of the Ancestors: The Life of a Zulu Traditional Healer.* Mbabane, Swaziland: Kamhlaba.

Mutwa, Credo. 1964. *Indaba, My Children.* Johannesburg: Blue Crane Books.

———. 1966. *Africa Is My Witness.* Johannesburg: Blue Crane Books.

———. 1996. *Song of the Stars: The Lore of a Zulu Shaman.* Barrytown, NY: Station Hill Openings.

———. 2003. *Zulu Shaman: Dreams, Prophecies, and Mysteries.* Merrimac, MA: Destiny.

Nene, Sibongile. 2006. "Sibongile Nene, Sangoma: African Traditional Healer." http://www.sangoma.cal.

Otto, Rudolf. 1923. *The Idea of the Holy,* trans. John W. Harvey. Oxford: Oxford University Press.

Somé, Malidoma Patrice. 1993. *Ritual: Power, Healing, and Community.* Portland, OR: Swan Raven & Co.

Stolow, Jeremy. 2005. "Religion and/as Media." *Theory, Culture and Society* 22(4): 119–145.

Sullivan, Lawrence. 1986. "Sound and Sense: Towards a Hermeneutics of Performance." *History of Religions* 26: 1–33.

Townsend, Joan B. 2004. "Core Shamanism and Neo-shamanism." In *Shamanism: An Encyclopedia of World Beliefs, Practices and Culture,* edited by Mariko Namba Walter and Eva Jane Neumann Fridman, 1:49–57. Santa Barbara, CA: ABC-CLIO.

Viall, Jeanne. 2004. "Claudia Uses Old Ways to Help with the New." *Cape Argus* (November 22): 13.

Wellness eJournal. 2001. http://www.compwellness.com/eJournal/2001/0131.htm.

Weyler, Rex. 2005. "Singer Interrupted by Life: Journeys with Ann Mortifee." *Shared Vision.* http://www.shared-vision.com/2005/sv1807/viewpoint1807.html.

Contributors

HAMADOU ADAMA is Professor of History at the University of Ngaoundéré in Cameroon.

J. KWABENA ASAMOAH-GYADU is Baëta-Grau Professor of Contemporary African Christianity and Pentecostal Theology at the Trinity Theological Seminary, Accra, Ghana.

SAMSON A. BEZABEH is currently a visiting fellow at the Afrika-Studiecentrum and the International Institute for Asian Studies both in Leiden.

JAMES R. BRENNAN is Associate Professor of History at the University of Illinois, Urbana-Champaign.

VICKI L. BRENNAN is Associate Professor of Religion at the University of Vermont.

DAVID CHIDESTER is Professor of Religious Studies and Director of the Institute for Comparative Religion in Southern Africa at the University of Cape Town, South Africa.

MARLEEN DE WITTE is a postdoctoral researcher at the Department of Sociology and Cultural Anthropology at the University of Amsterdam.

EHAB GALAL is Assistant Professor in Media and Society in the Middle East at the Department of Cross-Cultural and Regional Studies at the University of Copenhagen.

ROSALIND I. J. HACKETT is Professor and Head of Religious Studies and an adjunct in anthropology at the University of Tennessee, Knoxville.

MUHAMMED HARON is Associate Professor of Religious Studies at the University of Botswana.

BRIAN LARKIN is Associate Professor of Anthropology at Barnard College.

JOHANNES MERZ is a PhD candidate at Leiden University and an anthropology advisor for SIL International.

KATRIEN PYPE is Assistant Professor (BOF-ZAP) at the University of Leuven and a Fellow at the University of Birmingham.

BENJAMIN SOARES, an anthropologist, is Chair of the Research Staff at the Afrika-Studiecentrum in Leiden.

'ROTIMI TAIWO teaches English at Obafemi Awolowo University, Ile-Ife, Nigeria.

ASONZEH UKAH is a sociologist and historian of religion. He joined the University of Cape Town in 2013.

FRANCESCO ZAPPA is *Maître de conférences* (Assistant Professor) in Islamic Studies at Aix-Marseille University, France.

Index

Abbink, Jon, 267

Abdoulaye, Modibbo, 142, 152

Abubakar, Alhaji Muhammad Saad III, 259

Abu-Lughod, Lila, 118, 119

activists, 137; political, 30; religious, 2

Addis Ababa, 20, 278

Adeboye, Enoch, 201, 202n13

Adelaja, Sunday, 165, 168

advertising, 252, 276; religious, 55, 121, 159, 163, 165, 210, 224, 251–252, 254, 272; television, 175, 255. *See also* Advertising Practitioners Council of Nigeria

Advertising Practitioners Council of Nigeria (APCON), 246, 251–252, 253, 260, 262

aesthetic formation, 25, 29, 30, 32

affect, 117, 118, 119, 127, 129, 132, 133n2, 158, 268

Africa: East Africa, 20–22, 26, 27, 28; North Africa, 4, 9, 10, 171, 177; sub-Saharan, 4, 39, 40, 52, 118, 121; West Africa, 9, 40, 44–45, 47, 50, 56, 71, 99–101, 103, 106, 108, 110–111, 112n5, 228, 230. *See also* African Broadcasting Service; African "traditional" religion; culture, African; music, African

African Broadcasting Service (ABS), 24–25, 29, 33

African "traditional" religion, 6, 100, 207, 209–212, 213, 214, 215, 217, 220, 222, 223, 224n2, 224n5, 225n16

Afrikania Mission (Ghana), 6, 10, 208, 209, 211, 222; doctrine of, 212, 213, 216, 223

Ahidjo, Ahmadou, 138, 142, 152

Ahmed, Abadalla Said, 32

Ahmed, Aminu, 73

Akingbola, Erastus S. B., 260, 263n16

Al Jazeera, 175, 177, 183

Al Majd, 171, 172, 174, 178, 181–182, 185

Al Nas, 171, 173, 175, 177–178, 179

Al Rahma, 171, 173, 175, 177, 178

Alalake, Iyaladuke, 232–234, 236, 238, 241, 243n10

All India Radio, 21, 22

Alresalah, 171, 174, 175, 178, 179, 181, 182, 185

altars, 104, 105, 107, 218

Amartey, Cephas, 210

Ameve, Kofi, 213, 214–216, 217–221, 222

Amharic language, 11, 267, 279, 281n1

ancestors, 50, 101, 102, 104, 112, 212, 284, 285–286, 290, 292, 293, 294, 295, 296, 299. *See also* spirits, ancestral

Anderson, John W., 53, 58n3

animism, 65, 69, 70, 78n2

An-Nour (Cameroon), 148–151, 155n6

anthropology, 4, 52, 99, 101, 104, 112n1, 112n5, 230; linguistic, 10, 230, 239

Antoun, Richard, 267

Anwar, Auwalu, 72

Appadurai, Arjun, 280

Arab Broadcasting Committee, 23

Arab Satellite Television (ARAB SAT), 267

Arab Spring, 10, 177, 181

Arabic language, 20, 21, 22, 23, 25, 28, 29, 31, 35n47, 39–41, 45–46, 47, 48, 49, 51, 55, 56–57, 58n2, 68, 72, 77, 79n12, 140–142, 145–147, 148, 151, 153, 154, 171, 172–173, 178, 179, 185. *See also* books, Arabic; broadcasting, Arabic; education, Arabic; music, Arabic; schools, Arabic

Ashimolowo, Matthew, 163, 165, 166

Association Culturelle Islamique du Cameroun. *See* Islamic Cultural Association of Cameroon

Athumani, Kipanga, 24

audiocassettes. *See* cassettes, audio

Australia, 87, 193

authority, 23, 64, 239–240, 241, 267, 272, 287, 294; political, 139, 141, 152, 153; religious, 5, 7, 53, 66, 75, 141, 160, 163, 166, 193, 208, 246; royal, 63, 79n15; state, 9, 65, 138, 140, 153, 154, 155

Avaly, Doubla, 148, 150–151

Azhari, 171, 173, 175

Babangida, Ibrahim, 246

Bahri, Yunis al-, 20

Bakhtin, Mikhail, 239

Bamako, 39, 40, 41, 42, 50–51, 53, 57–58

Bambara language, 41, 42, 43, 44, 45, 46, 47, 48, 49, 52, 55, 56–57, 58n5, 59n15, 59n19, 59n25, 59n35

baptism, 120, 159

Barber, Karin, 122

Baron, Naomi S., 192